COMPUTER BOOK SERIES FROM IDG

Microsoft® Office 97 ~~...~~ with VBA For Du~~mmies~~

G000081490

Debugging Keys

Key	Command	What It Does
F8	Step Into	Runs next line of code
Shift+F8	Step Over	Runs called procedure as a unit
Ctrl+Shift+F8	Step Out	Runs remaining code in current procedure
Ctrl+F8	Run To Cursor	Continues code execution until the cursor is reached
F5	Run/Continue	Begins or continues execution of current code procedure
F9	Toggle Breakpoint	Sets or removes breakpoint from selected code statement
Ctrl+Shift+F9	Clear All Breakpoints	Removes all existing breakpoints
Shift+F9	Quick Watch	Sets up a watch on the fly while debugging
Ctrl+Break	Break	Stops your code during execution

Code Environment Shortcuts

Key	What It Does
Alt+Fll	Toggles between Office document and Visual Basic Editor in Word, Excel, and PowerPoint
F2	Opens the Object Browser
Ctrl+G	Opens the Immediate window
F7	Opens the code window for current object
F4	Opens or selects the Properties window
Ctrl+R	Opens or selects the Project Explorer window

IDG BOOKS WORLDWIDE

Cheat Sheet $2.95 value. Item 182-8.

For more information about IDG Books, call 1-800-762-2974.

...For Dummies: #1 Computer Book Series for Beginners

Microsoft® Office 97 Programming with VBA For Dummies®

Cheat Sheet

Conditions and Loops

```
Do While condition is true
'code statements
Loop


Do
'code statements
Loop While condition is true


Do Until condition is true
'code statements
Loop


Do
'code statements
Loop Until condition is true


For counter = start value To
end value
'code statements
Next


With object reference
'set properties and/or run
methods
End With


For Each element in a group
'code statements
Next
```

```
If condition is true Then do
  something


If condition is true Then
'code statements
End If


If condition is true Then
'code statements
ElseIf condition2 is true Then
'code statements
Else
'code statements
End If


Select Case expression
Case test_expression
'code statements
Case test_expression2
'code statements
Case Else
'code statements
End Select
```

To Find Specific Office 97 Team Info

Application	Basics (Object Model)	Advanced Stuff
Excel	Chapter 7	Chapters 18 and 19
Word	Chapter 8	Chapters 20 and 21
PowerPoint	Chapter 9	Chapter 22
Access	Chapter 10	Chapter 23

...For Dummies: #1 Computer Book Series for Beginners

References for the Rest of Us!®

COMPUTER BOOK SERIES FROM IDG

Are you intimidated and confused by computers? Do you find that traditional manuals are overloaded with technical details you'll never use? Do your friends and family always call you to fix simple problems on their PCs? Then the *...For Dummies*® computer book series from IDG Books Worldwide is for you.

...For Dummies books are written for those frustrated computer users who know they aren't really dumb but find that PC hardware, software, and indeed the unique vocabulary of computing make them feel helpless. *...For Dummies* books use a lighthearted approach, a down-to-earth style, and even cartoons and humorous icons to diffuse computer novices' fears and build their confidence. Lighthearted but not lightweight, these books are a perfect survival guide for anyone forced to use a computer.

> *"I like my copy so much I told friends; now they bought copies."*
>
> **Irene C., Orwell, Ohio**

> *"Quick, concise, nontechnical, and humorous."*
>
> **Jay A., Elburn, Illinois**

> *"Thanks, I needed this book. Now I can sleep at night."*
>
> **Robin F., British Columbia, Canada**

Already, millions of satisfied readers agree. They have made *...For Dummies* books the #1 introductory level computer book series and have written asking for more. So, if you're looking for the most fun and easy way to learn about computers, look to *...For Dummies* books to give you a helping hand.

5/97

MICROSOFT® OFFICE 97 PROGRAMMING WITH VBA FOR DUMMIES®

**by Karen Jaskolka
and Mike Gilbert**

Foreword by Mike Gunderloy

IDG Books Worldwide, Inc.
An International Data Group Company

Foster City, CA ♦ Chicago, IL ♦ Indianapolis, IN ♦ Southlake, TX

Microsoft® Office 97 Programming with VBA For Dummies®

Published by
IDG Books Worldwide, Inc.
An International Data Group Company
919 E. Hillsdale Blvd.
Suite 400
Foster City, CA 94404
www.idgbooks.com (IDG Books Worldwide Web site)
www.dummies.com (Dummies Press Web site)

Library of Congress Catalog Card No.: 96-80287

ISBN: 0-7645-0182-8

Printed in the United States of America

10 9 8 7 6 5 4 3 2 1

1B/TQ/QW/ZX/IN

Distributed in the United States by IDG Books Worldwide, Inc.

Distributed by Macmillan Canada for Canada; by Transworld Publishers Limited in the United Kingdom; by IDG Norge Books for Norway; by IDG Sweden Books for Sweden; by Woodslane Pty. Ltd. for Australia; by Woodslane Enterprises Ltd. for New Zealand; by Longman Singapore Publishers Ltd. for Singapore, Malaysia, Thailand, and Indonesia; by Simron Pty. Ltd. for South Africa; by Toppan Company Ltd. for Japan; by Distribuidora Cuspide for Argentina; by Livraria Cultura for Brazil; by Ediciencia S.A. for Ecuador; by Addison-Wesley Publishing Company for Korea; by Ediciones ZETA S.C.R. Ltda. for Peru; by WS Computer Publishing Corporation, Inc., for the Philippines; by Unalis Corporation for Taiwan; by Contemporanea de Ediciones for Venezuela; by Computer Book & Magazine Store for Puerto Rico; by Express Computer Distributors for the Caribbean and West Indies. Authorized Sales Agent: Anthony Rudkin Associates for the Middle East and North Africa.

For general information on IDG Books Worldwide's books in the U.S., please call our Consumer Customer Service department at 800-762-2974. For reseller information, including discounts and premium sales, please call our Reseller Customer Service department at 800-434-3422.

For information on where to purchase IDG Books Worldwide's books outside the U.S., please contact our International Sales department at 415-655-3200 or fax 415-655-3295.

For information on foreign language translations, please contact our Foreign & Subsidiary Rights department at 415-655-3021 or fax 415-655-3281.

For sales inquiries and special prices for bulk quantities, please contact our Sales department at 415-655-3200 or write to the address above.

For information on using IDG Books Worldwide's books in the classroom or for ordering examination copies, please contact our Educational Sales department at 800-434-2086 or fax 817-251-8174.

For press review copies, author interviews, or other publicity information, please contact our Public Relations department at 415-655-3000 or fax 415-655-3299.

For authorization to photocopy items for corporate, personal, or educational use, please contact Copyright Clearance Center, 222 Rosewood Drive, Danvers, MA 01923, or fax 508-750-4470.

is a trademark under exclusive license to IDG Books Worldwide, Inc., from International Data Group, Inc.

About the Authors

Karen Jaskolka and **Mike Gilbert** have spent the majority of their careers as database gurus who love developing applications by using Microsoft technologies. Together they bring the unique perspectives of both a corporate developer and an independent consultant to Office 97 VBA programming. Both Karen and Mike are trainers, technical writers, editors, and Microsoft Certified Developers.

Karen works for Trigon BlueCross BlueShield as a senior information center consultant; her role includes technical project management, custom application development, and intranet development. In addition, Karen is currently a speaker at Advisor *Devcon* conferences, writes for *Access/Office/VBA Advisor* magazine, and works as a technical reviewer, development editor, and contributing writer for various computer books. Her first love, however, is volleyball! (Actually, volleyball is second only to her wonderful husband and co-author.)

Mike is a senior consultant with MCW Technologies, focusing on the Microsoft suite of development products. He is co-author of the *Access 95 Developer's Handbook, Access 97 Developer's Handbook,* and *VBA Developer's Handbook,* all from Sybex. Mike is also a contributing editor to *Smart Access,* from Pinnacle Publications, and *Access/Office/VBA Advisor,* from Advisor Publications. In addition, Mike is a trainer for Application Developers Training Company, presenting classes aimed at Access, Visual Basic, and client-server application developers. He also speaks at many conferences and shows throughout the world, including *Tech*Ed* and Advisor *DevCon.*

Karen and Mike live in Richmond, Virginia, with their two cats, Chicago and Cairo. In their spare time away from their PCs, Karen and Mike enjoy snow skiing, playing volleyball and tennis, taking walks through the neighborhood, and dining out on their deck — and now they'll even have time to start swinging those golf clubs!

ABOUT IDG BOOKS WORLDWIDE

Welcome to the world of IDG Books Worldwide.

IDG Books Worldwide, Inc., is a subsidiary of International Data Group, the world's largest publisher of computer-related information and the leading global provider of information services on information technology. IDG was founded more than 25 years ago and now employs more than 8,500 people worldwide. IDG publishes more than 275 computer publications in over 75 countries (see listing below). More than 60 million people read one or more IDG publications each month.

Launched in 1990, IDG Books Worldwide is today the #1 publisher of best-selling computer books in the United States. We are proud to have received eight awards from the Computer Press Association in recognition of editorial excellence and three from *Computer Currents'* First Annual Readers' Choice Awards. Our best-selling *...For Dummies®* series has more than 30 million copies in print with translations in 30 languages. IDG Books Worldwide, through a joint venture with IDG's Hi-Tech Beijing, became the first U.S. publisher to publish a computer book in the People's Republic of China. In record time, IDG Books Worldwide has become the first choice for millions of readers around the world who want to learn how to better manage their businesses.

Our mission is simple: Every one of our books is designed to bring extra value and skill-building instructions to the reader. Our books are written by experts who understand and care about our readers. The knowledge base of our editorial staff comes from years of experience in publishing, education, and journalism — experience we use to produce books for the '90s. In short, we care about books, so we attract the best people. We devote special attention to details such as audience, interior design, use of icons, and illustrations. And because we use an efficient process of authoring, editing, and desktop publishing our books electronically, we can spend more time ensuring superior content and spend less time on the technicalities of making books.

You can count on our commitment to deliver high-quality books at competitive prices on topics you want to read about. At IDG Books Worldwide, we continue in the IDG tradition of delivering quality for more than 25 years. You'll find no better book on a subject than one from IDG Books Worldwide.

IDG BOOKS WORLDWIDE

John Kilcullen
John Kilcullen
CEO
IDG Books Worldwide, Inc.

Steven Berkowitz
Steven Berkowitz
President and Publisher
IDG Books Worldwide, Inc.

Eighth Annual
Computer Press
Awards ≥1992

Ninth Annual
Computer Press
Awards ≥1993

Tenth Annual
Computer Press
Awards ≥1994

Eleventh Annual
Computer Press
Awards ≥1995

IDG Books Worldwide, Inc., is a subsidiary of International Data Group, the world's largest publisher of computer-related information and the leading global provider of information services on information technology. International Data Group publishes over 275 computer publications in over 75 countries. Sixty million people read one or more International Data Group publications each month. International Data Group's publications include: **ARGENTINA:** Buyer's Guide, Computerworld Argentina, PC World Argentina; **AUSTRALIA:** Australian Macworld, Australian PC World, Australian Reseller News, Computerworld, IT Casebook, Network World, Publish, Webmaster; **AUSTRIA:** Computerwelt Osterreich, Networks Austria, PC Tip Austria; **BANGLADESH:** PC World Bangladesh; **BELARUS:** PC World Belarus; **BELGIUM:** Data News; **BRAZIL:** Annuário de Informática, Computerworld, Connections, Macworld, PC Player, PC World, Publish, Reseller News, Supergamepower; **BULGARIA:** Computerworld Bulgaria, Network World Bulgaria, PC & MacWorld Bulgaria; **CANADA:** CIO Canada, Client/Server World, ComputerWorld Canada, InfoWorld Canada, NetworkWorld Canada, WebWorld; **CHILE:** Computerworld Chile, PC World Chile; **COLOMBIA:** Computerworld Colombia, PC World Colombia; **COSTA RICA:** PC World Centro America; **THE CZECH AND SLOVAK REPUBLICS:** Computerworld Czechoslovakia, Macworld Czech Republic, PC World Czechoslovakia; **DENMARK:** Communications World Danmark, Computerworld Danmark, Macworld Danmark, PC World Danmark, Techworld Denmark; **DOMINICAN REPUBLIC:** PC World Republica Dominicana; **ECUADOR:** PC World Ecuador; **EGYPT:** Computerworld Middle East, PC World Middle East; **EL SALVADOR:** PC World Centro America; **FINLAND:** MikroPC, Tietoverkko, Tietoviikko; **FRANCE:** Distributique, Hebdo, Info PC, Le Monde Informatique, Macworld, Reseaux & Telecoms, WebMaster France; **GERMANY:** Computer Partner, Computerwoche, Computerwoche Extra, Computerwoche FOCUS, Global Online, Macwelt, PC Welt; **GREECE:** Amiga Computing, GamePro Greece, Multimedia World; **GUATEMALA:** PC World Centro America; **HONDURAS:** PC World Centro America; **HONG KONG:** Computerworld Hong Kong, PC World Hong Kong, Publish in Asia; **HUNGARY:** ABCD CD-ROM, Computerworld Szamitastechnika, Internetto online Magazine, PC World Hungary, PC-X Magazin Hungary; **ICELAND:** Tolvuheimur PC World Island; **INDIA:** Information Communications World, Information Systems Computerworld, PC World India, Publish in Asia; **INDONESIA:** InfoKomputer PC World, Komputek Computerworld, Publish in Asia; **IRELAND:** ComputerScope, PC Live!; **ISRAEL:** Macworld Israel, People & Computers/Computerworld; **ITALY:** Computerworld Italia, Macworld Italia, Networking Italia, PC World Italia; **JAPAN:** DTP World, Macworld Japan, Nikkei Personal Computing, OS/2 World Japan, SunWorld Japan, Windows NT World, Windows World Japan; **KENYA:** PC World East African; **KOREA:** Hi-Tech Information, Macworld Korea, PC World Korea; **MACEDONIA:** PC World Macedonia; **MALAYSIA:** Computerworld Malaysia, PC World Malaysia, Publish in Asia; **MALTA:** PC World Malta; **MEXICO:** Computerworld Mexico, PC World Mexico; **MYANMAR:** PC World Myanmar; **NETHERLANDS:** Computer! Totaal, LAN Internetworking Magazine, LAN World Buyers Guide, Macworld Netherlands, Net, WebWereld; **NEW ZEALAND:** Absolute Beginners Guide and Plain & Simple Series, Computer Buyer, Computer Industry Directory, Computerworld New Zealand, MTB, Network World, PC World New Zealand; **NICARAGUA:** PC World Centro America; **NORWAY:** Computerworld Norge, CW Rapport, Datamagasinet, Financial Rapport, Kursguide Norge, Macworld Norge, Multimediaworld Norge, PC World Ekspress Norge, PC World Nettverk, PC World Norge, PC World ProduktGuide Norge; **PAKISTAN:** Computerworld Pakistan; **PANAMA:** PC World Panama; **PEOPLE'S REPUBLIC OF CHINA:** China Computer Users, China Computerworld, China Infoworld, China Telecom World Weekly, Computer & Communication, Electronic Design China, Electronics Today, Electronics Weekly, Game Software, PC World China, Popular Computer Week, Software Weekly, Software World, Telecom World; **PERU:** Computerworld Peru, PC World Profesional Peru, PC World SoHo Peru; **PHILIPPINES:** Click!, Computerworld Philippines, PC World Philippines, Publish in Asia; **POLAND:** Computerworld Poland, Computerworld Special Report Poland, Cyber, Macworld Poland, Networld Poland, PC World Komputer; **PORTUGAL:** Cerebro/PC World, Computerworld/Correio Informático, Dealer World Portugal, Mac*In/PC*In Portugal, Multimedia World; **PUERTO RICO:** PC World Puerto Rico; **ROMANIA:** Computerworld Romania, PC World Romania, Telecom Romania; **RUSSIA:** Computerworld Russia, Mir PK, Publish, Seti; **SINGAPORE:** Computerworld Singapore, PC World Singapore, Publish in Asia; **SLOVENIA:** Monitor; **SOUTH AFRICA:** Computing SA, Network World SA, Software World SA; **SPAIN:** Communicaciones World España, Computerworld España, Dealer World España, Macworld España, PC World España; **SRI LANKA:** Infolink PC World; **SWEDEN:** CAP&Design, Computer Sweden, Corporate Computing Sweden, Internetworld Sweden, it.branschen, Macworld Sweden, MaxiData Sweden, MikroDatorn, Nätverk & Kommunikation, PC World Sweden, PCaktiv, Windows World Sweden; **SWITZERLAND:** Computerworld Schweiz, Macworld Schweiz, PCtip; **TAIWAN:** Computerworld Taiwan, Macworld Taiwan, NEW ViSiON/Publish, PC World Taiwan, Windows World Taiwan; **THAILAND:** Publish in Asia, Thai Computerworld; **TURKEY:** Computerworld Turkiye, Macworld Turkiye, Network World Turkiye, PC World Turkiye; **UKRAINE:** Computerworld Kiev, Multimedia World Ukraine, PC World Ukraine; **UNITED KINGDOM:** Acorn User UK, Amiga Action UK, Amiga Computing UK, Apple Talk UK Computing, Macworld, Parents and Computers UK, PC Advisor, PC Home, PSX Pro, The WEB; **UNITED STATES:** Cable in the Classroom, CIO Magazine, Computerworld, DOS World, Federal Computer Week, GamePro Magazine, InfoWorld, I-Way, Macworld, Network World, PC Games, PC World, Publish, Video Event, THE WEB Magazine, and WebMaster; online webzines: JavaWorld, NetscapeWorld, and SunWorld Online; **URUGUAY:** InfoWorld Uruguay; **VENEZUELA:** Computerworld Venezuela, PC World Venezuela; and **VIETNAM:** PC World Vietnam.   3/24/97

Dedication

To Karen's father, Richard Jaskolka (1940–1992), who shared our love for new technology and our philosophy of living each day to its fullest.

Authors' Acknowledgments

We finally did it, but not without the help and support of many important people. Our sincerest thanks to all the great folks who made this book possible:

- To our families and relatives who have provided oodles of love and support: Mom/Janice and Dave, Mom and Bob, Jazz (lil' brother Dave), the Sterrett family, and last but not least, Grandpa.

- To our friends and neighbors, who haven't seen much of us in the past few months while we've been working away diligently in our office, but have been kind enough to check in on us to make sure we're still alive.

- To the people responsible for getting us both onto the Microsoft development path: Professor Veda Storey and Gordon A. Rogers.

- To the fine people at Microsoft who helped us get the information we needed: Neil Charney, David Lazar, Scott Horn, and the many unidentified souls on the Office team.

- To Ken Getz, our friend and fellow guru, who is responsible for putting us in touch with IDG to write this book and who is a constant source of encouragement!

- To Mike Gunderloy, yet another friend and fellow guru, who wrote the amusing foreword for this book. You've added a lot of goodness to our lives.

- To Jill Pisoni, our acquisitions editor, who had faith in us from the very beginning and got the ball rolling.

- To Michael Bolinger, Tammy Castleman, and Gwenette Gaddis, our copy editors, who provided us with constructive editorial feedback to make this book a literary success.

- To Robert L. Bogue, our technical editor, who was kind enough to preview the book for technical accuracy. The responsibility for any errors, however, rests soley on our shoulders.

- To Robert Wallace, our project editor, who acted as the glue to put this whole thing together. Thanks, Robert, for your understanding, encouragement, and, of course, editorial assistance — despite your lingering illnesses. Get some rest, Robert!

- And, finally, to all of the people at IDG who worked diligently behind the scenes to make this book a reality.

Publisher's Acknowledgments

We're proud of this book; please send us your comments about it by using the Reader Response Card at the back of the book or by e-mailing us at feedback/dummies@idgbooks.com. Some of the people who helped bring this book to market include the following:

Acquisitions, Development, and Editorial

Project Editor: Robert H. Wallace

Senior Acquisitions Editor: Jill Pisoni

Media Development Manager: Joyce Pepple

Associate Permissions Editor:
Heather H. Dismore

Copy Editors: Michael Bolinger;
Tamara Castleman, Senior Copy Editor;
Gwenette Gaddis

Technical Editor: Robert L. Bogue

Editorial Manager: Leah P. Cameron

Editorial Assistant: Chris H. Collins

Production

Project Coordinator: Sherry Gomoll

Layout and Graphics: Lou Boudreau,
Dominique DeFelice, Angela F. Hunckler,
Drew R. Moore, Mark C. Owens,
Brent Savage

Proofreaders: Renee Kelty,
Nancy Reinhardt, Christine Sabooni,
Christine Berman, Joel Draper,
Nancy Price, Rob Springer

Indexer: Sherry Massey

Special Help:
Mark Kory, Media Development Intern;
Stephanie Koutek, Proof Editor

General and Administrative

IDG Books Worldwide, Inc.: John Kilcullen, CEO; Steven Berkowitz, President and Publisher

IDG Books Technology Publishing: Brenda McLaughlin, Senior Vice President and Group Publisher

Dummies Technology Press and Dummies Editorial: Diane Graves Steele, Vice President and Associate Publisher; Judith A. Taylor, Product Marketing Manager; Kristin A. Cocks, Editorial Director

Dummies Trade Press: Kathleen A. Welton, Vice President and Publisher

IDG Books Production for Dummies Press: Beth Jenkins, Production Director; Cindy L. Phipps, Supervisor of Project Coordination, Production Proofreading, and Indexing; Kathie S. Schutte, Supervisor of Page Layout; Shelley Lea, Supervisor of Graphics and Design; Debbie J. Gates, Production Systems Specialist; Tony Augsburger, Supervisor of Reprints and Bluelines; Leslie Popplewell, Media Archive Coordinator

Dummies Packaging and Book Design: Patti Sandez, Packaging Specialist; Lance Kayser, Packaging Assistant; Kavish + Kavish, Cover Design

♦

The publisher would like to give special thanks to Patrick J. McGovern,
without whom this book would not have been possible.

♦

Contents at a Glance

Cartoons at a Glance

By Rich Tennant

page 5

page 143

page 47

page 365

page 269

Fax: 508-546-7747 • E-mail: the5wave@tiac.net

Table of Contents

Foreword

A few years ago, I had this word processor. . . . "What's that," you say? "How many years ago?" Well, to put it this way: The desktop computer I was working on at the time had a hard drive with about 5 percent of the RAM that the laptop on which I'm writing this foreword had. (For those of you who don't like math puzzles, it was a 5MB hard drive — and yes, this laptop *is* on steroids.) Anyhow, I had this word processor that had, amazingly enough, a macro language. If you're curious, the program was named Sprint, and it was state-of-the-art, which of course prompted its non-Microsoft manufacturer to discontinue it.

I was publishing a magazine at the time, and let me say that I had a great time with that word processor. I eventually did one hard-core programming task in which I hooked up a macro that counted all the words in a document, so that I'd know when I had written enough and could go to the printer and hand them all my money. This macro was a marvel of complexity — a couple pages of code in a language based on C instead of on Basic. Just to prove that I still have what it takes technically, here's the same macro, translated to VBA for Microsoft Word 97:

```
Sub CountWords()
    Debug.Print ActiveDocument.Words.Count
End Sub
```

(Hmmm, only 232 words so far; I've got a ways to go yet with this Foreword.)

Maybe if I had Word 97 in those good old days, I could have written fast enough to keep a magazine afloat rather than spending my days programming macros, and so avoided a promising development career. A moral to this story is in there someplace. (Well, all this disregards how the hard drive of that old word processor-computer was too small to install the Word help files, let alone Word itself.)

Now, if you're reading this at work, make your boss leave the room. That's right — *you,* you the boss-person with the pointy hair. Out!

Okay, are we alone now? Good. Here's a secret for you: read this book and you, too, can do more work with less effort than ever before. Just imagine, your boss thinks you're slaving over a hot macro, struggling with help files, pounding out code, and all the while you're actually relaxing and reading another *...For Dummies* book. What could be sweeter? Just don't let on how easy it is, or the management team will want to replace you with a co-op student.

Oh Mr. or Ms. Boss? You can come back now. We were just talking about the basketball season. Honest.

By now you probably know that Office 97 is taking up hundreds of megabytes on your hard drive; every single one of those multiple millions of bytes (in numbers greater than ants at a picnic) are packed chock-full of functionality. By just noodling around with a mouse and keyboard, you can create cool charts in Excel, design Word documents with live jumps to the Internet, animate your PowerPoint presentations, and use Access reports to see the sales figures for a small food company. Pretty cool, huh? Now just imagine doing all that *programmatically!*

Yep, that's right. After you master VBA, you can do all the cool stuff in Office 97 without your hands even touching the keyboard. And I do mean *all.* One great strength of Office is that it has over 500 programmable objects (see Chapters 7–10; you weren't expecting technical details from the Foreword, were you?) that you can poke, prod, and make dance at your command. Good thing some of those objects are obscure, dull, and unimportant, or this book would so big that you could kill gophers with it. Every single one of these objects can be ordered around with VBA.

That's the key: VBA. Visual Basic for Applications. (Pronounce the "for" quietly because VBFA would be a pretty dopey acronym.) In the old days — say, a year or two back — you had to know Access Basic to program in Access, Word Basic to program in Word, and Excel Basic to program in Excel. And if you told people that you were programming in PowerPoint . . . well, you were just plain fibbing. Now, however, one size really does fit all. Work with VBA, and you can use any of the Office applications to hold your code. Plus, as an added bonus, you can also use Visio or SQA or lots of other applications from VBA licensees. I understand VBA for toasters is due out next year.

No more of this narrow specialization stuff for you — no way. If you've been developing in Access and your group needs some work done in Excel, you've already got the techniques firmly under control. (Just remember to tell your boss that you need to work hard to make the switch, and save the time to read more at your desk.) Think about how much more respect you can get as an Access-Excel-PowerPoint-and-Word developer than you get as a mere Access developer. Think of the raises. Heck, think of the fun you'll have. Remember I said that you could control everything? That even includes making the little paper-clip Office Assistant guy dance on command.

So what are you waiting for? I'm not the one who's going to show you all about VBA; I'm just writing this part about how cool it is. Turn the pages and get to the real meat of the book!

As for me, I'm still trying to figure out some way to make that word-count procedure complex enough so that it feels like I really did some work.

Mike Gunderloy

Introduction

● ●

*W*elcome to the amazing and breathtaking tour through Microsoft Office 97 programmability, featuring your tour guides Karen and Mike. We're here to talk about Office 97 Programming with Visual Basic for Applications (VBA). Now that VBA is the common development language throughout almost all of the Office products and is being licensed to third-party vendors, the time has come to buckle down and find out what this VBA stuff is all about. So we said, "Heck, why not make it fun and easy to understand VBA and throw in some humor to boot!"

We had fun writing this book, and we hope that you enjoy reading it. Both of us feel very strongly about the merits of Office 97 and the advancements made with its development environment and language.

Who Are You?

We wanted to write this book on VBA in the world of Microsoft Office especially for you, the developer who is new to VBA but has some understanding of programming. Our mission for this book is to provide you with the knowledge and tools that you need to begin capitalizing on VBA in Office 97.

Before You Start

A few ideas, concepts, and procedures must be in place before you jump into using VBA and this book, such as

- ✔ You must have Office 97 installed on your PC and made ready to rock and roll (or just work properly, whichever you prefer).

- ✔ We assume that you already possess some understanding of and proficiency with the Office products. If you are new to Office, we suggest that you first spend some time exploring the basics of the Office suite.

- ✔ Also, we assume (here we go, assuming yet again!) that you are not entirely new to the concept of programming. If you haven't programmed in any of the Office products in the past, that's okay. We firmly believe that your work in another programming language and your extremely logical mind means that you already have the capacity to understand VBA.

Reasons and Conventions

In many of the chapters found in Parts I, II, and III, we use only one of the Office 97 products to demonstrate how things work. For example, in Chapter 12 we use Word to show conditional statements, and in Chapter 13 we use Excel to practice looping constructs. We could have, however, easily used Excel, PowerPoint, or Access as examples for those chapters, because all these programs use VBA!

Generally, we use Word and Excel to show common VBA elements and constructs, mainly because these products (and Access) are likely to be the ones that you use the most. Our only hesitation with using Access more — and we do honestly love Access as much as its siblings — is that Access has a slightly different development environment, which you can read more about in Chapter 3.

Also, note that we include lots of VBA code in this book. Sometimes a single line of code won't fit on one line in the book; computer screens are much wider than book pages. When this happens, you see an underscore (_) at the end of a line of code. This character tells VBA that you're not done typing and that it needs to read the next line, as well. For example:

```
Y = InputBox("Please enter a number other " & _
  "than zero", "Value of Y")
```

If the example is one where we're asking you to type the code, make sure that you type the underscore, too.

Ports of Call

So, where is this guided tour taking you? Here's a rundown of what we cover in each of the parts in this book. Each chapter is self-contained, so you don't need to read the chapters in order. Jump around as often as you like. If, however, you can't bear to put the book down even for a second, you can enjoy reading the book from cover-to-cover, as well.

> ✔ **Part I: Introducing VBA, the Common Language** — In this section, we explain the big picture of how Office and VBA fit together. Chapter 1 introduces the Office 97 programs, or *teammates,* as we call them. Chapter 2 explains everything you wanted to know (and more) about where this VBA stuff came from. Chapter 3 wraps up this introductory part with the basics of the development environment found in the Office 97 suite.

✔ **Part II: Discovering the VBA Building Blocks** —The parts that create VBA can be thought of as plastic toy connecting blocks. Before you can go off and create a colorful plastic masterpiece, you need to be aware of the different blocks that are available to you. VBA programming is much the same way — you'll find it helpful to understand the basics about objects and how to use them before developing grandiose and powerful Office applications.

In Chapter 4, we introduce the concept of an object and how to refer to an object in code. We also introduce you to the Object Browser (Chapter 5), which continues to be your development friend no matter how much of a VBA guru you become. Chapter 6 focuses on explaining the new syntax that you need to understand when referring to objects in VBA, and Chapters 7–10 delve into the object models for each of the Office products.

✔ **Part III: Everything Else You Need to Understand About VBA** — This part covers the necessary components of VBA, including variables (Chapter 11), conditional statements (Chapter 12), looping constructs (Chapter 13), and your own custom procedures (Chapter 14). Chapter 15 focuses on built-in VBA functions that are at your disposal, and Chapter 16 introduces the basics of building user-interface forms for your applications. Chapter 17 ends this part with a discussion about debugging and bulletproofing your applications.

✔ **Part IV: Doing Cool Stuff with VBA and Office** — Strap yourself in, because we take you for an exciting ride through some of the cool, yet practical, things you can do with Office 97 and VBA. We identify some real-world tasks to focus on for this purpose, such as manipulating pivot tables (Chapter 18), creating charts (Chapter 19), running a hard-core search and replace (Chapter 20), augmenting mail merge (Chapter 21), creating dynamic slide-show presentations (Chapter 22), and automating reports (Chapter 23).

✔ **Part V: The Part of Tens** — No *...For Dummies* book is complete without The Part of Tens. This part contains more useful information as you venture forth in your Office development efforts. Contents include shedding light on the ODE, discussing migration issues if you are upgrading to Office 97, and mentioning VBA resources to check out.

It's on the Disk

This book comes with a disk full of sample files and any code we write. Throughout many of the examples, we utilize files included on the disk to demonstrate VBA concepts. If you are going to access any files from the disk, you must first copy them to your local hard drive. For that matter, a good idea is to install the disk contents so that all the files are ready for you. Although the answers to the examples are included on the disk (and we don't try to hide the answers from you), much more benefit is derived from the examples if you struggle through the code development yourself and then use ours as a reference.

A Guide to the Icons Used in This Book

As you read through this book, notice some of the neat little icons that help offset the text that we think you really ought to pay attention to.

A Tip is generally a piece of valuable and helpful information that you need to know. This information may even save you time and energy. Check it out!

When you see the Remember icon, check to see if the string is still wrapped around your finger. This icon indicates that this information is too important to forget or is a reminder of something you may have encountered in other chapters.

Sometimes, we're dying to give you more technical details than you may really need. Even though the information included next to the Technical Stuff icon is often incredibly interesting to programming nerds like us, you can skip this stuff if you like.

When you see this icon, please pay special attention to the information — reading it may save you from disaster. Text next to this icon covers the not-so-nice things that can happen to you while you're developing in VBA.

Did you notice that a disk is included with this book? Well, the On the Disk icon marks text that refers to something you'll find on the disk, such as a sample file.

Where to Go from Here

After you go through all the chapters in this book, as evidenced by a large number of dog-eared pages and a few proverbial coffee and doughnut stains, more work is ahead. The best thing you can do is to start using this stuff. Take the examples in Part IV of this book and expand upon them. See how far you can take your Office applications with VBA — you may be very surprised and pleased.

Also, don't hide away in a corner with your VBA code. Talk to other developers, either by meeting with them in person or online through the Internet. Online forums are a great place to see what everyone else in the development world is up to and are great sounding boards for your questions and ideas.

Part I
Introducing VBA, the Common Language

The 5th Wave   By Rich Tennant

All through High School he wouldn't talk to anyone - hardly said a word. Now he's graduating from an Ivy League college with an advanced degree in communications.

In this part . . .

Technology seems to be advancing so quickly nowadays that keeping up can be a challenge. To help run the race for new application knowledge, we welcome you to the world of Office 97 and all that the suite offers. This part covers the basics about each Office component. We can't predict the next set of winning Lotto numbers, but we can forecast some pleasant surprises swimming around in Office 97.

Have you heard the latest buzz about something called *VBA?* We hope to clear up any mystery surrounding this acronym and to provide you with a good foundation for understanding its evolution and role within the Office suite.

Then, look forward to visiting the VBA development environment, where you can fill up your toolboxes with lots of neat stuff and get ready to start writing cool applications that actually work!

Chapter 1

Welcome to Office 97

In This Chapter

▶ Finding out what's new and cool in Office 97

▶ Introducing the Office 97 Dream Team — the starting lineup

▶ Discussing what you can do with VBA in Office 97

A lot of buzz has been going around about the latest and greatest version of Microsoft Office. But what's all the hoopla about? Yes, everyone knows that they have just increased the value of Bill Gates' stock options by buying the dazzling new upgrade to Office. But what's in Office for you, the purchasing power?

If you have spent any time in older versions of Office, you may feel very much at home with the new release. You are also guaranteed to discover lots of new exciting features, both for end users and developers. To start off our discussion, we look at some generic changes that you'll be thrilled with. Because this is a book about VBA development, we don't have time to delve into all the new aspects of Office 97. Bummer, we know. But lots of other cool *...For Dummies* series books delve into the basics of each Office component. We, however, do our best to point out as much useful and cool stuff as we can in 400 pages or less! So much we'd like to say; so few pages to say it in. Such is the life of an author.

A Few New and Cool Things in Office 97

Yes, we know that Office 97 is a new version with lots of great bells and whistles, but you must be wondering what this great new version is going to do for you — the developer. Well, take a quick look:

 ✔ **Improved usability:** The Office Assistant can walk your users through tasks and assist in answering questions. (Heck, it's so helpful that maybe you'll have time for that vacation you've wanted to take.) Additionally, you have programmatic access to the Assistant. Imagine the fun you can have with this and the benefits it can bring to your applications!

✔ **Integrated Web technologies:** If you aren't hearing about the Internet and intranets within your company or from your customers, we'll eat our socks. As you know, an intensified focus is on the Internet, and more so on building intranets. Office 97 has stepped up to the plate and hit a grand slam! Office 97 provides the tools for turning corporate data into easily accessible information for your employees or customers. All of the Office 97 tools have the option to save files as HTML and can be used to create intranet components. Other Web technologies have been integrated into Office 97 — such as hyperlinks, searching capabilities (Office Web Search), and Web Browser integration.

✔ **Better integration:** Microsoft has always touted the easy integration of Office. They want to lead you to believe that all the components have existed harmoniously forever. True enough, you have always been able to do some integration with the Office components. (I'm sure that you've caught at least one of those marketing and sales demos showing all the cool stuff that you were unable to replicate when you got back to your PC.) If you haven't seen integration in any of the precursors to Office 97, just suffice it to say that integration is downright excellent now! This is largely due to the common language that we cheerlead about throughout the book. *Rah, rah, sis-boom bah!* We are excited and hope that you join us in the celebration.

✔ **VBA, VBA, VBA:** Microsoft has been talking about having a common development language — and the day has finally come! All the Office 97 components (with the noted exception of Outlook) use VBA. This is an exciting time for you — the developer. You can use one language for developing solutions with Microsoft technology. But wait, there's more. Microsoft is licensing the VBA language to third-party vendors. In turn, VBA is the development language in much more than Office! The language is integrated into products such as Visio, AutoCAD, and Photoshop. In fact, VBA has been licensed to 30+ companies! Because VBA is the focus of the book, you may find out more than you can imagine about VBA throughout each chapter! In Chapter 2, we lay the groundwork for VBA, such as explaining how the language evolved.

✔ **500+ Programmable Objects:** Office 97 exposes more than 500 programmable objects. Developers can build familiar solutions by customizing any Office 97 application or feature, including Outlook 97, OfficeArt, Office Command Bars, and the Office Assistant, which are all programmable. (If you are not familiar with what an object is, we venture into a lengthy, but fun, discussion in Chapter 4. Take a look if you like!) In Chapters 7–10 we expose a good chunk of these programmable objects as we look at Excel, Word, PowerPoint, and Access!

The Office 97 Dream Team

Now, we want to take this opportunity to introduce the *Office 97 dream team*.

Excel

Excel: Undoubtedly, this is the team member that will begin playing a much larger role this year. Excel has always been a good player on the Office team, providing great charts and pivot tables. But now, on the Office 97 team, Excel can very well be the team star! We expect increased court time for this seasoned player in 1997 and beyond.

With the robust object model in Excel and the focus on VBA development, we expect an increased number of application developers focusing their efforts on Excel, taking chart development, pivot table creation, and data analysis to new heights! Although VBA is not new to Excel, we believe that an awareness of the untapped benefits in Excel is emerging as we speak! Chapters 7, 18, and 19 detail Excel's flexibility and prowess.

Word

Word: Hands down, this team member, of all the Office team members, has shown the most improvement in the past year. Word is not just for word processing anymore! Word has experienced a major change — trading in its old pair of WordBasic shoes for a more modern and robust pair of VBA shoes!

Although previous versions of Word enjoyed the WordBasic development language, they can't hold a candle to the new and improved Word — now with VBA! Exciting things may start to happen! Watch for lots of court interaction between Word and the other dream team members. To check out this member's stat sheet, turn to Chapters 8, 20, and 21.

PowerPoint

PowerPoint: While we've already introduced Word as the most improved player, PowerPoint has improved, as well, but in a very different way. PowerPoint was last season's team manager that now has a place on the starting roster. Yes, the starting roster. You must be wondering what has caused this dramatic change.

PowerPoint has never enjoyed its own programming language and was forced to live vicariously through the rest of the Office players. This season, PowerPoint sports its proud new addition — VBA. What developers discover with the new capabilities of PowerPoint ought to prove exciting in the near future. Chapters 9 and 22 highlight PowerPoint's newest arrival — VBA.

Access

Access: Without question, Access is the team's most consistent player and the unanimously elected team captain. However, even though we expect a big showing this year, we anticipate that Access will start to be rivaled by some of the other players — now that other team members enjoy VBA. Access will continue to assist the other team members with special skills, such as data storage and querying.

As the Office team members start to catch up to Access in terms of the number of developers that use them for application development, we may even witness some diehard Access fans cheering on some of the other team players. This season, we do have unfortunate news that Access has not inherited some of the same development features as Word, Excel, and PowerPoint. Specifically, the other team members all enjoy the Visual Basic Editor (VBE) for writing and managing code, which you can read about in Chapter 3. Hopefully, the lack of the VBE won't affect the Access team morale! Chapters 10 and 23 detail the Access object model and some neat automating of reports using VBA.

Outlook

Outlook: This new addition to the Office team is in its first season anywhere. Outlook is the replacement for Schedule+ (which has retired its jersey) that also sports capabilities as an e-mail client and file management tool. Outlook, unlike the rest of the Office suite, does not have VBA. You may expect this absence to be a concern for the Dream Team, but Outlook will be able to hold its own development weight. Outlook enjoys a programming language with similar, although less robust, capabilities as VBA — it's called VB Script. Although Outlook has great potential as a team member, we don't discuss Outlook in this book. For more about Outlook, pick up a copy of *Microsoft Outlook For Dummies* by Bill Dyszel (also published by IDG Books Worldwide, Inc.).

What Can You Do with Office 97?

The possibilities are endless. Many people from various professions have capitalized on the strengths of Office to solve business problems. Isn't that what this suite is really all about? Making our daily work more accurate, more efficient, and more fun! That's where Office 97 can come in and make a difference. Office 97 is more than a database to store your customer information; it can be extended to be a contact management system. Office 97 is more than a word processor — it can be a sophisticated mail merge tool!

Here, we just take a quick rundown of some of the things people around the world are doing with Office. Actually, Microsoft keeps a record in the form of case studies. You can check out the latest case studies on the Microsoft Web site at `www.microsoft.com/officeDev/Cases/Cases.htm`

Some uses of Office 97 are obvious but worth mentioning. Specific applications that we've read about include tracking of criminal offenders, credentialing and monitoring of medical staff, assisting a legal practice with case management, and maintaining an on-line gallery of art. One of the most interesting case studies we found is the Houston Astros' Player Injury System, which tracks information about players' injuries and treatments through the Major and Minor Leagues. Think about these as you design your own applications.

Chapter 2
What's This VBA Thing, Anyway?

*I*n this book, we use many pages to discuss VBA, the programming language in Microsoft Office 97. In every other chapter our discussion revolves around doing something with VBA. This chapter is different from the others, though. In this one, we look at what VBA is, where it came from, and how it works. We invite you, therefore, to sit back, relax, and find out a little about the background of this most important programming language.

What Does VBA Do?

As important as VBA is, you may be surprised to find out how little it actually does. Although VBA is powerful, to be sure, it's basically worthless without a host application like Excel, Word, PowerPoint, or Office. The reason for this is that VBA is just a programming language. Without something to program, VBA isn't worth very much.

So, what does VBA do for you? To answer that question, take a look at what comprises VBA itself:

> ✔ **Development environment:** VBA gives you a development environment in which you can create your applications. This includes the VBA editor that you can read more about in Chapter 3 as well as a form designer that we cover in Chapter 16. Think of the development environment as your artist's studio.

✔ **Code editor and execution engine:** VBA also has a sophisticated code editor and execution engine. These two elements are the real guts of VBA — the parts that look at what you've typed, try to make sense of the words and symbols, and, when you tell them to, run the code.

✔ **Data types and functions:** A set of built-in data types and generic functions that perform simple calculations are part of VBA. These elements of VBA are things that many different types of applications need to do, such as adding two numbers or determining what the first character of a text string is.

✔ **Control of host applications:** Finally, the last thing VBA offers is the ability to control host applications like Excel, Word, PowerPoint, or Access. Exactly how this is done is explained in the section "The Architecture of VBA" later in this chapter.

Looking at what VBA *can* do, you don't see any abilities such as building charts or preparing reports. That's because VBA knows literally nothing about charts and reports. Only when VBA and a host application, such as Excel or Word, cooperate can those tasks be accomplished.

Is VBA a Macro Language?

If you've used *productivity applications* (a fancy term for word processors and spreadsheets) for a long time, you've undoubtedly come across various incarnations of macro languages. So, you ask yourself, "Is VBA a macro language?" Well, we can hear you asking yourself this and so we answer, "Yes." In fact, VBA is a lot more than a macro language.

To understand how VBA and macro languages compare you need to consider what a macro language is. (We know — you have *so* many questions!) In general terms a *macro language* is a language that allows you to easily and repeatedly execute a customized series of commands within your application. The following list takes each part of that definition and looks at them more closely:

✔ **Easily.** If you want to execute a series of commands in Excel, for example, you can certainly use the built-in menu command, toolbar buttons, and dialog boxes. This may not be easy, however, especially if the series of commands is a complex one, so most macro languages provide an easy mechanism for initiating these commands, such as giving the series a name that you can choose from a list later on.

✔ **Repeatedly.** Your ability to execute a series of commands over and over again is another important feature of macro languages. This repetition implies that the exact sequence of steps is stored somewhere, whether in a document file, an external database, or someplace else.

✔ **Series of commands.** Macro languages aren't very useful if they enable you to execute only a single command, are they? After all, you'd be just as well off picking the command from a built-in menu. To provide a benefit, macro languages let you specify numerous commands to execute in a particular order.

✔ **Within your application.** This final point is the most important. The whole point of a macro language is to help you use the application that the macro language lives in. In the past, however, macro languages have been limited to working with only one application.

So, is VBA a macro language? Of course, because you can use VBA to execute a series of commands in any Office 97 application over and over again. In fact, that's probably how you were introduced to VBA, by recording a series of commands that you then played back.

Although being able to record a series of commands and saving them as a macro is a really cool feature, we don't consider this ability essential to the definition of a macro language. A number of software programs (most of which you've probably never heard of) feature macros that must be created by hand. Bummer.

But Wait, There's More!

Now that you know that VBA is a macro language, is it something more? At risk of sounding like a quiz show host, the answer again is, "Yes." You see, in order to create really cool and useful applications with Office 97, you need to do more than just automate a few simple tasks. That's why VBA brings to the dance many features of a true programming language (which, of course, it is).

What kinds of things must VBA be able to do to be considered a real programming language?

✔ **Work with data.** Although this may seem like an obvious requirement, working with data means being able to store and manipulate information in your application. VBA enables you to do this by using data types and variables, the subject of Chapter 11.

✔ **Create generic procedures.** Imagine that you want to perform the same set of tasks on ten Excel worksheets. Now, imagine that you have to write a special macro for each spreadsheet. Sound like fun? Probably not. That's why a *real* programming language must allow you to create generic procedures — those that do similar things to different objects. You can find out more about how to create your own generic procedures in Chapter 14.

✔ **Interact with the outside world.** Just as programmers can't live on pizza alone (or something like that), you often can't do everything you want to do inside a single application, such as Excel. Occasionally, you need to see what's going on in the outside world (finding out, for instance, what day it is). VBA gives you lots of functions that you can use for this purpose. You can read about them in Chapter 16.

And, as if that weren't enough, VBA has lots more to offer after you've mastered the basics. Unfortunately we promised the publisher that we'd keep this book to less than 5,000 pages so we can't explain everything.

Tonight on Biography: VBA, the Common Language

Did you ever wonder where VBA came from — how it came to be? After all, software programs as big as VBA don't just *happen,* they evolve over time. So what are the roots of VBA? What does the VBA family tree look like?

As it turns out, VBA is the product of two different evolutionary paths in the computing universe: programming languages and macro languages. Although you can make the argument that a macro language *is* a programming language, when we use the term *programming language* we mean something that full-time programmers (as in *pocket-protectors 'r' us*) use to create complete applications. For the purposes of this discussion, *macro languages* are limited programming languages used to automate repetitive tasks in another computer program.

As you can guess from the name, Visual Basic for Applications (emphasis on *Basic*) derives many of its language features from the original BASIC language developed at Dartmouth College in the '70s. That today's VBA has such a distant ancestor is pretty amazing when you consider that, back in those days, the idea of a *personal computer* went hand-in-hand with terms like soldering iron, wire wrap, and breadboard.

Microsoft has long favored BASIC as a programming language. The company was literally founded on BASIC when Bill Gates and Paul Allen developed a version of the language for the Altair computer. The success of this version, which, by the way, came on paper tape, convinced Gates to drop out of Harvard and dominate the computer industry on his way to becoming the world's richest self-made man. (That's the abridged version, anyway.) It's no wonder, then, that a BASIC derivative is the programming language of many Microsoft applications.

Of course, BASIC took many years to reach the point it's at now. Along the way, the language was extended and enhanced to include new features and capabilities. This effort culminated in the now famous Visual Basic, the first widely popular development tool for creating Windows applications that uses BASIC as its programming language. Despite the popularity, Visual Basic (or VB for short) has been criticized by programmers who use other languages, such as C, because VB lacks many of the most powerful features of their favorite language. (What can you expect from devotees of a language identified by a single letter?) On the other hand, VB also lacks most of the complexity, as well, which makes it easy for other programmers to understand and use.

About the same time that the revolution in programming languages was taking place, another revolution was happening in macro languages. When macro languages first began to appear in Microsoft products, they were extremely rudimentary and single purposed. Each language was designed to automate tasks in a particular program and only that program. From an organizational point of view, the groups that plan and develop software programs (called *product groups*) at Microsoft had complete control over their products' macro languages. This singular control led to a multitude of different languages with varying features, capabilities, and syntax — in other words, chaos in macro land!

Some product groups, like those responsible for Word and Project, chose to base their macro languages on BASIC, just like VB. On the other hand, the Excel team obviously felt that BASIC was too easy to comprehend and so they developed the XLM macro language. Although extremely powerful compared to the rival of Excel at the time, Lotus 1-2-3, the XLM macro language was one of the most obtuse languages we've ever seen. (Nonetheless, XLM was the first Microsoft programming language we used.)

As Microsoft Office became more popular, Microsoft began to realize that Office could be used as a development platform. That is, people could use the Office programs as the starting point for a custom application, adding functionality through their macro languages. Unfortunately, Microsoft (and Bill Gates in particular) also realized that Office would not realize its full potential in this regard as long as it relied on a mishmash of different macro languages. At that point, Office was like a nice apartment furnished with garage sale furniture. Although some pieces may have had character, you could tell they weren't part of a matched set.

Gates, aware of the success of Visual Basic, decreed that Microsoft would create a *common macro language* for Microsoft Office based on VB. This common language would include a similar development environment for each Office application and, as much as possible, identical syntax, regardless of which application it was used in. This would mean you could share program code between the Office applications and Visual Basic.

So, like Moses coming down from the mountain, Microsoft managers and developers scurried about for many months and came up with what we know now as Visual Basic for Applications. VBA made its debut in 1993 in Excel 5.0 and, with further enhancements along the way, it's what you see now in Office 97. Now, isn't that a touching story?

VBA and Its Predecessors

If you're just now beginning to develop applications in Office, you may not realize just how fortunate you are. VBA is now the common development language for all the Office products (not to mention others like Microsoft Project, Visio, and AutoCAD), but this uniformity hasn't always been this way. Like a virus, VBA slowly invaded the Office products, replacing their proprietary macro languages with itself. Table 2-1 shows how VBA conquered various languages over time.

Table 2-1	Time and Versions Can't Stop the March of VBA			
Product	*Office 97*	*Office 95*	*Office 4.x*	*Long Ago*
Access	VBA	VBA	Access Basic	N/A
Excel	VBA	VBA	VBA	XLM
PowerPoint	VBA	None	None	None
Word	VBA	WordBasic	WordBasic	WordBasic
Outlook	VBScript	N/A	N/A	N/A

As you may guess from their names, some of the VBA predecessors were also based on BASIC (Access Basic and WordBasic, to be specific). Even so, these languages were, for the most part, incompatible with each other. This meant that you couldn't easily share code among applications, killing whatever enthusiasm for writing integrated applications early Office developers may have had.

By the way, you may be wondering what the entry for VBScript is all about. Well, to make a long story short, when Microsoft was developing applications and tools for the Internet, it needed a lightweight programming language for its web browser, Internet Explorer. What Microsoft wanted was a scripting language that web developers could use to accomplish simple tasks, such as hiding a text field if the user clicked a button. Again, Microsoft decided to use a BASIC derivative, this time, a stripped-down version of VBA called VBScript. Because Outlook was a new program and required lots of effort and brain power to construct, Microsoft decided to give Outlook VBScript as its macro language, rather than VBA. Giving Outlook VBA would have taken longer, threatening the ever-important *delivery schedule!*

The intention of Microsoft is to eventually upgrade Outlook to include the same version of VBA as the rest of Office. In fact, they may already have shipped a new version by the time you read this book. Of course, we don't mention Outlook in this book. That we don't mention Outlook only goes to show you that books about software can become obsolete as fast as the software itself.

The Architecture of VBA

Well, you can pretty much guess from the heading that this section is going to get a wee bit technical. Words such as *architecture, component,* and *infrastructure* are dead giveaways. If you want, you can skip this section, although we think that it can help your overall understanding of what makes a VBA application tick. So, get out your pocket protector and slide rule because here you go.

The one *huge* difference between VBA and its macro language predecessors is that VBA exists as a separate software component and is not actually part of any one program, such as Excel. Now, we know that VBA *looks* like it's part of Excel. After all, you can record macros in VBA by using Excel menus, you can get to the code from Excel, and VBA contains references to all kinds of Excel thingies (that's a technical term). But, trust us, VBA is not part of Excel.

So, how is this trick performed? How does Microsoft make VBA look like it is part of Excel when it's really a separate software program? To answer this question, we need to tell you a little bit about another piece of the technology pie called COM. *COM* stands for Component Object Model, but you don't have to remember that. The only thing you need to remember is that COM defines a standard way for different kinds of programs to talk to each other. Why do programs want to do this (other than the obvious reason that they get lonely on your hard disk)? Many reasons abound. Sometimes, the programs need to share data. Other times, one program needs to tell another program to do something that it can't do itself.

Don't confuse the term COM that refers to how programs communicate with COM files (such as COMMAND.COM) and COM Web domains (such as microsoft.com). In this chapter, COM refers to the way programs interact under Windows.

You can think of COM as the drive-up window at a bank. By using the microphone and speaker, you can talk with the teller who is inside the bank. A small, retractable drawer lets you share things (money, checks, receipts) with the teller. The drive-up window is your *interface* to the bank teller. COM defines an interface (several, in fact) that allows programs to communicate and share things, although the interfaces are much more strict than a bank's drive-up window. (Imagine if you could only speak to the teller by using a few phrases expressed in a strange language!)

When you open an Excel workbook that contains VBA code, Excel uses COM to *wake up* VBA and tell it to go to work. COM tells VBA where to find the code inside the Excel workbook file. After VBA loads the code, Excel asks VBA to tell what macros are defined by the code. Excel needs to ask VBA because Excel doesn't know anything about the code itself. To Excel, the VBA code is just a blob of data. Excel *needs* VBA to make sense of the VBA code. After Excel has obtained the list of macros, it can let you run one of them.

Now, this may all sound complicated but, fortunately, the entire process all happens behind the scenes. You never have to worry about this process. All these actions happen automatically whenever you open anything that contains VBA code.

At this point in the discussion, we want to show some sort of nebulous diagram. So, take a look at Figure 2-1. Ooh, isn't it impressive? Nebulous diagrams are great for explaining complex topics because they can be interpreted in many different ways without actually conveying any information. These diagrams are what we describe as *amazing content-free*.

Actually, Figure 2-1 does convey some information. First, we depict VBA and its host application as separate boxes. This means that they are separate software programs (but we just told you that a few paragraphs ago). Inside VBA is a set of built-in functions that you are likely to use often, regardless of the host application that you're trying to control. Inside the host application, on the other hand, is a set of what we call *objects*. Objects are the *things* that you control by using VBA. In the case of Excel, objects are things such as workbooks, worksheets, and charts. We go into lots of detail on objects in Chapters 4 through 10. Finally, the figure shows that COM is what bridges the gap between these two components.

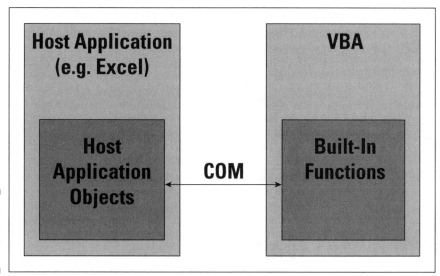

Figure 2-1:
Architecture
of a VBA
application.

When you write code in the VBA development environment you're using COM, too, albeit indirectly. That's because VBA doesn't know anything about the host application that you're trying to control. What VBA does know, however, is how to ask the host application about itself. VBA asks Excel, for instance, "What do you have that I can control?" Excel, being the cooperative type, answers, telling VBA all about workbooks, worksheets, charts, cells, and so forth. Armed with this knowledge, VBA can let you write code to control all of those things without having a fit and complaining that it doesn't know what you're talking about.

Actually, VBA doesn't really talk directly to Excel. Instead, VBA looks at a special file that Excel provides called a *type library*. A type library contains descriptions of all the things that VBA can control in an application and, because VBA doesn't have to launch the application to talk to this library, VBA can get the information much faster!

Where Is VBA Going?

Microsoft is not a company that sits on its laurels. Those busy little software beavers are furiously working to make VBA a better tool for creating applications. So, where is VBA going?

Well, first off, you can view the future of VBA right now, if you want to. Visual Basic 5.0 includes a slightly enhanced version of VBA, with a few more features. You don't need to be concerned about most of these features for a long, long, time because they are very advanced. In fact, many real programming nerds don't understand what these features are used for!

Another place VBA is going is into other applications. Microsoft has licensed the VBA environment to other software developers, including Visio, AutoDesk, Adobe, and Great Plains Software. Licensing VBA enables these companies to put VBA into their programs. So, just as you can open up the VBA editor from inside Excel now, you'll be able to open it up from a copy of Adobe PhotoShop in the future. Why is this good to know? Because all the skills you acquire from working with Office 97 can be translated (with a little change in mindset) to other programs. This knowledge makes you valuable to your company, which lets you keep your job and take the kids to Disney World every other year.

Where Are We Going?

Now that you know a little bit about what VBA is and how it got to where it is today, we hope that you'll enjoy using it more. We also hope this knowledge will help you understand why some things work the way that they do. Throughout other chapters of this book, we spend a lot of time in this book telling you how to do things.

Chapter 3

Where Does All That VBA Code Live?

*I*n this chapter, we discuss the development environment of Visual Basic for Applications (VBA) for the various Office products — Word, Excel, PowerPoint, and Access. Specifically, we present everything that you need to know about the new Visual Basic Editor (VBE) so that you can start writing code. We drill down into specifics about how to use the tools within the Visual Basic Editor, such as the Project Explorer, Properties settings, Option dialog boxes, and the Immediate Window. And soon, you will be on your merry way to using the VBE in Word, Excel, and PowerPoint.

Great, but aren't we forgetting about Access? Working with VBA would be all too easy if we could have one set of directions, right? As we started writing this book, it was an unpleasant realization that Access has a different development environment than the rest of its siblings. But, that's life. This really struck us as we were preparing some curry-flavored couscous for dinner a few nights ago. Preparing couscous for dinner is a lot like the Access predicament: Depending on where you are doing your cooking in MS Office 97, you must follow a different set of instructions. For example, we have some curry-flavored couscous that we like to have for dinner. The package contains more than one set of cooking instructions — for the stove, for the microwave, at low altitudes, at higher altitudes. If MS Office VBA is like using a microwave at sea level, then Access is like cooking on a Bunsen burner in orbit. Both are described as cooking couscous, but you definitely need a new set of instructions for outer-space couscous and VBA programming with Access.

Access 97 has not inherited the VBE for managing and writing code. After we complete our discussion about the other Office components in this chapter, we look at the specific differences that you deal with in Access.

Introducing the Visual Basic Editor

The Visual Basic Editor *(VBE)* needs no introduction. At last, a common development language has allowed a common development environment. Are you as excited as we are about this? Word, Excel, and PowerPoint now utilize the VBE for creating and managing VBA project code.

If you come from the land of Visual Basic, or have even visited there for a short time, you may find the VBE to be a bit like home. The VBE environment is modeled after Visual Basic. In fact, the VBE may even feel as good as your comfy old slippers. Even if you've *never* laid eyes on Visual Basic, finding out about the VBE and the VBA language can make you feel right at home if you ever decide to dabble in Visual Basic.

To introduce the VBE, we use Excel, although we can just as easily use Word or PowerPoint. When you are ready to write some VBA code or view existing code, you need to enter the VBA Development environment — the *VBE*.

To begin your tour of the VBE, follow these steps:

1. **Open Excel and a workbook of your choosing.**

   You can use our sample workbook, products.xls (located in C:\Dummies\Chapter 3\products.xls). The sample is based on the Northwind database. (If you prefer, you can use a blank workbook.)

2. **Choose Tools⇨Macro⇨Visual Basic Editor, as shown in Figure 3-1.**

After you jump in with both feet, you may feel very comfortable with the VBE. In fact, many of you may wonder how you ever lived without it! Imagining life without the VBE is kind of like imagining life before garage door openers, microwaves, and caller ID.

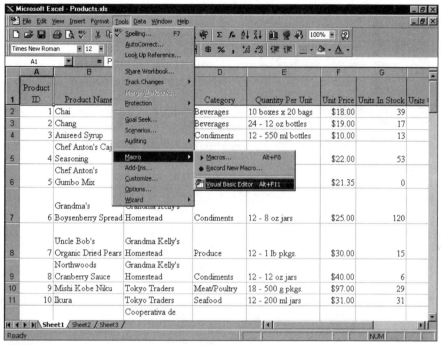

Figure 3-1:
Getting to
the Visual
Basic Editor.

Overall Project Properties

You can set properties for the entire Visual Basic project by using the
Project Properties dialog box, as shown in Figure 3-2. General properties
include the project name, project description, help file information, and
conditional compilation arguments. For right now, look at the overall
properties of the project. Microsoft divided the project's main properties
into two categories — General and Protection. To access your VBA project's
properties, do the following:

1. **In the VBE, choose Tools⇨VBAProject Properties from the menu bar.**

   If you do not have the VBE open, select Tools⇨Macro⇨Visual Basic
   Editor.

   The VBAProject Properties dialog box appears.

2. **Choose the appropriate option tab — either General or Protection.**

3. **Make necessary changes and click OK.**

Don't confuse the properties for the entire project with the individual
properties that you set through the Properties window. See the section "VBE
Windows" in this chapter for more details.

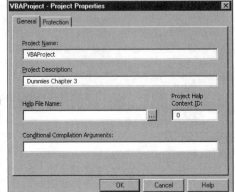

The default name for your project is VBAProject. If you change the name of
the project, the menu selection under the Tools menu and the shortcut
menu in Project Explorer changes accordingly.

General tab

In the General tab of the Project Properties dialog box, you find fields for the
Project Name, Project Description, Help File Name, Project Help Context ID,
and the Conditional Compilation Arguments. The project name, shown as
VBAProject in Figure 3-2, identifies your VBA project in the Windows Registry and the Object Browser (which we visit in Chapter 5). This must be a
unique name within the project and must not conflict with any references to
your project, such as the Office 8.0 Object Library.

To change the name of the project to *VBA* and see what happens:

1. **Choose Tools⇨VBAProject Properties from the menu bar or right-
   click to expose the shortcut menu in Project Explorer and select
   VBAProject Properties.**

   The VBAProject Properties dialog box appears.

2. **Click the General tab, if it's not currently being viewed.**

3. **In the Project Name field, delete the name VBAProject and type** VBA.

4. **Click OK.**

   You immediately get an error, shown in Figure 3-3, because this is the
   name of the Visual Basic for Applications library, which contains all of
   the built-in VBA functions.

5. **Click OK to close the error dialog box, which returns you to the Properties dialog box.**

6. **Change the Project Name to a valid entry, such as MyProject, and click OK.**

   This time the VBE accepts your project name change and closes the VBAProject Properties dialog box.

7. **Revisit the Tools menu and note that the menu selection that used to read as VBAProject Properties now reads MyProject Properties.**

 A valid project name is unique within the project and does not contain any spaces. The VBE lets you know if you have entered a name that conflicts with the name of any module, project, or object library as you saw in Step 4 of this example. If you try to put spaces in a project name, you receive a different error notifying you that it is not a legal object name.

Figure 3-3:
Visual
Basic lets
you know if
the project
name
that you
choose is
unaccept-
able.

 The *project name* is the name of the type library for your component. Great, but what's a type library? In basic terms, a *type library* (or *TypeLib*) contains the description of the objects and interfaces provided by your component.

Protection tab

Have your eyes been drawn to the Protection tab yet? Has the tab piqued your curiosity? As shown in Figure 3-4, the settings on the Protection tab enable you to lock your VBA project, which prevents others from making any modifications.

Check the Lock project for viewing box to protect your project from being viewed or edited. Only a valid password allows someone to view project properties. Then, set a password for the project and confirm that password. If you do not type in the same password in both the Password and Confirm password boxes, you receive an error message.

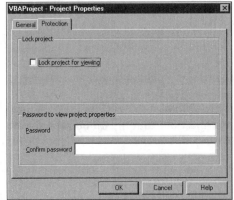

Figure 3-4:
Viewing the
Protection
settings for
a project.

If you set a password for the project but do not check the Lock project for viewing option, you are required to enter a password to open the Property window the next time that you open the project. Be sure to remember your password!

VBE Windows

When you first start out, the VBE does not even display a code window. As shown in Figure 3-5, you see a Project window (at the top left), which is referred to as the Project Explorer, a Properties window (at the bottom left), and the Immediate window (at the bottom right). Becoming familiar with the VBE interface is a lot to digest at once, so don't fret. We step through each window one at a time and point out what is important for you to know as we move forward. And heck, we do our best to make this introduction to the VBE fun!

If the Immediate window is not initially visible, select Immediate Window from the View menu.

Project Explorer

Need any assistance in managing your development project? *Project Explorer* can't whip your developers into shape or provide the team with lattes, but it does give you an overview of what's included in your project. At a very basic level, a project is a set of document objects from your application and modules, which act as containers for any VBA code you write.

Project Explorer   Standard toolbar

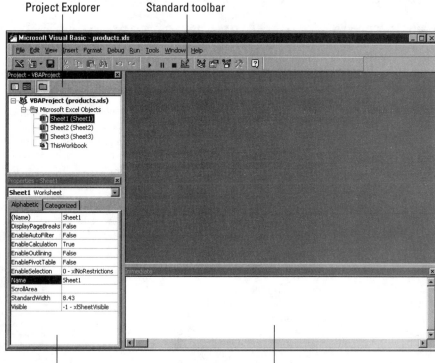

Project Explorer   Standard toolbar

Figure 3-5:
Touring the
Visual Basic
Editor for
the first
time.

Properties window   Immediate window

Project Explorer neatly groups your application objects (worksheets and charts for example), code objects (such as modules and class modules), and user forms. We know that some of these terms may be unfamiliar at this time, but for now you just need to know that the Project Explorer gives a visual representation of what is part of your overall development project. If you are dying to know more now about these unfamiliar objects, you can create code objects later in this chapter and in Chapter 14 or work with user forms in Chapter 17.

If you are using our example workbook, Products.xls, which is located in the C:\Dummies\Chapter 3 directory installed from the disk, all you see at this point are your Excel worksheets. You should see one folder for Microsoft Excel Objects, which includes the individual worksheets (Sheet1, Sheet2, and Sheet3) that comprise the workbook and our workbook object called *ThisWorkbook*. After you begin to flex your coding muscles by developing modules and user forms, these objects appear in additional folders in the Project window, as shown in Figure 3-6. We don't venture into more detail at this point, but do watch for it in Chapters 14 and 17 and beyond!

What's the Record New Macro selection all about?

If your eyes are drawn to the Record New Macro selection on the Tools⇨Macro menu, we have some good news and some bad news. First, the good news: Record New Macro is quite an amazing feature of Office 97. When you record a macro in Word, Excel, or PowerPoint, you are actually generating VBA code behind the scenes. Sounds greats, right?

The bad news is that, even though recorded macros are truly fantastic for single-use type functions, such as applying formatting to a document, recorded macros are generally not reusable. As a programmer, you live for reusable code, right? And besides, if recorded macros were the answer to a programmer's prayers, than we'd be out playing volleyball and not putting blood, sweat, and tears into this book about VBA programming.

Now, before you forget all about these recorded macros, please note that playing around with the macro recorder can be very valuable to those with little or no familiarity with Visual Basic or VBA. As you record your actions, you can see what VBA commands are generated. If you want to try this out, here are a few pointers:

1. Choose Tools⇨Macro⇨Record New Macro to begin recording your actions from either a Word document, an Excel workbook, or a PowerPoint presentation.

   Notice that the Stop Recording toolbar, which includes a Stop Recording button, is exposed.

2. Carry out a number of actions, such as applying formatting to your document and selecting various menu items.

   Note: Unfortunately, there are some limitations to the recording capabilities within Word. Although you can use your mouse to make menu selections, you can't use it to select text or move around your document.

3. Click the Stop Recording button when you are satisfied. This button is marked with a black square like the stop button on a boom box or CD player. If you are still unsure which button this is, you can hover your mouse over the toolbar and see which button is marked with the Stop Recording tooltip.

   Congratulations, you just successfully recorded a macro.

4. Choose Tools⇨Macro⇨Visual Basic Editor to open the VBE and view the code for what you've recorded.

Tip: If you decide to record any macros, the first macro that you record creates a new module in your VBA project. Any subsequent recorded macros can be added to this new module.

Although we do not discuss recorded macros throughout the other sections of the book, we would be remiss not to provide you with the basic information given here.

The neat hierarchical representation of your project objects in the Project Explorer makes managing your VBA project code and objects easy and maybe even fun (okay, we're pushing it a bit). If you have programmed in any Office component before, you can certainly welcome the change.

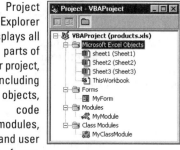

Figure 3-6:
Project
Explorer
displays all
parts of
your project,
including
objects,
code
modules,
and user
forms.

If you right-click on any element in Project Explorer, you have access to a shortcut menu, as shown in Figure 3-7. In the case of Excel, you can view the code related to a particular object (by selecting View Code) or toggle to the object itself in Excel (by selecting View Object).

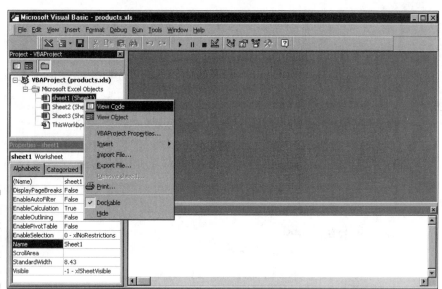

Figure 3-7:
The Project
Explorer
shortcut
menu.

Project properties

If you are thinking "so, what?" at this point, hold on. For each project object, such as individual Excel worksheets or Word documents, you can set a number of properties by using the *Properties window*. For example, for each worksheet in the workbook, you can change its name and determine whether or not it will be visible to the end user. As you become more familiar with Excel development, you will find more uses for these settings in the Properties window.

To view the properties of a specific object, click the object name in the Project window, and the Properties window provides the corresponding properties. To gain a little familiarity with the Properties window and how it can assist you, we go through a simple example of modifying an object property.

Often, you do not leave a worksheet named with its default name, such as Sheet1. By using the Properties window, you can change the sheet name. To do so, follow these steps:

1. **In Excel, open Products.xls, located in C:\Dummies\Chapter 3.**

   The Products.xls worksheet appears in Excel.

   If you haven't copied the disk files to your hard drive, you will not be able to make modifications to the Excel workbook.

2. **Choose Tools⇨Macros⇨Visual Basic Editor from the menu bar.**

   The Visual Basic Editor (VBE) appears on-screen.

3. **Click Sheet1 in the Project window.**

4. **Scroll down to the Name property in the Properties window.**

   The Name property is listed between EnableSelection and ScrollArea.

5. **Press Tab to go to the right column of the Properties window.**

   The Name property is now highlighted.

6. **Type nwind.**

   The column now contains nwind as the name of the worksheet.

7. **Press Ctrl+S to save your changes.**

You have successfully changed the name property of Sheet1, as well as the actual worksheet name in Excel, as shown in Figure 3-8.

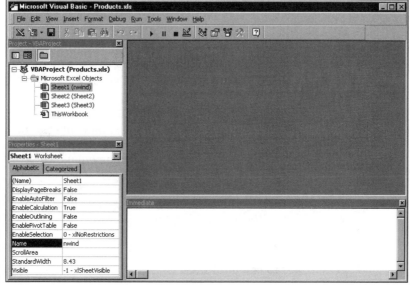

Figure 3-8:
Modifying
an object
property in
the VBE.

Using the Name property can be a bit confusing, because there is both a (Name) and Name property. The property we used in the prior series of steps refers to the real worksheet name in our Excel workbook, or the actual document name in Word. The *(Name) property* refers to what you call the worksheet in the VBE. In simpler terms, think of (Name) as your legal name and *Name* as your nickname.

When you need to do something important, such as file your taxes or apply for a mortgage, you need to use your legal name. But your accountant and your mortgage consultant can call you by your preferred nickname in conversation. To go back to VBA for a moment, if you want to do something with an object, you need to use the object's real name, which we see as (Name) in the Properties window. (Name) really isn't a property; it's just fact! The Name property without reference to the object (Name) is of no value.

Immediate response with the Immediate window

What on earth is an Immediate window? You can think of the Immediate window as VBA's command line. By using the Immediate window, you can run code immediately — before you plug your code into your user forms and application objects. The Immediate window also serves as a great testing bed for code!

The Immediate window serves you in a number of ways, including

- **Running your VBA code.**
- **Testing code that isn't working properly.**
- **Changing a code value (variable or property) while running your code.**
- **Viewing messages or progress statements.**

If you take with you nothing else from this chapter, you need to know how to run code from the Immediate window. Remember, if the Immediate window is not visible in the main VBE window, select Immediate window from the View menu to make it appear for your viewing pleasure.

Follow these steps to get the current date and carry out some simple arithmetic by using the Immediate window as your tool.

1. **In the Immediate window, type** ? Date().

2. **Press Enter to commit the code.**

   The current date (according to your PC) appears below the code line.

3. **To run one more command from the Immediate window, type** ?1+2.

4. **Press Enter.**

   The Immediate window displays the result of the addition – 3, as shown in Figure 3-9.

Date() is a built-in VBA function. In the same way that you ran this code function, you can run any VBA code you develop.

Figure 3-9:
Using the
Immediate
window
with some
simple
functions.

What about That Toolbar?

That the VBE has toolbars to give you quick access to environment features such as copying a selection or running the code currently in view should be of no surprise. Although you may be new to VBA, it is unlikely that you are new to Microsoft products. Some of these toolbar buttons may look very familiar, such as the Cut, Copy, and Paste buttons. Oh, and don't forget your friends Find, Undo, and Redo! These buttons need no explanation, but there are some new buttons specific to the VBE. Take a look at Figure 3-10, which shows the standard VBE toolbar (and Table 3-1 takes a quick look at some of those buttons as well). Although a few other toolbars are available, this is the toolbar that you use most often and consequently want to keep visible at all times.

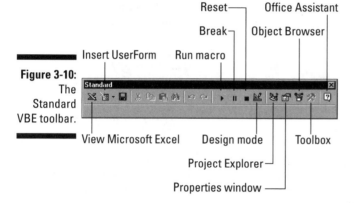

Figure 3-10: The Standard VBE toolbar.

Table 3-1	A Quick Look at Some VBE Toolbar Buttons
Toolbar Button	**What the Button Does for You**
View Microsoft Excel	Returns to your Excel workbook (or Word document or PowerPoint presentation).
Insert UserForm	Creates a user form for your application (see Chapter 17).
Run macro	Runs currently selected function or subroutine, referred to as *macros*.
Break	Inserts a break or pause into your code (see Chapter 18).
Reset	Resets your code after an error occurs (see Chapter 18).
Design mode	Places document in design mode (see Chapter 17).
Project Explorer	Opens the VBAProject window if it's closed, otherwise makes it the active window (see "Project Explorer" in this chapter).
Properties window	Opens the Properties window if it's closed, otherwise makes it the active window (see "Project properties" in this chapter).
Object Browser	Opens the Object Browser (see Chapter 5).
Toolbox	If applicable, opens the design toolbox for user forms design (see Chapter 17).
Office Assistant	Opens your favorite Office tour guide — the Office Assistant.

Where's the Beef? (Oops, We Mean the Code!)

Now that you are feeling more comfortable with the Visual Basic Editor (VBE), it's time to unleash the real fun. You must still be wondering where the heck the code is. That was, after all, what we promised this chapter would tell you. Because you haven't created any code yet for this workbook, the code window is hiding. Come out, come out, wherever you are.

Open a window! It's code in here!

To open a code window in VBE, select Code from the View menu or press F7. As shown in Figure 3-11, the code window is now ready for all the VBA you can find in this book!

In Figure 3-11, you see the VBE (including the code window) as it appears for Products.xls, which is the sample workbook we use throughout this chapter. If you are just joining us now, Products.xls is located in C:\Dummies\Chapter 3 directory installed from the disk.

Object Name   Procedure Name

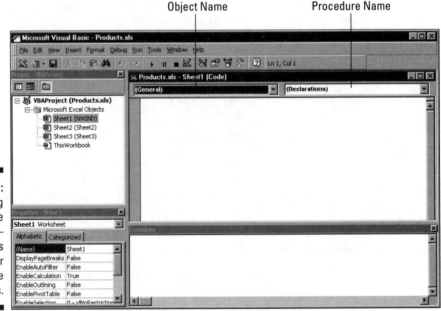

Figure 3-11:
Unhiding
the code
window —
this is
where your
VBA code
lives.

If the Code selection is disabled on the View menu, it is for a good reason: You can only open a code window if you have an object selected that can support its own code window. If you are using the sample Excel workbook, be sure that one of the worksheets is highlighted before you try to view the code window.

The code window is in view, so what's the big deal? True, at this point there is nothing exciting to see, at least until you start writing some code. For now, we just want to introduce you to a few features of the code window — the object name and procedure name drop-down lists.

The object-name list indicates what you are writing VBA code for, which may be a worksheet or a custom-built user form. The procedure name, after you start to write code, includes a list of existing code procedures written for the selected object. The procedure list always includes a (Declarations) section. Any values that you want to use throughout the entire module need to be placed here. If you think we're holding out on you and not giving you all the information — you are perceptive.

There's a lot more to say about the code window, but for now we just intend to give you a feeling of comfort with the VBE and introduce a few bells and whistles. We put a lot more detail into other chapters. In Chapter 11, we discuss declarations of various types and begin to enter code into the code window, and, in Chapter 14, we use the code window at full throttle.

But wait, we have a little bit more for you. You can actually open a code window for each object in your VBA project. By using our sample workbook, Products.xls, you can open as many as four code windows, as shown in Figure 3-12 — one for each worksheet (we have three) and one for the global workbook. After you start to create user forms, you can have a separate code window for each user form as well. So many code windows, so little time.

Now that you're a pro at viewing the code behind an object, such as a document or workbook, you probably want to know about some additional code — *modules*. In the Project Explorer section, we mentioned that modules are part of a VBA project, along with application objects and user forms. Modules are really the same as the code sitting behind a given application object but are accessible to all objects in a given project. Create a new module to give yourself a feel for what they really are:

1. **Open Excel if it's not already open.**

2. **Either leave the blank workbook open or open any sample workbook you'd like.**

3. **Choose Tools➪Macros➪Visual Basic Editor from the menu bar.**

   The VBE appears on-screen.

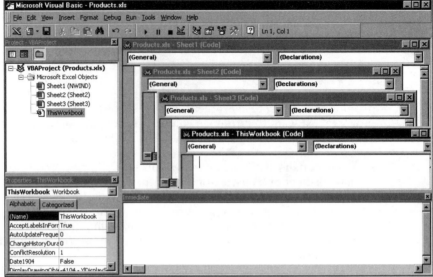

Figure 3-12:
Code
window
explosion —
a code
window for
each
object!

4. Choose Insert⊅Module.

A new module is created, and a code window is opened.

Once your new module is created, you can write lots of cool subroutines and functions, as you see in Chapter 14.

Code editor options you'll care about!

After you begin to utilize the Immediate window (in Chapter 4) and write functions and subroutines (in Chapter 14), you may realize the greatness of some of these code editor options. At last, writing code can be easy. No more memorization of arguments or referencing on-line help every 30 seconds. Put on your seatbelts and enjoy the ride.

First of all, we take a look at the Options dialog box and then we dive into the details. In Figure 3-13, you can see the Code Editor options, and Figure 3-14 shows the Editor Format tab options.

Remember, we are talking about coding options, which get set in the VBE. To access the Options dialog box, choose Tools⊅Options and choose the appropriate tab.

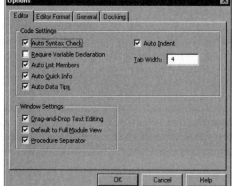

Figure 3-13:
The Code
Editor
Options
dialog box.

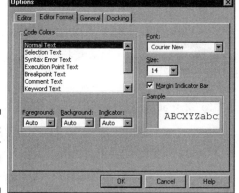

Figure 3-14:
Code Editor
Formatting
Settings.

Editor tab

The Code Settings available under the Editor tab provide a tremendous amount of value to the developer! These settings affect the Code window and the Immediate window:

- ✔ **Auto Syntax Check** — As the name suggests, checking this box means that your code syntax is automatically verified for accuracy as you enter a line of VBA code in the Code window.

- ✔ **Require Variable Declaration** — In Chapter 11, we delve into great detail about what variables are all about and how to declare them. Simply put for purposes of this introductory chapter, enabling this check box requires that you, the programmer, tell VBA up front what variables you want to use in your code. If the check box is selected, it automatically adds an Option Explicit statement to general declarations in any new module. We take a closer look at this option in Chapter 11 — we promise!

- ✔ **Auto List Member** — This check box enables an extremely cool feature that's new to Office 97. This option assists you in completing code statements in a logical fashion. You can think of this option as that person in your office that always completes your sentences for you! Don't worry, the auto list member feature isn't annoying at all, it's so helpful. If this feature tires you, turn it off. Sorry, we have no suggestions for annoying people who do the same. You can see the Auto List Member in action in Chapter 4.

- ✔ **Auto Quick Info** — Another cool feature! If you check this option, Office VBA assists you in writing your code by displaying the syntax for functions and their parameters as you type. Yep, you guessed it. We look at this feature in Chapter 4.

- ✔ **Auto Data Tips** — Keep this check box under your hat until you attempt to debug your code. (See Chapter 18 for more on this feature.) While in Break mode, Auto Data Tips displays the value of the variable as you hover over it with your cursor.

- ✔ **Auto Indent** — Many programmers like to indent their code to make it more readable. Check this box and, after you tab a line of code, all subsequent lines start at that tab position. Cool, huh? Oh, we remember the days of doing this manually.

- ✔ **Tab Width** — By using this field, you can set your desired tab width, which can range from 1 to 32 spaces. The default is 4 spaces.

The following Window Settings may be of interest to you as well, but are dim in comparison to the code settings in the preceding list:

- ✔ **Drag-and-Drop Text Editing** — Checking this box makes VBE similar to what you have today in Word, for example, in that you can drag and drop text around your document. In the VBE, this option allows you to drag and drop items from the current code and from the code window into the Immediate or Watch windows.

- ✔ **Default to Full Module View** — In the code window, you can opt to view your module code one procedure at a time or as a scrollable list of all your cool code! If you turn on this option while a module is open, it does not toggle the way the module is currently viewed. In other words, this option sets the default view of newly created modules, not existing ones.

- ✔ **Procedure Separator** — As a matter of personal preference, you can enable this check box to display separator bars that appear at the end of each procedure in the code window.

Editor format tab

Another welcomed inclusion with the VBA language is color-coded code. If you've never programmed in a language that recognized different types of code and applied a color scheme to them, you are in for a treat. These formatting options allow you to specify the appearance of your Visual Basic code.

Without going into painful detail, you can let your inner artist out and make decisions about how things appear in the code window, such as background and foreground colors, text colors, font types and sizes, and more. As shown in Figure 3-14, you can set many formatting options. You can make no right or wrong selections — only those that make you a happy programmer! Be sure that you take a gander at these options.

Now, What about Access?

Good question. We wish we could offer some explanation as to why Access 97 did not inherit the same development tools as the rest of its Office siblings. Perhaps Microsoft did not want to change the development environment Access has enjoyed since its birth. Nonetheless, here we highlight the items unique to Access that you need to know as you develop using VBA in Access.

Getting to the code

In Access 97, your VBA code is stored in modules just as it is in the other Office components. What is unusual is that you can access the code in your Access database in different ways. First, we need to point out that code can actually live in three separate places within Access — in modules, behind forms, and behind reports. Code behind a form or report is referred to as a *class module,* which distinguishes it from a general use module. In the VBE, modules and class modules can all be viewed as part of a VBA Project. (Refer to Figure 3-3.) Unfortunately, Access has no equivalent project window. Module code and class module code do not live together, so as you may expect, getting to different addresses requires different sets of directions.

All the great VBA code you develop is stored in modules. See Chapter 14 for more about those elements.

In the other Office components, recorded macros are actually VBA code, but the same does not hold true with Access. Access has two separate entities — macros and modules. Modules are built in VBA, macros are not. Access macros are outside the scope of this book, but you are not missing anything — trust us. VBA is the way to go!

When you open an Access database, you are immediately greeted by the database window, which sports various tabs, including the Modules tab, as shown in Figure 3-15.

Figure 3-15:
The
Modules
tab of the
Database
window.

From the Modules tab, you can either create a new module by using the New button or view the code contained in an existing module by selecting the module and pressing the Design button. For purposes of exploring the Access development environment, we use the Wine List database, which contains a small sampling of wines. Wine List.mdb was created using an Access wizard and is available on the disk in the C:\Dummies\Chapter 3 directory.

Create a new module in this database by opening Access and doing the following:

1. **Open the WineList.mdb that you have copied to your local hard drive from the disk.**

2. **From the Modules tab, click New.**

   A module window opens with a default name of Module1, as shown in Figure 3-16. Save the module with a more meaningful name.

3. **Choose File⇨Save, enter a module name in the Save As dialog box, and click OK.**

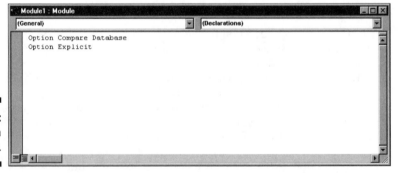

Figure 3-16:
Creating a
new module.

Notice that the new module already has two lines of code — Option Compare Database and Option Explicit. These lines are included automatically based on default option settings within Access. When the Option Compare Database statement is included in a module, strings are sorted and compared based on the local language. For databases used in America, this statement is English-U.S.; databases for use in other nations may use different statements. The Option Explicit statement indicates that you need to explicitly declare variables before you use them (see Chapter 11 for more details).

De-bug, de-window, de-code (Debug window)

Unlike the development environment of Word, Excel, and PowerPoint, Access only has a main code window and its own version of the Immediate window — the Debug window. When you first begin writing module code, the Debug window is not visible, so choose View⇨Debug Window.

The Debug Window, shown in Figure 3-17 with some code already in it, doesn't look like the Immediate window that we visit in the "VBE Windows" section of this chapter. In the top half of the Debug window, you see some unusual tabs — Locals and Watch. These come in handy when you start to debug your code. Not that we'd ever write buggy code, right? We explore the debugging functionality (Local and Watch variables) in Chapter 18.

Using the Debug Window in Access is essentially the same as using the Immediate window in the other Office components. Try a simple exercise by using the Debug window to gain some familiarity. Remember, the lower half of the Debug window is the Immediate pane (where you can type your code).

1. Place your cursor in the Immediate pane of the Debug window.

2. Type ? date, time.

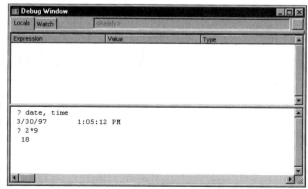

Figure 3-17: The Debug window in action.

3. **Press Enter to commit the code.**

   The current date (according to your PC) and time appear below the code line.

4. **To run one more command from the Debug window, type** ? 2*9 **and press Enter.**

   The Debug Window displays the result of the multiplication — 18, as shown in Figure 3-17.

More peculiarities — coding options and toolbar

In our discussion of the VBE, we point out the different coding options that you can set and provide a brief look at the VBE toolbar. As you may have guessed, coding options are set a bit differently in Access. Although you can set similar options and select similar toolbar buttons, Access is different enough to warrant a brief excursion through module coding options and the Visual Basic toolbar.

Now, return to the database window and open an existing module.

1. **To return to the Database Window, choose Window⇨ WineList:Database.**

2. **From the Modules tab, select the Global Code module.**

3. **Click Design.**

   The Global Code module opens in design mode, as shown in Figure 3-18.

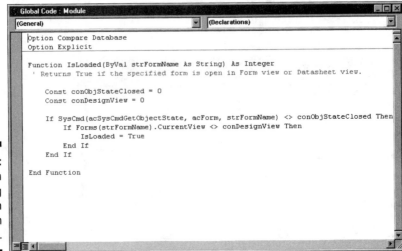

Figure 3-18: Opening an existing module in design mode.

```
Global Code : Module                                              _ □ X
(General)                            ▼   (Declarations)                    ▼
Option Compare Database
Option Explicit

Function IsLoaded(ByVal strFormName As String) As Integer
  ' Returns True if the specified form is open in Form view or Datasheet view.

    Const conObjStateClosed = 0
    Const conDesignView = 0

    If SysCmd(acSysCmdGetObjectState, acForm, strFormName) <> conObjStateClosed Then
        If Forms(strFormName).CurrentView <> conDesignView Then
            IsLoaded = True
        End If
    End If

End Function
```

Other than the fact that we're in Access right now, the code looks similar to what you see in the Visual Basic Editor code window for the other Office products. As you may expect, the nicely indented code and color coding come compliments of some option settings. Access has a different dialog box for setting code editing and formatting options, as shown in Figure 3-19. Unlike in the VBE, all the code settings are under one option tab (Module).

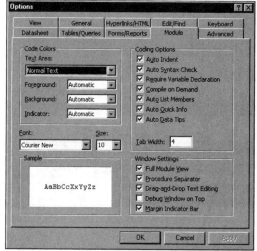

Figure 3-19:
The module
coding
options.

To view current settings for the module code:

1. Select Options from the Tools menu.

This can be opened from within the Database window or while editing module code.

2. Click the Module tab.

Now you can view the code option settings, as shown in Figure 3-20.

The majority of the options may look familiar, because these settings are similar to those for the VBE. The challenge may be figuring out where a particular option setting can be found in the Access Option dialog box versus the VBE Option dialog box.

You may have also noticed that Access has a slightly different toolbar at the top of the main window for working with your module code, as shown in Figure 3-20. Look at Table 3-2 for brief explanations of some of the toolbar buttons.

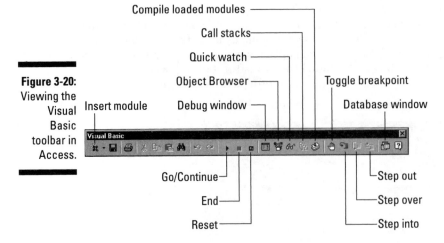

Figure 3-20:
Viewing the
Visual
Basic
toolbar in
Access.

Compile loaded modules

Call stacks

Quick watch

Object Browser

Toggle breakpoint

Insert module

Debug window

Database window

Go/Continue

End

Reset

Step out

Step over

Step into

Table 3-2	A Quick Look at the Access Visual Basic Toolbar Buttons
Toolbar Button	*What It Does for You*
Insert module	Inserts a new module, class module, or procedure. Select the one that you want from the pick list.
Go/Continue	Runs currently selected function or subroutine, or continues execution if in break mode.
End	End execution of code currently running.
Reset	Resets your code after an error occurs.
Debug window	Opens the Debug window if it's not already open.
Object Browser	Opens the Object Browser. In Chapter 5, we discuss your friend the Object Browser in much detail.
Quick watch	Gives you the value of any expression while in Break mode.
Call stack	Provides a list of the most recently called procedures to assist with your debugging efforts.
Compile loaded modules	Checks loaded modules for syntax problems and compiles them into pseudo-code.
Toggle breakpoint	Sets and clears breaks in your module code.
Step into	While in break mode, executes one line of code at a time in consecutive order.

Toolbar Button	What It Does for You
Step over	While in break mode, runs one line of code at a time, with the exception of procedure calls within procedures. These calls are executed as a unit.
Step out	Runs the rest of the current procedure, and then returns to the calling procedure.
Database window	Brings the Database window into view.

Many of these toolbar buttons pertain to debugging your VBA code and are covered in greater detail in Chapter 18.

Code behind forms and reports

Before we leave our discussion of the Access development environment, you may recall that VBA code can live in three separate places — in modules, behind forms, and behind reports. Now that you are comfortable with finding module code, take a look at the code behind forms and reports.

By using our sample database, Wine List, we open the code module (referred to as a class module) behind the Wine List form.

1. Open Access if it's not already open.

2. Open our sample database, WineList.mdb.

The file is located in the C:\Dummies\Chapter 3 directory.

3. In the Database window, click the Forms tab.

4. Select the Wine List form and click Design.

5. Click the Code toolbar button or choose View➪Code.

As you can see in Figure 3-21, a number of code procedures are stored behind the Wine List form. Even though we opened a code window in a different manner, the development environment is still the same as what we experience in the other Microsoft programs. You have the same toolbar and menu selections as seen with a regular module, such as those that you work with in the "Getting to the code" section in this chapter.

A quicker way to access the code behind a form or report is to select the form or report in the database window and then click the Code button on the main toolbar, or select Code from the View menu. Both the module window and the form will be opened in design mode for you.

If you are still curious about how to get to the code behind a report, you can simply select the report and choose View➪Code. To view the code behind the Wine By Type report using the WineList.mdb sample database, do this:

1. Click the **Reports** tab in the Database window.

2. Select the **Wine By Type** report and click **Design**.

3. Click the Code toolbar button or choose <u>V</u>iew⇨<u>C</u>ode.

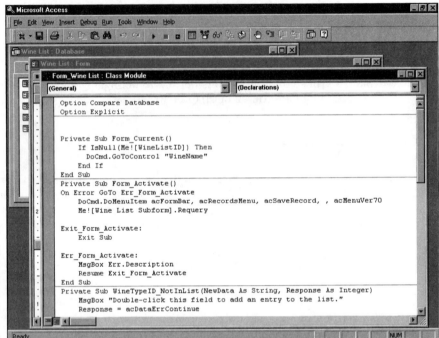

Figure 3-21:
Viewing
code
behind an
Access
form.

Part II
Discovering the VBA Building Blocks

The 5th Wave   By Rich Tennant

In this part . . .

Time to discover the building blocks of VBA. Before you can jump in and start pumping out beautiful applications, the basics about objects and syntax require some attention — and practice. Think of discovering the basics in terms of learning to walk before you enter that 18-mile marathon!

Objects are everywhere throughout the Office components — they make it possible to do many things in VBA. Drill down into each chapter to discover more than you ever imagined about the raw power of objects!

Chapter 4

It Slices, It Dices, It's an Object!

*N*o, this chapter is not about Ginsu knives. In this chapter, we establish concepts that are the bases for other chapters in this book by explaining the importance of objects. Before you can dive in and write VBA code in Office 97, you need to acquire an understanding about what objects are, how they apply to VBA, and what fun things they can do.

Discovering Objects

Take a look around you. Objects are everywhere! You are holding a book object right now and are likely sitting on a chair or a couch object. After reading this chapter, you may consider visiting the refrigerator object, which is full of delightful beverage objects.

An *object* can be a person, place, or thing. What does this discussion on objects have to do with Office 97? Well, as you may have guessed, objects are in every Office 97 component. Not real, physical objects like books or refrigerators, but conceptual objects — the things that make up an Office 97 application. Document objects are in Word, workbook objects are in Excel, and presentation objects are in PowerPoint — and that is just the beginning. (If curiosity is killing you, or if you already know what an object is about, you can turn to Chapters 7 through 10 for details about each Office component's object model.)

Objects are the keys to automating tasks in Office 97. Put another way, you can say that objects are the basic materials for building VBA code. After you have acquired an understanding of how to work with objects (and which ones are available), you will be well on your way to getting your money's worth out of Office 97. Throughout this book, and starting right now in this chapter, we focus on programmatic control of objects using VBA code.

What can objects do?

All objects, whether they are real or part of a software program, can be described by what they look like and how they act. For example, if your friend asks you about your new car, you may tell her what color it is, how large the engine is, and how fast it can go. In programming terms the things that describe an object's appearance are called *properties* and the things than an object can do, its behaviors, are called *methods*.

Properties describe the physical or personality characteristic of an object. For example, a Word document has many properties such as its name, a total number of paragraphs, and whether or not it is password protected. Methods are things that an object can do. For example, a Word document can be saved, closed, and spell-checked, which are all considered methods of the document.

Current events

Before we venture into a discussion about methods and properties, we want to give you a few moments of exposure to events. *Events* are loosely related to methods in that both refer to an action that the object takes. The difference is that a method is a way for you to tell an object, "do something," whereas an event, on the other hand, is an object's way of telling you, "hey, I'm doing something." For example, a Word document has exactly three events: New, Open, and Close, which occur when a document is first created, opened, and then closed. Events are important to us because we can write VBA code that runs whenever an event occurs. In Chapter 14, we dive deeper into the subject of events and how to use them to trigger your VBA code.

Even if you are not yet comfortable with the concept of objects yet, keep reading this chapter. As you find out more about an object's methods and properties, any confusion over what objects are all about should clear up.

The cat object: A practical example of methods and properties

We want to talk about our cat Chicago. (No, he's not named after the city. His owners are certified computer nerds that love Microsoft technology.) Chicago is an extremely friendly black Siamese cat that just celebrated his third birthday. These descriptions or explanations about Chicago are really his properties. Again, properties either describe an object's physical characteristics or provide general facts. We just discussed four different properties — disposition, fur color, breed, and age.

In addition to being cute, Chicago leads a very interesting life. His day consists of various activities, such as eating, sleeping, annoying his *father,* destroying curling ribbon, and the occasional yakking of his cat food. All these activities are things that Chicago can do, or what in-the-know computer types would call his methods. If you want to describe Chicago's behaviors in technical terms, you can say that he has five methods: Eat, Sleep, Annoy, Destroy, and, occasionally, Yak.

Method madness

You can begin to take advantage of all the objects in Office 97 when you know how to invoke object methods. Take a look at a few code samples that demonstrate how using an object's methods can be easy. For example, the following code closes the active Word document:

```
ActiveDocument.Close
```

In this example, ActiveDocument is the object and Close is the method. Notice that the two words are separated by a dot (.). Normally, things on the left side of the dot are objects and things on the right hand side are properties and methods. In this case, we are applying the Close method to the ActiveDocument object.

To use this code in a Microsoft Word file, open a Word document and do this:

1. **Choose Tools⇨Macro⇨Visual Basic Editor.**

   You can also press Alt+F11. The Visual Basic Editor appears.

2. **To open the Immediate window, if it's not already open, press Ctrl+G.**

   The Immediate window appears.

3. **Type** `ActiveDocument.Close` **in the Immediate window.**

   Notice that as soon as you press the dot (.) after ActiveDocument, a list of methods and properties appears for the ActiveDocument object, as shown in Figure 4-1. You can choose to select Close from the listing.

4. Press Enter.

When you press enter you commit the Close command, which closes
the current Word document.

We are sure you'll agree that the automatic prompting of a list of valid
methods and properties for a given object is quite remarkable. As we
discuss in Chapter 3, this is an available option called Auto List Members.
To turn on this option, choose Tools➪Options to open the Options dialog
box in the Visual Basic Editor (VBE). Under the Code Settings section on the
Editor tab, verify that the Auto List Members option is turned on.

This next example is very similar to the Word example, but we use the
ActiveWorkbook object found in Excel and its PrintPreview method.
ActiveWorkbook refers to the Excel workbook that is currently being viewed.
To print this workbook in preview mode, you need to apply the PrintPreview
method to the ActiveWorkbook object with the following code:

```
ActiveWorkbook.PrintPreview
```

Open any workbook in Excel and follow these steps to see what we mean:

1. Choose Tools➪Macro➪Visual Basic Editor.

The Visual Basic Editor appears.

2. If it's not already open, press Ctrl+G to open the Immediate window.

The Immediate window appears.

3. Type `ActiveWorkbook.PrintPreview` **in the Immediate window.**

4. Press Enter.

When you press Enter, you commit your command to print your
workbook in preview mode.

Now, take a look at a more complex example. In the previous two code
snippets, you simply tell an object to do something, and it does what is
asked of it. That's all you need to do because the object has all the information it requires to perform the action. Sometimes, however, the object doesn't
have all the information it needs and you have to supply the information

when you invoke the method. You wouldn't imagine inviting someone to your house without providing them with comprehensive directions — so, equally, you don't want to neglect to provide a method with whatever information it requires.

Consider the act of saving a Word document. You can't just tell the document to save itself without also telling the document what name it should save itself under. Therefore, when using the SaveAs method of a document, you must also include the name of the file to save to, which is the FileName *argument*. An argument is simply a piece of information. Here's an example:

```
ActiveDocument.SaveAs FileName:="MyWordDoc.doc"
```

In this code snippet, you are calling the SaveAs method of the ActiveDocument object. The rest of the statement tells the object the name of the file to save to: MyWordDoc.doc.

Because a method may have lots of different arguments you can include the argument's name along with the value. That's what the funny := characters do. In our example, these characters tell the SaveAs method that the value of the FileName argument is MyWordDoc.doc.

To try saving a file with VBA code, open any document in Microsoft Word and follow these steps:

1. **Open the Immediate window in the Visual Basic Editor.**

   See the preceding steps in this section if you don't know how to open this window in the VBE.

2. **Type** ActiveDocument.SaveAs **and then hit the spacebar.**

   As soon as you hit the spacebar, you are prompted with an argument listing for the SaveAs method, as shown in Figure 4-2. Optional arguments are contained in brackets, such as [optional argument].

3. **Type** FileName:= "MyWordDoc.doc".

   When you type this code, you complete the ActiveDocument.SaveAs command. You can optionally include a full path designation as well, such as "C:\Data\MyWordDoc.doc".

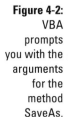

Figure 4-2:
VBA
prompts
you with the
arguments
for the
method
SaveAs.

4. Press Enter.

This action commits your command to save the current Word document.

The option setting called Auto Quick Info assists you in writing your code by displaying information about the arguments that a method accepts. You may have noticed the information prompt for the SaveAs method in Step 3 of the previous list. To turn on Auto Quick Info, open the Options dialog box in the VBE by choosing Tools➪Options. Under the Code Settings section on the Editor tab, verify that the Auto Quick Info option is turned on.

If you do not provide a complete path when you use the SaveAs method in Word, your documents are saved in your default documents directory. This default is set to the C:\My Documents directory unless you explicitly change it in the Options dialog box found in Word. To open the dialog box, choose Tools➪Options from the menu bar and then click the File Locations tab. Use the modify button to change the default directory for your documents.

Here's another example. To use the Open method of the Documents object to open a Word document, follow these steps:

1. **Open the Immediate window in the Visual Basic Editor.**

2. **Type** `Documents.Open` **and then hit the spacebar.**

3. **Type** `FileName:= "filename".`

   This action completes the command, and the FileName is the only required argument. For example, if your document is named CoolStuff.doc and is located in the C:\MyStuff directory, you type `FileName:= "C:\MyStuff\CoolStuff.doc"` for the argument.

4. **Press Enter.**

   When you press Enter, you commit the command, and the document that you specified opens.

Method arguments are covered in more detail in Chapter 14. For your purpose here, just remember that when you see := the text to the left is an argument name and whatever is to the right is the argument value.

When you enter method arguments, the argument that you are currently entering is in boldface type, so you can follow the syntax as you type.

Properties and plots of land

Now, take a look at how to refer to properties in VBA code. In Word, you have the option of having spelling errors signaled by red squiggly under-lines. Spelling errors are sure to jump off your computer screen. To hide spelling errors in your document, you can set the appropriate option manually by using the Options dialog box (under the Spelling & Grammar tab) or you can set the ShowSpellingErrors option through VBA.

To hide spelling errors in a document (and practice setting properties through VBA), do the following:

1. **Open any document in Word and be sure that the document includes some spelling errors.**

   Your misspelled words should be underlined with the red-squiggly underlines.

2. **Choose <u>T</u>ools⇨<u>M</u>acro⇨<u>V</u>isual Basic Editor.**

   The Visual Basic Editor (VBE) appears.

3. **Press Ctrl+G to open the Immediate window.**

   The Immediate window may already be in view when you open the VBE. Notice that the document you opened is represented by ThisDocument in the Project Explorer.

4. **Type** `ThisDocument.ShowSpellingError=False` **in the Immediate window.**

   Notice that as soon as you type the = another value list appears with the valid values for the ShowSpellingErrors property of the object ThisDocument, as shown in Figure 4-3.

5. **Press Enter to commit your VBA command.**

   After you press Enter, press Alt+F11 to switch back to your Word document. Your misspelled words should no longer be marked within your document.

The list of valid property settings is part of the Auto List Members functionality set in the Options dialog box in the VBE. For the ShowSpellingErrors property, only a true or false value makes sense. By taking advantage of Auto List Members, you can save yourself debugging time down the road.

Look at another example that actually changes some characteristics of your document. In the following code snippet, you set the style of the currently selected area to the Heading1 style. The object is Selection, and Style is the property. The Selection object is defined by the area currently highlighted, or selected, in a Word document:

```
Selection.Style = "Heading 1"
```

Figure 4-3:
Setting a
document
property
with VBA.

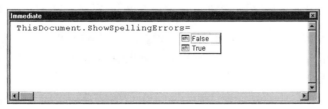

Notice that this is a little different than our method example in the preceding section. With a method you just tell the object to do the method. A property, on the other hand, represents some characteristic of the object that you can change. To do that, you need to tell the object what to change the property to. In the example above, the code says, "Okay, Selection object, change your Style property to the value Heading 1."

To change the style property of a selected area in a Word document, do the following:

1. **Open any document in Word and select a block of text.**

   To highlight text, click and drag with the mouse or hold down the Shift key and use the arrow keys.

2. **Choose Ṯools➪Macro➪Ⅴisual Basic Editor.**

   The Visual Basic Editor (VBE) appears.

3. **Press Ctrl+G to open the Immediate window.**

   The Immediate window may already be in view when you open the VBE.

4. **Type** `Selection.Style = Heading 1` **in the Immediate window.**

5. **Press Enter to commit your VBA command.**

After you press Enter, press Alt+F11 to switch back to your Word document. Your selected text should now be in the Heading 1 style.

Sometimes setting a property can be a bit more complicated, as shown in the following example:

```
Selection.Font.Size = 12
```

Not all object references are as simple as the name of the object followed by the method or property. In the above code, you set the font size property for the selected text in our document. What is unusual is that although Font is a property of the Selection object, it is also an object that has properties of its own, Size being one of them. Simply put, objects can contain other objects. In this case, the Selection object contains the Font object. The Font object in turn has a number of properties, such as size and color. In this example, Selection is the object, Font is both a property and an object, and Size is the property. We have set the font size of the current selected area to 12 points.

Enough talk. Try a similar example by following these steps:

1. **Open any document in Word and select a block of text.**

   To highlight text, click and drag with the mouse or hold down the Shift key and use the arrow keys.

2. **Choose Tools➪Macro➪Visual Basic Editor.**

   The Visual Basic Editor (VBE) appears.

3. **Press Ctrl+G to open the Immediate window.**

   The Immediate window may already be in view when you open the VBE.

4. **Type** `Selection.Font.Bold = True` **in the Immediate window**.

5. **Press Enter to commit your VBA command.**

   After you have done this, switch back to your Word document to see that your selected area is now bold. You have set the font bold property to true.

In Chapter 6, we devote much more time to explaining the syntax that you need to abide by in VBA. We explain dots, bangs, colons, and more. Try not to concern yourself with syntax at this stage of the game. Focus instead on how VBA defines methods, objects, and properties.

Getting object properties

In Chapter 11, variables are the topic, as well as how to use VBA code to get the value of properties and methods. At this stage, however, you can sneak a peak at getting and setting object properties by using an Immediate window in the Visual Basic Editor from any of the Office components. The Immediate window, shown in Figure 4-4, demonstrates how easily you can set and retrieve property values. First, you set the value of the ActiveCell to "rain, rain, go away." You can also ask the ActiveCell what value it contains by posing the question: ?ActiveCell.Value.

You may have noticed that we used the ? to print the contents of the ActiveCell in the Immediate window. The ? is a shortcut for Print or Debug.Print, which you may be familiar with from other programming languages.

Try to set and get an object's property value by following these steps:

1. **Open Excel and then open the Visual Basic Editor.**

   The Immediate window appears. If not, press Ctrl+G to bring up the window.

2. **In the Immediate window type** `ActiveCell.Value = "rain, rain, go away"`.

3. **Press Enter and press Alt+F11 to return to the open worksheet.**

   You see the currently active cell now filled with the value or text that you put in your command. You have successfully set an object's value property.

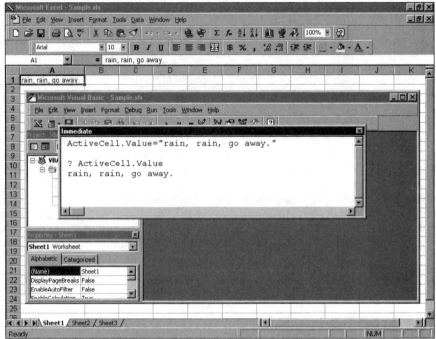

4. Type ?ActiveCell.Value **in the Immediate window.**

When you press Enter, it returns the value of the active cell, which is "rain, rain, go away."

You have successfully retrieved an object's value property. Congratulations!

Object Gangs (Or, Object Collections)

Many times objects don't exist on their own. Instead they hang out in gangs, or collections. A *collection* is a group of other similar objects. Each object in the collection may have different characteristics but it is fundamentally the same thing as other objects in the collection. In practical terms, think about buying a dozen eggs in your local supermarket. When you make your grocery list, you simply put down eggs, not 12 eggs. You are buying a collection of eggs that consists of 12 egg objects. Each egg may have different characteristics such as size, color, and weight, but each is still an egg.

In Excel, for example, the Workbooks collection contains all the open Workbook objects. In Word, the Documents collection contains all the open Document objects. Take a look at how you can use collections to gather information.

Collections have their own methods and properties. For example, by using the Documents collection object, you can check the Count property to see how many documents are currently open, as shown in the following line of code:

```
?Documents.Count
```

To get a count of the number of Excel workbooks currently open, start Excel, open one or more workbooks, and follow these steps:

1. **Open the Immediate window in the Visual Basic Editor.**

    Refer to the steps at the beginning of this chapter in the section "Method madness" to pull up the VBE and the Immediate window if you need assistance.

2. **Type** ?Workbooks.Count **and then press Enter.**

    The Immediate window returns the appropriate number that corresponds to how many workbooks you currently have open.

Collections also have methods, such as the Open method. As shown in the next code snippet, the Documents collection object has an Open method. In some instances, methods require you to provide some additional information in the form of arguments. In this example, the Open method needs to know what document file you want to open. (You may have tried this before you knew what an object collection was all about.)

```
Documents.Open FileName:="C:\Data\Annual Sales.doc"
```

All collections have a Count property that tells you how many objects are in the collection, but not all share the same methods. For example, while it makes sense for the Documents collection to have an Open method, it doesn't make sense for a collection like Paragraphs to have an Open method.

You can utilize collections in another way. Each member or item in an object collection is given a unique number that identifies its position in the collection. The first item added to the collection can be assigned the number 1, the second, 2, and so on. You can use this number to refer to a specific object in the collection. For example, if you want to print the name of the first Document object in the Documents collection you can use code like this:

```
?Documents(1).Name
```

This code returns the name of the first document that you opened after starting Word. You can find out the number of open Word documents and subsequently the name of them by opening Microsoft Word, opening up a few of your documents, and following these steps:

1. **Press Alt+F11 to open the VBE and then press Ctrl+G to pull up the Immediate window.**

2. **Type** `?Documents.Count` **in the Immediate window.**

   Performing this action gives you a count of the number of open documents.

3. **Type** `?Documents(1).Name` **to find the name of one of your documents.**

   This action returns the name of the first document that you opened. You can then type `?Documents(2).Name`, `Documents(3).Name`, and so on, to find the names of your other documents.

You can try these steps with Excel workbooks, PowerPoint presentations, and Access forms. If you feel brave, give these steps a try. Doing so can help you become more familiar with writing VBA code for each of the Office components.

In the above example, the first item in a collection is given the number 1. This is the case in Excel, Word, and PowerPoint. However, Access is a strange and mysterious creature, and it starts numbering at 0. Therefore, the first item in the Access Forms collection is referred to as Forms(0), not Forms(1).

If you do not know the number of an object in a collection but you know the object's name, you can use the name instead. Consider the following example:

```
Documents("PoorlySpelled.doc").CheckSpelling
```

Here, you refer to a document object called "PoorlySpelled.doc" and invoke the CheckSpelling method. You can try this yourself by opening a Word document and following these steps:

1. **Press Alt+F11 to open the VBE and then press Ctrl+G to pull up the Immediate window if it's not already open.**

2. **Type** `Documents("MyDocument.doc").CheckSpelling`**, where MyDocument.doc is your document's name, in the Immediate window.**

3. **Press Enter.**

   This action runs spell-checking on your selected document.

Chapter 5

Your Friend the Object Browser

In This Chapter

▶ Introducing the Object Browser

▶ Finding out how to use this tool

▶ Exploring an application's objects

*I*n Chapter 4, we discuss the importance of objects and briefly touch upon properties and methods enjoyed by objects. The Object Browser assists you, the developer, in referencing various object types and their associated features. In this chapter, we begin with a brief dissection of the Object Browser (hey, better than that frog in tenth-grade Biology class), and then we look at specific benefits that it can bring to your development efforts in Office 97.

What Is the Object Browser All About?

At a very basic level, the Object Browser can be thought of as the VBA card catalog. You can find out about various characteristics of objects, such as their properties, methods, and events, by browsing through the Object Browser. In fact, the Object Browser is more than a card catalog for VBA. The Object Browser is the window into all objects living in Office, OLE Automation libraries, and the Microsoft Forms library, as well as the specific Office component library that you are developing your application in.

The Object Browser actually serves two purposes — browsing and searching. In more amusing terms, think of the Object Browser as your shopping partner. Put out of your mind the fact that the store — the object store — may not be that exciting. Besides, your shopping buddy makes window-shopping easy and fun. The Object Browser's easy-to-use dialog box provides great browsing capabilities through the objects available to your VBA project. Sounds great so far, but is there more? Of course there is, otherwise we wouldn't have asked!

Now, consider going out shopping with a specific goal in mind, perhaps that perfect pair of shoes or a model race car. When you are out on the hunt, window-shopping isn't usually of interest. If you have an idea of what you are looking for, your shopping partner can lead you straight to those shoes or that car. Likewise, the Object Browser is not omniscient, unfortunately, so you need to provide some clues as to what you are looking for. Ready to go shopping now?

In more techno-weenie language, the Object Browser displays the classes, properties, methods, events, and constants available from various object libraries (such as Office, PowerPoint, and VBA) and any neat code procedures in your VBA project. Start off with finding the Object Browser, which is accessible from the development environment within each Office component.

Starting the Object Browser and Sizing up Its Parts

In Word, Excel, and PowerPoint, you access the Object Browser from the Visual Basic Editor (VBE). After you load a document, spreadsheet, or presentation, follow these steps:

1. **Choose Tools⇨Macro to open the VBE.**

   The VBE appears within your document, workbook, or presentation.

2. **Choose View⇨Object Browser or press F2.**

   The Object Browser, as shown in Figure 5-1, comes out from its usual hiding place.

You can also open the Object Browser with the simple click of the Object Browser button on the toolbar. The Object Browser is the button that looks as if shapes are escaping from an open box.

If you are using Access, you first need to open a module in design mode to enter the development environment, which is discussed in Chapter 3. From there, as with the other Office components, you can select Object Browser from the View menu or press F2 to open the Object Browser. The Object Browser works the same across all the Office components; it only differs in how you open the dialog box from within Access.

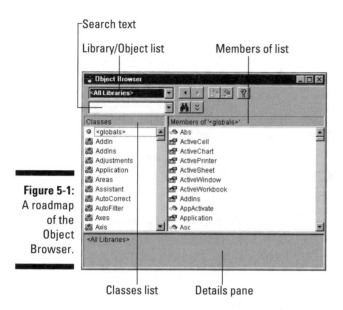

Search text

Library/Object list   Members of list

Figure 5-1:
A roadmap
of the
Object
Browser.

Classes list   Details pane

In Figure 5-1, we note the main portions of the Object Browser. The Library/
Project list displays the referenced libraries for the project in which you are
currently working. By default, the selected library/project is <All Libraries>,
which allows you to view objects from all of the available libraries at once.
In most cases, you want to focus on one library at a time. To do so, you can
select the desired library from the drop-down list that shows <All Libraries>
in the figure.

The Excel example

To gain some familiarity with the Object Browser, you can see what objects
are available to Excel. Follow these steps:

1. Open a workbook in Excel.

2. Choose Tools⇔Macro⇔Visual Basic Editor.

 The Visual Basic Editor appears.

3. Choose View⇔Object Browser from the menu bar, or press F2.

 At this point, the Object Browser looks as it does in Figure 5-1.

**4. Click the drop-down list of libraries and projects to see what is
 available to Excel.**

 The libraries list is the one that has <All Libraries> as the default. After
 you click this list, you see a number of libraries, including Office, VBA,
 and Microsoft Forms (MSForms), as shown in Figure 5-2.

5. Select Excel from the list.

This action populates the Classes listing with objects from the Excel Object Library. Notice that the Details pane (at the bottom of the Object Browser dialog box) indicates the name and location of the source, which is the Microsoft Excel 8.0 Object Library located by default in C:\Program Files\Microsoft Office\Office\EXCEL8.OLB. If your Excel Object Library is located elsewhere, it's okay. This difference just means that you did not accept the default installation path.

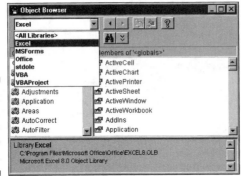

Figure 5-2:
Exploring
the libraries
available to
Excel.

Classes list

You can view all of the available classes within the library or project that you select in the Project/Libraries box. These classes aren't like History or Calculus 101 classes, but rather are types of objects. Notice the entry of <globals> at the top of the Classes list. The <globals> selection gives you a list of globally accessible members in the Members of list box.

If you select a Class in your VBA Project code and neglect to specify a member, you get the default member if one is available. In the Members of list box, a small bluish-aqua marble identifies default members. Microsoft claims that defaults are marked by an asterisk (*), but all we've found are marbles. In addition to the visual cue, the default member is noted in the Details pane. See the section "Those funny symbols" in this chapter for more about the Details pane.

Pick up the Excel example from the section "The Excel example" in this chapter. Now that you are looking at the Excel library, you may want to browse through the classes in the Classes list. A number of the objects (classes) are similar across the Office components, such as AddIns, AutoCorrect, Dialogs, Hyperlinks, and Shapes. Although these components are similar in name, the usage within each component can differ. We also have a number of Excel specific objects, such as Worksheets, PivotTables, and Charts.

Checking out referenced libraries

We know that the library/project list displays the referenced libraries, but how do you know what's referenced and what's not? You can select References from the Tools menu to open the References dialog box, as shown in the figure below. The References dialog box determines which libraries are available to your VBA project and which ones are currently loaded. After a library is loaded into your VBA project, you can browse the library's object offerings. Libraries are easily added or removed by toggling the check box next to each library's name in the Available References list box.

Ever hear of having too much of a good thing? Well, while it's great to add various libraries to your project, it only makes sense to include those that you are actually using. To remove references to unused libraries, you can clear the check box for those references. As a bonus, your project will compile faster without these extraneous libraries. Keep in mind, however, that you can't remove a reference for an item that is used in your project.

Members only

This Members list box displays the elements (or members) of the class selected in the Classes list box. These members can be grouped by type or listed alphabetically.

To modify the member list order, follow these steps:

1. **Right-click anywhere on the Object Browser dialog box to expose the shortcut menu.**

   If you have your mouse set up to use the right button for regular functions (as many left-handed people do), then you want to left-click to expose the menu in question.

2. **Set the check toggle on the Group Members command as you desire.**

   If the Group Members command is checked, members are grouped by type — all events are listed together and so on. If the command is left unchecked, all members are sorted in alphabetical order.

Next, view the members of the Excel's chart object to see what is available. First, make sure that you have the Object Browser open (in Excel) with the Excel library selected. Select Chart from the Classes list to expose the members of the chart object in the Members of list, as shown in Figure 5-3.

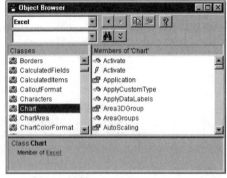

Figure 5-3:
Browsing
the
members of
the Chart
object.

Bolding, bolding, over the open sea. In the Object Browser, the use of bolding generally indicates something grand. Specifically, if code is written for a class, that class name appears in bold. If a class's underlying methods, properties, events, or constants have code written for them, they appear bold as well.

Details pane

Residing at the bottom of the Object Browser dialog box, the Details pane, as its name implies, gives some additional information about the particular class member. This pane shows the definition of the member and includes a hyperlink to the class or library to which the member hangs out with. You can also see what type the member is. Members can be functions, properties, methods, or even events.

If you have the Excel Chart object selected (see the "Members only" section in this chapter), you can browse through its members. After you select a member, the Details pane changes to reflect information on the selected member. For example, if you select the ApplyDataLabels method from the Members of list, the Details pane shows the syntax for the ApplyDataLabels subroutine and includes hyperlinks to its parent class (Excel.Chart) as well as a link to the values for XLDataLabelsType.

You can copy or drag text from the Details pane to a code window. Cool!

Those funny symbols

When you start using the Object Browser, you may notice all the funny symbols floating around in the Classes list, Members of list, and Search Results. The symbols are intended to give you a visual cue indicating object or element type. We can try to make the funny symbols fun, as shown in Table 5-1, where we introduce all of the symbols. Actually, after you understand the symbols that the Object Browser employs, the Browser will be much more useful for you.

Table 5-1		Explaining Those Funny Symbols	
Symbol	*Name*	*Looks Like a . . .*	*What It Means*
🖼	Class	Picture frame hung on your wall with colored duct tape	Specifies an object type, such as chart or document
🔲	Const(ant)	The female end of an extension cord	Available values for use in code
⊙	Default	Bluish-aqua marble	Identifies which member needs to be used in code if a class is used without a member specification
📇	Enum	Pair of tickets to see your favorite NBA team	List of numbers or constants
�/	Event	How Ben Franklin discovered electricity	Something that happens, such as opening a document (Open event)
🖘	Method	Fluorescent green eraser flying through the air	Procedure (subroutine or function) that carries out some set of instructions
🧩	Module	Poorly assembled tinker toy	Collection of code procedures
🖼	Property	Parental hand pointing to bad grade on report card	Characteristic of an object

Watch for these symbols when using the Object Browser — they may come in handy!

Search-O-Rama

Take a gander at the coolest part of the Object Browser — the Search Text box. Figure 5-4 points out the search-related features of the Object Browser.

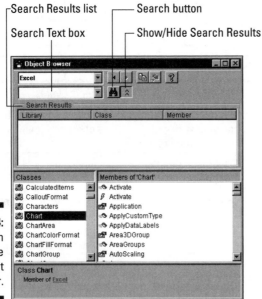

Search Results list — Search button

Search Text box — Show/Hide Search Results

Figure 5-4:
The Search
team of the
Object
Browser.

No one, we don't care how much of a techno-weenie he may be, knows all the methods and properties available for every single object available within Office and other libraries. If you know someone who does, they have entirely too much time on their hands.

Anyway, you inevitably will need to carry out some task and think that there ought to be a method to do it, but you won't have a clue as to what it may be. Or perhaps your buddy John mentioned a cool property setting for an Excel worksheet, such as MakeDisappear. In any event, you don't have the specifics but can use the Search Text box to help out.

To use the Search Text box, enter a string that you want to use in your search. You can type or choose the string you want. After you start to take advantage of the search capabilities, the Search Text box remembers the last four search strings that you entered until you close the project. To assist your searches of strings, you can employ the standard wildcards (* and ?) used in Visual Basic. If you want to search for a whole word, set the Find Whole Word Only option available on the shortcut menu.

After you enter a search string, you can press the Search button to begin the search of the libraries for the class or property, method, event, or constant that matches the string that you typed in the Search Text box and open the Search Results pane with the appropriate list of information.

If the Search Results pane is not visible, you can use the Show/Hide Search Results button to open the Search Results pane. Actually, this button works as a toggle, so you can make the decision whether or not you want to review the results of your searches.

The Search Results list displays the library, class, and member that are found as a result of your search. Either the class or member contain your search string. The Search Results pane follows your move. As you change the selection in the Project/Library box, the Search Results pane is refreshed with the new information. These results appear in alphabetical order.

For your viewing pleasure, you can adjust the size of various parts of the Object Browser dialog box. Size adjustments can be made by using the split bars, which are located between the Classes and Members of boxes, under the Search Results list, and above the Details pane.

Enough talk, time to walk by using the search capabilities. For this example, pick up the example from "The Excel example" earlier in the chapter.

   1. **In the Excel Visual Basic Editor, open the Object Browser, if it's not already open.**

   2. **Locate the Search string text box and type** print.

   3. **Press the Search button to start your search.**

      After your search has been completed, the Search Results list appears (if it wasn't already open) with any class or member that matches the search criteria.

Notice that the Object Browser has inserted wildcards behind the scenes and finds all members with the word *print* in them. For example, when you type in print in the Search string text box, the Object Browsers interprets that as *print*.

Browse through the Search results list. A few entries include the BeforePrint event and the PrintArea property. Done? Cool. In Figure 5-5, you can see the search results in the Search Result list. This list includes the name of each library, class (object types), and member (property, method, event, or constant) that meets the search criteria.

Figure 5-5:
Trying out
the search
tools.

Other Buttons and Zippers

The Go Back and Go Forward buttons are obvious, aren't they? Use the Go Back button to view your previous selections in the Classes and Members of lists. With each click of the button, you move back one selection until you are at the end of the list! Use the Go Forward button in the same way, but to move forward through previous selections.

The Copy to Clipboard button is one of our old standbys in every Microsoft product. Copying to the beloved Windows Clipboard can save you time, energy, and brain cells. If you click this button, your program copies the current selection from the Members of list or the Details pane to the Clipboard.

If you have written custom procedures and you select them in the Object Browser, the Show Definition button moves you to the place in the Code window where your procedure is defined.

Another great feature of the Object Browser dialog box is the Help button. You can easily find context-sensitive help for whatever you select in the Classes or the Members of list. This help can also be invoked by pressing F1.

Another cool help feature of the Object Browser is the ability to bring up context-sensitive help. If you press Shift+F2 on a method or property name, the Help dialog box appears with its focus on the particular information that you are interested in. We have even better news for you — Shift+F2 also works in code windows and the Immediate window.

Chapter 6

Dot. Bang! You're Dead — Bizarre Syntax Explained

. . . .

In This Chapter

▶ Finding out why VBA uses funny characters in its code

▶ Understanding what the dot is and what it does

▶ Discovering when a property can also be an object

▶ Seeing how to use the dot with object collections

▶ Finding out what default members are and why to love them

▶ Finding out when to use brackets (other than when putting up a shelf)

▶ Discovering how (and when) to put a bang in your code

. . . .

*I*n Chapters 4 and 5 we introduce the wonderful world of objects. Chapters 7 through 10 look at some of the coolest objects in the Office suite — ones that you need to do all the neat things that you've been planning. In this chapter, though, we discuss the thorny issue of how you reference objects in your VBA code. Specifically, how do you tell VBA which of the many thousands of objects you want to control?

To answer this question you need to become familiar with a whole cast of seemingly innocuous characters: the dot (.), the bang (!), parentheses, and brackets. In this chapter we attempt to answer the ages-old questions of what these characters are and how they're used. In other words, here we tackle the problem of *VBA object syntax!*

Why Do You Need These Odd Symbols?

You may be asking yourself why you need these little characters at all. What purpose do they serve? You need them because they give VBA a clue as to what you want to do. Building an application by using Office 97 is all about controlling objects. *Objects* are things in an application like Excel that you can control by using VBA. Objects have characteristics, called *properties*, and behaviors, called *methods*. In order to write code to control objects you need a way to distinguish an object from its properties and methods. That's what these characters do. You can see some simple examples in Chapter 4 involving Word documents and Excel worksheets. We dive deeper into the issue in this chapter.

What confuses many people is that there are two characters, the dot (which is sometimes called a period by non-geeks) and the bang (also known as an exclamation point), and under some circumstances they are interchangeable. We hope to put to rest any confusion you may have.

Dotting Your Objects

Take a look at the dot character. It's the one that you use most often. In fact, you really need to use poor old bang in only a few situations.

In VBA, the dot is known as a separator character. This ought to come as no surprise because you use the dot (called a period) to separate sentences when you write. What does the dot separate in VBA? Well, you can use it to separate three things:

1. You can separate an object from one of its properties.

2. You can separate an object from one of its methods.

3. You can separate an object from one of its objects.

Although this may seem like a small list, you can create powerful VBA statements by combining these uses. But we're getting ahead of ourselves. Now, take a look at the first two uses for the dot character.

Chapter 4 demonstrates several examples of using the dot character with an object's properties and methods, but it doesn't really explain all the permutations of this versatile little character. To see what we mean, start with these simple steps:

1. Launch Microsoft Word.

The Word main window appears, containing a black document.

2. Press Alt+F11 to open the Visual Basic Editor.

3. **If the Immediate window isn't open, choose View⇨Immediate Window to open it.**

4. **In the Immediate window, type the following and press Enter:**

```
?Application.Name
```

In order to make VBA do anything, you need to press Enter after typing a line of code into the Immediate window.

This action prints the value of Word's Application object's name property. (The question mark is shorthand for the Print command.) Not surprisingly, the result is *Microsoft Word.* And, as you can see, our friend the dot character sits right smack in the middle of the statement. Here, the dot separates an object (Application) from one of its many properties (Name, in this case).

Notice that the statement begins with an object (forget about the ? character). Anytime you write code like this the thing to the left of the dot will be an object and the thing to the right will be a property. (Except when the property is an object, but more about that later in the section titled "Objects are properties!")

Likewise, you use the dot to separate an object from one of its methods. The following statement tells Word to execute its Quit method, which causes the program to terminate. (*Don't run the code,* however, or you'll have to restart Word!)

```
Application.Quit
```

Once again, the pattern is *object-dot-property* or *object-dot-method.* If you remember nothing else about the dot character, remember this pattern. Chapters 18 through 23 show you how to put these statements to use in places other than the Immediate window.

Objects within objects

In big, complex applications like Microsoft Word, objects sometimes contain other objects. Why is this? Well, objects are very nice containers for information (which you know as properties). When something is so complicated that it requires lots of information to describe it, you can encapsulate some of that information in a second object that is *contained* in the first object to simplify your objects. The two objects are often referred to as *parent* and *child.* Our friend the dot is used to separate the two objects.

Containment is only part of the story. Sometimes the word containment doesn't really describe the relationship between the objects. For example, the font characteristics mentioned next aren't really contained by an object but are an extremely important part of objects. You may see lots of other examples of objects containing other objects where the term contained really doesn't fit. However, grouping the characteristics of one object inside another object still makes sense, even if the word contained doesn't.

Take, for example, the font characteristic of text in a Word document. You can say a number of different things about the font, including its name, size, weight (normal, bold, and so on), and whether or not it's underlined. Rather than make each of these elements a direct property of the text, Word creates a Font object, which is contained by the text.

To prove that Word actually performs this task, go back to the Immediate window (which you open via the steps found in the section "Dotting Your Objects" in this chapter) and type the following:

```
?Selection.Font
```

After you press Enter, an error message from VBA appears (some silly complaint about the object not supporting a particular property or method). What VBA is trying to tell you (and what would be obvious if VBA knew how to communicate in plain English) is that Font is not a property of the selection but an object that the selection contains. If you want VBA to print something, you need to supply a property of the Font object, such as its Name. Try to run the following, slightly different line of code from the Immediate window:

```
?Selection.Font.Name
```

VBA responds with a font name, such as Times New Roman. In this example, you see a pair of dots; the first one separates one object from another while the second separates an object from its property. Big applications like Word often have several levels of nested objects, requiring lots of dots. Consider the following line of code:

```
?ActiveDocument.Background.Fill.BackColor
```

In this example, ActiveDocument, Background, and Fill are all objects. BackColor is a property of the Fill object.

At first, this way of referring to properties may seem confusing, but it's actually very clear after you get used to it. You may ask yourself, for instance, *what is the Fill object to which we refer?* If you read the statement from right to left, you can easily see that it's the fill of the background of the active document. That's because the ActiveDocument object precedes the Background object, and the Background object precedes the Fill object, and they're all separated by dot characters. This means that the ActiveDocument contains the Background object, which contains the Fill object, whose BackColor property you're inspecting! Isn't this cool?

Objects are properties!

Okay, so now you've seen how you can use the dot character to separate two objects. Well, guess what — the objects we've been talking about are themselves properties! That's right, you really have only two uses for the dot character because the third one is really the same as the first.

What are we talking about, you ask? How do we know the objects are really properties? To get the answer just look in the VBA Object Browser. (Press F2 in the Visual Basic Editor and you can open the Object Browser quickly.) Figure 6-1 shows the Object Browser open to Word's Selection object. In the Members of list, you can see that we've highlighted the Font property. We know that it's a property because of the little icon next to the name and because it says so at the bottom of the window. So, yes, Font is a property of a Document object.

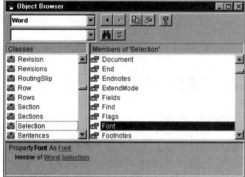

Figure 6-1: Font is a property and an object.

But wait, what about all that rubbish about Font being an object? As it turns out, Font is an object. To prove Font's object nature, look at the Details pane at the bottom of the Object Browser window. The pane tells you that the data type of the property is Font. Font is another type of Word object. How do we know it's an object? Our first clue is that the underlined text is green. (We know that the text doesn't *look* green in this black-and-white book, but bear with us.) This coloration means that we can click on it to get more information. If we click on it, the Object Browser changes the selection to show what you see in Figure 6-2 — information on the Font object. In this case you see a list of the object's properties and methods.

If you scroll down in the Members of list like we did, you see an entry for the Name property. If you look at the Details pane, you can see that the data type is String. This property is plain, old text, not an object.

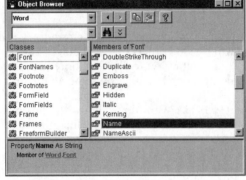

Figure 6-2:
You can
easily
jump to
information
on the Font
object.

If you're a fan of the original *Saturday Night Live*, you may remember a fictitious product called Shimmer the cast once promoted in a skit. Shimmer had the unique quality of being both a floor wax *and* a creamy whipped topping. So you can see that, like Shimmer, you may come across elements in VBA that are two things in one: both properties and objects!

Parentheses, Numbers, and Names

If you have read the previous sections of this chapter, you have a pretty good idea of how to use the dot for properties and methods. Another related use of the dot is with collections of objects. Remember that collections are gangs of objects that like to hang out together. They like hanging out together because they're so similar. Word, for instance, maintains a collection of open documents. All the objects in the collection are similar (they're all documents), but they may have different properties. If you want to modify one of the documents in the collection, you need to tell VBA which one.

You can use either of two basic ways to refer to an object in a collection. You can pick the object out by its name or by its position in the collection. Both methods utilize two close friends of the dot, the parentheses. You use the parentheses with the name of a collection to tell VBA with which object in the collection you want to work. Try to run the following line of code from the Immediate window. The code tells VBA to print the name of the first document in the collection of open documents in Word:

```
?Application.Documents(1).Name
```

This statement is very similar to the ones that we show you in the section "Dotting Your Objects." The line begins with an object, Application. This time, however, the first dot character in the example separates the object from a collection it contains instead of a single object. The concept is the same, however. Documents is a property of Word's Application object that refers to a collection of other objects.

Even though a collection contains a bunch of objects, it also contains properties, such as Count, and methods. So, a collection is still considered an object. If you want a complete list of a collection's properties and methods, look it up in the Object Browser.

Now, what about those parentheses? As we mentioned before, you use them to tell VBA which object you want to work with. In the above example, we use a number inside the parentheses. We did that because we want to refer to a worksheet based on its position in the collection. You can think of a collection as a bunch of objects standing in a police lineup. You can pick out the criminal by number.

We can use the worksheet's name just as easily. If you don't believe us, try to enter the following line of code in the Immediate window:

```
?Application.Documents("Document1").Name
```

Provided that you have an open document named Document1, VBA prints the text "Document1" to the Immediate window. Either way, the result is a reference to a particular object in the collection. We know that the result is an object because if it wasn't we wouldn't be able to tack on the property at the end.

In case you're wondering about those parentheses, any member of an object (property or method) can accept what are called *arguments*. Arguments let you customize the way a property or method works. In the case of collections, supplying a different argument results in a different object of the collection. You can find out more about arguments, and how you can add them to custom VBA procedures that you write, in Chapter 14.

Default Properties and Methods (Or, A Way to Write Less Code!)

Hopefully, the syntax for referring to objects in a collection makes sense to you. Taken by itself, a code fragment such as Documents(1) ought to be self-explanatory. The word *Documents* refers to a bunch of objects (it's plural), and the number 1 is the object that you want to use. As in life, however, things aren't exactly as they seem. You see, Documents(1) really isn't the correct syntax for referring to objects in a collection. This code fragment only works because of a neat VBA trick known as a default method.

According to the VBA book of etiquette, the proper way to refer to an object in a collection is by using a property or method of that collection. If the truth be known, the Documents collection has a method called Item that accepts an object's name or position and returns a reference to it. But because Item is designated as the collection's default method you don't have to use it if you don't want to. That's what a *default property* or *method* is — one that you can leave out of your code if you want to. Used effectively this default method results in lots less typing!

What this means is that the following two lines of code are identical in their function:

```
?Application.Documents.Item(1).Name
?Application.Documents(1).Name
```

To avoid confusion and utter chaos, an object can only have one default member, either a property or a method. So how do you know what the default property or method is? The easiest way is to use the Object Browser. Figure 6-3 shows the VBA Object Browser opened to the Documents object. (Remember that a collection is also an object.) If you look carefully, you can see a small blue circle next to the icon for the Item method. (Okay, so it's light gray in the book.) This circle is the indicator for the default member. Notice that none of the other entries in the list have little blue/gray circles. That's because an object can only have a single default member.

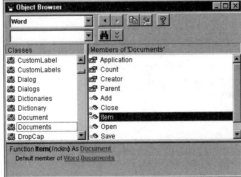

Figure 6-3:
The blue circle signifies a default property or method.

The method's description, shown in the pane at the bottom of the Object Browser window, also includes the information that the method is, in fact, the object's default member.

Most collection objects feature an Item property or method that is also their default member. In most cases, this feature allows you to use the shortcut described above to refer to objects in the collection.

As you start to write your own VBA code to control Office applications, you can take advantage of default properties and methods to save yourself some typing. To demonstrate how, try these steps:

1. **Type some text into Document1 open in Microsoft Word.**

2. **Highlight some of that text.**

3. **Switch to the Visual Basic Editor and type the following code in the Immediate window:**

```
?Selection.Text
```

4. **Press Enter.**

VBA prints the text that you highlighted. Now, delete the `.Text` from the end of the statement and run it again.

VBA prints the same thing. Why? You know the answer — because Text is the Selection object's default property. Now, anytime you need to use the text of the current selection (or any other part of a document, for that matter) you can leave off the final .Text. Think of how much typing that omission can save you over the course of several years!

Most of the time, the Microsoft programmers were pretty smart when designing the Office objects and picked default properties or methods where they made sense. For example, when an object has a property like Name, Text, or Value, chances are it also is the default property. Be sure to check this out in the Object Browser when you start to write your own VBA code.

Now Comes the Big Bang

In this chapter, we spend a lot of time discussing the dot character, forgetting about poor old bang. Before getting into a deep discussion of the bang character, though, how about a quick joke? Can you guess what this is?

!!!!!!!

It's a machine gun! Get it? Okay, maybe the joke isn't that funny. In any event, the reason we haven't given the bang character much ink is because you can use it in only a few places. In fact, you can survive without ever using it, relying on the dot character to see you through all your VBA coding adventures. Nonetheless, the bang does show up in a variety of places, including sample code, on-line help, and other books and magazine articles. So, in an effort to keep you up-to-date and informed, here is the straight scoop on the bang.

The bang character was invented as a special shortcut for referring to an object's default property or method. You see, it's used most often to refer to objects in a collection. If you are reading this chapter from the opening page to the closing page, you know from reading the previous sections that you can use other ways to refer to objects in a collection, so why another one? Why does it rain when you want to go to the beach? It just does. A good explanation may exist, but we don't know what it is.

Anyway, you can use the bang character if the following are true:

1. An object has a default property or method.

2. The property or method accepts a single argument which can be expressed as text.

In most cases, the only time that these conditions are met is when you're dealing with collections. In the section "Default Properties and Methods," we explain that you use a method or property to refer to an object and that method or property is usually the object's default member. You can also refer to objects by name, which is a text string.

This means that you can use the bang character to refer to objects in a collection if you really want to. You use the bang by placing it between the collection name and the name of an object in the collection. Try to run the following line of code from the Immediate window:

```
?Application.Documents!Document1.Name
```

VBA prints Document1, the name of the document. This statement should look familiar, despite the bang. The statement is almost like this one, which you can see in the section "Default Properties and Methods":

```
?Application.Documents("Document1").Name
```

Take away the quotes and parentheses and slip in a bang and the two statements are identical.

If you do decide to use the bang character you need to beware of object names that include spaces or other special characters that make VBA grumpy. VBA gets grumpy when you include spaces in an object name because it normally uses spaces to break up parts of a VBA statement. When a space really belongs to a single part of the statement, VBA gets really confused. For instance, consider the following line of code, which has no hope of actually working:

```
?Application.Documents!My Cool Document.doc.Name
```

The name of the document is My Cool Document.doc, a perfectly valid long file name. The problem is that, as it stands, this statement confuses the heck out of VBA. First off, VBA interprets the spaces in the document name as gaps between multiple parts of the statement. Second, the dot character between Document and doc is the file system character designating the file extension. VBA, however, tries to interpret it as an object/property separator, failing miserably in its attempt.

But the document name is valid, so how can you use it with VBA? The answer, if you absolutely must use a bang, is to enclose the document name in square brackets. That's right, VBA has two more special characters that you need to remember! Square brackets are a way of telling VBA to treat everything inside them as a single unit and not to try and break it apart. So, the correct version of the above statement is this:

```
?Application.Documents![My Cool Document.doc].Name
```

Notice how the entire file name is inside the brackets. Of course, you don't need to be concerned about this if you stick to using parentheses. You see, parentheses act like brackets automatically. VBA treats everything inside them as a single unit. So, you can rewrite the prior statement using parentheses, making it look like this:

```
?Application.Documents("My Cool Document.doc").Name
```

If your brain is beginning to hurt, you're not alone. Our advice is to stick with the parentheses whenever you need to refer to objects and forget about the bang altogether.

A Comment from the Peanut Gallery

In this final section of the chapter, we need to tell you about one more strange and special character that you see a lot of in the chapters to come — the apostrophe. *Apostrophes* (') are used to denote *comments* in your code. Programmers use comments to tell other programmers (and sometimes even themselves) what the code does. We highly recommend that you add comments to your code as you write it, so that you'll know what the code snipped does when you look at it again.

You can include comments in your code on a line all by themselves or on lines that contain VBA code. VBA treats everything to the right of the apostrophe as a comment. The following code shows the two ways that you can use comments:

```
' This is a comment by itself
x = 10     ' I'm a comment, too
```

To bang or not to bang

You don't see the bang character used very much with Excel, PowerPoint, or Word. You see Access examples that use it, however. Why is this? Because the bang character is most useful when you use a number of default properties or methods in a row within a single VBA statement. When you write code to modify data in an Access database, you use objects that have default members that lend themselves to this.

Specifically, you use an object called a Recordset, which essentially represents the results of a database query. Each Recordset object has a Fields collection containing one object for each field in the result set. To get at the actual data, you need to reference a single field by using the collection's Item method. Under normal circumstances such a reference requires a statement like the following:

```
?Recordset.Fields.Item("CustomerID").
  Value
```

But, because the Fields collection is the default property of a Recordset, and the Item method is the default method of the Fields collection, you can collapse the statement down to something much more convenient:

```
?Recordset!CustomerID
```

(Note that Value is also the default property of a Field object.) This works because Access objects, such as the Recordset, have default members that refer to other objects, which have default members that refer to other objects, which . . . well, you get the picture. More often than not, the default members of Excel, PowerPoint, and Word objects are just plain old values (not other objects) so the bang character is not all that useful.

When you type a comment into the VBA editor, VBA turns the text green so that you can easily tell what's a comment and what isn't. Like we said, try to add comments (while the purpose of the statement is fresh in your mind) as you write your code. Writing comments as you go is a whole lot easier than adding comments later on.

Chapter 7

Analyzing Excel Objects

• •

In This Chapter

▶ Getting started with Excel objects

▶ Introducing the Application object

▶ Exploring workbooks and worksheets

▶ Having fun with the Range object

• •

*R*eady for some excitement? This is the first in a series of chapters that discuss the object models within each of the Office components and point out the most commonly used objects. In this chapter, we focus our efforts on Excel. Before venturing into this chapter, or the subsequent chapters on Word, PowerPoint, and Access, you need to be comfortable with the concept of an object. If not, take a moment to read Chapter 4.

Excel offers a robust and expansive object model, including objects such as workbooks, worksheets, ranges, charts, and pivot tables. In this chapter, we lay the groundwork for using the basic objects. In Chapters 18 and 19, we delve into more detail about some more advanced Excel objects, including pivot tables and charts.

Introducing the Excel Object Model

Excel has enjoyed its own object model for many versions now. As with all the Office components, all objects are born from the mother or creator object — the Application object. Actually, the Application object represents the entire Microsoft Excel application. Using the Application object, we can gather basic information about Excel, such as its version, location, and other application-wide settings and options. The Application object also contains properties that track the current workbook (ActiveWorkbook) and current worksheet (ActiveSheet).

If you are still in a fog and we are losing you, launch Microsoft Excel and use the following steps to look at the available methods and properties of the Application object within Excel. This may feel familiar if you followed us through Chapter 4.

1. **Press ALT+F11 or choose** **Tools**➪**Macro**➪**Visual Basic Editor to open the Visual Basic Editor.**

2. **If the Immediate window isn't already open, choose** **View**➪**Immediate window to open it.**

3. **In the Immediate window, type** `?Application.` **to expose the automatic listing of members available to the Application object, as shown in Figure 7-1.**

   Over 180 properties and methods are available in this listing.

Figure 7-1:
The Application object's Bag of Tricks.

 If you do not see a listing as soon as you type the . (dot) after Application, you do not have the Auto List Members option turned on. This option can be set in the Options dialog box (Tools➪Options), on the Editor tab under the Code Settings section.

 You can use the Object Browser to browse or shop through objects and their respective properties, methods, and events. These functions of the Object Browser are discussed in detail in Chapter 5.

Browse through the listing and see if you can guess which properties and methods are specific to Excel and which are common across the Office suite. (*Hint:* Only Excel has workbooks, worksheets, and charts, while all the Office components share the Office Assistant and utilize Add-Ins.)

 In the preceding Step 3, you type `?Application` followed by the dot syntax (.) to expose the member list. (If the member list is not visible, see the preceding Tip.) If you type `Application` without the preceding question mark (?), you still see the member list. In general, if you want to print something, such as a property setting, to the Immediate window, you want to precede your object with a question mark. If, however, you want to set a property or launch a method, a question mark only causes syntax problems.

The Application Object Example

Before we examine specific Excel objects, we want you to look at one example using the Application object in Excel. One of the properties available to the Application object is RecentFiles, which tracks the names and locations of the most recently accessed workbooks.

1. **In Excel, choose File⇨New to create a new workbook.**

   A blank workbook appears with a default name of Book1. If you have created other new workbooks in the same session of Excel, the default name may be Book2, Book3, and so on.

2. **Select File⇨Save to save the new workbook.**

   The Save As dialog box prompts you for a name.

3. **Type a name that you can remember, such as** MyWorkbook.xls, **into the Save As dialog box.**

4. **Select File⇨Close to close the workbook.**

   Are you wondering why we are going to all this trouble to create a new workbook, save it, and then close it? The RecentFiles property tracks only those files that have been opened and subsequently closed. By creating our own workbook, we get a firsthand view of how this works.

5. **In the Immediate window, type**
   `?Application.RecentFiles(1).Name` **to print the name of the workbook that you just created, saved, and closed.**

   The directory to which you saved your workbook is now considered the current directory, so Excel just returns the workbook file name without a path. Try this again by using the index number of 2 in the next step.

6. **Type** `?Application.RecentFiles(2).Name` **in the Immediate window.**

   If you have used Excel before, which is a pretty good bet, this line of code returns the name and path of the second to last Workbook that you had open.

7. **Type** `Application.RecentFiles(1).Open` **in the Immediate window.**

   The Open method re-opens the most recently opened Excel workbook. If you toggle back to Excel, your new workbook that you created in this series of steps is open again.

The Open method only works if the file you reference has maintained the same name and continues to live in the same location. If either the name or the location changes, this method results in an error indicating that Excel can't find the workbook. So, if your workbook is going through an identity crisis and has recently changed its name or address, forget any notion that you have of using the Open method.

You do not need to precede the command in Step 7 with a question mark because you are executing the Open method of the RecentFiles object.

You can continue this exercise using different index values, but at some point you get an error message indicating that the subscript is out of range. This error means that Excel has no more information to give you. Actually, Excel stores the names and locations of a finite number of workbooks that you can control. By using the Options dialog box you can set the number of recently used files that are listed under the File menu and therefore accessible via VBA code. By default, this number is set to four (4). To set this option, locate the *Recently used file list* entry under the General tab of the Options dialog box.

Workbooks and Worksheets

Before we begin our discussion on workbooks and worksheets, take a look at the basic structure of how these are related. As mentioned earlier, the Application object is at the top of the object hierarchy, followed by the Workbooks collection, the Worksheets collection, and then the Range object as depicted in Figure 7-2. This diagram depicts one possible progression down the object slide. Wee! This progression ought to make perfect sense if you look at how Excel works. Excel (the Application) is made up of workbooks. Workbooks in turn are made up of one or many worksheets, and within worksheets you can have one or more ranges.

Figure 7-2:
An abbreviated object hierarchy of select Excel objects.

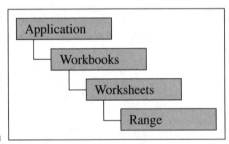

Singular or plural — which is it?

Time to end the confusion here. We have all sorts of objects flying around, such as workbooks and worksheets, as well as a workbook and a worksheet. As we already mentioned, Workbooks refers to the collection of all currently open workbooks, whereas a workbook is a member of that collection. The Workbooks collection is like a cookie jar, and each individual workbook is a cookie. The cookie jar can be filled with cookies, have just a single cookie, or be plumb out of cookies. The Workbooks collection can have one or many workbook objects. In fact, you can have no workbooks in the collection, indicating that you have no open workbooks.

In general, when referring to the entire collection, use the plural object. However, you also use the collection object to refer to a specific workbook in the collection, such as `Application.Workbooks("MyWorkbook.xls")`. In this example, you are referring to MyWorkbook.xls, which is a member of the Workbooks collection.

The best way to understand is to do, so here you go. Follow these steps:

1. **Open Excel if it's not already open, and close any open workbooks so that you get a fresh start.**

2. **Open the Sales.xls workbook, which is available in C:\Dummies\Chapter 7 directory installed from the disk.**

   This workbook includes an extract from the Northwind sample data-base that ships with Access 97. If you haven't copied this workbook to your local hard drive yet, now is a good time. You can't modify the files while they are on the disk — it's write-protected.

3. **Next, open Product.xls located in the same directory.**

4. **Press Alt+F11 to open the Visual Basic Editor.**

5. **If it's not already visible, select <u>V</u>iew⇨<u>I</u>mmediate window in the Visual Basic Editor to open the Immediate window.**

6. **In the Immediate window, type** `?Application.Workbooks.Count` **to discover the number of workbooks currently open in Excel.**

   This ought to return a value of 2. If you are unsure about the result, refer back to Excel and see how many workbooks are actually open according to the Window menu.

In the above step, you retrieve a count of all workbooks in the Work-books collection. Other methods and properties pertain to the entire collection as well, such as the Close method which closes all open workbooks in one easy command — Application.Workbooks.Close. You can also add a new workbook by using the command Application .Workbooks.Add. Check out what methods and properties are available to you for the Workbooks collection.

Now, you know how many workbooks are open. Great, but what work-books are they? You can find that out by using the Name property of the Workbooks collection, with a small catch. You need to specify for which element or member of the collection that you want to retrieve the name.

7. **Type** `?Application.Workbooks(1).Name` **in the Immediate window.**

   This command ought to return Sales.xls because that was the first workbook that you opened in Step 2.

You may have noticed that when you refer to a specific workbook in the Workbooks collection, you see a different list of methods and properties. You simply have a wider range of possibilities when referring to a specific workbook, such as printing or saving the workbook. Take a moment to look through the available features.

Try the same command as in Step 6 but use an index of 2.

8. **Type** `?Application.Workbooks(2).Name` **in the Immediate window.**

This returns Product.xls.

Because only two workbooks are open, using an index value of 3 yields a subscript out-of-range error. This indicates that a third workbook is not open.

Looking for a shortcut? Technically, you don't need to explicitly type in the Application object when referencing workbooks and worksheets; the Application object is assumed if you do not include it, so save yourself some typing! For example, ?Workbooks.Count works the same as ?Application.Workbooks.Count.

Referring to collection members

You can refer to a member of a collection in two ways — using index numbers or explicit names. In the preceding section, you can find out how to use an index number to refer to a workbook (Application.Workbooks(1), for example) within the Workbooks collection. These index numbers are assigned when you open or create workbooks within Excel. The first workbook that you open or create receives the index number 1, the next receives a 2, and so on. No workbook escapes this index numbering schema. Even hidden workbooks are indexed.

Now, you may be wondering if you can change the index number of a workbook. The only way to get a new index number is to close an open workbook. Upon doing that, all the index numbers shift accordingly. If you close Sales.xls in the example in the preceding section, Products.xls becomes Workbooks(1), whereas it is Workbooks(2) when Sales.xls is open.

When you activate a workbook, you do not change its index number. Workbook index numbers only change when a change is made to the Workbooks collection, specifically, from one workbook dropping out of the order. Then, and only then, can an open workbook's index number change.

Okay, so if the first workbook that you open or create is referred to as Workbooks(1) then what about the last one? Good question. To refer to the last workbook opened or created, you use Workbooks(Workbooks.Count). A little unusual, but keep in mind that you can find the total number of workbooks opened if you check the Count property of the Workbooks collection.

Index numbers are useful, and save on typing, if you know the index number of your intended workbook. You can also refer to a specific workbook by simply calling it by name, such as Workbooks("Sales.xls"), and unlike your cat, the workbooks actually come when you call!

Pick up the example from the section "Singular or plural — which is it?" in this chapter. We assume that you have the two workbooks open, but if not, please re-open Sales.xls and Products.xls in that order. If Sales.xls is the first workbook opened, you can refer to it as Application.Workbooks(1) or Application.Workbooks("Sales.xls"). Follow these steps:

1. **Type** `Application.Workbooks(1).PrintPreview` **in the Immediate window to apply the Print Preview method to Sales.xls.**

   This activates Excel and brings Sales.xls up in print preview. Now, try this by using the explicit name of the workbook.

2. **Type** `Application.Workbooks("Sales.xls").PrintPreview.`

   You experience the exact same behavior as in the previous step. If not, check your spelling.

This entire discussion on referring to collection members extends to the Worksheets collection and Worksheet object. If you want to refer to a worksheet in the Worksheets collection, refer to it as

```
Application.Workbooks(index number).Worksheets(index number)
```

Alternatively, you can leave out the implied Application object to save some keystrokes: `Workbooks(index number).Worksheets(index number)`.

If you want to find out how many worksheets are in Sales.xls and what they are named, try this:

1. **Type** `?Workbooks("Sales.xls").Worksheets.Count` **in the Immediate window.**

   This returns a result of 2.

2. **Next, retrieve the worksheet names by typing the following in the Immediate window:**

```
?Workbooks("Sales.xls").Worksheets(1).Name & _
    " and " & Workbooks("Sales.xls").Worksheets(2).Name
```

   This returns the result Beverage Sales and Produce Sales, which are the correct names of the two worksheets in the Sales.xls workbook.

Hopefully, the last example didn't throw you for a loop. We simply put two commands and a text string together with ampersands (&). You can separate these as two distinct commands and execute them one at a time.

Before leaving this section, here're a few more things to try:

1. **In the Immediate window, type** `Workbooks("Sales.xls").Activate.`

   This makes Sales.xls the current workbook. You can verify that Sales.xls is now active if you type in `?ActiveWorkbook.Name`.

2. **Add a new worksheet to this workbook by typing** `Worksheets.Add.`

   This adds Sheet1 to the Sales.xls workbook and places it in the left-most position. Now, you can rename Sheet1.

3. **Type** `Worksheets("Sheet1").name="MyNewSheet"` **in the Immediate window.**

   Check Sales.xls in Excel to see that the name change worked.

Did you notice that when you typed Worksheets("Sheet1") followed by the dot (.) that no list of methods or properties appeared as you are accustomed to? For some reason, VBA can't determine what type of object Worksheets("Sheet1") is, so it is unable to give you a pick list. We agree that it is quite frustrating, but this is how Excel was designed. You can still type in the appropriate method or property as you normally do.

For your last trick, suppose that you want to move this new worksheet to the right of the Produce Sales worksheet. Type the following in the Immediate window:

```
Worksheets("MyNewSheet").Move after:= _
  Worksheets("Produce Sales")
```

(Refer back to Excel to verify that the new worksheet has indeed moved after the Produce Sales worksheet.) Notice that the Move method of the Worksheets collection accepts an argument — after. Alternatively, you can tell VBA which worksheet to place MyNewSheet before rather than after. It's all a matter of choice.

Active workbooks and worksheets

In other examples in this chapter, you explicitly identify which workbook or worksheet to use. However, sometimes you don't need to identify an index number or a specific name. You can use the ActiveWorkbook property of the Application object to refer to the workbook that is currently active or the ActiveSheet to refer to the current worksheet. For example, `?Application.ActiveWorkbook.Name` returns the name of the workbook that is currently active in Excel.

Not sure which workbook is active, or how to make one active? Pick up the example from the section "Singular or plural — which is it?" in this chapter. We assume that you have the two workbooks open, but if not, open Sales.xls and Products.xls in that order and take a walk through these steps:

1. **In Excel, ensure that you can see Products.xls.**

   If this workbook is not immediately visible, select it from the Window menu if it is still open but waiting in the background for you. This action makes Products.xls the active workbook in Excel.

2. **If you do not have the Visual Basic Editor open, use the shortcut key Alt+F11 to open it from within Excel.**

3. **In the Immediate window, type** `?ActiveWorkbook.Name` **to return the name of the currently active workbook in Excel.**

   This workbook ought to be Products.xls. Now, suppose that you want to activate Sales.xls instead.

4. **In the Immediate window, type** `Workbooks("Sales.xls").Activate.`

   If you switch back to Excel, you see Sales.xls rather than Products.xls. Sales.xls is now the active workbook.

If you don't believe us, you can check it out yourself if you type `?ActiveWorkbook.Name` in the Immediate window of the Visual Basic Editor. The active workbook has changed from Products.xls to Sales.xls.

Now, that wasn't so bad, was it? You can try similar things with the ActiveSheet property of the Worksheets collection. For example, continuing on with our example you can see what worksheet is currently active in the Sales.xls workbook. Type `?Workbooks("Sales.xls").ActiveSheet.Name` and the Immediate window returns the currently viewable worksheet in Sales.xls. Actually, because the ActiveWorkbook is assumed when VBA sees ActiveSheet, you can just type `?ActiveSheet.Name` to yield the same results. Neat, huh?

If you are wondering why we didn't have you use the ActiveWorksheet property, you may be surprised to find out that it does not exist. The ActiveSheet property, which you used above, can refer to either a worksheet or a chart.

We know, you can't handle another way to refer to a workbook. Enough is enough, but we have one more to tell you about. Excel has a property called ThisWorkbook that returns the workbook in which your Visual Basic code is actually running. Most of the time, ThisWorkbook is the same as the ActiveWorkbook. When isn't it the active workbook, you ask? Without entering into painful technical detail, if an Excel add-in is called by the active workbook, the ThisWorkbook property returns the name of the add-in workbook. Confusing, huh? Well, when and if you start to use Excel add-ins, then you can worry about understanding this. Take a look at *Excel 97 Programming For Windows For Dummies* by John Walkenbach (also published by IDG Books Worldwide, Inc.) for more information.

Home, Home on the Range

The Range object is likely the most important object in Excel. What exactly is a range? Well, this range is not related to golf balls (as in a driving range) or cooking (as in a stove-top range). A *range* is a block of cells containing one or more contiguous blocks of cells, or if you want to get fancy, a 3-D range which contains cells through multiple worksheets. A range can contain multiple columns and rows, or just a single cell. As you can see, a range can come in many shapes and sizes. A range object has a number of available methods and properties such as cells and offset, which we define later in this chapter.

When you identify a range, and refer to it in your VBA code, you can be explicit about the range address, such as "C10:C20" or a predefined named range, such as "MyRange", which designates a particular block of cells.

Explicit range addresses

When we say *explicit range address*, we mean the beginning and ending cell numbers for a range of values in a table. You can use this address to identify a range in your VBA code. To see what we mean, start out with some examples by using the example workbooks from the section "Singular or plural — which is it?" in this chapter. We assume that you have the two workbooks open in Excel 97, but if not, please open Sales.xls and Products.xls in that order. Make Sales.xls active and then follow these steps:

1. **If you do not have the Visual Basic Editor open, use the shortcut key ALT+F11 to open it from within Excel.**

2. **Type** `?ActiveSheet.Range("A1").Value` **in the Immediate window.**

   This returns the value in cell A1 of the active sheet in the active workbook. In our case, this returns "Product Name" which is the first cell in the Beverage Sales worksheet in Sales.xls. You can even set the values for a range of cells; see the next step.

3. **In the Immediate window, type** `Worksheets("MyNewSheet").Activate` **to insure that our newly created worksheet is the current one.**

4. **Next, type** `Range("A1").Value = "100"` **which can represent your hourly consulting or yardwork rate.**

This command sets cell A1 to the number 100. In and of itself, not earth shattering, but the fact that you can do this type of thing programmatically is really cool. After you are into the swing of writing subroutine and incorporating looping and conditional statements, the possibilities are nearly endless.

5. **Type** `Range("A2:A10").Formula = "=A1*2"` **into the Immediate window.**

In this step, you're propagating a formula. Check MyNewSheet to see your handiwork. If all goes well, cell A1 contains your constant value of 100, whereas cells A2–A10 contain formulas that are relative to their rows. For example, cell A2 contains the formula "A1*2", while cell A3's formula is "A2*2".

Are you still staring at Step 4 of the last example and wondering how and why Excel changed A1 to A2, A3, and so on? Excel is smart enough to know that A1 is a relative reference and handled it accordingly. In the above example, you referred to cells by using the A1 style, which is likely what you are most familiar with, but you can also refer to cells absolutely. Consider the following ways that you can refer to cell A1: A1, $A$1, $A1, and A$1. The presence of a $ preceding a column or row value locks that specific value when you copy the formula, making it an *absolute value*. So, if you are storing a constant in cell A1 and planning on using this value in formulas, you want to use $A$1 to refer to the constant. By doing so, if the formula is copied, your constant value is maintained.

The $ notation works great when you enter formulas and values into a worksheet manually; however, after you start to use code to populate worksheet cells, you want to find out about another type of relative referencing — *R1C1 notation*. For instance, cell A1 can also be referred to as R1C1. If you programmatically set formulas and want to use relative references, you want to use R1C1 notation. For example, RC[-1] refers to a cell in the same row but one column to the left, hence the -1 indicator. Similarly, R[1]C[1] refers to a cell one row over and one column down.

Name that range

You can refer to a range explicitly like you do in the preceding example, or you can call it by a given name that you can define. Try to refer to a range explicitly in this new way to give yourself an idea how this works. For this example, say that you want to use the Sales.xls workbook as modified in the section "Explicit range addresses" prior to this section. By using the Add method of the Names collection (which contains all existing named ranges in the current workbook), you can name a range by using VBA code.

1. **In the Immediate window, type** `ActiveSheet.Names.Add Name:="MyNamedRange", RefersTo:="=$A$2:$A$10".`

   This code creates a named range "MyNamedRange" that refers to the nine cells (A2 through A10). You also can check the Define Name dialog box to search for your new named range.

2. **Switch to Excel and select Insert⇨Name⇨Define to open the Define Name dialog box, as shown in Figure 7-3.**

   You see the new named range "MyNamedRange" which refers to the correct cells.

   Notice that when you select the range A2:A10 on the worksheet, the name of this range appears in the name box, as shown in Figure 7-3.

   If your named range was created as planned, ensure that you anchored the cells by using the dollar signs ($), such as $A$2:$A$10. If you did not use the absolute referencing (this is what the dollar signs do), you instead created a named range that was relative to your current cell position on the worksheet.

   Now, you can use the named range to refer to cells A2:A10 and set various properties, such as interior settings.

3. **Type** `Range("MyNamedRange").Interior.ColorIndex=3` **in the Immediate window.**

   This changes the interior color of cells A2:A10 to red. Refer to Excel Visual Basic Help for a listing of the default colors and their respective index numbers. Finally, you can clear the contents of this range by using the ClearContents method.

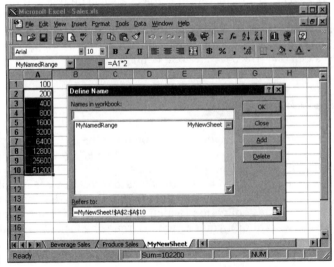

Figure 7-3: Viewing the named ranges with the Define Name dialog box.

4. Type `Range("MyNamedRange").ClearContents.`

Cells A2 through A10 are now blank.

Every property or method that returns a range is relative to the object that precedes it. For example, consider the range defined by the following code: `ActiveWorkbook.ActiveSheet.Range("A2:B5").Cells(1,1)`. `Cells(1,1)` refers to the Range("A2:B5") which is located on the ActiveSheet of the ActiveWorkbook in the Excel application.

When you use the Range property without an object qualifier (that is, an object to the left of the dot syntax "."), as you do in Steps 2 and 3, the Range property returns a range on the active sheet. If, however, the active sheet isn't a worksheet, the method fails. To be 100 percent sure that you don't crash and burn with your Range command (without an object qualifier), use the Activate method to activate a worksheet before you use the Range property.

Range object versus Range property

If you've read and performed the steps of earlier sections in this chapter, you've already seen some assorted uses of the Range object and its Range property. A Range (the Range object) is a set of one or more cells. The Range object can be a column, a single cell, or an entire worksheet. Also, the Range object has a number of methods (such as AutoFormat and Sort) and properties (such as Worksheet, Columns, Rows, and Address). In VBA, to get a Range object to control you call the Range property of a worksheet. For example, `?Worksheets("MyNewSheet").Range("A1").Value` prints the value in cell A1 on the MyNewSheet worksheet. You need to call the worksheet's Range property to VBA that you mean cell A1 on that worksheet as opposed to another.

Although you can refer to a range with A1-style notation, such as Range("A1") or a named range, such as Range("MyNamedRange"), you can not use R1C1-style notation. R1C1 notation is another form of relative referencing, but don't worry about that. Just tuck this information away for that rainy day when you use R1C1 notation to refer to Range and your code doesn't work.

Cells property

Look at the Cells property of the Range object. A range, as you already know, can be defined by cells of a Range object. Within a given range, you may want to refer to a specific cell. Consider the range area of "A10:B20". You can use the syntax `Cells(row, column)` where row is the row index and column is the column index, to isolate a particular cell within the range. For example, you may want to find the value of a cell in a given range that is two rows down and two columns over as shown in the following code snippet.

```
?ActiveWorkbook.ActiveSheet.Range("A10:B20"). _
  Cells(2,2).Value
```

When you know exactly what cell you want to get or set the value of, you may decide to simply identify the cell in the Range property, such as Range("A1") to return cell A1. However, there may be times when the Cells property is more convenient because you can use a variable for the row or column. The following example sets the value of a cell within the range, but uses variables *x* and *y* to determine the actual row and column.

```
ActiveWorkbook.ActiveSheet.Range("A1:C5"). _
  Cells(x, y).Value
```

Forgive us for discussing variables without providing a full explanation of them; Chapter 11 is devoted entirely to variables so you may want to refer to that chapter now if you can't wait! In a nutshell, the variables *x* and *y* are theoretically set to some numeric values in your VBA code.

After a worksheet has been activated, such as by calling the command ActiveWorkbook.Worksheets("MySheet").Activate, the Cells property can be used without an explicit worksheet declaration. Without the declaration, the cells property returns a cell on the active worksheet.

With the Cells property, you can specify a cell by its row and column within a given range. The Offset property is similar in that it accepts a row and column as seen with its syntax Offset(row, column). However, with the Offset property the row and column values specify how many rows and columns to offset (or move) from the range to return a range. Confused by this? Give us a chance to explain, because this is a handy little property.

The following example selects the cell two rows down and four columns over from cell A1 in the ActiveSheet.

```
ActiveSheet.Range("A1").Offset(2,4).Select
```

This example provides a simple illustration of offsetting a single cell. You can also offset a range of cells to physically move a selection block. For example, if you enter ActiveSheet.Range("A1:B2").Offset(1,1).Select, the cells B2:C3 are selected. How did this happen? Well, you asked Excel to select a range of cells (four cells to be exact) over one column and down one row.

Enough talk right? Give some of this a try with one of our sample workbooks. Follow these steps:

1. **If it's not already open, open the Sales.xls workbook that you use throughout the chapter and ensure that it's the active workbook.**

   Active refers to the workbook that you see when you switch to Excel.

2. **If you do not have the Visual Basic Editor open, use the shortcut key ALT+F11 to open it from within Excel.**

3. **In the Immediate window, type**
   `ActiveWorkbook.Worksheets("Produce Sales").Activate.`

   This makes Produce Sales the active worksheet.

4. **Next, set the current selection to cells A1:B2 and type**
   `Range("A1:B2").Select` **in the Immediate window.**

   If you flip back to Excel (such as by using Alt+Tab), you see this block of four cells selected in the Produce Sales worksheet.

   After you have a range of cells selected (meaning that the range is the current selection), you can start to use the Selection object to refer to the range.

A common error when writing code is to assume that the workbook or worksheet you want to reference is the active one. In our current example, you did activate the proper worksheet before sending commands, which is good programming. When you write applications, keep this in mind: End users are unpredictable! If an end user changes the active workbook or worksheet and then runs your code, your code may fail, or even change an unsuspecting worksheet. To play it safe, ensure that your code is running on the right workbook or worksheet by referring it explicitly in your code statements, such as Workbooks("MyWorkbook"). Worksheets("MyWorksheet"). Keep in mind that this does not just apply to Excel. The same rules hold for PowerPoint, Word, and Access.

5. **You can access property values of individual cells within the selection. To find the value of each cell in the range, type**
   `?Selection.Cells(1,1).Value.`

   This returns "Product Name" to the Immediate window which is the actual content of cell A1, which resides in the first row and first column of the selected area. Keep in mind that if the selected range is B5:D10, the same command provides the value of cell B5.

Offset property

Ready to try to use the Offset property? We start simple by finding out which cell is two rows over and three rows down from a given cell. If it's not already open, open the Sales.xls workbook that you use throughout the chapter and ensure that it's the active workbook. Then follow these steps:

1. **Type** `?Cells(1,1).Offset(2,3).Address` **in the Immediate window.**

   This returns the cell address of $D$3. You can also check the value of this cell with the following command: ?Cells(1,1).Offset(2,3).Value.

   Notice that even though you are checking a value of a cell outside the current selection, the current selection remains intact. To verify this, return to Excel. The same four cells are still highlighted.

   One last trick. If you use the offset property, you can actually move the selected range over by one row and one column.

2. **Type** `Selection.Offset(1,1).Select` **in the Immediate window.**

   Now, cells B2:C3 are the current selection. If you flip back to Excel, the highlighted area has moved down one row and one column but still maintained the same number of cells.

3. **Type** `?Selection.Address` **in the Immediate window.**

   If everything goes as planned in your example, this line returns $B$2:$C$3, which is the address of the current selection.

You can't select a cell that isn't on the active sheet. If you are uncertain whether the sheet is active, use the Worksheets("MySheet").Activate before you send any commands at it.

Chapter 8

A Word About Word Objects

• •

In This Chapter

▶ Getting started with Word Objects

▶ Checking out the Application object

▶ Introducing the Range object

▶ Using the object model to have fun with tables!

▶ Explaining templates

▶ Modifying template contents

• •

*I*n case you haven't heard yet, the big news in Word 97 is that it *finally* has an object model and subsequently a real programming environment, too. If you are saying to yourself "An object model? What's that all about?," then take a few moments to read about objects in Chapter 4 before taking this object model tour with us.

After you dive into developing Word applications with its robust object model, you'll wonder how developers survived without Word 97. Word offers a rich object model, including objects such as documents, templates, paragraphs, and bookmarks. In this chapter, we cover some of the basic objects. If you are left thirsting for more cool stuff using the Word object model, we suggest that you explore Chapters 20 and 21.

An Object Model Explosion

Unlike Word's friend PowerPoint that is brand new to an object model, Word has always enjoyed an object model. But why then did we make the crack that Word finally has an object model? Previous versions of Word have exactly one object — the Word.Basic object. Actually, if you only developed within Word, you may not have known about the Word.Basic object. In the times of the single object model, you only needed to reference the Word.Basic object when accessing Word from other applications. Word.Basic, like the Farmer in the Dell's cheese, stood alone.

In Word 97, the object model has been expanded to include real objects like Documents, Templates, and CommandBars, as seen in Figure 8-1. What a transformation, like the caterpillar to butterfly! But wait, there is more. Using the Document object, you can reach additional objects such as tables, styles, bookmarks, and sentences that may be included in the document.

We thought it would be helpful to provide you with the quick steps that you can take to view Word's object model in on-line help. Start off by opening Word and then doing the following:

1. **Choose Help⇨Contents and Index.**

   The Help Topics dialog box opens.

2. **Click on the Contents tab if it's not already selected.**

3. **Locate the Microsoft Word Visual Basic Reference book, which is near the end of the reference book list, and double-click it to expose its contents.**

   Actually, only one entry exists — the Visual Basic reference.

4. **Select the Visual Basic reference and click the Display button.**

   Doing so launches the Help Topics dialog box for Word Visual Basic.

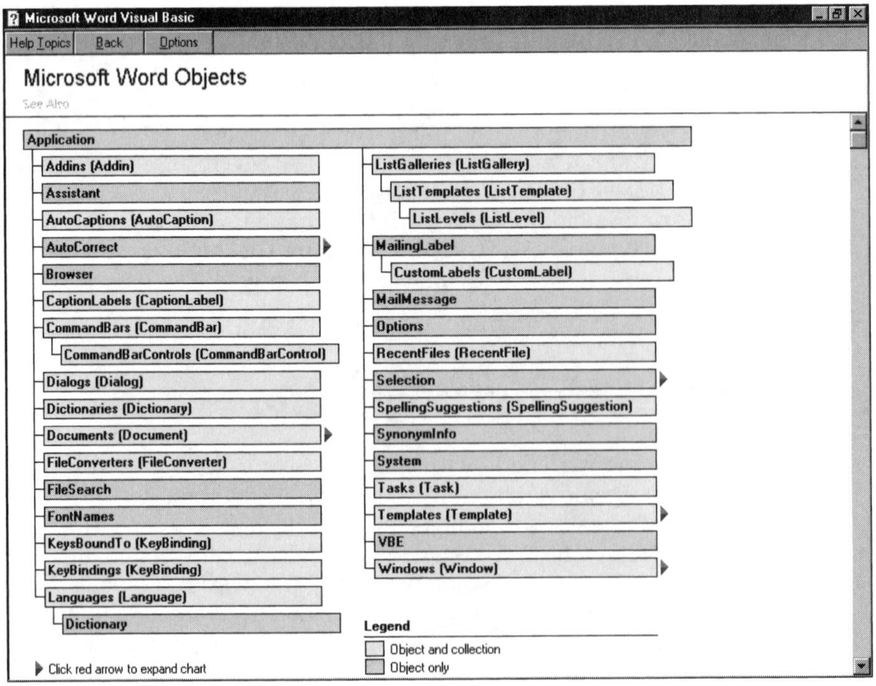

Figure 8-1: Looking at Word's object model.

5. **Select the Index tab if it's not already selected.**

6. **Type** object **in the empty text box located at the top of the dialog box.**

   Notice that as soon as you start typing, the index entry list box moves to the items matching your entry. After you finish typing **object**, you view the object-related entries in online help.

7. **Select object hierarchy in the index entry listing and then click the Display button.**

   Word's object model is now visible, as shown in Figure 8-1. By using this help dialog box you can drill down into various objects for more information and assistance.

Using on-line help is one way of exploring Word's object model. You may also want to take advantage of the Object Browser, which we discuss in Chapter 5.

In Chapter 26, we discuss migration issues from previous Office versions. If you have developed solutions in older versions of Word, or have a chance of inheriting an old solution from your Aunt Betty or the guy a few cubes away, take a moment to read the brief tips on Word 97 migration.

The Mother of All Word Objects

Each of the Office components starts out with the *Application object,* which is the launching pad for all other objects. Word is no exception. By using the Application object, you can set options for Word and gather information about the current environment, such as how many documents are open and what application you are using (Word? Excel? PowerPoint?).

Take a look at a few examples that use the Application object.

1. **Launch Microsoft Word.**

   When you first open Word, a blank document (affectionately named Doucment1) appears. You can either leave this one open or open any other document.

2. **Open the Visual Basic Editor by pressing ALT+F11 or by choosing Tools⇨Macro⇨Visual Basic Editor.**

3. **If the Immediate window is not already visible, open it by choosing View⇨Immediate Window.**

4. **In the Immediate window, type** ?Application.Name **and then press Enter.**

Doing so returns `Microsoft Word` to the Immediate window, which indicates the application is Word, but you knew that, right?

Next, you need to get a count of the number of documents open in Word right now. You know that the answer is 1, because you actually opened the document, but go ahead and see what VBA has to say.

5. In the Immediate Window, type `?Application.Documents.Count` **and press Enter.**

Doing so returns the correct number of documents open to the Immediate window.

Remember that the Documents collection, which contains all the currently open documents, is a sub-object of the Application object. You invoked the Count property of the collection to get the result. In the section "Working with Document Objects and Their Children" later in this chapter, we explore the Documents object and its sub-objects.

You are likely to already be familiar with the Options dialog box in Word that allows you to customize your Word environment. You have the ability to modify save settings, viewing options, and more. By using VBA and the Application object, you can check whether an option is set or not, and then correct it if needed.

6. In the Immediate window, type
`?Application.Options.VirusProtection` **and then press Enter.**

Doing so returns True or False to the Immediate window, which tells you whether the Macro Virus Protection option is set in the general option settings.

Word is very susceptible to viruses. Unless you've been living under a rock, we're sure that you have either experienced the Concept virus or know someone who has. Even when you think you've killed it, it still appears to be lurking! The concept virus attacks the Normal.dot file. Ouch! If Macro Virus Protection is on, you receive a warning that a document you are about to open has macros that could contain viruses. This warning is not a substitute for installing antivirus software on your desktop, but provides an extra level of security for Word users. If you are new to Word or even if you're not and you are wondering what Normal.dot is, we lift the fog in the section "Checking out templates" later in this chapter.

Working with Document Objects and Their Children

By using the Document object, you have access to various aspects of your Word documents, including your page setup, document text, and tables. As an example, by using VBA you can alter the page orientation of a document. The following code snippet, that can be run from the Immediate window, sets the page orientation to landscape for the first document in the documents collection.

```
Documents(1).PageSetup.Orientation = wdOrientLandscape
```

We could be here all day playing with document settings using VBA. To prevent insomnia (you can thank us later), we highlight the more useful and more interesting parts of the Document object.

How about adding a hyperlink programmatically? With all the emphasis on corporate intranets and the Internet, it certainly can't hurt to toss this knowledge into your bag of tricks. This code snippet adds a hyperlink to the selection to your current document and sets the address to a document file on your hard drive.

```
ActiveDocument.Hyperlinks.Add Anchor:=Selection.Range, _
    Address:="c:\My Documents\Cool Document.doc"
```

The address in the ActiveDocument.Hyperlinks.Add statement can also be a Web address such as http:\\www.microsoft.com.

In case you are unclear about what ActiveDocument refers to, relax a moment. The Application object has a number of properties, including *ActiveDocument*, which is the document that is currently in view within Word. If you are typing words into a Word document, for example, it is considered the active document. If you toggled over to the Visual Basic Editor and checked the ActiveDocument property of the Application object, it would return the name of your document.

Using a range

No, we aren't talk about the kind of ranges used to cook food, although we don't need much prodding to think about food. A *range* is a designated area in your Word document. A range can be a paragraph, two paragraphs, a few words, or even the entire document. A range is a contiguous area in a document that is defined by a starting and ending character position. For example, you could have a range that starts at position 0 and ends at position 10.

Unlike bookmarks that are persistent objects, Range objects only exist while the procedure that defined it is running. You may think that a range is the same as the selection object. The two are similar, although you can only have one selection, whereas you can have multiple ranges within a document.

Range objects are independent of the selection object, which means you can have your cake and eat it, too. In nonfood terms, you can define and manipulate a range without changing the current selection.

In this next example, you can define a Range object in the current or active document, determine what text it contains, and check its characteristics.

1. **Launch Microsoft Word and open Sample.doc found in C:\Dummies\Chapter 7 installed from the disk.**

2. **Open the Visual Basic Editor by pressing ALT+F11.**

3. **If the Immediate window is not already visible, choose View⇨ Immediate Window to open it.**

4. **Type** `?ActiveDocument.Paragraphs(1).Range.Text` **in the Immediate window and press Enter.**

   This line of code defines the range as the first paragraph and checks the text property of the range. The code returns "A Word About Word Viruses," which is the text of the first paragraph in Sample.doc, to the Immediate window. Try this step again without using the Text property.

5. **Type** `?ActiveDocument.Paragraphs(1).Range` **in the Immediate window and press Enter.**

   The result should be the same as in Step 4. Because you did not specify a property, VBA used the default property, which is Text. As the next step shows, you can even check the properties of the range, such as whether or not the range is bolded.

6. **Type** `?ActiveDocument.Paragraphs(1).Range.Bold` **in the Immediate window and press Enter.**

   Doing so returns a zero (0) if the range is not bold and a negative one (–1) if it is bold. In the case of Sample.doc, the first paragraph is typed in a bold font, so the code returns –1.

   To finish up with ranges, why not change the text stored in the range?

7. **Type** `ActiveDocument.Paragraphs(1).Range.Text="Replacement text!"` **in the Immediate window and press Enter.**

This line of code replaces the current text of the first paragraph with whatever you set the text property equal to.

Working with tables

By using a sample document that contains a refrigerator inventory table, you can use the object model to gather various information about the table, such as the number of columns and rows. You can also apply a sort, modify the table contents, and add rows and columns. Ready for some fun?

1. **Open the sample Word document (Inventory.doc).**

This file contains a listing of produce contents in our refrigerator, as seen in Figure 8-2. The file is located in the C:\Dummies\Chapter 8 directory installed from the disk. (Actually, we have more beverages in our refrigerator than anything else, but we wouldn't want to bring up beer when you are concentrating so hard on Word objects!)

Inventory.doc

Refrigerator Inventory (Perishables).

Item	Quantity	Estimated Shelf Life	Purchase Date
Romaine	1	10 days	4/1/97
Tomatoes	4	4 days	4/8/97
Asparagus	1 bunch	5 days	4/1/97
Green Beans	½ lb.	5 days	4/8/97
Cucumber	2	1 week	4/8/97
Fresh Basil	1 bunch	2 weeks	4/1/97
Ginger Root	1	2 weeks	4/3/97
Carrots	2 lb bag	1 month	4/1/97
Celery	1 bunch	3 weeks	3/30/97
Red Pepper	1	1 week	4/8/97

Figure 8-2: The before shot of our inventory table.

2. **Open the Visual Basic Editor.**

If you've done any programming at all by using this book, you've likely memorized this step by now, but if not, press ALT+F11 as a shortcut to open the Visual Basic Editor. If you prefer to use the menus, go right ahead.

3. **Type** ?ActiveDocument.Tables(1).Columns.Count **in the Immedi-ate window and then press Enter.**

Doing so gives you a result of 4, because the inventory table has four (4) columns.

If you receive a run-time error, such as the one shown in Figure 8-3, then Inventory.doc is not the active document, and the document that is active does not have a table, resulting in this error. Don't be alarmed; just check to see which document is active by toggling over to Word. The document that is in view is the active document.

See Chapter 17 for information on preventing run-time errors such as this one.

Figure 8-3:
You may
receive this
error dialog
box if
something
doesn't go
right with
your code.

Now see how many rows the table has.

4. **Type** ?ActiveDocument.Tables(1).Rows.Count **in the Immediate window and press Enter.**

The table has eleven rows (ten food items plus the column heading), so you see a result of 11.

This example uses the ActiveDocument object. If you have more than one document open, the active document may not be the document you expect. To be more precise, and to avoid any possible runtime errors, you can replace ActiveDocument with Documents("Inventory.doc") as is used in the next example.

Now that you have mastered getting information about a table, how about adding a column to the table, entering information, and then sorting the table based on date? Using the Inventory.doc example from the last set of steps in this section, add a new column to store planned use of the produce items.

1. **In the Immediate window, type**
   `Documents("Inventory.doc").Tables(1).Columns.Add` **and press Enter.**

   This code adds a new column at the end of the inventory table. Next, add a column heading to the new column by selecting the cell and entering text.

2. **Type** `Documents("Inventory.doc").Tables(1).Cell(1,5).Select` **in the Immediate window and press Enter.**

   After the cell is selected, you can use the Selection object to set the column heading by using the Text property.

3. **Type** `Selection.Text="Planned Use"` **in the Immediate window and press Enter.**

   If you go back to the document, you see the new column with its new heading text. Adding a new row is as easy as adding a new column, so why not try that, too?

4. **Type** `Documents("Inventory.doc").Tables(1).Rows.Add` **in the Immediate window and press Enter.**

   Doing so adds a new row to the bottom of the table. By using code, you can easily continue this example by entering text into the table.

5. **Type** `Documents("Inventory.doc").Tables(1).Cell(12,1).Select` **in the Immediate window and press Enter.**

   This action selects the first cell in the new row.

6. **Type** `Selection.Text ="New food item"` **in the Immediate window and press Enter to add text to the item column.**

   You can also apply a sort to the table by using VBA.

7. **Type** `Documents("Inventory.doc").Tables(1).Sort` **in the Immediate window and press Enter.**

   The Inventory table is then sorted by the first column entries. Again, you can get more advanced and select multiple columns to sort on.

   One last trick. By using VBA, you can easily apply flashier formatting to the table.

8. **Type** `Documents("Inventory.doc").Tables(1).AutoFormat` **in the Immediate window and press Enter.**

   After completing all these steps, your inventory table should look like the one depicted in Figure 8-4.

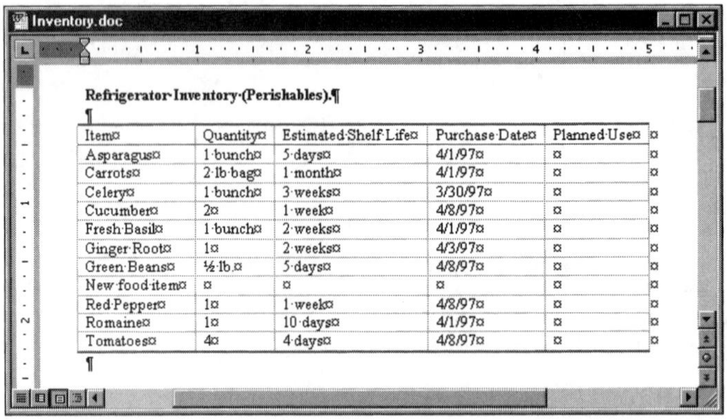
Inventory.doc

Refrigerator Inventory (Perishables).

Item	Quantity	Estimated Shelf Life	Purchase Date	Planned Use
Asparagus	1 bunch	5 days	4/1/97	
Carrots	2 lb bag	1 month	4/1/97	
Celery	1 bunch	3 weeks	3/30/97	
Cucumber	2	1 week	4/8/97	
Fresh Basil	1 bunch	2 weeks	4/1/97	
Ginger Root	1	2 weeks	4/3/97	
Green Beans	½ lb.	5 days	4/8/97	
New food item				
Red Pepper	1	1 week	4/8/97	
Romaine	1	10 days	4/1/97	
Tomatoes	4	4 days	4/8/97	

Figure 8-4: The after shot of our inventory table.

Hopefully the discussion and examples of using the Table object have left you with a number of ideas. The bottom line is that anything you can do manually, such as adding rows and columns to tables, can be handled programmatically with VBA. Cool, huh?

Checking out templates

If you plan to be a serious Word developer, you need to understand a little about templates. Before Word 97, the only way to distribute a Word application was via a template because Word documents could not store code. In today's new world, you can store code directly in a Word document, but after you read a bit about templates, we think you'll agree that they remain very important in Word 97.

A *template,* denoted by the `.dot` extension, looks like a regular document on the surface. You can think of templates as a storage unit for your styles, AutoText entries, customized toolbars, boilerplate text and graphics, and VBA code that are used by your documents.

As a developer, templates are extremely useful because, as we already mentioned, they are a great means of distributing a Word application. By implementing your Word application with templates, your end users can load your template as an add-in and have the code always available, rather than having to open a specific Word document.

Earlier in this chapter, we mentioned the Normal template (Normal.dot). The Normal template is a general-purpose template for documents that is used each time you create a new document or modify an existing one. The Normal template is different from other templates you create because it is available to any and all documents, whereas, other templates need to be explicitly loaded (added in) before their goods can be used.

If you want to attach to another template, open a Word document and follow these easy steps:

1. **Choose Tools⇨Templates and Add-Ins.**

   The Templates and Add-Ins dialog box appears.

2. **In the Document template section, click the Attach button.**

   The Attach Template dialog box appears.

3. **Select a template in the Attach Template dialog box and click Open.**

   This returns you to the Templates and Add-Ins dialog box.

4. **Click OK to close the Templates and Add-Ins dialog box.**

   The document now has access to any styles or code associated with the template file.

Actually, you can do the same thing through code by using the AddIns object. The AddIns object has an Add method that you can use to make a template or add-in available in Word and optionally install it. If you have a template called MyTemplate.dot, you can add it to the Add-Ins list (and get it installed) by using the following code:

```
AddIns.Add _
FileName:="C:\Templates\Other\MyTemplate.dot", _
Install:=True
```

The line continuation character (an underscore like this: _) can be used to make your code easier to read. We've used it in this book to avoid any confusion over what needs to be typed on one or more lines.

Now that you know a bit about templates, go ahead and see what the Word object model offers with its templates. You already know that you are using a template, the Normal template, even when you're just writing a simple memo. Take a look at what's hiding under the covers. Before beginning these steps, be sure that you have Word opened (this is a Word chapter, right?).

1. **Open a document and type in any sentence.**

   For fun, you can type in **Lions and Tigers and Bears, Oh My!**

2. **Open the Visual Basic Editor, if it's not already open by pressing ALT+F11.**

3. **Type** ? `Templates(1).AutoTextEntries.Count` **in the Immediate window and press Enter.**

This action returns 44 to the Immediate window, because a nice assortment of AutoText comes right out of the box with Word. If you have been taking advantage of AutoText entries, your number may be higher.

Next, you can use the Add method of the AutoTextEntries and create your own AutoText entry with VBA code. Now this is cool!

4. **In the Immediate window, type** `Templates(1).AutoTextEntries.Add Name:="Fun AutoText",Range:=ActiveDocument.Sentences(1)` **and press Enter.**

Doing so adds the first sentence of your active document to the AutoText entries under the name `Fun AutoText`.

The Immediate window can be frustrating. When you follow along with the example to add an AutoText entry, nothing appears to happen after you press Enter to commit the line of code. If you type the code in correctly, the only reassurance Word gives that your code worked is not giving you an error message. Wouldn't it be nice if the Immediate window told you if the entry executed properly? C'est la vie!

5. **To check if your AutoText entry was really added, type** `?Templates(1).AutoTextEntries.Item("Fun AutoText")` **in the Immediate window and press Enter.**

This code returns the first sentence of the active document to the Immediate window. The entry is now stored away in your AutoText entries for future use. Obviously, AutoText is just one of the many items you can get to programmatically by using the object model. Hopefully, this example has gotten the juices flowing as to the possibilities that await.

Your templates are stored in a Templates subdirectory under \Program Files\Microsoft Office, if you accept the installation defaults. If you're not sure if you accepted the defaults, you can check where the Normal.dot lives. You know it's activated as soon as you open Word, so check it out with some VBA code.

In the Immediate window, type **? Templates("Normal.dot").Path**. The full path to the Normal template is the result, which likely will be C:\Program Files\Microsoft Office\Templates.

Did we slide one past you by using Templates("Normal.dot").Path, rather than Templates(1).Path that we have been using? In the case where the Normal template is the only one loaded, Templates(1) is set to Normal.dot. However, if multiple templates are in use, the index numbers can vary.

Chapter 9

Presenting PowerPoint Objects

• •

In This Chapter

▶ Getting started with PowerPoint

▶ Creating new presentations

▶ Making presentations look snazzy

▶ Adding slides to presentation

▶ Adding text to the slides

▶ Launching a slide show

• •

*A*t first, it may seem odd for a presentation program to have its own programming language. After all, what kind of program can revolve around slides? Actually, the decision by Microsoft to add VBA to PowerPoint makes a great deal of sense. Many organizations need to create slide presentations on a regular basis. Having a way to automate the process makes the organizations more productive. In this chapter, we explore the basic elements of Microsoft PowerPoint from a programmer's perspective and introduce you to the objects you can use to construct your own slide-show maker!

The PowerPoint VBA help file may come in handy while working through the examples in this chapter. If you installed Office 97 by using the Typical option, however, you may not have installed the help file. If you press F1 while in the Visual Basic Editor, rerun the setup program and install the *Programming Help* option for PowerPoint.

It's the Same Object Model, Only Different

As we explain how to write VBA code to control PowerPoint, you may notice that on the surface, PowerPoint bears a strong resemblance to its Office teammates. In fact, PowerPoint features an Application object through which you can get at all of the other objects that relate to slide presentations.

To check this out, follow these steps:

1. **Launch Microsoft PowerPoint.**

   The Startup dialog box appears in the main PowerPoint window.

2. **Select Blank Presentation from the Startup dialog box and click OK.**

   PowerPoint then creates a presentation file. The New Slide dialog box appears.

3. **Click OK in the New Slide dialog box.**

   The default New Slide settings are okay for this example, so you don't have to change any of the settings in that box.

4. **Press Alt+F11 to display the Visual Basic Editor (VBE).**

   The main VBE window appears.

5. **Open the Immediate window, if it's not already visible, by choosing View⇨Immediate window.**

6. **Type the following code in the Immediate window:**

   ```
   ?Application.Name
   ```

7. **Press Enter to run the code.**

VBA should return the string Microsoft PowerPoint to the Immediate window. Exciting, isn't it? Not really, but it does demonstrate the consistency that exists between Office applications.

You may have noticed that when you entered the text "?Application." in the Immediate window, VBA did not display a list of the Application object's properties and methods. This is because PowerPoint defines its Application object by using the generic Object data type instead of a particular data type like the other Office products do. (We discuss data types in more detail in Chapter 11.) Because PowerPoint won't tell VBA what type of object an Application is, VBA can't display the list of properties and methods.

The PowerPoint Application object has a number of other properties like Caption, Path, Version, and Visible. If you want some more practice working with the Immediate window you can try using these properties, as shown in Figure 9-1.

The Application object is where most of the similarities end. That's because the main thing that you manipulate by using PowerPoint is a slide presentation, as opposed to a document or a spreadsheet. Specifically, the PowerPoint

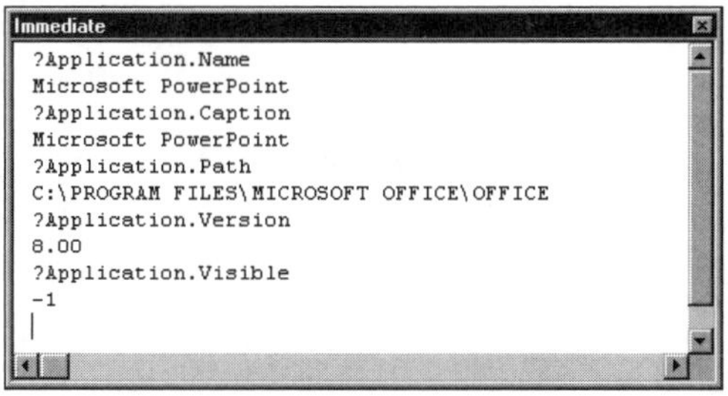

Figure 9-1:
Experi-
menting
with
PowerPoint's
Application
object.

```
Immediate                                    [X]
?Application.Name
Microsoft PowerPoint
?Application.Caption
Microsoft PowerPoint
?Application.Path
C:\PROGRAM FILES\MICROSOFT OFFICE\OFFICE
?Application.Version
8.00
?Application.Visible
-1
|
```

Application object contains a collection of Presentations. You can test the
Presentations collection by typing the following line of code into the Immediate window:

```
?Application.Presentations.Count
```

VBA should print the number 1 unless you've created a new presentation or
opened an existing one.

Working with Presentations

In PowerPoint a *presentation* is a group of slides. Each slide can conform to a
predefined layout or it can be completely free form. The most common use
for a PowerPoint presentation is for an on-screen show, usually using some
type of projection equipment. You can, however, print slides if you'd like. Of
course, these days printed presentations are becoming about as common as
$5^1/_4$-inch diskettes.

You can do several things with presentation, the most common being adding
new slides. We talk about slides in the section, "Slip Sliding Away" later in
this chapter. In addition to adding slides, though, you can change several
settings that affect all the slides in your presentation. Using these settings
effectively helps you create slide presentations more quickly and gives your
presentations a consistent look. The next few sections explain some of the
ways you can alter several slides (or an entire presentation) at once.

Applying a design template

Normally, all the slides in a presentation need to have the same overall style.
If they don't, then looking at the presentation would be very distracting.
Imagine watching a nightly news program where every story's subtitle was
in a different font and color. The reports wouldn't look like they came from
the same program, would they? The same goes for slide presentations.

To help you maintain consistency in your slide presentations, PowerPoint lets you apply a design template to your presentation. A *design template* is really just another presentation with preset options like font, color scheme, and background. When you apply a design template to a presentation, the presentation inherits all the characteristics of the template. You can try this feature out yourself by following the steps described next.

Before you do the following series of steps, you need to have a blank PowerPoint presentation open. See Steps 1–3 in the section "It's the Same Object Model, Only Different" earlier in this chapter if you need help getting started.

1. **Type some text to the title slide of the blank presentation.**

   Your slide should look very similar to the one shown in Figure 9-2.

2. **Type the following code from the Immediate window (make sure that you type all the code on one line):**

```
ActivePresentation.ApplyTemplate "C:\Program
        Files\Microsoft Office\Templates\Presentation
        Designs\NOTEBOOK.POT"
```

3. **Press Enter.**

   VBA runs the line of code.

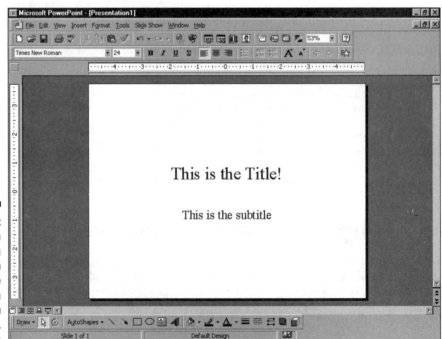

Figure 9-2:
A plain vanilla presentation before applying a design template.

REMEMBER

If you installed Office 97 in another directory, this code won't work for you unless you replace the path name shown in the code with the path name that's correct for your computer. (Now, you know why we always accept the defaults!)

TECHNICAL STUFF

POT is the file extension for a PowerPoint template file, as opposed to *PPT,* which is a normal PowerPoint presentation file. You can turn a regular presentation into a template just by choosing File⇨Save As and then choosing the Presentation Template option from the list of file types.

If everything worked correctly, your presentation should now look like the snazzy number shown in Figure 9-3. If it didn't work, try it again standing on one foot and whistling the theme from *The X-Files* (it works for us).

In addition to the background bitmap, which is obvious, a design template changes the fonts and color scheme for the presentation. You can also control these separately.

After you apply a template, PowerPoint tracks the name of that template should you ever want to know what it is. To see what we mean, you need to use the file modified in the section, "Applying a design template" earlier in this chapter. Try running the following code from the Immediate window:

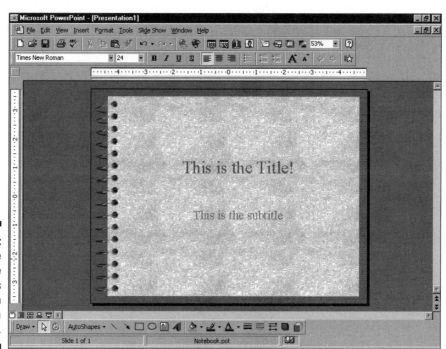

Figure 9-3:
In the world of ice cream, this presentation is a banana split.

```
?ActivePresentation.TemplateName
```

VBA returns just the template name to the Immediate window, without including the path where the template stored.

PowerPoint doesn't limit you to using POT files as design templates. You can use a normal PPT file if you want. This ability comes in especially handy when you want to copy the format of a presentation created by you or a colleague.

Saving presentations

After you've spent a great deal of time and effort creating a slide presentation, you'll likely want to save your work. You may also want to save your work periodically if you're making lots of modifications. A PowerPoint Presentation object has two methods that fill this need quite nicely — SaveAs and Save. As you may imagine, the SaveAs method is used to save a presentation with a particular name. You must use this method the first time you save the presentation, and you can use it at other times to save the presentation under a new name. You only use the Save method after calling SaveAs at least once. Otherwise VBA doesn't know what filename to use.

To see what we mean, you need to use the file modified in the section "Applying a design template" earlier in this chapter. Save that presentation by executing the following line of code in the Immediate window:

```
ActivePresentation.SaveAs "C:\TEST.ppt"
```

You should hear you, hard drive whir for a bit, and the PowerPoint window should change to reflect the new file name for the presentation.

You can now see how smart a presentation is about knowing its own name. Try running each of the following statements from the Immediate window:

```
?ActivePresentation.Name
?ActivePresentation.Path
?ActivePresentation.FullName
```

VBA should print the presentation's file name, the directory where it's saved, and the complete path and file name.

Juggling presentations, new and old

At the start of this chapter, you created a new presentation by hand. You can also create new presentations by using VBA code. For example, try running the following code, which executes the Add method of the Presentations collection:

```
Presentations.Add
```

As you may expect, this action creates a new presentation. If you have created and modified the sample file that we've been using throughout this chapter, you should now have two open presentations, the one you just saved and a new one.

PowerPoint takes a *tabula rasa* (blank slate) approach when you create new presentations by using VBA code. New presentations are created without slides. You'll need to add them yourself by using the techniques described in the next section.

Now that you have a second presentation, try closing the first one by using VBA code. Because it's no longer the active presentation, you have to tell VBA which presentation to close by using the Presentations collection. Run the following code from the Immediate window:

```
Presentations("Test.ppt").Close
```

Notice how the name of the presentation is used to identify it. This value is the same one returned by VBA when you ran the code ?ActivePresentation. Name from the Immediate window.

Referring to objects in collections by name rather than number is always the safer route. The number indicates an object's position in the collection — something that may change as you work with the collection.

You've now seen how to create a new presentation, save it, and close it. To complete the grand slam, run the following code, which reopens the test presentation:

```
Presentations.Open "C:\Test.ppt"
```

This code tells the Presentations collection to go and find the TEST.ppt file on the hard disk and open it.

If you are going to continue with the rest of the examples in this chapter, switch from the VBE to PowerPoint and close the new presentation (not TEST.ppt) that you created earlier.

Slip Sliding Away

Because a presentation is nothing without some slides, we sensibly spend a good deal of time exploring slides and showing you how to create and modify them. After you have a bunch of slides assembled, we can show you how to put them on display with a slide show.

You can perform the steps in this chapter by using the file TEST.ppt that is created in the section "Working with Presentations" earlier in this chapter.

Now, how do you think you would modify the slides in a presentation by using VBA? If you guessed the Slides collection, you're right. (If the term *collection* throws you, refer to Chapter 4 for a little help.) Each presentation has a Slides collection that you can use to add new slides and modify existing ones. For instance, to find out how many slides are contained in the test presentation, execute this statement from the Immediate window:

```
?ActivePresentation.Slides.Count
```

Because we haven't added any additional slides yet, the result is 1.

If you're going to be creating slide presentations from scratch, or adding slides to existing presentations, you're going to need to know how to create slides. PowerPoint provides you with a handy method of the Slides collection (called Add) that creates a new slide in a particular presentation. (Microsoft uses the same names for methods that do the same things; for example the Presentations collection also has an Add method.)

Before you use the Add method, however, you need to know two crucial pieces of information — what type of slide you want to create and where in the presentation you want to put it. PowerPoint won't let you create a new slide without this information. PowerPoint is not purposely trying to make your life more difficult — making these choices when you create the slide helps you out later on.

What flavor would you like?

PowerPoint gives you a choice of 24 different slide types, and these are the same choices you see in the New Slide dialog box. Figure 9-4 shows the New Slide dialog box with 12 of the choices displayed. The panel at the dialog's lower right corner gives a description of the file type.

For your convenience, we've painstakingly illustrated all 24 slide varieties in Figure 9-5. We added numbers to help you match the slide layouts with the entries in Table 9-1.

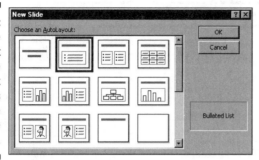

Figure 9-4: The PowerPoint New Slide dialog box shows half the available choices.

Figure 9-5: A complete list of all the slide types.

Table 9-1		What All Those Slide Types Are
Number	*Constant*	*Description of Slide Type*
1	ppLayoutTitle	Standard opening slide — title and subtitle
2	ppLayoutText	Standard bulleted text slide
3	ppLayoutTwoColumnText	Two columns of bullet text
4	ppLayoutTable	Contains a table of information
5	ppLayoutTextAndChart	Bulleted text and a small chart
6	ppLayoutChartAndText	A small chart with bulleted text
7	ppLayoutOrgchart	Contains an organizational chart
8	ppLayoutChart	Contains a large embedded chart
9	ppLayoutTextAndClipart	Bulleted text and a small graphic
10	ppLayoutClipartAndText	A small graphic with bulleted text
11	ppLayoutTitleOnly	Contains only a title
12	ppLayoutBlank	Duh, it's blank!
13	ppLayoutTextAndObject	Bulleted text and an embedded object (like a spreadsheet)

(continued)

Table 9-1 *(continued)*

Number	Constant	Description of Slide Type
14	ppLayoutObjectAndText	An embedded object with bulleted text
15	ppLayoutLargeObject	A really large embedded object with no title
16	ppLayoutObject	A large embedded object with a title
17	ppLayoutTextAndMediaClip	Bulleted text and a media object (like an AVI file)
18	ppLayoutMediaClipAndText	A media object with bulleted text
19	ppLayoutObjectOverText	A small embedded object over bulleted text
20	ppLayoutTextOverObject	Bulleted text over a small embedded object
21	ppLayoutTextAndTwoObjects	Bulleted text next to two small embedded objects
22	ppLayoutTwoObjectsAndText	Two small embedded objects next to bulleted text
23	ppLayoutTwoObjectsOverText	Two small embedded objects over bulleted text
24	ppLayoutFourObjects	Four small embedded objects

The Constant column in Table 9-1 contains the entry in the list that appears when you type the Add method into a code window. You can choose to use the number listed in the Number column or pick the constant name from the list.

Please go to the end of the presentation

The other required piece of information, the slide position, is simply where you want the new slide to go. The first slide is position 1, the second is 2, and so on. Unfortunately, no easy way exists to tell PowerPoint to "put it at the end" but the end is always the number of slides in the presentation plus one. To figure out how many slides you have, you use the Count property of the Slides collection.

You can perform the steps in this chapter by using the file TEST.ppt that is created in the section "Working with Presentations" earlier in this chapter.

Try creating a new slide of bulleted text by running the following line of code from the Immediate window (it's a long one — make sure to enter it all on one line):

```
ActivePresentation.Slides.Add
            ActivePresentation.Slides.Count + 1,
            ppLayoutText
```

Now, switch from VBE to PowerPoint and locate the new slide. (You may have to click the scroll bar to move to the next slide.) You should see a blank bulleted text slide like the one shown in Figure 9-6. Because you haven't added any text yet (that's next), you see the placeholders where the text will go.

Great! You've just created a new slide. You can create a different slide type by entering a different constant or number as the last argument of the Add method. You can also position the new slide anywhere in the presentation by choosing a different number for the first argument (just don't pick a number greater than the number of slides plus one).

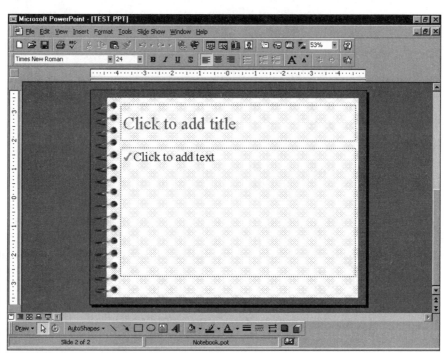

Figure 9-6:
A newborn slide created by using VBA.

But wait, you say, the slide doesn't contain any text. In its current state the slide is — to be delicate — less than informative. That's true, but to add text, you need to know about slide shapes first. We discuss shapes in the section "Whipping Shapes into Your Slides" — which just happens to be next!

Whipping Shapes into Your Slides

One thing that distinguishes PowerPoint from the other Office 97 applications is that the document objects it manipulates (slides) have no strict structure. Word documents can be thought of as simply blocks of text, Excel spreadsheets have cells arranged in rows and columns, and Access uses highly structured database tables.

Microsoft decided that PowerPoint had to be different and made the program's slides completely free-form. They can contain text, graphics, sound and video, even embedded documents from other applications. These objects can be placed just about anywhere on a slide that you want. To accommodate all this free-wheeling creativity, PowerPoint features generic objects called *shapes* that can contain everything you could possibly put on a slide. For example, you can create squares, rectangles, text boxes, lines, and lots of other funny-looking shapes. Furthermore, most shapes can contain text. Every slide has a Shapes collection that you can use to manipulate all the "things" on the slide.

Getting in shape for free

One benefit to choosing the layout carefully when creating a new slide is that all but one style comes with shapes already on the slide. If all you want to do, for example, is add a title and some bulleted text, then you're halfway home. To test this theory, run the following code from the Immediate window:

```
?ActivePresentation.Slides(2).Shapes.Count
```

Note that Slides(2) refers to the new bulleted text slide that you created earlier. VBA prints 2, which refers to the two text placeholders that are included automatically on a slide of this type.

By convention, if a slide has a title, the title is the first shape in the collection. Therefore you can run the following code to find out what kind of shape the title is:

```
?ActivePresentation.Slides(2).Shapes(1).Type
```

VBA responds by printing the number 14, which corresponds to the place-holder shape type. Placeholders are used on new slides to help you position standard text elements.

To get a complete list of different shape types, look up the Shape object in VBA's Object Browser. Click the Type property and then the green under-lined MsoShapeType in the Details pane. (For more about the Object Browser, see Chapter 5.)

Frames, ranges, text . . . you've got to be kidding!

Now that you know to reference the shape, you're ready to add some text. Ah, if it were just that simple! You see, PowerPoint shapes are very compli-cated little doodads. Not only can they contain text, but the text can be aligned horizontally and vertically, have different tab stops, and can be formatted in different ways. In order to provide an organized and manage-able way to work with these attributes by using VBA code, the industrious Microsoft programmers created two cool object types: TextFrames and TextRanges.

Every shape that can contain text (most can) includes a *TextFrame* property that gives you access to text positioning properties like orientation and margins. This object, in turn, has a *TextRange* property that allows you to control the formatting of text the shape actually contains. The TextRange object's default property is *Text,* the actual letters inside the shape. So, if all you want to do is to add text to a shape by using the default alignment and format properties, you can use this simple, albeit long, statement (which, by the way, needs to be entered all on one line):

```
ActivePresentation.Slides(2).Shapes(1).TextFrame.
TextRange.Text = "A Slide Title"
```

Whew! Now that's a mouthful! It would be nice if PowerPoint had thrown a few more default properties in there, but no such luck. If you want to change the text inside a shape, you gotta put up with a lot of code.

Stupid text tricks

Despite the fact that adding text to a slide can be a pain, all those objects provide you with quite a bit of functionality. By using the TextFrame object's properties, you can adjust the margins for the invisible box that contains the text. You can also decide how the text is anchored. Where you *anchor* text (top, bottom, or middle) determines where it's displayed when you change the size of the shape. Finally, you can control how PowerPoint wraps the text inside the shape.

All of these properties correspond to options on the Text Box tab of the Format AutoShape dialog box shown in Figure 9-7. You access this dialog box by right-clicking a shape and selecting Format Aut<u>o</u>Shape from the popup menu.

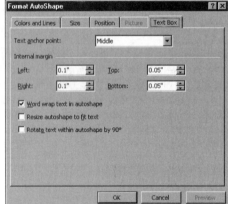

Figure 9-7:
TextFrame
properties
map to
options
on this
dialog box.

The TextRange object is even more interesting. Just like the Microsoft Word Range object, a TextRange object can refer to any block of text, from a single character to the entire contents of a shape. You use the TextRange object's properties and methods to alter the contents and formatting of the text.

Before you do the following series of steps, you need to have a blank PowerPoint presentation open. See Steps 1–3 in the section "It's the Same Object Model, Only Different" earlier in this chapter if you need help getting started.

To show off the power of the TextRange object, follow these steps:

1. **Execute the following line of code from the Immediate window:**

```
ActivePresentation.Slides(2).Shapes(2).TextFrame.
TextRange.Text = "Point Number 1"
```

The code adds some bullet text to the slide.

2. Now run the following code:

```
ActivePresentation.Slides(2).Shapes(2).TextFrame.
TextRange.InsertAfter vbCrLf
```

This code starts a new line; vbCrLf is a VBA constant that means "insert a carriage return and line feed."

3. Now run this code:

```
ActivePresentation.Slides(2).Shapes(2).TextFrame.
TextRange.InsertAfter "This is a minor point"
```

The previous code adds some more text on the new line.

4. Lastly, run this code:

```
ActivePresentation.Slides(2).Shapes(2).TextFrame.
TextRange.Words(7).Font.Italic = True
```

The code formats the word minor in italics.

This example contains two things that you need to note. First, you can use the Text property to change the entire contents of a TextRange. If you want to add additional text, however, you must use the InsertAfter (or InsertBefore) method.

Second, a TextRange object has several methods that you can use to divide up the entire text into smaller chunks. These methods include Characters, Lines, Paragraphs, Runs (no jokes, please), Sentences, and Words. Each of these methods returns another TextRange object. You used this convenience to your advantage in the example by changing a font characteristic — in this case, setting a word in italics.

You put your indent in, you put your indent out . . .

The last stupid text trick we'll show you how to make PowerPoint perform is changing the indent level of one of the lines in the slide's bulleted text. You do so by changing the IndentLevel of a TextRange object. Even though the sample slide contains several lines of text, indenting one of them is easy.

Run the line of code shown below from the Immediate window. (Make sure to type it all on one line!) Doing so indents the second line of text one tab stop by setting its IndentLevel property to 2.

```
ActivePresentation.Slides(2).Shapes(2).TextFrame.
TextRange.Paragraphs(2).IndentLevel = 2
```

Your sample slide should now look like the one shown in Figure 9-8. Notice the indented second line and the word minor in italics.

Show Me the Slides!

Of course, creating a slide presentation is only part of the PowerPoint story. At some point, you'll want to show off your hard work to a (hopefully) appreciative audience. In Chapter 22, we spend a great deal of time showing you how to make your presentations come alive. In the meantime, however, run the following code from the Immediate window, sit back, and enjoy the show!

```
ActivePresentation.SlideShowSettings.Run
```

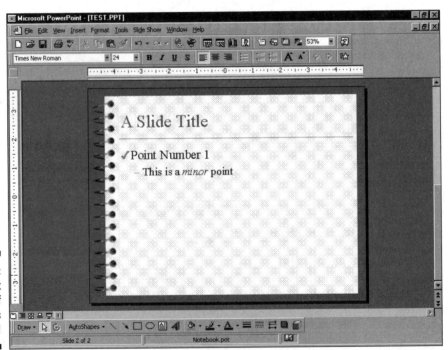

Figure 9-8: Perhaps not a work of art, but it's pretty good!

Chapter 10

Accessing Access Objects

As we pointed out in other chapters, Access is the odd application of the Office 97 bunch. If you've ever heard the Rolling Stones' tune, "You Can't Always Get What You Want," you'll understand how we feel about Access. Access shares many characteristics with its Office brethren, but it is also odd and quirky at times. This quirkiness is probably because Access has been around for quite some time. Also, because it already featured a development language based on BASIC, Access did not get a chance to "reinvent" itself when VBA came along. Nonetheless, get ready to take this sometimes convoluted journey and behold what Access has to offer.

To point out some of the basic programming techniques for Microsoft Access, we use the Northwind Traders sample database that ships as part of the product. We chose this database because it has several objects to play with and because everyone who has Access 97 has a copy.

Do Command Dot What?

We must confess that one aspect of programming with Access is absolutely vital, yet completely ludicrous. The problem arises because, as you may know, you can program Access in two ways: macros (boo! hiss!) and VBA. We like VBA and, given the choice, would use it all the time. Unfortunately macros do some things that don't have *direct* VBA equivalents. We empha-size *direct* because although you do write VBA code to perform these actions, you do so using an odd little device called the *DoCmd object* (pro-nounced *dew*-cuh-mand). Simply stated, DoCmd is a way to call macro actions from VBA.

Unfortunately, you use DoCmd all the time. We say unfortunate because DoCmd is a single object that must try to cope with about 40 macro actions. As such, the DoCmd syntax is hard to understand and remember.

How DoCmd works

To understand how DoCmd works you at least have to look at a macro. (We know — it's hard to force yourself.) Figure 10-1 shows a macro in design view with a number of different actions. You can see from the figure that the macro is made up of three different commands: Hourglass, OpenForm, and Maximize. You also see the macro action list open to the Hourglass action, and the argument pane at the bottom of the window shows the action's one argument, Hourglass On.

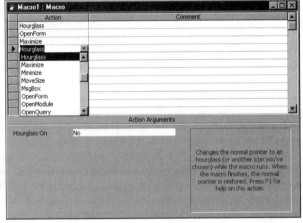

Figure 10-1:
You just can't get rid of those pesky macros.

DoCmd works by treating all the actions in the list as methods. If the action requires arguments (like Hourglass does), you pass the arguments to the method. Sounds simple, right? Okay, try one by following these steps:

1. Launch Microsoft Access.

2. Open the Northwind Traders sample database.

The filename is Northwind.mdb, and it is located in the Samples subdirectory of your Office directory. (After opening the database, you may need to close the opening screen if you haven't turned it off.)

3. To open the Debug window, press Ctrl+G.

4. Enter the following code (but don't press Enter):

```
DoCmd.
```

You should see the pop-up list of methods, as shown in Figure 10-2.

5. Type the letter h to highlight the Hourglass method and press the space key.

Access displays the argument list for the Hourglass method (it has just one).

6. Type True **as the argument and press Enter.**

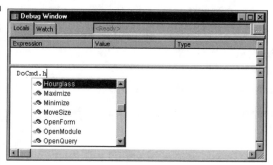

Figure 10-2: You can see which macro actions DoCmd supports as you write code.

Your mouse should now be displaying the hourglass cursor. If you want to turn the hourglass off, just run the following code in the Debug window:

```
DoCmd.Hourglass False
```

A more complex DoCmd example

The previous example was a simple one because Hourglass only accepts a single argument. Now try something more complex — closing a form. The DoCmd object has a Close method that you can use to close not only forms but also any type of Access object. You can use the method in two ways, to close the active object, whatever it is, or to close a particular object.

The syntax to close the active object is actually very simple:

```
DoCmd.Close
```

Unfortunately, you shouldn't really rely on the object that you want to close to be active. Access is not quite as smart as you are and does not know what you want to close. A better way is to tell Access exactly what you want to close. To do so, you need to supply a bit more information when you call the Close method. Try the following:

1. **From Access, open the Employees form in the sample database.**

   After all, you need something to close.

2. **Select the Immediate window and type the following code (but don't press Enter just yet):**

   ```
   DoCmd.Close
   ```

3. **Press the space key.**

   You should see the argument list for the Close method as well as a list of values you can enter. (See Figure 10-3.)

4. **Select acForm from the list of values and type** `","`.

5. **Now type the word** `"Employees"`, **including the quotation marks, and press Enter.**

   The complete line of code as it appears on your screen is

   ```
   DoCmd.Close acForm, "Employees"
   ```

   Just like magic, the Employees form disappears after you press Enter.

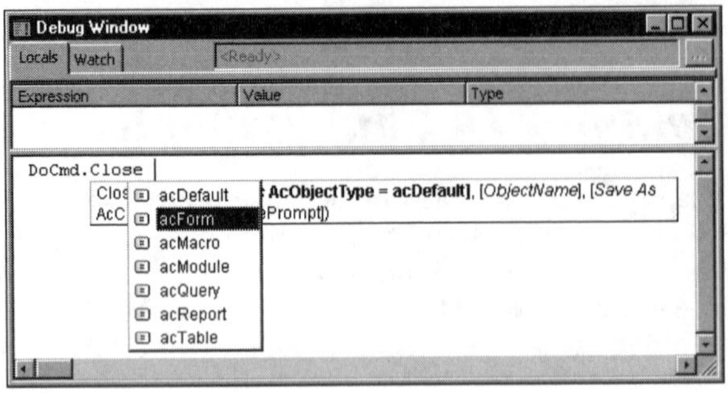

Figure 10-3: You can choose the type of object you want to close from the list that appears.

Hopefully by now, you are getting the hang of using DoCmd. Think of DoCmd as a little helper that can run macro actions for you. You tell it what you want done and it runs off to do it. The next section shows you how to tell DoCmd to open a form. (After all, closing a form isn't exactly possible if you don't have one open.)

Opening Forms with DoCmd

Probably the most common use for the DoCmd object is to open a form. Yes, that's right, the only way to open a form in Access by using VBA is by calling DoCmd with another method, OpenForm.

Unlike Hourglass and Close, the OpenForm method accepts many arguments (fortunately you rarely have to supply them all). By passing along additional information you can tell DoCmd which form to open, how to open it (as an icon, for example), and what data you want to display.

Start with something simple

Follow the steps shown below to try a simple example that opens the Northwind Traders Employees form.

You must be in Access 97 with the Debug window open to do these steps. Press Ctrl+G to open the Debug window.

1. **Select the Immediate window in Access and move the cursor to a blank line.**

2. **Enter the following line of VBA code, but don't press Enter:**

```
DoCmd.OpenForm
```

3. **Type a space.**

   VBA displays the argument list for the OpenForm method. Big, isn't it? Figure 10-4 shows the argument list. The first argument is the name of the form you want to open.

4. **Type** `"Employees"`**, including the quotation marks, followed by a comma, in the Immediate window.**

   VBA displays a list of constants for the second argument.

5. **Select acNormal from the list of constants.**

   This constant tells VBA to open the form in normal view; that is, just like you had opened it yourself from the database window. The other values tell VBA to open the form in design view (acDesign), datasheet view (acFormDS), or print preview (acPreview). You should now have a line of VBA code that looks like this:

```
DoCmd.OpenForm "Employees", acNormal
```

6. Press Enter to execute the line of code.

VBA opens the Employees form.

Figure 10-4:
The many
OpenForm
arguments
that let you
control how
a form is
opened.

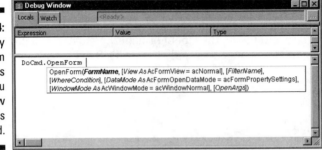

Form filtration

If you've followed the steps in this section up to this point, you should be ready to perform some more advanced tricks by using the OpenForm method.

How about filtering the data when opening the form? If you have forms that contain a great deal of data, sometimes finding the information you want is difficult. Like water filtration systems that remove undesirable contaminants, forms can have filters that show only the information you're interested in. Doesn't that sound Brita, er, better than pouring over oceans of data?

You use the OpenForm method's third and fourth arguments to filter data on a form. You can specify the name of a saved filter query as the third argument and/or a filter string as the fourth argument. Try a simple example of each, starting with a saved filter query.

1. Start by closing the Employees form (from the last set of steps in this section) if it's still open.

You won't be using that form for this example because applying a filter to a document with only nine records hardly makes sense.

2. Open the Orders form in the Northwinds database.

You start by creating a saved filter query, and then you apply it by using the OpenForm method. Unless you've changed the data in the database, the first order that you see on the form should use Speedy as the shipper.

3. Right-click the mouse on the Speedy check box in the Ship Via field.

Access displays a shortcut menu containing filtering commands.

4. Select the Filter by Selection command from the shortcut menu.

Doing so applies a filter that shows only those orders shipped by Speedy. At the bottom of the form, you should see that the record count has changed to 249 (Filtered). Figure 10-5 illustrates the Orders form after the filter has been applied.

The next step is to save this filter as a query in the database. This action involves opening the Advanced Filter window that looks exactly like the query design window.

5. Choose Records⇨Filter⇨Advanced Filter/Sort.

This step opens the Advanced Filter window. You should see that a filter has been applied to the ShipVia field. Figure 10-6 shows the Advanced Filter window. Note the criteria of 1 under the ShipVia field.

6. Choose File⇨Save As Query and enter `Speedy Orders` **in the Save As Query dialog box that appears.**

Press Enter or click the OK button to save the filter as a query. You're now ready to apply this filter by using VBA code and the OpenForm method.

7. Close the Advanced Filter window by choosing File⇨Close.

8. Close the Orders form by choosing File⇨Close.

9. Now, open or select the Immediate window by pressing Ctrl+G.

10. Place the cursor on a blank line in the Immediate window and enter the following line of code:

```
DoCmd.OpenForm "Orders", acNormal, "Speedy Orders"
```

11. Press Enter to execute the statement.

VBA opens the form *and* applies the filter at the same time. You should see the Orders form displaying only those orders shipped by Speedy.

Figure 10-5:
Applying a filter restricts the records that Access displays on the form.

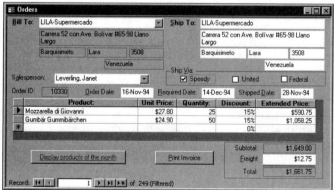

Figure 10-6:
By
opening the
Advanced
Filter
window
after
applying a
filter you
can save it
as a query.

Filters on the fly

Although saved filter queries are powerful, they aren't always practical. For example, what if you wanted to look at the orders that were placed on a particular date? If you have a great deal of data, creating separate saved filters for each date that you may want to look at just doesn't make sense (unless you are really, really bored!). Instead, what you want is for someone to choose a date when you open the form. The fourth argument to OpenForm allows you to do just that.

Instead of the name of a saved filter query, you supply a filter string. If you've written queries by using their native tongue, SQL, filter strings should seem very familiar. They're just SQL WHERE clauses without the word, "WHERE." (*SQL,* pronounced like *sequel,* stands for Structured Query Language — another successful attempt by computer programmers to create an obtuse language that very few people fully understand.) If you're no SQL guru, *filter strings* are just combinations of fields and the values you want to find in them. You can create filter strings by using the following formula:

```
field name operator Expression
```

Field name is the name of a field in the form's record source; that is, the table, query, or SQL statement the form is based on. The operator is often an equal sign (=) but can also be any of these: >, <, >=, <=, and <>. You can even use complex SQL functions like BETWEEN and LIKE, but, hey, this book is about VBA, not queries. Finally, the expression can be a simple value or a complex expression involving other fields, mathematical operators, and other cool stuff. You can also combine individual filter strings by using the AND and OR operators.

To demonstrate how to use a filter string, follow these steps to open the Orders form with a filter that shows only those orders placed on February 23, 1996.

1. **Close the Orders form if it's still open from the previous set of steps in this section.**

2. **Open the Debug window by pressing Ctrl+G.**

3. **Place the cursor on a blank line in the Debug window and enter the following line of VBA code:**

```
DoCmd.OpenForm "Orders", , , "OrderDate = #2/23/96#"
```

4. **Press Enter to execute the line of code.**

   VBA opens the form to the first of three orders placed on February 23, 1996.

Pretty neat, huh? All you have to do the next time you run the code is to choose a new date. You don't need to create a saved filter query. In fact, if you want to see something really cool, try this:

1. **Leaving the Orders form open, select the Debug window again.**

2. **Highlight the 3 in 2/23/96 and type the number** 6, **changing the date to 2/26/96.**

3. **Press Enter.**

   The code is executed again and, wonder of wonders, the new filter string is applied to the form. The form now contains only two records, those orders placed on February 26!

 You can also use the ApplyFilter method of the DoCmd object to apply a filter to an open form. Furthermore, you can use the ApplyFilter method with tables and reports in addition to forms. For more information, consult the online help on the ApplyFilter method.

The Form's the Thing

Of all the VBA code you'll write in Access, the majority (at least starting out) will involve Access forms, for good reason. Access forms are what form the basis for an application. They're how the user interacts with the data. Now don't get us wrong. Tables and queries are very important to the overall application, but after you design them in your laboratory (you do have your own lab, don't you?), your users rarely need to even know they exist.

If you've read the preceding sections, you've already seen how you can open and close forms and how to apply filters to them to restrict the data they display. After a form is open, however, you can write VBA to manipulate its properties and all of its controls.

More forms than the government

In Chapter 6, we discuss various methods for referring to objects. Access forms are objects, so they obey the rules we outline in that chapter. If you're not comfortable with these rules, we suggest you flip back to Chapter 6 for a quick review.

You refer to forms in Access by using the Forms collection. The Forms collection is always available when you're writing and running VBA code and consists of all the forms that are currently open. ***Note:*** You can only write code to control forms that are already open. If a form isn't open, you can use the OpenForm method described in the section "Start with something simple" earlier in this chapter to open it.

After a form has been opened, you can refer to it in VBA by using any of the methods explained in Chapter 6 for objects in a collection. For example, assuming the Orders form is the only open form, any of the following statements would return its name to the Immediate window:

```
?Forms!Orders.Name
?Forms("Orders").Name
?Forms(0).Name
```

Notice that the last statement uses the number zero to refer to the Orders form. For some reason known only to Microsoft, Access collections start numbering objects at 0 rather than 1 like the rest of Office does. In our example, the Orders form is the first item in the Forms collection so it's numbered zero. Cumbersome as it may be, try to remember this convention when writing VBA code to control Access.

Some simple form tricks

If you read the section immediately prior to this one, you now know how to reference an open form in Access. What's next? Actually, you'll likely only want to do a few things with the form itself. Most of the things you'll need to do concern controls on the form, the subject of the next section. Here we highlight using VBA to control Access forms by using a few simple form properties and methods.

First off, sometimes you'll want to make a form invisible — hiding it, in other words. If the form contains a great deal of data, it may take a long time to open. Your users may not appreciate this behavior if they constantly close and open forms. You may, therefore want to hide the form instead of closing it. You do so by setting the form's Visible property. To try this out, follow the steps below:

1. **If you've been following the previous steps in this section, make sure that the Orders form is closed.**

2. **Highlight the Debug window by pressing Ctrl+G.**

3. **Place the cursor on a blank line in the Debug window and type the following line of code; press Enter when you're done:**

```
DoCmd.OpenForm "Orders"
```

VBA opens the Orders form. So far, so good.

4. **Now execute this statement in the Debug window:**

```
Forms("Orders").Visible = False
```

The Orders form disappears, leaving you back at the Debug window. Next comes the cool part.

5. **Use the arrow keys or mouse to place the cursor at the end of the line containing the OpenForm method that you entered in Step 3.**

6. **Press Enter to run the code again.**

VBA displays the Orders form. Isn't that nifty? OpenForm has two uses: to open a closed form and to display a hidden form. (Of course, you could have set the form's Visible property back to True, but why bother? OpenForm works just as well.)

Setting a form's Visible property to False has the same effect as choosing Window⇨Hide. In fact, if you choose the Window⇨Unhide command after hiding a window, you'll see the window in the list that appears.

Another common requirement is the need to requery a form to show any new records that have been added to an underlying table since the form was opened. This step is necessary because when you open an Access form, it looks at the records in the database only once before displaying them. If new records are added, say by another user or even another part of the program, they don't show up on the form until you requery it. Fortunately, Access forms have a Requery method that accomplishes this task.

To see how this feature works, follow these steps:

1. **If you've been following the examples in earlier sections and have the Orders form open, close it now.**

2. **Open the Customers form and move to the last record.**

   You can do so by clicking the Last button on the navigation bar or by choosing Edit⇨Goto⇨Last. Unless you've made changes to the data, you should be on record 91 of 91 and the customer's company name should read Wolski Zajazd.

3. **Press F11 to switch back to the database window, click on the Tables tab, and open the Customers table.**

   Once again, the record indicator at the bottom of the window should report that the table contains 91 records.

4. **Move to the new record input area in the datasheet by clicking the New button on the navigation bar or by choosing Edit⇨Goto ⇨New.**

5. **Type AAAAA in the Customer ID field, AAAAA Company in the Company Name field, and leave the other fields blank.**

   Your datasheet should look like the one shown in Figure 10-7.

6. **Save the record by pressing Shift+Enter or by choosing Records⇨Save Record.**

   You just saved the new record to the Customers table.

7. **Close the Customers table and switch back to the Customers form.**

   Note that the form still says the table contains only 91 records, even though you just added a new one. (You can go back to the first record but don't expect to find AAAAA Company there. The first record is still Alfreds Futterkiste.) This is because a form never looks at new records until you tell it to. We show you how to do so in the next steps.

8. **Select the Debug window by pressing Ctrl+G.**

   If you can, move the Debug window so that you can see the Customer form behind it.

9. **Move the cursor to a blank line in the Debug window and type the following line of code:**

   ```
   Forms("Customers").Requery
   ```

10. **Press Enter to execute the statement.**

    After a bit of hard disk whirring, Access updates the Customer form. AAAAA Company is now the first record displayed and the record count indicator reads 92 records. Figure 10-8 shows the results.

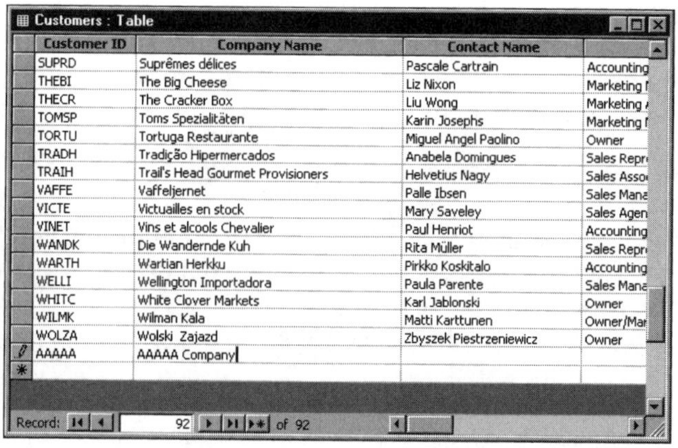

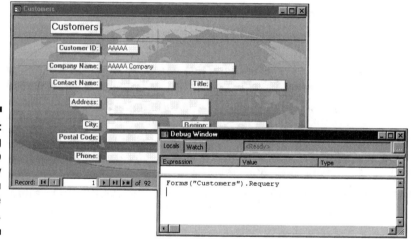

Figure 10-7:
You can
add a new
record
to the
Customers
table, but it
won't show
up on the
form!

Figure 10-8:
After telling
the form to
requery
itself, you
can see the
new record.

Controlling Controls

The final section of this chapter deals with controls. Every form you create
is likely going to have many controls, some that are bound to fields in the
form's record source and some that are not. You will write a great deal of
VBA code to manipulate controls, usually to retrieve or set their values.

Getting values

Suppose you have a form open on the screen and you need to find out the
value in one of its controls. Doing so is easy, thanks to the way a form keeps
track of its controls. Each form object (we talk about those earlier in this

chapter) has a collection of control objects. Each control, in turn, has a Value property that returns the value stored in the control. Because you're an expert on referencing objects, you know that you can print the value of a control called LastName on the Customers form by using this line of code:

```
?Forms("Customers").Controls("CompanyName").Value
```

"But wait," you say. "Can't I take advantage of default properties?" In fact, you can. Because the Controls collection is the default property of a form and the Value property is the default property of a control, you can condense the statement down to the following:

```
?Forms("Customers")("CompanyName")
```

or even this:

```
?Forms!Customers!CompanyName
```

Try using this feature by completing the following steps:

1. **If you've been following the other examples in this chapter, make sure that the Customers form is still open (open it if it's not).**

   If you've followed the steps in this chapter up to this point, AAAAA Company should be the first customer shown. If you didn't add customer AAAAA then go back to the example in the section titled "Some simple form tricks" and do so.

2. **Activate the Debug window by pressing Ctrl+G.**

3. **Place the cursor on a blank line in the Debug window and type the following line of code, pressing Enter to run it when you're done:**

```
?Forms!Customers!CompanyName
```

   VBA returns AAAAA Company to the Debug window.

Those sneaky list boxes

Retrieving values from controls like text boxes, check boxes, and option groups is pretty straightforward because what you see is what you get. The value in a text box is what returns to the Debug window when you ask VBA for the Value property. List and combo boxes, on the other hand, are a different story. These controls often store one value but display another.

To demonstrate the strange nature of list and combo boxes, the following steps describe how to print the Value property of a combo box on the Northwind Traders Products form.

1. **Close any open forms.**

2. **Open the Products form.**

   The vital statistics for the first product, Chai (whatever that is), are shown. Figure 10-9 shows the form, complete with the distracting background bitmap. Notice the value of the Category combo box, Beverages.

3. **Open the Debug window by pressing Ctrl+G.**

4. **Place the cursor on a blank line in the Debug window and type the following line of code, pressing Enter to execute it:**

   ```
   ?Forms!Products!CategoryID.Value
   ```

   CategoryID is the actual name of the control, even though the label says Category.

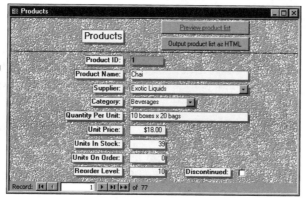

Figure 10-9:
Even though the Category field says Beverages, its value is 1.

VBA returns the number 1 to the Debug window, rather than the string Beverages. What's up with that? Well, you see the combo box is getting its data from a query based on the Categories table. Specifically it's extracting the CategoryID and CategoryName fields. The combo box is storing the value from the CategoryID field (a number) in the CategoryID field of the Products table. (In Access-speak, we say that the combo box is *bound* to the CategoryID column from the Categories table.) The column width of this column is set to zero, however, so the first column doesn't show up on the form. Access only displays the second column, CategoryName.

So, how can you get the actual text? Access combo and list boxes have a Column property that returns the contents of any column, not just the bound one. To use it, you supply the column number as an argument. (Of course, Access being Access, the columns are numbered starting at zero!)

With the Products form still open, execute the following statement from the Debug window:

```
?Forms!Products!CategoryID.Column(1)
```

VBA correctly returns Beverages to the Debug window.

In Access 97, as opposed to previous versions of Access, Microsoft enhanced the Column argument, allowing you to pass a row number as the second argument (starting with zero, of course). This feature allows you to find out the value of any piece of data in the combo box.

Setting values

Setting the value of a control is accomplished just like setting any other property. (Value is just a property, after all!) You reference the control and set it equal to an expression, which could be a simple value or something more complex.

The only thing you need to keep in mind is that when you set the value of a bound control, you're changing data on the form! Whoop! Whoop! Imagine red lights flashing overhead. Make sure that's what you want to do when you write VBA code that modifies control values.

To see what we mean, follow these steps:

1. **With the Products form open from the prior set of steps in this section, select the Debug window and place the cursor on a blank line.**

2. **Enter the following line of code in the Debug window:**

   ```
   Forms!Products!UnitPrice = 19.50
   ```

3. **Now switch back to the Products form.**

   The Unit Price field has been changed to $19.50. Although it may not be apparent, the Chai record is now *dirty*, which means that you've changed data that has not been saved back to the database.

To save the record, press the Page Down key. Before moving to the next record (Chang), Access saves your change to the current record.

Now press the Page Up key to go back to Chai. (Sounds like a Bob Hope–Bing Crosby movie, doesn't it?) Notice that, indeed, Access saved the unit price value of $19.50.

Part III
Everything Else You Need to Understand about VBA

In this part . . .

*J*ust when you think you're ready to hit the road, you realize that you need to stop by the ATM and that you better fill up with gas. What does this have to do with VBA programming, you ask? Well, after you become armed with knowledge of the Office products, you need to acquire some fundamentals before beginning your development efforts — basics that range from creating code in the development environment to declaring a variable. In this part, you add skills to your development toolbox, such as the ability to make decisions while your code is running and the know-how to repeat lines of code over and over again.

Chapter 11

A Variable's Life

*W*e must warn you up front — discussing variables is not all that stimulating. In this chapter, we cover the basics of how to create and use variables within your VBA code. Plenty of opportunity abounds in later chapters to try out everything that we discuss here.

Some of our examples are within code procedures, so if this is completely foreign to you, consider jumping to Chapter 14, which discusses the guts of code procedures as well as how to create them.

All You Need Is Love and Variables

Okay, you bought in on the needing love, but what on earth are variables and why do we need them? A variable is simply a bucket that holds a piece of information.

Remember back to ninth-grade algebra class. Do you recall that darn x that kept appearing in your equations? Well, x is really a variable in mathematical terms that stores a numeric value. Consider 2x=8. In this case, the variable x represents a value that when multiplied by 2 totals 8. In the case of algebra, the variable x usually takes on only one value, whereas a variable in VBA can do just that — vary!

If our algebra example leaves you yearning for another example, we can talk about why a variable is like a bucket. Consider what you can use a bucket for. You can store items in it, fill it with water and wash your car, or perhaps even use it as a planter. In any event, you use the bucket to store something that you want to hold onto for a given length of time. Further, at times the bucket may be empty, longing to store something. With variables in VBA, you can have an empty variable.

Variables have names, which are often more descriptive than the *x* used in math class. Variable names must begin with a letter, be less than 256 characters, and can't contain any weird characters such as periods, ampersands, or those characters that typically make up not-so-nice words in cartoon language, such as *!@#. One last naming rule: variables that hang out in the same area (that is, within the same *scope*) must be unique. In this chapter, we discuss variable scoping and what is meant by it in the section "Variable Scoping."

Why do you need variables? You won't always have all the answers when you start to write your VBA code. Variables help you to write flexible, reusable code. Throughout this chapter, you can see some examples of variable usage.

Selecting a Storage Container

Variables can come in many different shapes and sizes that are intended to store different kinds of data. As an example, think about how many different food storage containers you have in your home. These plastic storage gems come in sizes small enough to fit a few jellybeans and large enough to store a few boxes of cereal. Then, some containers are intended to store dry goods and others for liquids. Some containers can be put in the freezer and some in the microwave.

Well, variables come in difference types and sizes too. Some variables hold string values, such as Company Name, while others hold numeric values or dates.

Variables can be declared as one of the following data types: *Boolean, byte, Integer, Long, Currency, Single, Double, Date, String* (for variable-length or fixed-length strings), *Object,* or *Variant.* If you do not specify a data type, the variant data type is assigned by default. You can also create a user-defined type by using the Type statement. Table 11-1 lists out the various data types that a variable can store. It's not exciting stuff, we admit that, but very useful for you to know. Don't fret; we won't have a quiz later.

Table 11-1		Data Types
Data Type	*Storage Size*	*Range of Valid Values*
Byte	1 byte	0 to 255
Boolean	2 bytes	True or False
Integer	2 bytes	−32,768 to 32,767
Long	4 bytes	−2,147,483,648 to 2,147,483,647
Single	4 bytes	Extremely large numbers
Double (double-precision floating-point)	8 bytes	Obscenely large numbers
Currency (scaled integer)	8 bytes	−$922,337,203,685,477.5808 to $922,337,203,685,477.5808 (enough to track Bill Gates' net worth!)
Decimal	14 bytes	Very large numbers with up to 28 decimal places
Date	8 bytes	January 1, 100 to December 31, 9999 (apparently the century change will not cause any concern here!)
Object	4 bytes	Any Object reference
String (variable-length)	10 bytes + string length	0 to approximately 2 billion
String (fixed-length)	Length of string	1 to approximately 65,400
Variant (with numbers)	16 bytes	Any numeric value up to the range of a Double
Variant (with characters)	22 bytes + string length	Same range as for variable-length string

Still awake? We have one more data type to mention. You may decide to create your own user-defined data type if none of the ones listed in Table 11-1 suit you or you have some special needs. With user-defined types, storage size depends on the requirements of each element and range varies by element data type. To create a user-defined data type, you declare the type in the Declarations section of a code module as seen in the following code example:

```
Type Employee    ' Create user-defined type.
    EmployeeNum ID As Integer
    Name As String * 20
    HireDate As Date
End Type
```

Using a user-defined type enables you to store related pieces of information in one variable, as with our Employee type. The Employee data type contains an integer, a fixed width string, and a date.

Table 11-1 shows that, essentially, you have a wide selection of data types for your variables. You want to do your best to select the appropriate type, or rather the best-fitting type. To store a yes or no response in a string field when a Boolean type is available is obviously wasteful.

When it's time to set up your variables, think about the range of values that the variable can store, whether the variable is a string, numeric, date, or other (if you even know) and then make the best selection that you can.

Conceiving a Variable

By now (if you have read this chapter straight through from the beginning), you have a general idea about what a variable is and why it is useful. Next, you need to know how to give birth to a variable and begin its life cycle, or *declare a variable*. To declare a variable, you simply dimension it by using the Dim keyword, such as Dim X. Be aware that variables are declared within code procedures. (See Chapter 14 if you're unfamiliar with the Module window, subroutines, and functions.) Also, variables are not declared in the Immediate window; unlike other chapters in which we utilize that window, now we need to do something different.

You can even declare more than one variable in one line of code, such as:

```
Dim X, Y
```

What data types are variables *X* and *Y* in the preceding code snippet? They are both variants because we did not explicitly declare a data type for them. Variant is the default data type for variables in VBA.

Next, you can declare a variable with a specific data type. You can explicitly declare *X* as an integer and *Y* as a variant by using the As keyword.

```
Dim X as Integer, Y as Variant
```

Variables must be declared within a code procedure. As an example, you may have a subroutine that looks like the following:

```
Sub DoSomething()
    'Declaring variables
    Dim UnitPrice As Currency, Quantity as Integer
    Dim Msg As String
    Dim StartDate as Date
```

```
     'Code goes after variable declarations
End Sub
```

In this subroutine, we declare four variables and their respective data types. These variables are available for use by this subroutine and only this subroutine (see the section "Variable Scoping" for more details).

It's always a good idea to document your code, as we have done in the preceding subroutine. The single quote is the symbol VBA recognizes as a comment marker.

Using Your Variables

After your variables are declared, using your variables is a breeze. You can set your variables or check their current values. To set your variables, simply use the following syntax:

```
VariableName=Value
```

The following example shows how we set four different variables with four different data types. Notice that strings are enclosed (or *delimited*) in quotes and dates in pound signs. All the numeric data types, however, require no delimiters when setting values as seen in UnitPrice and Quantity.

```
Sub DoSomething()
    'Declaring variables
    Dim UnitPrice As Currency, Quantity as Integer
    Dim Msg As String
    Dim StartDate As Date
    'Setting variable values
    UnitPrice=100
    Quantity=2
    Msg="This is a message"
    StartDate=#01/01/1998#
    'Additional code placed here
End Sub
```

In this chapter's section "A Different Kind of Variable — Object Variables," we talk about how to declare and set *object variables* (which differ from run-of-the-mill variables). Now it's your turn to work with variables by opening Excel and following these steps:

1. **Choose File⇨New to start with a clean workbook.**

2. **Press Alt+F11 to open the Visual Basic Editor.**

3. Choose Insert⇨Module to create a new module.

A new storage bin for your procedures (Module1) is created.

4. In the Code Window, type `Dim MyFirstVar As Integer`**.**

Look at Figure 11-1 for an example of this declaration. This statement declares a variable of the integer data type. Notice that you can select the appropriate data type from the list box. Now, in the Immediate window, you can have some fun with this new variable that you created.

5. Type `?MyFirstVar` **in the Immediate window.**

This returns nothing to the Immediate window, because you haven't yet given the variable a value.

6. Next, type `MyFirstVar=100` **and then type** `?MyFirstVar` **to check the value of MyFirstVar again.**

This time 100 returns to the Immediate window. You can even do some fancy things with variables, such as multiplying them by a number.

7. Type `MyFirstVar = MyFirstVar*2` **in the Immediate window and then type** `?MyFirstVar` **to check the variable's current value.**

This returns 200 to the Immediate window, as shown in Figure 11-2.

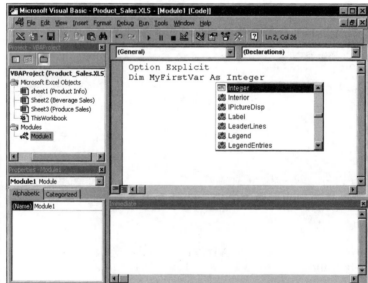

Figure 11-1:
A view of the Visual Basic Editor with your new module and variable declaration.

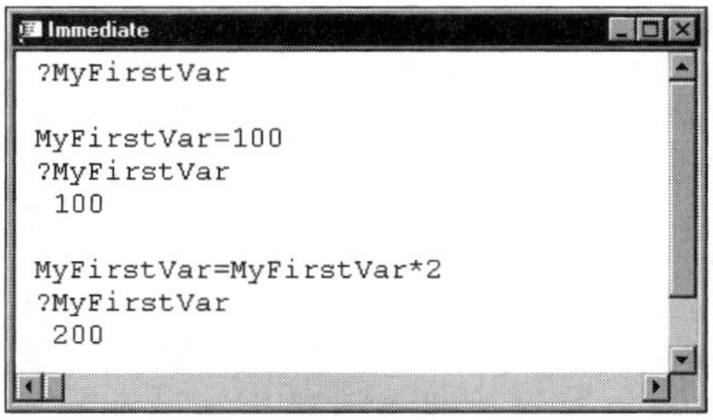

Figure 11-2:
Your
commands
as shown
in the
Immediate
window.

```
Immediate                          _□×
?MyFirstVar

MyFirstVar=100
?MyFirstVar
 100

MyFirstVar=MyFirstVar*2
?MyFirstVar
 200
```

Variable Scoping

Scoping refers to the extent to which a variable can be accessed. You can work with three scoping levels: the procedure-level, the private module-level, and the public module-level. Variables with *procedure-level scope* are only available to the procedure that declared them and can't be seen by other functions and subroutines. In the example found in the section "Using Your Variables," the four variables declared in the subroutine DoSomething have a procedure-level scope.

In case you find our use of the terms procedure, functions, and subroutines confusing, here are some definitions to clear the air. A *procedure* is simply a code construct. *Functions* and *subroutines* are two types of procedures.

If you want to use variables within a given module, you can declare them in the Declarations section of the specific module. Any variables declared in the Declarations section are available to all procedures within the module, but not to procedures in other modules in the VBA project. This is called *module-level scoping*. As an example, look at this sample listing for a module:

```
'Declarations Section
Dim EmpSalary as Currency

Sub DisplaySalary()
    Msgbox "CurrentSalary is " & EmpSalary
End Sub

Sub PerformanceIncrease()
    Dim NewSalary As Currency
    NewSalary = 2000 + EmpSalary
End Sub
```

In this code listing, the variable EmpSalary is declared in the Declarations section of the module, making the variable accessible to both subroutines. NewSalary, however, is declared within the PerformanceIncrease subroutine and therefore has procedure-level scope.

Any variable declared at the module level using the Dim statement is private by definition. You can optionally include the Private keyword if you think that it makes your code easier to read, such as Private EmpSalary As Currency. Remember, private variables can be used only by procedures in the same module.

However, in some instances subroutines and functions in other modules need to access the EmpSalary variable. To accommodate this you can make EmpSalary a public variable using the Public keyword, as seen in the following code:

```
'Include in Declarations section of any module.
Public EmpSalary As Currency
```

Without the Public keyword, the variable EmpSalary can only be available to the module in which it is declared. By declaring EmpSalary publicly, it can be seen and accessed by all modules and hence has *public module-level scope*.

With all this said about variable scoping, we haven't yet addressed how long a variable's value is accessible. If you declare a variable within a procedure, it only exists as long as the procedure is running. After the procedure ends, the variable no longer contains any value. This is the default behavior you can expect with variables, unless you make your variables static.

An interesting concept — static variables. But is anything more annoying than a bad case of static cling? Fortunately, a static variable is quite handy to have sticking around. You can declare a variable as *static* to preserve its value once a procedure has ended, such as Static MyVar As String. Under normal circumstances, variables maintain their value for the life of the procedure and lose it as soon as the End Sub or End Function command executes. Static variables, on the other hand, maintain their values.

Do static variables maintain a value forever? Not exactly. A static variable lives for the duration of your application or program that you are running. For example, if you have some code behind an Excel workbook, your static variables are maintained while that workbook remains open.

To Declare or Not to Declare, That Is the Question

Now, regarding how to declare your variables, we have a small confession to make. You can actually declare your variables in two ways — *explicitly* and *implicitly*. In the preceding two sections, you find out how to use the Dim keyword to declare your variables. You can also use the Private and Public statements to explicitly declare variables if you want to effect the variable's scope. In summary, when you use Dim, Private, or Public to declare variables, the variables are declared explicitly.

Implicit declaration

To see how implicit declaration works, take a look at the following example:

```
'Declarations Section
'Nothing declared here

Sub PerformanceIncrease()
    'Nothing declared here
    NewSalary = 2000 + EmpSalary
End Sub
```

In this example, two variables that we haven't declared are in use. NewSalary and EmpSalary are declared on-the-fly (implicitly) after they are used in the procedure. If you think that this is a much easier way to declare variables, you are mistaken. Sure, on the front end it's easier to just create and use variables as you need them; however, you are likely to pay for that convenience later. For example, consider this example that uses implicit variable declaration:

```
Sub WhyImplictIsBad()
    NewVar=100
    NewVar = NewVar*2
    MsgBox "The value of NewVar is " & NewVat
End Sub
```

The subroutine WhyImplicitIsBad does not work as you may anticipate. After you modify the value of NewVar you attempt to display the result with the MsgBox command, but this does not work properly. Why?

If you noticed the typo in line 4 of the code, then kudos to you. In fact, yes, a typo is in the MsgBox command line. We are displaying the value of NewVat, not NewVar. Sure, to find the problem in this small example is easy, but after you start to write complex procedures with hundreds of lines of code, finding silly problems like this can take a lot of time and energy.

Don't think that you can just compile the code to catch this error. In this case, in which we aren't requiring explicit variable declaration, VBA has no problem with the way the code appears. If we had required explicit variable declaration, we would have started off the subroutine by declaring the variable NewVar. As soon as we mistyped NewVar as NewVat, VBA would have gotten cranky and let us know about it with a message saying that the variable is not defined.

Option Explicit

The good news is that this can all be avoided if you include one simple statement in our code — Option Explicit. When Option Explicit appears in a module, you must explicitly declare all variables before using them with either Dim, Private, Public, or Static statements. If you attempt to use an undeclared variable name, as we do in the preceding example, you encounter an error at compile time. In fact, any misspelled variable names are detected as well. To use Option Explicit, place this command in the Declarations section of your modules. (See Chapter 14 for more about modules and how to use them.)

Can't remember to place Option Explicit in all your modules? You can have VBA take care of it for you. You can use an option setting to require variable declaration. When this option is turned on it automatically places the Option Explicit statement in all new modules that you create. To check this setting, choose Tools⇨Options and locate Require Variable Declaration under the Editor tab.

If you don't use the Option Explicit statement, all undeclared variables are of Variant type. As noted throughout this chapter, declaring your variables with the most appropriate data type is best. Variables declared as Variants require more memory resources than most other variables. Leaving undeclared variables as the default Variant type may cause your application to run less efficiently as it potentially can with explicitly declared variables of a specific data type.

A Different Kind of Variable — Object Variables

An object variable is one variable type not quite like the others. An object variable stores a *pointer* to an object, such as an Access form, a Word document, an Excel workbook, or a PowerPoint presentation. A pointer is a way to tell VBA which object you want to control. You can think of object variables as more complex than their counterparts, such as string variables or integer variables that store simple pieces of information.

To start out with, you declare object variables in the same way that you do a normal variable. For example, to declare an Access form you type `Dim f As Form`, where *f* is the name of the variable and *Form* is the type of object.

What is different is how object variables are set with an appropriate value. To demonstrate this, look at the following code example in which we declare two variables, set their values, and then display the results with a series of MsgBox statements.

```
'Declarations section
Option Explicit

Sub ObjectPlay()
    'Declare Object variables
    Dim wb As Workbook
    Dim ws As Worksheet

    'Set Object variables
    Set wb = Application.ActiveWorkbook
    Set ws = wb.ActiveSheet

    'Display names of active workbook and worksheet
    MsgBox "Current workbook is " & wb.Name
    MsgBox "Current worksheet is " & ws.Name

End Sub
```

To set an object variable, you use the keyword Set prior to actually setting the variable equal to a specific object. In the code example, we declare the variable WB as a workbook object. By using the Set keyword, we store a pointer to the ActiveWorkbook in Excel.

Using an object variable

What's really neat about object variables is that you can treat them exactly the same as the object to which they refer. You have access to the properties and methods of the underlying object. Look again at the preceding code example. After we set the variables *wb* and *ws* to the ActiveWorkbook and ActiveSheet respectively, we use the Name property of each of these object variables. The code ws.Name returns the name of the ActiveWorkbook.

If you use an object variable without declaring it first, the data type of the object variable is Variant by default.

Want to try this out? In Chapter 14, we discuss how to write module code and we don't intend to replicate that information here, but we think that it would be beneficial to start Excel and try out this object example:

1. **Open the sample workbook, Produce_Sales.xls.**

   This workbook is installed from the diskette that comes with this book in the C:\Dummies\Chapter 11 directory.

2. **Press Alt+F11 to open the Visual Basic Editor and choose Insert⇨Module to create a new module.**

   After you do this, a new module (Module1) is created.

3. **In the Code Window, type** Sub ObjectPlay() **and press Enter.**

   As soon as you do, notice that the code window separates your subroutine from the Declarations section and ends the End Sub command.

4. **Continue to enter the code between the Sub and End Sub commands as seen in the code listing in the section "A Different Kind of Variable — Object Variables."**

   When you finish typing, your code looks like the code in Figure 11-3. Now you can try out the code and see whether you declared and set the object variables properly.

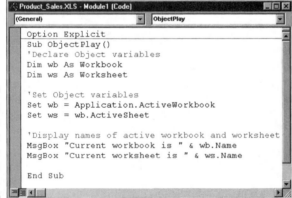

Figure 11-3:
The
ObjectPlay
subroutine
in the code
window.

```
Option Explicit
Sub ObjectPlay()
'Declare Object variables
Dim wb As Workbook
Dim ws As Worksheet

'Set Object variables
Set wb = Application.ActiveWorkbook
Set ws = wb.ActiveSheet

'Display names of active workbook and worksheet
MsgBox "Current workbook is " & wb.Name
MsgBox "Current worksheet is " & ws.Name

End Sub
```

5. **To run the ObjectPlay subroutine, click the Run button on the toolbar.**

   If you forget which button is which, choose Run⇨Run Sub/UserForm.

   When the code hits the MsgBox commands, it displays a message box in Excel with the appropriate information, as shown in Figure 11-4.

Figure 11-4 displays the name of the ActiveWorkbook, which is Product_Sales.xls in this example.

Figure 11-4:
The MsgBox command pops up a message in Excel.

House cleaning

When you are done using your object variable, as a matter of cleanliness (and efficient resource usage) you need to remove the relationship between the object variable and the object. To do this, set the object variable equal to the keyword Nothing as seen in the following example:

```
Set MyObject = Nothing
```

When you set an object variable equal to Nothing, the association of the object variable with any specific object is discontinued.

Constants — No Variables Needed

Yes, this is a chapter on variables, but you also need to understand what constants are all about. A *constant,* as its name implies, is a type of variable that maintains a constant value. When you declare a constant, you should assign it a meaningful name that makes the constant easier to refer to in your VBA code.

To declare a constant, such as a tax rate, use the keyword Const to set its value. For example, Const TaxRate=0.045. After the TaxRate constant is declared, it can't be modified or assigned a new value. If the tax rate changes, you must physically change the Const statement to reflect the appropriate rate.

You declare constants in the Declarations section of a module or within a specific procedure or at the top of a module. By default, any constant that you declare in a module is private. If you want to declare a public constant, you need to precede the Const statement with the Public keyword. The following example declares the Public constant MarkUpRate as an Integer and assigns it the value .025:

```
Public Const MarkUpRate As Integer = .025
```

Constants can be declared as one of the following data types: Boolean, Byte, Integer, Long, Currency, Single, Double, Date, String, or Variant (refer to Table 11-1 for a description of these data types). Because you already know the value of a constant, you can specify the data type in a Const statement. As with variables, you can declare several constants in one statement.

To ensure that you are comfortable with the concept of a constant and how to use it in your VBA code, consider this simple subroutine that calculates some simple interest on a loan.

```
Sub HowMuchDoYouOwe()
'Declare some constants
Const SimpleInterestRate = 0.09
Const Amount = 10000, LoanedOn = #1/1/97#

'Declare variable to use in calculation
Dim Days As Integer, OweYou As Currency

'Calculate elapsed days
Days = DateDiff("d", LoanedOn, Date)

'Calculate current interest owed & display it!
OweYou = (SimpleInterestRate / 365) * Days * Amount
MsgBox "I owe you " & OweYou & " in interest."
End Sub
```

In this subroutine, we begin by setting up three constants. (Notice that you only use the keyword Const once when declaring two constants on the same line of code.) Then, after setting up some variables to use within the subroutine, we use the DateDiff function to calculate the number of days that have elapsed since the loan was made. Finally, using both variables and the constants we set, we determined the amount of interest owed as of today's date and displayed the value in a message box. As you can see, you can use constants just as you would use variables.

Chapter 12

Conditioning Your Code

. . . .

In This Chapter

▶ Exploring If..Then statements

▶ Introducing the Immediate If

▶ Casing the joint with Case statements

▶ Deciding on a conditioner

. . . .

*I*t is quite unlikely that you own one outfit that is appropriate for every occasion. You'd feel quite comfortable in a tee-shirt and jeans for a backyard picnic, but rather out of place at a wedding. Conversely, a formal gown or tuxedo may fit the bill for that wedding, but would be rather cumbersome for the backyard gathering. It makes sense to wear a different outfit for different types of occasions. Similarly, depending on the conditions in your application, you may choose to run different code.

With the use of the various conditioning statements, you can plan for the various actions that your user may take as well as the current environment of your application. VBA provides you with two basic conditioning constructs — If..Then..End If and Select Case..End Select. In this chapter, you have the opportunity to try both of these out. The value of using conditional statements should be readily apparent. If you have previous programming experience, these constructs may already be familiar to you.

For those of you that are not sure about this new stuff we're jabbering about — why do you need conditional statements? Essentially, these statements allow you to plan for different *conditions* that can occur within your application. For example, consider an application that asks you a yes/no question. Depending on your response, the application takes a different course of action. In real-life terms, think about your commute to work. If the highway has no delays, then you are likely to travel that route because it's generally faster. However, if the traffic situation on the highway looks grim, then you take the back roads to work.

If..Then . . . What?

Breaking the commute scenario we just described into computer lingo helps demonstrate the If..Then..Else construct, the first stop on our conditioning tour. In computing terms you'd code your commuting decision in the following way:

```
If Highway_Delays=False Then
     Travel on the highway
Else
     Travel on the back roads
End If
```

If there are no highway delays, then the expression Highway_Delays=False results in a true condition, whereas delays cause this expression to be false. After the condition is checked, a travel decision is made to either travel the highway or the back roads. If this is confusing, this code may be easier to understand if this is completely new to you.

```
If Highway_Delays=True Then
     Travel on the back roads
Else
     Travel on the highway
End If
```

In this case, you check first for traffic delays. If there are delays, then the back roads are traveled, whereas not meeting the condition leaves you with a highway commute. This is essentially the same as the previous code listing; we have simply changed what condition we are checking first and reordered the code under the appropriate condition check.

Another way to check for traffic is by using the Not function. By evaluating Not(Highway_Delays) you can test the condition. If no traffic is on the highway, Not(Highway_Delays) returns a true condition. Although using the Not function is an efficient way to check the condition in this case, it can be a bit confusing because it's really a double negative. After you use this function a few times, you may prefer it over more verbose alternatives.

We think you will agree that using the If..Then constructs is really rather easy. Simply talk through the actions you want and put the information into this structure. As you may have guessed, about as many flavors of If..Then statements are available as selections in the ice cream section of your grocer's freezer. Okay, maybe we are exaggerating slightly, but a bunch of different constructs are available for you to explore.

Using If..Then statements

Start with the basic If..Then statement, which is a one-liner. You use the simple If..Then statement as follows:

```
If condition is true Then take some action
```

Here are a few examples. Consider an application that asks for user input. At some point, if you ask the user a question, you may want the application to react, such as

```
If response="no" Then End Sub
```

In this case, a response of "no" terminates the code procedure that this statement is a part of. Secondly, if you are using Access you may want to check the value of the user currently logged on. If the current user is SysAdmin, you give a special greeting with the following code snippet:

```
If CurrentUser()="SysAdmin" Then MsgBox "Welcome Admin!!"
```

Using If..Then..End If

These single If..Then statements are great, but they are not always adequate for your application. You can rewrite this example by using the next construct in the family — If..Then..End If, which we think you'll agree is easier to read and allows you room to grow your code. At this point, you are only taking one action if the condition is true, but additional statements can be placed between the If and End If lines of code.

```
If CurrentUser()="SysAdmin" Then
    MsgBox "Welcome Admin!!"
End If
```

In the preceding example, to use a single line of code to test the condition and take some action is obviously more efficient. The If..End If construct works the same, but takes more coding. On a computer-nerd level, if coding efficiently in as few lines of code as possible is important to you, the one-liner is your best bet when possible. If you make bets with your buddies as to how many lines of code it takes to deliver a set amount of functionality, the one-liner can help you win the Name That Code Procedure game. You remember, don't you? This game is a spin-off on the old *Name That Tune* game show.

Keep in mind that if you decide to use the one-liner If..Then statement and later down the road you decide to take more than one action, you will be faced with some rework!

Okay, then why do we have this If..Then..End If construct? The limitation of the single statement is that you can only take one action, which in the above example was to put up a message box for the end user. With the If..Then..End If construct, however, you can have as many statements as you want as a result of the condition being met. Consider this example:

```
If DueDate>Date() Then
    MsgBox "You have missed your deadline on this!"
    Overdue = True
    'Run some other code
End If
```

You could not have accomplished this with a single line of code! The next in the family lineup is a variation on a theme. In the previous examples, you only check one condition and then follow a course of action if and only if the condition is true. Often, you want to take a different course of action depending on the result of the condition test. The syntax for this construct is as follows:

```
If condition is true Then
    'Do some stuff
Else
    'Do something else, indicates condition not met
End If
```

In this case, if the condition is not true your code runs any statements that you include under the Else statement. Alternatively, you can explicitly check if the condition is false (ElseIf condition is false).

Using If..Then..ElseIf..End If

In some instances you may want to check the value of a certain item, which has more than one outcome. Consider some code that checks the color of a stoplight that you are approaching. A simple If..Then..End If won't do in this case. We need to use If..Then..ElseIf..End If, the last member of the family that we want to introduce to you. The only real new clause here is the ElseIf statement, which works just like the If statement. In this next example, we start off by checking if the light is green. If it isn't, we move through the code and then check to see if the light is yellow. If we still have no luck, we execute the code in the Else clause.

```
If StopLight_Color="green" Then
    MsgBox "All systems go! Go for the green!"

ElseIf StopLight_Color="yellow" Then
    MsgBox "The light turned yellow, please proceed
    with caution"

Else
    MsgBox "The light is some color other than
    green or yellow"

End If
```

Be sure that you type each MsgBox statement as one line of code, not on two separate lines as seen in the code listing. It is only broken in the code listing because of page-width constraints.

For purposes of displaying this code in this chapter, we could not use a line continuation character in the middle of the string. We could have, however, defined a string variable to store the message we want to display and create the message by using more than one line of code, as shown in the following code snippet. Then we could use the MsgBox statement with the string variable Msg.

```
Dim Msg As String    'Declare string at top of subroutine
Msg = "The light turned yellow, please proceed "
Msg = Msg & " with caution"
MsgBox Msg
```

To gain some familiarity with the use of the If..Then statement, you can enter this stoplight check code into a function or subroutine within one of your Office applications. For demonstrative purposes, we walk you through a test of this code within Word.

1. **Open Word if it's not already running.**

   You must have a document open, which can be just a blank document waiting for text.

2. **Press Alt+F11 to open the Visual Basic Editor.**

3. **Choose** <u>I</u>nsert⇨<u>M</u>odule.

   A new code window is opened.

4. **Type** `Sub Test (StopLight_Color As String)` **in the code window and press Enter.**

   You have just created a new subroutine. Notice that VBA automatically puts the End Sub command at the end of your new procedure.

5. Complete the Test subroutine by typing the If..Then constructs that test for the stoplight color and give advice via a message box.

This code block is found in this section, directly under the heading "Using If..Then..Elself..End If."

6. Press Ctrl+G to open the Immediate window if it's not already visible.

7. Type `Test("green")` **to test this code from the Immediate window.**

This returns the message box stating "All systems go! Go for the green!" You can repeat this test by using other colors, such as yellow and red. A yellow light returns a message box that indicates the end user can proceed with caution, while a red or other colored light returns another message.

With this particular function, you want to know the color of the stoplight and are unlikely to be concerned if the light is *yellow* or *Yellow*. Interestingly enough, depending on the options you have set, the function can actually fail if you feed Test("Yellow") as opposed to Test("yellow"). However, if Option Compare Text is placed in the Declarations section of the affected module, strings can be compared with no concern for case.

If..Then statements leaving the nest

When you start to get fancy with your code logic, you may find a need to have multiple levels of If..Then statements in your VBA code. These If..Then levels are referred to as nested commands. In the following example, if the stoplight we are facing is yellow, we then check to see if a speed trap is set up, which as you may expect affects your decision to run the yellow light.

```
If StopLight_Color="green" Then
    MsgBox "All systems go! Go for the green!"

ElseIf StopLight_Color="yellow" Then

    If Not(Speed_Trap) Then
        GoThruLight=true
        Msgbox "Keep going, but be careful if light
          is nearing red."
    Else
        GoThruLight=false
        MsgBox "The light turned yellow, please slow
          down and come to a complete stop"
    End If
```

```
Else
    MsgBox "The light is some color other than green
    or yellow."

End If
```

As you can see, we have nested an If..Then construct in the ElseIf part of the code snippet to handle the light-running logic. If the stoplight is never yellow, you never execute the nested If..Then clause.

An Immediate If

There is one last If-type statement called an Immediate If statement, or IIf. An IIf statement can be thought of as a one-stop-shopping statement. In one line, you can check if a condition is true and then carry out an action if it is true or an alternative action if it is false. The IIF combines an If..Then..Else..End If construct folded into one neat little convenient line.

However, convenience has its price. The IIf has the same limitation as the single statement for If..Then. You can only carry out one action for each condition. Here, we use the commuting example carried throughout the section "If..Then . . . What?" in this chapter. The following code snippet checks the delays and then returns the appropriate route to work to a string variable, Msg. From here, the result string would likely be passed onto another code procedure or command, such as a MsgBox statement that informs you of the correct path to work.

```
Msg = IIf(Not(Highway_delays), "Highway", "Back Roads")
```

The general syntax for the Immediate If statement is as follows:

```
IIf(condition, true, false)
```

After VBA evaluates the condition, either the true or false statement or value is evaluated. This can result in either an expression or a value.

Here's a brief example of how you actually use the Immediate If in your VBA code. Because IIf returns a result, you set the function equal to a variable.

```
Function MyFunction (Sales As Single)
    Dim SalesResult as String
    SalesResult = IIf(Sales>100000, "Great job!", _
"Keep plugging.")
    MsgBox SalesResult
End Function
```

The IIf statement evaluates both true and false expressions, even though it returns only one of them. If one of the expressions results in an error, such as division by zero, you may not see the behavior that you expect. When you test your code, a good idea is to test both the true and false expressions to ward off this type of unanticipated bite.

Do you want to give this a try? Although we haven't written any functions yet, you can immediately try out the Immediate If in the Immediate window.

1. **From within Word, press Alt+F11 to open the Visual Basic Editor.**

You can also try this out in Excel, PowerPoint, or Access, because this is all just basic VBA (no object specifics). Keep in mind, however, that Access has a Debug window, not an Immediate window (see Chapter 10 for more about the peculiarities of Access).

2. **In the Immediate window, type the following series of statements and press Enter:**

```
y=50000
x=IIf(y>100000,"Great job!","Keep plugging.")
? x
```

After setting y=50000, the Immediate If statement checks to see if y is greater than 100000. If y>100000, the variable x is set to "Great job!", whereas if y<=100000, x is set to "Keep plugging." When you check the value of x, it returns the string "Keep plugging." to the Immediate window.

To test that our code snippet really works, and that the x returning the correct string value isn't a fluke, try setting y to a value over 100,000.

3. **In the Immediate window, type these three statements and press Enter to continue this example:**

```
y=150000
x=IIf(y>100000,"Great job!","Keep plugging.")
?x
```

This returns the string "Great job!" to the Immediate window, because the condition y>100,000 is true.

You can even have embedded or nested IIf statements, such as

```
X = IIf(x>100,IIf(y>200,"Fuzzy","Wuzzy"),"Was a bear")
```

In this silly code snippet, if x is greater that 100, then the next IIf statement is evaluated and is returned as the result of the parent IIf. If x is less than or equal to 100, the string "Was a bear" is returned by the IIf statement.

Case Statements

The If..Then family of conditional constructs is great, but there may come a
point when using it becomes unwieldy or impractical. Consider a situation
where you need to check which option value has been selected and take
appropriate action, such as this example:

```
Sub SomeFunc(MyValue as Integer)

If MyValue=1 Then
    'Do something for 1

ElseIf MyValue=2 Then
    'Do something for 2

ElseIf MyValue=3 Then
    'Do something for 3

ElseIf MyValue=4 Then
    'Do something for 4

ElseIf MyValue=5 Then
    'Do something for 5

Else
    'Do something completely different

End If
End Sub
```

As you can see, this can get quite tedious and in this instance we only check
for five (5) different values. There can easily be 10, 20, or even more values
for which to search.

A Case statement is an alternate way to code this subroutine which often is
a better way to represent multiple values. In the next example code snippet,
we've rewritten the subroutine SomeFunc from the preceding example to
use the Case statements:

```
Sub SomeFunc(MyValue as Integer)

Select Case MyValue
    Case 1
'Do something for 1
    Case 2
```

(continued)

(continued)

```
'Do something for 1
    Case 3
'Do something for 1
    Case 4
'Do something for 1
    Case 5
'Do something for 1
    Case Else
End Select

End Sub
```

As you can see, the general syntax for using the Case statements is as follows:

```
Select Case expression
    Case test_expression
        'Do something if the expression matches this case
    Case test_expression_2
        'Do something if the expression matches this case
    'More Cases to test...
End Select
```

The *expression* in the Select Case statement is the value that you are searching for within your Case statements that ultimately decides your course of action. This expression can be either a numeric or string expression. After you know what you are looking for, each Case statement is checked for the appropriate expression match.

Next, all the code that follows the matched Case statement begins to execute and continues until the next Case statement is encountered. At this point, the Case construct completes its work and your code continues to execute after the End Select statement. It is important to note, however, that if more than one Case statement matches the expression you are seeking, only the statements that follow the first match are executed. Yet another good argument for thoroughly testing your code. In Chapter 17, we spend some time discussing how to test and debug your code.

In this example, we use simple equality case statements. In each of the five (5) cases, we look for an exact match. Alternatively, you can construct an expression such as Case >5, Case Is Null, or Case <=12.

When Case is better

Perhaps the benefits of the Case construct are not readily apparent when you compare the SomeFunc subroutine written with If..Then..End If statements to the SomeFunc subroutine that utilizes Select Case..End Select. Actually, you can argue that the Case statements are not much better than the If..Then constructs in this example, but give this next scenario a test-drive.

```
Select Case MyCase
    Case 0
        'A set of actions when the value is 0
    Case 1 to 10
        'Another set of actions when then value is 1
        'through 10
    Case 12, 14, 17
        'Yet one more set of actions when then
        'value is 12, 14, or 17
    Case Is > 20
        'Actions to be carried out when MyCase>20
    Case Else
        'Do something completely different
End Select
```

In this case (no pun intended we assure you), you can easily check the value of the case expression and take appropriate action. You can simply look for a single value, as you see with Case 0. Then, with Case 1 To 10, you search for a range of numbers. If MyCase is 12, 14, or 17, the third group of actions is executed, and finally, if MyCase is greater than 20, you have a final set of actions.

But what if none of these cases yield a match? For this special circumstance, you have the Case Else statement. If no other matches are found, the Case Else wins and its actions are carried out.

Using Case

To gain some experience with the Case statements, you can create a simple procedure in any of the Office products. For this example, we continue to use Word, even though this procedure can work the same in Excel, PowerPoint, or Access.

1. Open Word if it's not already running.

You need to have a document open, which can be just a blank document waiting for text.

2. **Press ALT+F11 to open the Visual Basic Editor.**

3. **Choose Insert⇨Module.**

   If you have an existing module (perhaps from a previous exercise), you can add to it rather than create a new module. The choice is yours.

4. **Type** `Sub HowOld (Age As Integer)` **in the code window and press Enter.**

   You have just created a new subroutine. Notice that VBA automatically puts the End Sub command at the end of your new procedure.

5. **In between the** `Sub HowOld()` **and** `End Sub` **statements, type the following code:**

```
Dim Msg as String
Select Case Age
    Case 0 To 3
        Msg="It's still diaper time."
    Case 4
        Msg="Getting ready for school."
    Case 5 To 18
        Msg="Getting an education."
    Case Is >18
        Msg="On their own"
End Select
Debug.Print Msg
```

   Now, you can test out your new procedure.

6. **Choose View⇨Immediate Window to open the Immediate window.**

7. **Type** `HowOld(2)`.

   After this is commited, the phrase "It's still diaper time" is returned to the Immediate window with the Debug.Print command.

Try other values, such as HowOld(4), HowOld(5), and HowOld(21), and verify the results with your code, as shown in Figure 12-1.

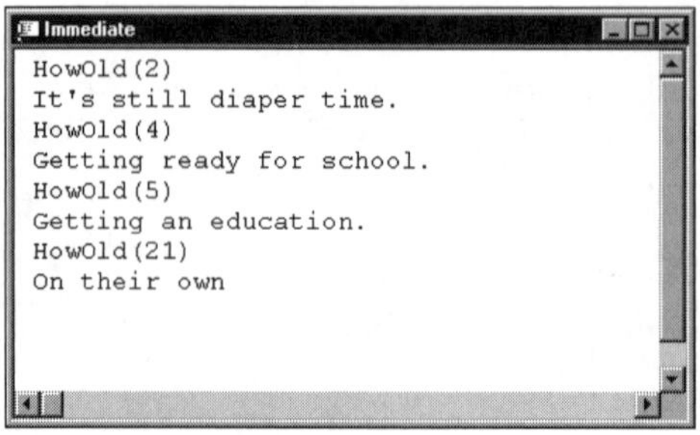

Figure 12-1:
Testing out
a Select
Case
construct.

```
Immediate                                    _ □ ×
HowOld(2)
It's still diaper time.
HowOld(4)
Getting ready for school.
HowOld(5)
Getting an education.
HowOld(21)
On their own
```

In this chapter, you can see simple expressions in each Case statement, such as Case 3 or Case 1 To 5. You can alternatively include multiple expressions or ranges in any given Case clause, such as the following example:

```
Case 1, 3 To 9, 12 To 15, Is > 20
```

You can accomplish a similar thing with string expressions by using explicit strings, as well as variables that store string values. For example, the following code statement is a valid Case statement which compares the case expression to a single letter, a range of letters, and the variable, MyStr:

```
Case "A", "E" To "M", MyStr
```

Deciding on a Conditioner (Making the Case–If..Then Decision)

So when do you want to use the Case statements rather than If..Then constructs? You need to consider two factors when you make this decision — the number of possible values and the number of conditions you want to test.

✔ Generally, the more possible values you want to check for, the more appropriate a Case statement becomes. The Case statements are easier to work with when you have some complex expressions and cases where multiple results yield the same set of actions, such as Case 1 To 10, 20, 30 does thirty push-ups. This is more difficult to accomplish by using an If..Then construct. If, however, you only need to test one or two values, an If..Then construct is a better selection.

✔ Another decision criteria for selecting a construct is how many conditions you need to check. Consider how a Case statement works. Each Case statement contains different values that are tested against a single variable, which is identified in the Select Case statement. An If..Then construct, on the other hand, can conceivably check for different conditions at each step along the way, which makes it the obvious choice for checking more than one condition as you go.

If you consider both factors and still can't decide which construct to use, don't fret about it. There isn't always a right choice of a conditioning construct. Sometimes, which construct you use doesn't really matter for a given procedure — it's just a personal preference.

When you specify a range of values, you can use the Is keyword with a comparison operator, such as Case Is >10. If you do not include the Is keyword, it is automatically inserted.

As with the If..Then constructs, Select Case statements can be nested. (See the section "If..Then statements leaving the nest" in this chapter for more information about nesting. Don't forget that each nested Select Case statement must have a matching End Select statement. If you neglect this duty, aliens will come down and stomp on your code. Actually, you may just get an error; we can't seem to verify under which conditions the aliens arrive.

Chapter 13

Loop-de-Loop

· ·

In This Chapter

▶ Sporting a loop for every season, or is it reason?

▶ Staying out of a bad loop situation

▶ Using For..Next constructs

▶ Building nested loops (Yes, you can!)

▶ Saving coding time with the With..End With construct

▶ Handling groups of data or objects with the For Each..Next?

· ·

*W*hat is looping? Why do we need it? *Looping,* or processing through the same lines of code multiple times, is often useful. A number of looping constructs are available to assist you. Loops come in all sorts of shapes and sizes, including For..Next, Do While, Do Until, With..End With, For Each..Next, and While..Wend. Some loops execute a set number of times, and others watch for a particular condition to be true or no longer true. You can even find a loop that only executes once. Actually, some loops never get a chance to come out and play.

How Not to Loop

Before venturing into discussions on looping, we need to take a look at how not to loop. Consider this following example:

```
Do Until PigsFly=True
    'Code to execute
Loop
```

When this looping construct is encountered, execution begins and then continues until the condition is true. In this case, it is unlikely that pigs will ever fly, so you may find yourself in an endless loop. You may want to have a contingency plan for this type of scenario. If you really think that you can get the pig to fly, perhaps you can give him 100 tries to get in the air, and then if nothing happens, leave the loop.

```
Do Until PigsFly=True
    NumTry=NumTry+1
    If NumTry>100 Then Exit Do
    'Code to execute
Loop
```

In this scenario, if the loop has executed more than 100 times, and if pigs still aren't flying, the loop is exited using the Exit Do command.

Do You Think We're Loopy?

We want to tell you about four different varieties of Do loops. They are all essentially the same, but differ in whether the code is executed at least once and how to check for the condition. The lineup includes

```
Do While..Loop
Do..Loop While
Do Until..Loop
Do..Loop Until
```

The *Do loops* repeat a block of statements either *while* a certain condition is True or *until* a condition becomes True. Take a look at each of these loops.

If the condition for a Do While or Do Until loop is Null, then VBA treats the statement as if it had the value False. Remember, a Null value really means that there is no known value for the condition.

While you're at it, keep looping

Start by looking at the Do-While loops, which come in two lovely varieties. This Do loop executes the code within the loop while the specified condition is true. In real-life terms, think about playing a pick-up game of hoops (also called *basketball* by some folks). You decide to play while you're having fun. As soon as the fun is over, either because you've lost interest or your opponents become jerks, you stop playing.

```
Do While condition is true
    'Do some cool stuff like running a few lines of code
Loop
```

When the Do statement is encountered and if the condition you set is true, the loop begins executing. If, however, the condition is false from the beginning, the loop is bypassed and code execution resumes after the Loop statement. You may have already noticed that, unlike the For..Next loops discussed in the section "For My Next Trick" later in this chapter, no counter value is being incremented or controlling the number of times the loop is executed in the Do loop. With the Do loops, everything is based on a specific condition being true or false.

The second flavor of the Do-While loop is different in that the loop begins executing before any condition is checked. Also, a Do..Loop While loop always executes at least one time.

```
Do
      'Do some cool stuff like running a few lines of code
Loop While condition is true
```

To assist you in understanding the Do-While looping construct, follow this example:

1. **Open Excel if it's not already running.**

2. **Start the Visual Basic Editor (VBE) by choosing Tools⇨Macro⇨Visual Basic Editor.**

   The VBE is opened.

3. **Create a new module by choosing Insert⇨Module.**

4. **Type** Sub MyFirstWhileLoop( ) **and press Enter.**

   Notice that as soon as you commit the line, an End Sub automatically appears. Now, you can enter any code within the Sub and End Sub statements.

5. **Type in the following code in between the Sub and End Sub statements:**

```
Dim x, y
x = 1
y = 20
Do While x < y
      Debug.Print "Loop # " & x & ": " & x, y
      x = x + 1
Loop
```

This example is nothing fancy, but illustrates the point. Inside the Do-While loop, *x* is incremented by one each time the loop runs. When *x* is no longer less than *y*, the loop execution ends.

6. If the Immediate window is not already open, open it by choosing View⇨Immediate Window.

Doing so enables you to see the Debug.Print statements when you run the code procedure.

7. Place your cursor in the code procedure and click the Run button on the toolbar.

Check the Immediate window to see the values of *x* and *y* for each pass through the Do loop. The loop is executed 19 times, and then is halted because *x* has caught up to *y!*

Alternatively, if you want to ensure that the code within the loop is executed at least once, you can substitute in the Do..Loop While construct, as seen in the following code listing.

```
Do
    Debug.Print "Loop # " & x & ": " & x, y
    x = x + 1
Loop While x < y
```

In this particular scenario, it really doesn't matter which Do-While loop you use. In both cases, the code executes the same number of times. However, if you need to ensure at least one execution, and you aren't certain if a condition is going to be tried right off the bat, use the Do..Loop While construct.

Okay, you have a good feeling for Do-While loops. Then why do you need these Do-Until looping constructs and when is Do Until better than a Do While loop? Truly it's a matter of personal preference how you want to write your code. Chances are that either the Do-While or Do-Until loop will make more sense to you, and you'll stick with your preferred construct.

All the code for this chapter that takes place in Excel is included in the Code module of Sample.xls, which is accessible via the VBE. We have preceded all our procedures with a DM so you can tell what we coded and you won't have to worry about any duplicate procedure names.

Do this until you drop loop

Next, consider the Do-Until looping constructs, which come in two flavors just like the Do-While loops. These Do loops execute the code within the loop until the specified condition is true. In real-life terms, think about a pick-up game of basketball. You may have some looping logic in your mind that says that you'll play basketball *until* you are about ready to pass out from exhaustion. When you reach exhaustion, you stop playing. The basic construct of the Do-Until Loop is as follows:

```
Do Until condition is true
    'Do some cool stuff like running a few lines of code
Loop
```

If the condition is true when you enter the loop, the code is never executed. If the condition is not true, the loop begins execution and continues looping as long as the conditions remain false. Once the condition becomes true, the loop is terminated. Generally, you use the Do-Until loop when you anticipate the condition to be false to start with and expect the condition to change while the loop is executing.

As you may have guessed, the other Do-Until loop flavor is as follows:

```
Do
    'Do some cool stuff like running a few lines of code
Loop Until condition is true
```

This Do..Loop Until begins executing as soon as the Do statement is encountered. The condition is not checked until the Loop Until statement, at which point the code continues executing if the condition is not true or terminates if the condition is true. Remember, the Do..Loop Until loop always executes at least one time.

Notice the MyFirstWhileLoop subroutine we looked at in the section "While you're at it, keep looping" (found earlier in the chapter). You can substitute in a Do Until..Loop for the Do While..Loop, as seen in the following code procedure:

```
Sub MyFirstUntilLoop()
    Dim x, y
    x = 1
    y = 20
    Do Until x >= y
        Debug.Print "Loop # " & x & ": " & x, y
        x = x + 1
    Loop
End Sub
```

The first thing you should notice is that you need to rewrite the way you check for the condition. If you had left it as Do-Until x < y, then the loop would never run because *x* starts off less than *y*. As you can see though, the code is still essentially the same. The code can be written as a Do-While or Do-Until loop. All that needs to change is the way you test for your condition.

Stuck in an endless loop? Don't despair, simply press Esc or Ctrl+Break to end the torture.

Exit the Do loops

Breaking out of a Do Loop is as easy as pie. Simply include an Exit Do statement where you want to leave the loop. For example, you may want to exit the loop when a certain condition is true, other than the one that is checked by the Do Loop. Generally, you include an exit clause to handle unexpected circumstances in your code. In the basketball example we mention earlier, perhaps your playing logic would look like the following:

```
Do While I'm having fun
    'Check to see if I'm hurt, although unlikely
    If I get hurt Then Exit Do
Loop
```

Any number of Exit Do statements may be placed anywhere in the Do..Loop as an alternate way to exit a Do Loop. Exit Do is often used after evaluating some condition, as seen in our little code example. Often you see an If..Then statement in which a condition is checked and, if true, the Exit Do statement terminates the current Do loop.

For My Next Trick

Many of you may already be familiar with the For..Next loop. This loop is useful for iterating through a set of code statements a predetermined number of times. The basic syntax can be seen in the following bare-bones example:

```
For x= 1 To 5
    'Do something
Next
```

In this construct, x represents the counter value that keeps track of how many times the code is executed. The counter value *x* migrates from the starting value of 1 to the ending value of 5. When the Next statement is encountered, the counter value is increased by 1.

The loop continues executing as long as the counter value is less than the ending value. Each time the loop is executed, all code between the For and Next statements runs, unless an ending statement is encountered. (We get to exiting loops momentarily.) The simple For..Next construct we just showed you runs exactly 5 times — once for each counter value, which evaluates to 1, 2, 3 , 4, and then, finally, 5.

The counter, start, and end values are all required parts of the For..Next construct and must be a number or a variable storing a number. Rather than hard code in the starting and ending values, you can use variables as seen in this code snippet:

```
For x= StartVal To EndVal
    'Do something
Next
```

Notice that the counter is incremented automatically. You do not need to include code to increment the counter by one.

Sometimes you may include a *Step* keyword to increment the counter by something other than one, such as in the following code listing:

```
For x= 1 To 5 Step 2
    'Do something
Next
```

In this case, the Step keyword causes this loop to only execute 3 times. It executes the first time when the counter value is 1, and then increments the counter by 2 when the Next statement is encountered. The loop executes again for the counter value of 3 and then again for 5.

You may decide to go backwards down the steps. Be careful and hold onto the railing! Your For statement may appear something like the following:

```
For x=100 to 1 Step -5
```

Notice that you do not need to specify a step value in a For..Next statement. If you do not included a Step, a step of 1 is assumed.

We do not recommend changing the value of your counter from within the For..Next loop. Doing so can lead to code errors, such as an endless loop, that are quite difficult to debug.

Consider the following For..Next loop. Do you see how this code listing can lead to problems?

```
For x= 1 To 10
    'Do some neat stuff with VBA code
    x= 3
Next
```

If the problem didn't jump out at you, take a look at what happens to the counter value *x* during the For..Next loop. We intend this loop to run 10 times, because the starting counter value is set to 1 and the ending value is set to 10. When the For..Next loop begins, *x* is equal to 1; however, in the third line, *x* is set to 3. When the Next statement is reached, the loop continues and increments *x* to 4.

But after the loop begins once more at the For statement, we run into the statement that sets *x* equal to 3 again. At this point, VBA gets stuck in an endless loop. Our counter value, *x*, will never reach 10, because we keep setting it to 3 each time the loop is executed. The moral of this story is that you should never, *never* change the value of your counter value within a For..Next loop — doing so just may be a cardinal sin. I'll have to check that out for you. In the meantime, play it safe and vow never to do this!

Get me outta here

Sometimes running through your For..Next loop as many times as you had planned just doesn't make sense. Yes, you can use a trap door to break out of the loop. The statement Exit For terminates the For..Next loop immediately, no matter what counter value you are currently on. In fact, you can have as many Exit For statements as you'd like, and they can be placed anywhere in the loop. Generally, Exit For commands are used after evaluating some expression or condition, such as If Johnny is tired Then Exit For. Here's an example of how you may use an Exit For command:

```
Sub SimpleLoop()
    Dim x, y
    y = 1
    For x = 1 To 10
        y = y * x
        Debug.Print x, y
        If y > 100 Then Exit For
    Next
End Sub
```

This simple procedure sets up two variables *x*, which acts as the counter value of the For..Next loop, and *y*, a variable that we modify. The For..Next loop is originally intended to execute 10 times, as seen by the starting and ending values. The variable *y* is multiplied by the current value of *x* each time the loop is executed. Before the loop ends, check to see if *y* is greater than 100. If it is, the For..Next loop is terminated with the Exit For statement.

Why not try creating this subroutine in VBA? Because we use Word as our platform for VBA testing in Chapter 12, here we use Excel for most of our examples. Keep in mind, however, that the rules and syntax you read about in this chapter also apply to Word, PowerPoint, and Access.

1. **Open Excel if it's not already running.**

2. **Start the Visual Basic Editor by choosing Tools➪Macro➪Visual Basic Editor.**

   The VBE is opened.

3. **Create a new module by choosing Insert➪Module.**

4. **Type** Sub SimpleLoop() **and press Enter.**

   Notice that as soon as you commit the line, an End Sub automatically appears. Now, you can enter any code within the Sub and End Sub statements.

5. **Type in the following simple loop code:**

```
Sub SimpleLoop()
    Dim x, y
    y = 1
    For x = 1 To 10
        y = y * x
        Debug.Print x, y
        If y > 100 Then Exit For
    Next
End Sub
```

6. **Choose View➪Immediate Window.**

   You want to open the Immediate window before you test out this code so that you can see the values being returned to this window.

7. **Run your new subroutine by pressing the Run button on the toolbar.**

   If you aren't comfortable with the toolbar buttons, you can choose Run➪Macro while in the Immediate window and then choose SimpleLoop from the Macros dialog box and press Run.

   Check the output in the Immediate window, which should mirror what is seen in Figure 13-1.

To use the Run button on the toolbar to start your procedure, your cursor needs to be in the code window and inside the subroutine or function that you want to run.

Figure 13-1:
Testing a
Simple
For..Next
Loop.

Kick 'em out of the nest

So far, we've shown you simple For..Next constructs, but they can get as complex as you'd like. On some occasions, you may need to nest your For..Next loops by placing one For..Next loop within another as seen in the following code listing. Be sure that both counters are their own separate values and have their own name.

```
For OuterLoop = 1 To 25
    For MiddleLoop = 1 To 5
        For InnerLoop = 1 To 100
            'Do something interesting with code
        Next InnerLoop
    Next MiddleLoop
Next OuterLoop
```

Did you notice that in this code sample that the Next statements include the counter name? Although this argument is optional, including the counter name with its Next statement makes your code easier to read when you start nested For..Next loops.

Although not required, including the counter in your Next statements can save you debugging pain down the road.

With..End With

We think that you'll agree that this looping construct is one that will grow near and dear to your programming heart. Have you gone through the pain of setting multiple properties for an object? In Chapter 4, we set object properties one at a time, which can become a pain with all the repetitive typing. Why so much typing, you ask? Well, you need to include a full reference to the object for each property you want to modify.

Stop the presses! The With..End With construct is the answer to your prayers and eliminates the pain. This looping construct lets you to run a series of statements without having to specify your object each time.

First, take a look at the basic syntax involved.

```
With object reference
    .property=value
    .method
End With
```

By using the With statement you specify an object (or user-defined type). The great thing about this construct is that you include the object reference once and only once! Within the construct, you can include one or many code statements that begin with the dot syntax (.) and are followed by the property that you want to set or the method you want to execute. For example, one statement may be .ClearContents, if your object is a range of cells. To make your code complete, the End With statement signals that the construct is complete.

Not only does the With..End With construct save you typing, but your code runs faster. Hmm, sounds like having your cake and eating it, too.

Next, look at a more practical example, in which you apply some formatting to a range of cells on a specified worksheet. First you set a reference to the worksheet and set the range as the object reference. Then you can apply bold formatting, increase the font size to 16, set the interior color of the cells to blue, and set the column widths to 20.

```
Sub WithYou()
Dim WK As Worksheet
Set WK = ActiveWorkbook.Worksheets("Produce Sales")
```

(continued)

(continued)

```
With WK.Range("A1:D1")
    .Font.Bold = True
    .Font.Size = 16
    .Interior.Color = RGB(0, 0, 255)
    .ColumnWidth = 20
    'Any other property settings or method execution
End With

End Sub
```

Without the With..End With construct, you have to repeat the object reference for each and every property setting!

You may have noticed that you needed to repeat the .Font for purposes of setting the bolding and the size. Actually, by using nested With statements, you can write this differently, resulting in greater efficiency and less typing. Are you smiling yet? Maybe a sheepish grin?

```
With WK.Range("A1:D1")
    With .Font
        .Bold = True
        .Size = 16
    End With
    .Interior.Color = RGB(0, 0, 255)
    .ColumnWidth = 20
    'Any other property settings or method execution
End With
```

Setting the object reference in a With construct is a one-shot deal. A With statement can only affect one object and once you have entered the territory of a With block, the object specification can't be altered, not even by your neighborhood tailor.

Jumping in and out of With blocks can be hazardous to the health of your application. If somehow you execute statements in a With block without executing either the With or End With statement, unpredictable behavior may result. Proceed with caution if you start using the With..End With unconventionally.

Using is believing, so now give the With..End With a try. For this example, you need access to C:Dummies\Chapter 13\Sample.xls, which can be installed from the disk included with this book. Keep in mind that the disk is write-protected, so you cannot modify files on the disk; you need to copy this workbook locally if you haven't already.

1. **Open Excel if it's not already running.**

2. **Open C:\Dummies\Chapter 13\Sample.xls.**

The file is on the disk included with this book.

3. **Start the VBE by choosing Tools⇨Macro⇨Visual Basic Editor.**

   The VBE is opened.

4. **Create a new module by choosing Insert⇨Module.**

5. **Type** Sub WithYou() **and press Enter.**

6. **Complete the WithYou subroutine by typing the following statements:**

```
Dim WK As Worksheet
Set WK = ActiveWorkbook.Worksheets("Produce Sales")

With WK.Range("A1:D1")
    .Font.Bold = True
    .Font.Size = 16
    .Interior.Color = RGB(0, 0, 255)
    .ColumnWidth = 20
    'Any other property settings or method execution
End With
```

First, we declare an object variable to store a worksheet and then set the variable to the worksheet Produce Sales in the current (or *active*) workbook. At this point we are ready to construct the With..End With statements. The object reference is set to a range of cells ("A1:D1") on the worksheet stored in variable WK.

Notice that after the object reference is set in the With statement, entering code is easy because pressing the dot (.) opens a pick list of valid properties and methods, as seen in Figure 13-2.

7. **Test your code by pressing the Run button while your cursor is in the** WithYou() **subroutine.**

If you switch back to Excel, you can see the effects of running the WithYou() subroutine. Your worksheet should look similar to the one shown in Figure 13-3.

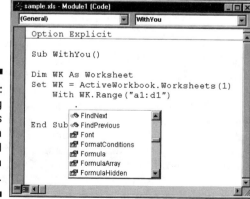

Figure 13-2:
Entering
statements
in a
With..End
With
construct.

Figure 13-3:
A newly
formatted
worksheet
compliments
of our With..
End With
subroutine.

	A	B	C	D
1	Product Name	Quantity Sold	Sales	Cost
2	Longlife Tofu	297	$2,566.00	$2,970.00
3	Manjimup Dried	886	$44,742.60	$46,958.00
4	Rössle Sauerkraut	640	$26,865.60	$29,184.00
5	Tofu	404	$8,630.40	$9,393.00
6	Uncle Bob's	763	$22,464.00	$22,890.00
7				
8				
9				

sample.xls — Produce Sales

Do Something for Each of These Do-Hickeys

We want to tell you about another exciting looping construct. The *For Each..Next construct* enables you to loop through a set of code statements for each element in an array or collection. Take a look at the basic syntax, which closely resembles the For..Next looping construct.

```
For Each element in a group
    'Do some neat stuff on all elements in an array _
    'or a collection
Next
```

The *element* is essentially a variable that is used to iterate through the elements of the *array* or collection, whereas the *group* represents the name of the array or collection. (Collections are discussed in the "Object Gangs" section of Chapter 4.) Seeing For Each..Next loops in action may make it easier to understand.

Unfamiliar with arrays? Simply stated an array is a group of similar data elements that are stored in a single variable. You can think of an array as your front hall closet. Within the closet, you store similar items in a certain order. If you ask your friend to get you an element from your closet, you may say something like, "Can you get me the coat second from the left?" You are indicating a position, or what is referred to as an *index* in array-lingo. All elements of an array are denoted by an index number. For example, you could stuff the days of the week into an array called Days (6), where the elements would be Days(0)=Sunday, Days(1)=Monday, and so forth.

The For..Each loop is entered if there is at least one element in the group. On the first pass through the loop, the statement is run for the first element in the group. When the Next statement is reached, the counter is incremented to the next item in the group. The loop continues execution until no more elements or members are present in the collection or array.

For example, consider an Access application that you have built in which you want to toggle the visibility of all controls on a given form. If you don't know the names of all the controls (which would be tedious anyway), you can use the For Each..Next loop to cycle thorough all controls on a given form as seen in the following example:

```
Sub ToggleControls()
    Dim ctr As Control
    DoCmd.OpenForm "Wine List", acDesign
    For Each ctr In Forms![Wine List].Controls
        ctr.Visible = Not(ctr.Visible)
    Next
    DoCmd.Close acDefault, , acSaveYes

End Sub
```

This simple example opens the form in design mode and then cycles through each control on the form by using the Controls collection. Then it sets the visible property of each control to false (if it's currently visible) or true (if it's currently hidden). After you have looped through all controls on the form, the loop is terminated and code resumes execution after the Next statement.

To avoid any problems after you start using the For Each..Next, you need to have the correct data type for your elements. When using arrays elements, they must be declared as *variants* (Dim element as Variant). For collections, if the elements are not variant variables, they must be either a generic or specific object variable. Remember, when a variable is declared as a variant data type, it can handle any type of data — strings, integers, or whatever you throw its way. For more information on data types, refer to Chapter 11.

Want to give the For Each..Next construct a try? For purposes of this example, you can use any database you'd like. May we suggest the Wine database included on the diskette that you may have already used in Chapter 3. Simply copy the database down to your local drive, if you have not already done so. As a reminder, it's located in C:\Dummies\Chapter 13\ Wine List.mdb.

1. **Open Access if it's not already running.**

2. **Open the Wine List database.**

    The database is in C:\Dummies\Chapter 13.

3. **Create a new module for your code by choosing Insert➪Module.**

    A new module window is opened for you.

4. **Type** Sub ToggleControls() **and press Enter.**

    Notice that the End Sub statement is added for you automatically.

5. Type in the following code listing in between the Sub and End Sub statements.

```
Dim ctr As Control
DoCmd.OpenForm "Wine List", acDesign
For Each ctr In Forms![Wine List].Controls
    ctr.Visible = Not(ctr.Visible)
Next
DoCmd.Close acDefault, , acSaveYes
```

Notice that you need to include brackets around the form name, Wine List, because it has an embedded space. Refer to Chapter 6 to brush up on your VBA syntax, including the use of brackets to handle spaces in object names.

6. Run the code to test it out by choosing <u>R</u>un⇨Go/<u>C</u>ontinue.

Assuming that you have the correct form name, you should see the form opened in design mode briefly while the code is executing. Check out your handiwork by opening the Wine List form. You won't see any controls on the form if the code worked properly.

7. Run the code a second time to make all the controls visible again. Verify that this happens by opening the form again.

As with the regular flavor of the For-Next loops, you can exit a For Each..Next Loop before it is finished by using the Exit For statement. For example, you may want to end execution of the loop if an error occurs, or when a certain condition is true. In the following snippet, we check to see if a certain form is open in Access, which will not mix well with the code we want to run against it, so we exit the loop.

```
Sub TestForBadForm()
Dim frm as Form
For Each frm In Application.Forms
    If frm.Name = "frmWillCauseAppToExplode" Then
        Exit For
    End If
    'Run some code related to this open form in Access
Next
End Sub
```

In Access, the Forms collection contains all the forms that are currently open. If no forms are open, the collection is empty.

While..Wend

Never seen this construct before? Actually, it has been around a long time but isn't used as much as it once was. The While..Wend works similarly to the Do While looping constructs as seen in this syntax example:

```
While condition is true
    'Run some code
Wend
```

When the loop is entered, the condition is checked. If the given condition is true, a series of statements is executed. After the condition is no longer true, the loop is terminated and code execution resumes after the Wend statement. As with the other looping constructs, While..Wend loops can be nested.

You likely will not see many While..Wend loops, because the Do loops are generally preferred. The Do Loops tend to be more flexible and include an easier way to terminate execution.

No specific command exists to terminate a While..Wend loop prematurely, but you can work around this problem. If a particular situation occurs that makes you want to end the loop, simply set the condition to false.

Chapter 14

Subs and Functions and Arguments, Oh My!

. . . .

In This Chapter

▶ Understanding what procedures are and why you should use them

▶ Telling the difference between a sub and a function

▶ Creating your own subroutines and functions

▶ Making your procedures more useful with arguments

. . . .

*I*n chapters prior to this one, we focus on the VBA Immediate window as the primary mechanism for running code. Although this method is fine for testing and understanding purposes, using your applications would certainly be awkward for your users if they could only execute one line of code at a time!

What you need is a convenient way to run a whole bunch of statements at once, thus allowing your users to sit back, watch, and be impressed with your incredible development skills. This chapter introduces subroutines and functions, VBA's storage units for your code. Along the way, we also mention some really cool companions of subroutines and functions: arguments.

A Crate for Your Code

You can think of *subroutines* and *functions* as containers for VBA code. We also talk of *modules* as containers for code, but modules are merely the warehouses, keeping your VBA code safe until you're ready to use it. Inside a module, code is divided into smaller containers called either subroutines or functions. Why two names? We're coming to that. (If the terms are confusing for you, developers sometimes refer to both subroutines and functions as *procedures*.)

Unlike a module, which warehouses the code, procedures enable you to execute several lines of code, one after the other. You can think of them as crates in the warehouse that you can fill with code to make finding and running easier later on. When you're ready to run the code, you tell VBA which crate the code is stored in and VBA retrieves and executes it.

Figure 14-1 shows what this structure may look like using our warehouse metaphor. The big box is the warehouse; inside the warehouse are several crates, each labeled with a different name. When you want to run some code, you tell VBA how to find it by the label on the crate. VBA locates the crate, opens it, and runs the code inside.

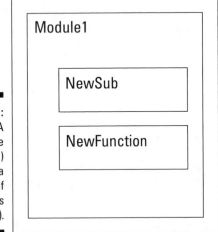

Figure 14-1:
Each VBA
warehouse
(module)
contains a
stack of
crates
(procedures).

Of course you don't actually see crates when you look inside a module, so what do you see? Look at Figure 14-2. It shows a module open in design view. Those thin lines you see stretching across the width of the window are used to separate procedures in the module. Each chunk of code in between is either a function or a subroutine. (You can probably guess which is which if you try.)

Why Use Procedures?

Actually, you have a number of good reasons to use procedures. We've already said that, unless you intend have your users enter VBA code in the Immediate window by hand, you must use them. They are where you put code that you want VBA to run. But other reasons exist, as well.

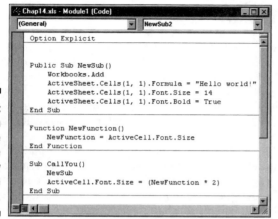

```
Chap14.xls - Module1 (Code)
(General)                          NewSub2

    Option Explicit


    Public Sub NewSub()
        Workbooks.Add
        ActiveSheet.Cells(1, 1).Formula = "Hello world!"
        ActiveSheet.Cells(1, 1).Font.Size = 14
        ActiveSheet.Cells(1, 1).Font.Bold = True
    End Sub

    Function NewFunction()
        NewFunction = ActiveCell.Font.Size
    End Function

    Sub CallYou()
        NewSub
        ActiveCell.Font.Size = (NewFunction * 2)
    End Sub
```

Figure 14-2:
The thin
lines in the
module
window
separate
procedures.

First off, procedures let you divide up code into manageable chunks designed for a specific purpose. Any application is going to have many different things to do. Having a single chunk of code that could adequately cope
with it all would be nearly impossible. By using many different procedures,
you can create specialized pieces of VBA code to accomplish varying tasks,
like looking for important terms in a Word document, or highlighting negative numbers in an Excel worksheet.

Second, procedures allow you to take code that fulfills a very specific need
and alter it so it can cope with a wider variety of circumstances. For instance, suppose you have written (or recorded, for that matter), a chunk of
VBA that looks for the words Declaration of Independence in a document
called History.doc and italicizes them. Although the code may work fine with
History.doc, you would have to make several modifications to it if you
wanted to italicize other words in other documents. Procedures (through
the use of arguments, a subject we discuss shortly) enable you to make the
functionality generic enough to work with any words in any document.

Finally, procedures let you easily share your fine-crafted VBA code with your
friends and colleagues. After all, you're going to create many neat bits of
functionality for your own applications. Sharing your accomplishments with
others is nice. (Plus, it shows off how smart you are!) Procedures enable
you to share by providing the crate with which to ship your code. If your
code was not divided into little crates, but was instead spread out all over
the floor of the warehouse, giving it to others would be much harder.

When to Use a Sub

Because VBA knows you wouldn't want things to be *too* easy to understand, it gives you the option of creating two different types of procedures: subroutines (called *subs* for short) and functions. Why these two? Actually these days, there is no good reason. Many moons ago there used to be a good reason involving different syntax requirements, but that reason is now just another distant memory (meaning we aren't going to discuss it).

However, one significant difference still remains between functions and subs. Functions can return values and subs can't. You can create a function that performs some type of calculation, for instance, and the function gives you the result. (We cover just exactly how this is done shortly.) Though you can do the same types of things in a sub that you can in a function, a sub can never return a result. The difference between the two should become clear as you delve deeper into the chapter.

Creating a Procedure

You can create procedures several different ways. Which one you use is a matter of taste and style. To give you the full menu to choose from, we cover all the different ways to create a procedure in VBA.

Point and click procedures

Until you get experienced with the exact syntax for defining procedures, you may want to ask VBA for a little help. VBA has a special dialog box that you can use to create procedures. The dialog box lets you choose a name for the procedure and select from various options. For a little practice in using the dialog box, follow these steps:

1. **Launch Microsoft Excel.**

2. **Open the sample file for this chapter,** Chap14.xls, **located in the C:\Dummies\Chapter 14 directory.**

3. **Press Alt+F11 to open the Visual Basic Editor.**

   The Project window for Chap14.xls appears, and you may see a module window or two.

4. **Choose Insert⇨Module.**

   VBA inserts a new module into the project.

5. **Choose Insert⇨Procedure.**

   VBA displays the Add Procedure dialog box as shown in Figure 14-3.

6. Type the name NewSub **in the Name box and click OK.**

(Don't worry about the other options. We'll get around to explaining them soon enough.)

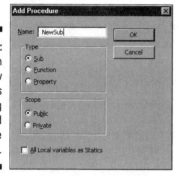

Figure 14-3:
You can create new procedures by using the Add Procedure dialog box.

After you click OK, the dialog box disappears and VBA creates a new procedure for you in the new module. Figure 14-4 shows what this looks like. You can see that it used the name you provided as the name for the procedure.

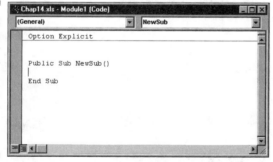

Figure 14-4:
VBA writes the code for you after you make selections in the New Procedure dialog box.

Going it alone

As you get more experienced with VBA, you may find that the New Procedure dialog box actually becomes more of a hindrance than a help. This is especially true if you're in the process of typing code into a module window. Fortunately, you can create a new procedure in another (and we think easier) way. You can type one directly into the module window. To demonstrate, follow these steps to create a new function:

Before following this next series of steps, note that you must perform all the steps preceding this series within the section "Creating a Procedure." Each of the steps in this section builds on the previous set.

1. **Make sure that the new module window (the one containing your NewSub procedure) is active.**

2. **Use the down arrow to position the cursor on the line *after* the words** End Sub.

3. **Type the following text into the module window (but don't press Enter just yet):**

```
function NewFunction as integer
```

The module window looks like the one shown in Figure 14-5.

4. **Press Enter.**

Like magic, VBA creates a new function in the module window based on the information you provided. (VBA even fixes up capitalization.) You should now see the code shown in Figure 14-6.

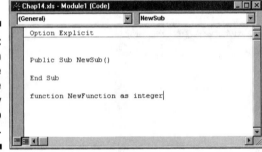

Figure 14-5: You can also create a procedure just by starting to type it.

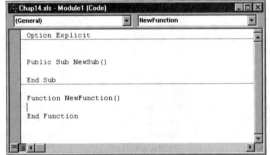

Figure 14-6: When you press Enter, VBA fills in the missing information.

Event-urous procedures

Before we give you the lowdown on procedures and all their options, we're going to look at the final way to create a new procedure. Because this method is easier to demonstrate first and then explain, follow these steps:

Before following this next series of steps, note that you must perform all the steps preceding this series within the section "Creating a Procedure." Each of the steps in this section builds on the previous set.

1. Highlight the ThisWorkbook **entry in the VBE Project window by clicking the phrase with the mouse.**

2. Choose <u>V</u>iew⇨<u>C</u>ode.

VBA opens a module window for the ThisWorkbook object like the one shown in Figure 14-7.

At the top of the window are two drop-down list boxes. The one on the left is called the Object list.

3. Select the Workbook object from the Object list.

VBA immediately adds some code to the module, as shown in Figure 14-8.

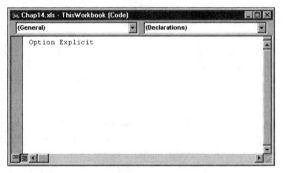

Figure 14-7: Each object in a VBA project can have a code module associated with it.

Figure 14-8: When you select an object from the list, VBA creates a special procedure in the module.

What you see in Figure 14-8 is called an *event procedure*. Event procedures are special subroutines that VBA calls automatically in response to some kind of event. What kind of event, you ask? Well, each object may have many events that correspond to things that happen to the object.

In our example, VBA has added a procedure for the Excel workbook's Open event. You can tell it's the Open event because the word Open is displayed in the right-hand list box. You can also tell from looking at the name of the procedure, Workbook_Open. VBA always, always names event procedures by using the object and event names separated by an underscore. Oh, by the way, event procedures are always subroutines, never functions.

Don't ever rename an event procedure. If you do, you'll break the link between the event and the VBA code that runs when the event occurs. Of course, you can reestablish the link by renaming the procedure back to its original name.

If you quickly want to see what events an object supports, select it from the Object list and then open the other list box. You'll see a list of all the events to which you can attach VBA code. Those events that already have VBA code attached to them are highlighted in bold.

The Anatomy of a Procedure

Now that you've created a few procedures of your own, it's time to step back and discuss the anatomy of procedures. Take out your rubber gloves and scalpel, you're going to dissect a few subroutines and functions to see what makes them work. (You didn't just eat lunch, did you?)

Figure 14-9 shows the first procedure you created by using the New Procedure dialog box, NewSub, laid out on the examination table. Its outer skin has been peeled back and its internal organs have been labeled. The same thing has been done to the function that you created by hand, NewFunction, in Figure 14-10. Each of the organs is explained in detail in our lab report — er, that is, Table 14-1.

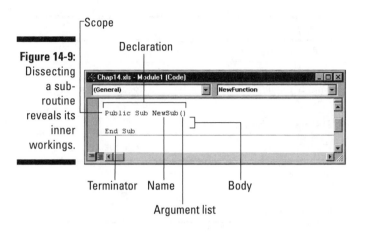

Figure 14-9:
Dissecting
a sub-
routine
reveals its
inner
workings.

Scope
Declaration
Terminator   Name   Body
Argument list

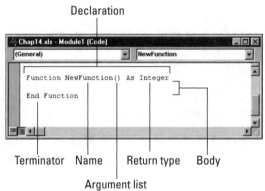

Figure 14-10:
A function
is similar
to a sub-
routine, but
it also
includes a
return type.

Declaration
Terminator   Name   Return type   Body
Argument list

Table 14-1	Each Procedure "Organ" and What It Does
Organ	**Purpose**
Declaration	The entire first line of the procedure is called the Declaration. It defines the procedure's name, scope, arguments, and, for functions, its return type.
Body	The lines between the declaration and the body and the terminator make up the procedure's body. The body is where you put the VBA code statements that you want the procedure to execute.
Terminator	All procedures are terminated by an End statement (either End Sub or End Function). The terminator tells VBA where one procedure stops and another begins.

(continued)

Table 14-1 *(continued)*

Organ	Purpose
Scope	We discuss scope in the body of the chapter. You can specify Public, Private, or nothing. Scope defines what other procedures can see and call the procedure.
Name	The name of the procedure.
Argument list	If a procedure has any arguments, they go inside the parentheses. For argumentless procedures the parentheses are empty.
Return type	This feature only applies to functions. It tells VBA the data type of the function's result.

The Declaration of Subs and Functions

Although not as significant as the document crafted by Thomas Jefferson, the declaration of a sub or function is important to VBA. It is a contract that you must draft between VBA and your code. This declaration defines the procedure to VBA, telling VBA what the procedure should be called, the information it requires to operate, and what type of value it will return. When it comes time to use the function or sub in your code, VBA expects you to abide by the contract. If you don't, VBA informs you of the violation by using an error dialog box.

Among other things, the declaration includes the procedure name. As you can see from the Figures 14-9 and 14-10, the declaration comes right after the Function or Sub keyword. An important consideration when choosing a name is to make sure that it's unique. Choosing a procedure name is kind of like naming your child. If you give your child the same name as someone else's, everyone gets confused. When you go outside and yell, "Kaitlyn! Time for dinner!" you're liable to wind up with a kitchen full of kids. (Kaitlyn is a *very* popular name in our neighborhood.)

The same thing happens when you have two procedures with the same name. If you tell VBA to execute one of them, it gets confused and tells you it doesn't know which procedure you mean. To avoid this problem, make sure that the name you choose is unique.

In actuality, you can have more than one procedure with the same name. To do so, you must create each in a separate module and preface the Sub or Function keyword with the word Private. *Private* tells VBA that only other procedures in the same module can see the procedure. Private is the opposite of Public, which is the default for procedures. _Public_ means that everybody can see the procedure, so in that case, the procedure must have a unique name.

Besides the name, a procedure declaration includes an argument list and, if the procedure is a function, a return type. We discuss arguments a little later in this chapter. The _return type_ tells VBA what data type the function returns. You may already be familiar with VBA data types like String or Integer. If not, we discuss them in Chapter 11. A good idea is to always tell VBA what the return type is. That way, VBA can make sure that you've used the function appropriately elsewhere in your code.

Don't Just Stand There — Do Something!

So far, so good, but as it stands, the sub and function you've created don't do anything useful. In fact, they don't do anything at all. Why not? They don't contain any VBA code, of course! So get ready to fill the crates with some goodies.

We all live in a mellow subroutine

If you've been reading the book up to this point, you know that most of the interaction we've shown with VBA code is via the Immediate window. By using the Immediate window, you can run one line of VBA code at a time. It should therefore come as no shock that you can execute those statements, one after the other, by placing them inside the body of a procedure. In effect, by implanting statements in the body of a procedure, you control what it does. (Note that this practice is completely unrelated to the microchips the government implants in the bodies of its citizens to control their behavior.)

To demonstrate, add some VBA code to the NewSub subroutine by following these steps:

Before following this next series of steps, note that you must perform all the steps preceding this series within the section "Creating a Procedure." Each of the steps in this section builds on the previous set.

1. **Switch back to the VBE and select the module window containing the NewSub procedure.**

2. **Type the following four lines of VBA code (each one on a separate line) in the body of the procedure.**

   That is, type the code _after_ the line containing the words Sub NewSub and _before_ End Sub. Your procedure should now look something like the one shown in Figure 14-11.

Figure 14-11:
Getting a
procedure
to do
something
means
adding
some VBA
code.

```
 Chap14.xls - Module1 [Code]                                    _ □ ×
 (General)                          ▼   NewSub                         ▼
                                                                       ▲

      Public Sub NewSub()
          Workbooks.Add
          ActiveSheet.Cells(1, 1).Formula = "Hello world!"
          ActiveSheet.Cells(1, 1).Font.Size = 14
          ActiveSheet.Cells(1, 1).Font.Bold = True
      End Sub
                                                                       ▼
 ▤▤ ◀                                                              ▶  /
```

```
Workbooks.Add
ActiveSheet.Cells(1, 1).Formula = "Hello world!"
ActiveSheet.Cells(1, 1).Font.Size = 14
ActiveSheet.Cells(1, 1).Font.Bold = True
```

You'll notice from Figure 14-11 that we've indented the VBA code inside the body of the procedure. We think doing so makes the code easier to read. If you indent one line of code in a module (using the Tab key) and press Enter, VBA indents the next line automatically, just beneath the line above it.

This functional family

You make a function work the same way you do a subroutine — by adding code to the body of the procedure. In fact, you can do the same sorts of things in a function as you can in a subroutine. Then why bother with a function? As we said earlier, functions can return values. To return a value you must, at some point in the function, write a statement that sets the name of the function equal to the value you want to return. (We know this sounds weird but bear with us.)

To demonstrate, add some code to the function you created by following the next set of steps.

Before following this next series of steps, note that you must perform all the steps preceding this series within the section "Creating a Procedure." Each of the steps in this section builds on the previous set.

1. **Highlight the code window and place the cursor inside the body of the NewFunction function.**

2. **Type the following line of VBA code:**

```
NewFunction = ActiveCell.Font.Size
```

Figure 14-12:
Returning a
value from
a function
means
setting the
function
name equal
to the value.

Your code module should now look like the one shown in Figure 14-12. Note that, again, we've indented the actual VBA code somewhat.

This piece of code means that wherever VBA sees a reference to the function, it will replace the function with the font size of the active cell. Why? Because you're telling VBA that that's what the function is equal to. Of course, this is a very simple function. As you delve deeper into VBA, its mathematical operators, and its built-in functions, you'll write functions that are more complex.

Making Procedures Go

If these are your first procedures ever, you'll notice that VBA didn't respond by running each statement as you entered it. In fact, VBA won't do anything until you tell it to. So how do you do that? You have several choices.

Your friend the Immediate window

You can call any procedure (a sub or a function) from the Immediate window.

Before following this next series of steps, note that you must perform all the steps preceding this series within the section "Don't Just Stand There — Do Something!" The steps in this section build on that previous set.

1. **Open the Immediate window if it's not already showing by choosing <u>V</u>iew⇨<u>I</u>mmediate Window.**

2. **Type the following line of code into the Immediate window and press Enter:**

```
NewSub
```

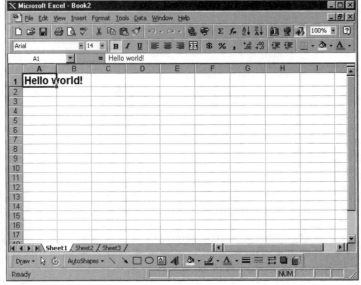

Figure 14-13:
Running the
subroutine
makes all
sorts of
changes
to the
worksheet.

VBA hesitates for a moment and then returns control to the Immediate window.

The hesitation you may have noticed (if your computer isn't the latest and greatest) was caused by VBA running each line of code in the procedure. Switch back to Excel and take a look at the results. We've illustrated them in Figure 14-13. A new workbook is open in Excel with the words Hello World! proudly emblazoned in cell A1.

Functions are treated a little bit differently. Although you can call them like subroutines (just by typing their name in the Immediate window), VBA won't report back on the values they return unless you include the ? character. If you read earlier chapters you know that a question mark in the Immediate window is a shortcut for the Print command, meaning, "Print the results of what I type next."

To run a function, therefore, you need to type the following statement in the Immediate window (go ahead, give it a try):

```
?NewFunction
```

VBA responds by printing the size of the font in the active cell (14 if you didn't select another cell).

Subroutines are macros!

You can also run the procedure through the Excel Macros dialog box. This method is a more common way of launching procedures from the end user's point of view. Follow the steps listed below to run the NewSub procedure from Microsoft Excel.

1. **Press Alt+Tab to switch back to Excel.**

2. **Choose Tools⇨Macro⇨Macros.**

   Excel displays the Macros dialog box as shown in Figure 14-14.

3. **Select the NewSub procedure from the list and click the Run button.**

   Excel runs the NewSub procedure.

Figure 14-14:
The subroutines you create can be called from the Macros dialog box.

As far as Excel, Word, and PowerPoint are concerned, a macro is any VBA subroutine that does not accept any arguments. Functions, even if they don't accept arguments, cannot be called by using the Macros dialog box. If you're wondering why we don't include Access in this statement, take a look at Chapter 10; that chapter explains how Access differs from its Office 97 kin.

I'll call you

Though your users are likely to initiate actions in your application, you may also need to call procedures from other procedures. In VBA, one procedure can call another. The syntax for calling a procedure from inside another is basically the same as it is in the Immediate window. With that in mind, we're going to show you how to create another procedure that calls the two existing ones.

Before following this next series of steps, note that you must perform all the steps preceding this series within the section "Don't Just Stand There — Do Something!" The steps in this section build on those previous sets.

1. **Highlight the code window that contains the two existing procedures.**

2. **Use the down arrow key (or the mouse) to position the cursor at the very bottom of the window, after the last** End Sub **statement.**

3. **Create a new procedure by entering the following line of code:**

```
Sub CallYou
```

VBA adds the parentheses and End Sub statement for you.

4. **Place the cursor inside the body of the new procedure and type the following two lines of VBA code:**

```
NewSub
ActiveCell.Font.Size = (NewFunction * 2)
```

After entering the code, your new function should look like the one shown in Figure 14-15.

Figure 14-15:
This new procedure shows you how to call other procedures from your code.

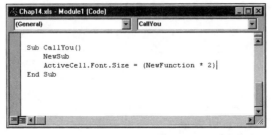

Now, go ahead and run the new procedure by entering CallYou in the Immediate window. When you press Enter, VBA runs the CallYou procedure. The CallYou procedure, in turn, calls the NewSub procedure that creates another new Excel workbook and places text into cell A1 on the first worksheet. After running NewSub, the CallYou procedure changes the font size of the active cell. The size that is used is the result of the NewFunction function multiplied by two. Though this is a simplistic example, we hope you can see how you can start an entire chain of events made up of different procedures simply by calling one function or subroutine.

The return of the event procedure

Earlier in this chapter we discussed event procedures. Although these procedures are created for you by VBA (based on an object and its events), they are still procedures. It should come as no shock that you can call other subs and functions from them.

To demonstrate how to call subs and functions from procedures, we've created a Microsoft Forms button on the sample worksheet for this chapter. Figure 14-16 shows the worksheet with the button smack-dab in the middle of it. The steps listed below show you how to call a procedure when a user clicks the button by adding code to the event procedure for its Click event.

Don't worry about how the button got there. We discuss how to create dialog boxes and other controls by using Microsoft Forms in Chapter 17.

1. **Switch to Microsoft Excel.**

2. **Select the sample workbook that we developed for this chapter,** Chap14.xls **installed from the sample disk.**

3. **Right-click any toolbar to open the toolbar context menu.**

   The toolbar context menu shows all the available toolbars.

Figure 14-16: Adding code to the event procedure for this button is just one more way to call procedures.

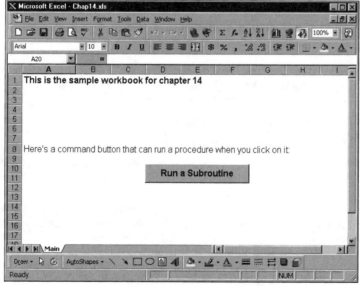

4. Select the Control Toolbox command on the context menu.

Doing so opens the Control Toolbox toolbar that contains tools for creating buttons and other controls.

5. Click the Design Mode button.

The Design Mode button looks like a set of drawing tools and is the first button on the toolbar. When you click the button, VBA lets you edit controls that are already on the worksheet. Note that when you click the button it stays depressed until you click it again.

6. Right-click the command button on the worksheet and select <u>V</u>iew Code from the pop-up menu that appears.

Doing so takes you to the VBE and opens the code module from the worksheet. VBA will also create an event procedure for the button's Click event. Figure 14-17 shows what the empty event procedure looks like.

7. Type the following line of code into the event procedure:

```
NewSub
```

8. Switch back to Excel again.

The command button on the worksheet should still be selected and the Design Mode button on the Control Toolbox toolbar should still be depressed.

9. Click the Design Mode button.

It should pop back out to its normal state.

10. Close the Control Toolbox toolbar by clicking the close button in the upper-right corner or by right-clicking the toolbar and selecting Control Toolbox from the pop-up menu.

You're now ready to test the procedure.

11. Click the command button.

VBA calls the button's event procedure, which in turn calls the NewSub subroutine, which creates a new workbook.

As you start constructing the user interface for your applications, you'll plug in your custom VBA code by using the event procedures of objects like buttons, forms, and text boxes.

Figure 14-17:
When you
select View
Code for an
object, VBA
displays its
event
procedure.

When Arguments Are Useful

Historically, arguments are something people have tended to avoid. (Do you remember the last time you *discussed* whose turn it was to take out the garbage?) In VBA, however, *arguments* are generally good things. That's because they aren't disagreements you have with VBA but, instead, ways to send additional information to procedures you create.

Why would you want to send additional information to a procedure? We mentioned earlier that procedures allow you to take a very specific functionality and generalize it. You do so by using arguments. Consider the subroutine that is created at the beginning of this chapter. It creates a new workbook and sticks some very specific text into it. You can easily modify the procedure to accept the text and font size as arguments, letting you decide what to put on the worksheet at the time the procedure is called.

Start at the top

You create arguments by typing some code into the parentheses at the top of a procedure, otherwise known as its declaration. (You knew those parentheses were there for a reason, didn't you?) The code you type looks almost like a variable declaration (flip back to Chapter 11 if you need more information). In fact, arguments are like variables in that they hold values that you can use inside the procedure. The difference is that you declare them along with the procedure (without using a Dim statement) and the values are set by whatever process calls your procedure.

Arguments must have a unique name inside the procedure (just like variables), and you should define the type of data that they will hold. Procedures can have more than one argument. Each one is separated by a comma inside the parentheses.

Arguing with a subroutine

To show you how to use arguments, complete the following steps to create a generic version of the NewSub subroutine. This version will accept three pieces of information as arguments: the text to enter on the worksheet, the font size for the text, and whether or not the font should be bold.

Before following this next series of steps, note that you must perform all the steps preceding this series within the section "Don't Just Stand There — Do Something!" The steps in this section build on those previous sets.

1. **Switch to the VBE and select a module window.**

2. **Use the down arrow key (or the mouse) to move the cursor to the last, blank line at the bottom of the module (after the last End Sub statement).**

3. **Enter the following code (but don't press Enter just yet):**

   ```
   Sub NewSub2 (
   ```

   Notice the open parentheses. This marks the start of the argument list.

4. **Now, create the first argument by typing the following code. Again, don't press Enter.**

   This argument is used to store the text that the procedure eventually enters on the new worksheet.

   ```
   strText As String,
   ```

5. **Next, create the second argument (that controls the font size) by typing the code shown here:**

   ```
   intSize As Integer,
   ```

6. **Finally, create the third and last argument by typing this code:**

   ```
   fBold As Boolean
   ```

   You are finished defining the argument list.

7. **Type) to finish off the list and press Enter.**

   VBA creates a new procedure, adding the text End Sub two lines below the declaration.

   Now, you need to add the VBA code that the procedure is to run.

8. **Enter the following four lines of code into the body of the procedure (note how the arguments are used):**

```
Workbooks.Add
ActiveSheet.Cells(1, 1).Formula = strText
ActiveSheet.Cells(1, 1).Font.Size = intSize
ActiveSheet.Cells(1, 1).Font.Bold = fBold
```

Now, you should have a new procedure that looks like the one shown in Figure 14-18. Because the argument list makes the procedure declaration rather long, we used a *line continuation character* (the underscore) to break it into two lines.

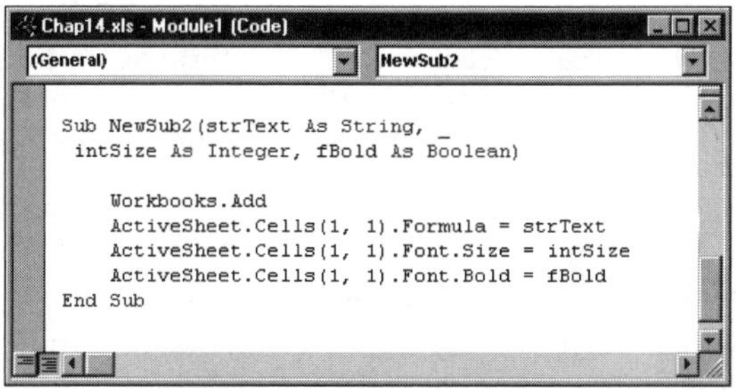

Figure 14-18:
Using this generic procedure, you can control text attributes at runtime.

```
Chap14.xls - Module1 (Code)
(General)                              NewSub2

Sub NewSub2(strText As String, _
  intSize As Integer, fBold As Boolean)

    Workbooks.Add
    ActiveSheet.Cells(1, 1).Formula = strText
    ActiveSheet.Cells(1, 1).Font.Size = intSize
    ActiveSheet.Cells(1, 1).Font.Bold = fBold
End Sub
```

Calling argumentative procedures

After you create a procedure that accepts arguments, you can't call it just by using its name the way you do in earlier examples in this chapter. If you do, VBA growls at you with an error message, Argument is not optional. So, to make VBA happy, you need to pass the information expected by the procedure on the line of code where you call it.

With subroutines, you can pass each piece of information by typing it after the subroutine name, separating each piece of information with a comma. For example, to run the NewSub2 procedure, enter the following line of VBA code in the Immediate window and press Enter:

```
NewSub2 "Cool Stuff!", 18, False
```

If you switch back to Microsoft Excel, you'll see that VBA has created yet another new workbook and placed the text Cool Stuff! in cell A1. VBA has also changed the font size to 18 points but did not make the text bold. All of that information was provided by you when you called the procedure. Try it again with different values by executing this line of code:

```
NewSub2 "Really Cool!", 24, True
```

You should be getting the idea by now. By changing the inputs to the procedure, you change the output as well. Is this cool or what?

Of course, the same rules apply when calling a procedure from VBA code instead of the Immediate window. Follow the procedure with the bits of information required by its arguments.

The data types of the information you pass to the procedure must be compatible with the arguments as they are defined in the procedure. If you try to pass the wrong data type (for example, by trying to pass a text string when the procedure expects a number), VBA complains with an error dialog box.

The last thing we need to mention is that when you call a function that has arguments, you must enclose the argument values in parentheses. Therefore, suppose the function you created earlier in this section accepted a single, numeric argument. (We know it doesn't, but imagine that it does.) You would then call the function from the Immediate window using code like this:

```
?NewFunction(100)
```

In later chapters of the book, we provide lots and lots of examples for creating procedures. Just try to follow the simple guidelines in this chapter and you'll do just fine.

Chapter 15

Using VBA Built-in Functions

In This Chapter

▶ See what functions VBA provides

▶ Try out several useful built-in functions

▶ Use functions to interact with users

*I*f you decided to skip the last few chapters you missed a great deal of fascinating information on how to write your own functions and subroutines using VBA (things like variables and control structures). Not only can you create your own functions, but VBA also offers many built-in functions, as well. To use a carpentry metaphor, VBA provides you with the wood and tools to build your own house, but it offers you some prefabricated components, too. You can mix and match these components with the raw materials to build just the house you want. This chapter introduces several categories of built-in functions and shows you how to use many of them.

We have to assume in this chapter that you have some knowledge about writing VBA code. You need to understand how to write your own procedures, use variables, and create simple control structures. If you bypassed earlier chapters and are uncomfortable with the last sentence, perhaps you should take some time to review the material in Chapters 11 through 14.

Before We Go Any Further

We should state right off that we can't *possibly* cover all the built-in functions that VBA has to offer. VBA simply has way too many. What we attempt to do is introduce you to a few of the most useful — the ones we use most often and think you will, too. But if we don't discuss anything that meets your particular needs, VBA has resources that you can consult: on-line help and the Object Browser. These should be your first lines of attack when trying to find information. For a complete and handy reference you can also check out a copy of *VBA For Dummies Quick Reference*.

Figure 15-1 shows the Object Browser open to VBA's library. (If you're not sure how to use the Object Browser, check out Chapter 5.) Several categories of functions are in the Classes list. We highlight those in Table 15-1 and provided a clue as to the functions that comprise each category.

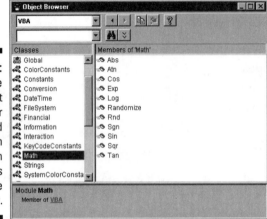

Figure 15-1: Use the Object Browser to find information on built-in functions that we don't cover.

Table 15-1	Categories of VBA Built-in Functions
Category	*Description*
Conversion	Functions for converting between data types (such as to convert a string containing a number to an actual number)
DateTime	Functions that return and manipulate dates and times
FileSystem	Functions that provide information about and that manipulate files
Financial	Functions for computing financial values such as Net Present Value
Information	Functions that provide information about variables and data
Interaction	Functions that let you interact with the user and capture user input
Math	Functions for performing complex mathematical computations such as finding the natural log of a number
Strings	Functions for manipulating text data

You can see why we can't cover everything. This book would be so big it would violate the Consumer Product Safety Commission's limit on book size and weight. So remember, like the title of Chapter 5 says, the Object Browser is your friend. Call on it often when you need to find a function that does what you want.

Keeping the User Involved

Naturally, your users are extremely computer savvy and trust your programs completely. You can create programs that can run unattended for decades with no user input. But other programmers often need to interact directly with the user to gather information and provide feedback. VBA offers these programmers several functions for doing that, as later sections show.

Putting Messages in a Box

The most widely used function is MsgBox. You use MsgBox to display informational (and sometimes annoying) dialog boxes. You supply the text, title, and a few options that control what buttons and icons are displayed. The function then returns a value that tells you what button the user clicked. If all you need to do is display a simple message, you can tell MsgBox to do so with no other options. For instance, the line of code shown below creates a dialog box containing the text Hello there! and an OK button (try running it from the Immediate window if you don't believe us):

```
MsgBox "Hello there!"
```

While this code does work, it's not very exciting. To dress up the dialog box a bit, you can add an icon (like an exclamation point). To do so, pass one of the VBA MsgBox icon constants as the second argument:

```
MsgBox "Hello there!", vbExclamation
```

VBA pops up a list of the constants when you type the comma in the statement above. Your other options are a question mark (vbQuestion), a stop sign (vbCritical), and an information symbol (vbInformation).

Another thing you may want to do is tell VBA what the title of the dialog box should be. To do so, you pass a text string as the third argument. If you don't supply a title, VBA uses the name of the host application, such as Microsoft Excel. Here's an example of a completely customized dialog box:

```
MsgBox "Hello there!", vbExclamation, "My Cool App"
```

Figure 15-2 shows what happens if you run this line of code from the Immediate window while using VBA in Excel. VBA pops up the dialog box on top of Excel. Note the exclamation point icon and the title of the dialog box.

Figure 15-2:
Now you,
too, can
create
annoying
dialog
boxes.

Button it up

That's very nice, but what about the buttons? So far we've only told you how to create an OK button in a dialog box, but you can construct dialog boxes with various combinations of OK, Cancel, Yes, No, Abort, Retry, and Ignore buttons. How? You pass another constant as the second argument, adding it to the icon constant. This formula may sound weird, but it works. Try to run the following line of code from the Immediate window:

```
MsgBox "Format your hard drive?", vbQuestion + vbYesNo
```

Figure 15-3 shows the result. Note that the dialog box has a question mark icon and Yes and No buttons. Again, VBA helps you out by opening a list of constants and leaving it open as you type. If you scroll through the list, you can see vbYesNo and other constants, such as vbOKOnly, vbOKCancel, vbAbortRetryIgnore, vbRetryCancel, and vbYesNoCancel.

Figure 15-3:
You can use
MsgBox to
get user
input, too.

Great, but how do you tell which button the user clicked? The answer lies in the fact that MsgBox is really a function that can return a value. The value it returns is a number that corresponds to the button selected by the user. To see this feature in action, try running this slightly modified line of code from the Immediate window (note that we've added the ? symbol and enclosed the arguments in parentheses):

```
?MsgBox("Format your hard drive?", vbQuestion + vbYesNo)
```

If you run the code several times, you should notice that VBA prints different values, depending on which button you clicked: 6 for Yes and 7 for No. Constants exist for each button that you can use in your code. Normally you check the return value of the function by using an If..Then or a Select Case statement. For instance, the following procedure first displays the question and then another message, depending on the user's selection:

```
Sub MaybeFormat()
    Dim intResponse As Integer

    intResponse = MsgBox("Format your hard drive?", _
     vbQuestion + vbYesNo)

    If intResponse = vbYes Then
        MsgBox " You're drive is toast!", vbExclamation
    Else
        MsgBox "Wimp.", vbInformation
    End If
End Sub
```

The underscore in the previous example is VBA's *line continuation character.* When you can't or don't want to fit a long code statement on a single line, you can include a space and an underscore to continue the statement on the next line.

InputBox — when you need more

Of course, creating a MsgBox only works in certain situations. Sometimes you need to ask the user more than yes/no questions. The function InputBox lets you ask the user for typed information. InputBox is easier to demonstrate than explain, so run this statement from the Immediate window:

```
?InputBox("Enter a value:", "Type It", "Default")
```

Figure 15-4 shows what you'll see when you run the code. It's a dialog box with an area where the user can type something.

When you called InputBox, you passed it three pieces of information. The first thing you told it was what message to display to the user. Usually, you give users some sort of directions concerning what data they should enter.

The next information you pass InputBox is the dialog box title. In our example, we used the string "Type It". Figure 15-4 shows that InputBox used this string as the title. If you don't supply a title (the parameter is optional), VBA just uses the host application's name, for instance, "Microsoft Excel".

Figure 15-4:
You use
InputBox
to create
dialog boxes
like this one.

Finally, the third piece of information you can pass to InputBox is a default value that appears in the edit box. Default values are useful if you can guess what the user will most likely enter. If the user likes the default value, he or she can simply click the OK button to select it. Of course, the user can also overwrite the default value with something else.

InputBox returns a text string. If the user clicks the OK button, InputBox returns whatever is in the edit box on the dialog box. If the user clicks the Cancel button, however, InputBox returns an empty string. (An *empty string* is a string that contains no characters, represented by two double quotes with nothing in between, " ".) You should check the value returned by InputBox to make sure that the user clicked OK before continuing. For example, the following procedure prompts the user to type a value, checks to see if the user did, and issues a warning message if the user didn't.

```
Sub GetAName()
    Dim strName As String

    ' Ask the user for a name
    strName = InputBox("Enter a name below:", _
      "Enter Name", "Type something here")

    ' Check to see if they did
    If strName = "" Then

        ' If not, issue a warning
        MsgBox "Hey! You didn't enter anything."
    Else

        ' If they did, display it
        MsgBox "You entered " & strName & "."
    End If
End Sub
```

InputBox is useful for getting single, typed values from the user. If you need to get more information, InputBox is not so useful. Displaying one dialog box after another can be quite annoying. Instead, you should create a custom dialog box by using the user forms described in Chapter 16.

Number Crunching

What would we do with computers if we didn't have numbers to crunch? VBA includes bushels of functions that operate on numbers. Most, however, are only used in a few circumstances. For instance, VBA includes a whole category of financial functions like IRR, FV, MIRR, NPV, and SLN. (They sound a little like the Muppets' Swedish Chef if you say them real fast.)

These, and the math functions like Sin, Cos, and Tan, fall into the bigger category of, "If you need them, you'll find out how to use them." In other words, we won't bore you with examples of computing the net present value of a series of cash flows for the sake of the one person reading this book who cares (sorry, whoever you are). Furthermore, we don't remember enough about geometry to know what a cosine is (much less what it's used for). Instead, we're going to look at a few commonly used numeric functions.

What's your sign?

No, we're not talking about the zodiac. VBA has two functions for dealing with the sign of a number; that is, whether the number is positive or negative. The Sgn function tells you a number's sign, returning –1 for negative numbers, 1 for positive numbers, and 0 for the number zero. Test this function by running the following code from the Immediate window:

```
?Sgn(-100), Sgn(100), Sgn(0)
```

Sgn is useful in functions where you need to control the sign of numbers inputted by the user. The following code listing shows a very simple subroutine that uses the InputBox function to request a number from the user. If the number is negative (determined by calling Sgn), the procedure displays a warning message.

```
Sub OnlyPositive()
    Dim varResult As Variant

    ' Get a value from the user
    varResult = InputBox("Enter a number:")

    ' Test to see if it's negative
    If Sgn(varResult) = -1 Then

        ' If it is, display a message
        MsgBox "No negative numbers, please."
    End If
End Sub
```

If you do wind up with a negative number, you can always convert it to a positive one by using the Abs function. Abs (for *absolute value*) takes any number and returns it as positive. Run this from the Immediate window:

```
?Abs(-100), Abs(100)
```

VBA prints the same value, 100. With a negative number, VBA computes the absolute value. With a positive number, VBA leaves it positive.

Spin the wheel of VBA

Another commonly used function is Rnd, which returns a random number between 0 and 1. Actually the number isn't really random. VBA produces the same sequence of semi-random numbers each time you use Rnd. Thus, most people use Rnd in conjunction with another VBA function, Randomize. Randomize sets the starting point in the sequence of numbers based on your computer's clock. So, even though the sequence of numbers returned by Rnd isn't really random, they appear to be if you vary the starting point.

To use these functions you should call Randomize before calling Rnd for the first time. After that, don't call it again. To test the Rnd function, open the Immediate window and run the Randomize function simply by typing **Randomize** in the window and pressing Enter. Next, run the following code:

```
?Rnd()
```

VBA should print a number between 0 and 1, such as 0.1858419. Run the function a few more times. VBA prints different numbers.

Most people like to think of random numbers as whole numbers that fall within a certain range. You can use the Rnd function to create these by using a formula that multiplies the result of the function by the total range of possible values. Specifically, the formula looks like this:

```
number = CInt((upper - lower + 1) * Rnd() + lower)
```

In this case, upper is the highest possible value and lower is the lowest possible value. CInt is a function that takes the result (which includes fractional numbers) and converts it to an integer. Therefore, suppose you needed to produce a random number between 5 and 20. You can use a statement like the following:

```
?CInt((20 - 5 + 1) * Rnd() + 5)
```

Or, to simplify things

```
?CInt(16 * Rnd() + 5)
```

Run this line of code from the Immediate window a few times and observe the results. If you run it enough times, you'll eventually see each number from 5 through 20, but no others.

It's a String Thing

You'll need to play with strings (blobs of text) a lot in VBA. In fact, when it comes to string data, you'll slice, dice, chop, graft, mix, and swap letters, words, and entire paragraphs! Fortunately, VBA offers a lovely variety of string functions to help you.

Up and down and up and down and . . .

We're going to start you out with some simple functions. VBA has two functions called UCase and LCase that can take any string and turn it into all uppercase or lowercase letters. Just give 'em a string and they do the work. Run this line of code from the Immediate window:

```
?UCase("Let us pump you up!")
```

VBA prints all the letters in uppercase. (It doesn't do anything to the punctuation, though.) Now try this one:

```
?LCase("On no, I'm SHRINKING!")
```

VBA prints all the letters in lowercase. (What'd you expect, dancing bears?)

Leaner strings in only one line!

Incredibly, VBA has three functions just for trimming spaces from the ends of a string. If you find yourself staring at an overweight string like, " Mmmmm. Spaces! ", you can put it on a crash diet with your choice of LTrim, RTrim, or plain, ol' Trim. The first two functions whack spaces from the left or right sides of a string, respectively. Trim is the heavy hitter of the bunch, chopping the dead wood from both sides *at once*!

Run each of the following lines of code from the Immediate window one at a time. The asterisks on each side of the function show you where the spaces still live. Figure 15-5 shows what the results look like.

```
?"*" & "         Mmmmm. Spaces!        " & "*"
?"*" & LTrim("        Mmmmm. Spaces!        ") & "*"
?"*" & RTrim("        Mmmmm. Spaces!        ") & "*"
?"*" & Trim("        Mmmmm. Spaces!        ") & "*"
```

```
Immediate                                                    ×
?"*" & "         Mmmmm. Spaces!         " & "*"
*       Mmmmm. Spaces!        *

?"*" & LTrim("        Mmmmm. Spaces!        ") & "*"
*Mmmmm. Spaces!        *

?"*" & RTrim("        Mmmmm. Spaces!        ") & "*"
*       Mmmmm. Spaces!*

?"*" & Trim("        Mmmmm. Spaces!        ") & "*"
*Mmmmm. Spaces!*
```

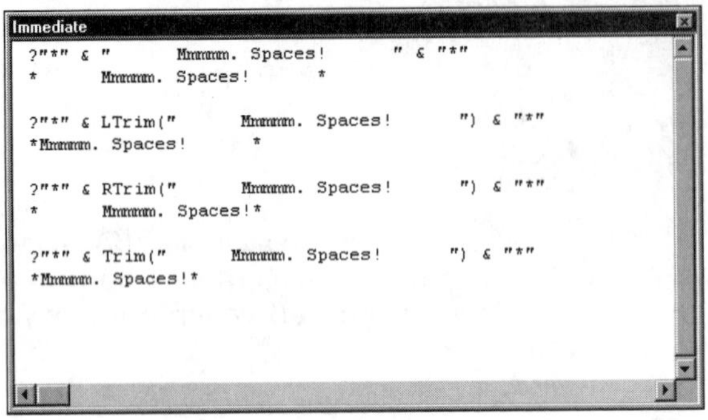

Figure 15-5:
Now you
see spaces,
now you
don't.

Left? Right? Make up your mind!

One of the most common tasks is grabbing the left or right portion of a string. For instance, if you have a part number like "BN1004" you may want to get the two left-hand characters. Use the Left function. Feed it the string and the number of letters you want:

```
?Left("BN1004", 2)
```

Or, maybe you want the four right-hand letters. Try this:

```
?Right("BN1004", 4)
```

Of course, it's not always that simple. Sometimes, the left or right ends won't do and you need letters from the middle of a string. If that's the case, check out the Mid function. Like Left and Right, you feed Mid a string, but you also feed it the letter to start with (by its position in the string) and the number of letters you want. The following line of code extracts the letters "10" from the part number by starting at the third letter in:

```
?Mid("BN1004", 3, 2)
```

Little string, where are you?

Suppose that you want to split a string containing someone's full name into first and last names. But if you don't know in advance what the name is going to be, what are you going to do?

The answer in this case is the VBA InStr function. InStr examines one string while looking for another. If it finds the second string, it tells you where it found the string by returning the position of the first character in the string. As an example, consider the string, "Abraham Lincoln". How might you split this into two parts? You look for the space in between, of course. Try running the following line of code from the Immediate window:

```
?InStr("Abraham Lincoln", " ")
```

VBA returns 8, the position of the space in the former President's name. Given this information, you can break up the string. Don't believe us? The following subroutine uses the InStr function to find the space and then uses Left, Right, and Len to display the first and last names.

```
Sub GetNames()
    Dim strFullName As String
    Dim strFirstName As String
    Dim strLastName As String
    Dim intPosition As Integer

    ' Store the full name
    strFullName = "Abraham Lincoln"

    ' Find the space
    intPosition = InStr(strFullName, " ")

    ' Find and display the first name
    strFirstName = Left(strFullName, intPosition - 1)
    MsgBox strFirstName, vbInformation

    ' Find and display the last name
    strLastName = Mid(strFullName, intPosition + 1)
    MsgBox strLastName, vbInformation
End Sub
```

How to Get a Date

Every book on programming should have a section like this. And, no, it's not what you think. We're talking about calendar dates! Many applications need to manipulate dates. By using VBA you can modify dates in many ways.

Before we get into specific functions, we should tell you that for simple operations, you don't need to call any procedures. Because VBA stores dates and times internally as numbers, you can perform numerical operations on them. For instance, the following line of code, run from the Immediate window, displays the date and time for one week from now:

```
?Now() + 7
```

Here you're adding seven days to the value returned from the Now function. You can probably guess what the function does.

I want it now!

VBA has three functions that give you the current date and time, according to the tiny clock inside your computer. Why three? Because you may want both the date *and* the time, or one or the other. The function that returns both pieces of the puzzle is called Now. We used this function in the preceding example. The other two functions are called, appropriately, Date and Time. Run the following from the Immediate window:

```
?Now(), Date() + Time()
```

VBA should print the identical date and time twice.

Present, past, and future

Though we just said that you don't need to use a function to add or subtract date values, VBA does include two functions for doing just that. These functions are useful when you want to add or subtract a certain number of time units to a date/time value, or when you want to find out by how many units two values differ. The two functions are called DateAdd and DateDiff. DateAdd adds a certain number of units (which you specify) to a date/time value. For instance, suppose that you want to find out what the time will be exactly 45 minutes from now. You can use the following line of code:

```
?DateAdd("n", 45, Time())
```

DateAdd accepts a unit of measurement ("n" in the above example), the number of units, and a date/time value. VBA makes you specify the unit of measurement by using a secret code. Fortunately we've broken the code and listed each unit in Table 15-2.

Table 15-2	Use These Codes with DateAdd and DateDiff
Setting	**Description**
yyyy	Year
q	Quarter

Setting	Description
m	Month
y	Day of year
d	Day
w	Weekday
ww	Week
h	Hour
n	Minute
s	Second

You use this statement to find out the date nine months from now:

```
?DateAdd("m", 9, Date())
```

DateDiff works in basically the opposite direction. You give DateDiff two date/time values and a unit of measurement, and it tells you by how many units the two values differ. For instance, suppose you want to find out how many days you've been alive. You can use a statement like the following (assuming that you were born on February 23, 1969, that is):

```
?DateDiff("d", #2/23/69#, Date())
```

The only thing you need to remember is that the smaller of the two dates and/or times should be listed first if you want a positive result. If you reverse the order, the result will be negative.

Dialing Information

The last category of functions we're going to cover are those that provide you with information that you can use in your programs. We also discuss functions that let you convert between data types — something you'll need to do often.

Name that data!

From time to time especially you will find yourself wondering, "What type of data is that?" especially when using functions like InputBox. Suppose that you asked users to type a number. How do you know if what they typed is really a number? To answer such questions, call on some VBA functions.

To answer the question posed in the preceding paragraph, use the IsNumeric function. IsNumeric takes any expression — a number, string, or whatever — and tells you if the expression is truly a number (or at least can be interpreted as one). IsNumeric returns True if the expression or False if it's not. That makes a perfect candidate for use in an If..Then statement.

The following procedure asks the user to type a number by using the InputBox function. If the user follows directions (like all your users do, right?), the procedure displays the number's square root by using the Sqr function. If the user makes a mistake, the procedure complains. Try running the procedure from the Immediate window.

```
Sub FindSquareRoot()
    Dim strNumber As String

    ' Get a number from the user
    strNumber = InputBox("Enter a number:")

    ' Test to see if it's really a number
    If IsNumeric(strNumber) Then

        ' If it is, display its square root
        MsgBox "The square root of " & strNumber & _
        " is " & Sqr(strNumber)
    Else
        ' If it's not, whine to the user
        MsgBox "Hey! That's not a number!"
    End If
End Sub
```

VBA has several other "Is" functions such as IsArray, IsDate, IsEmpty, and IsNull. You can look them up in online help to see how to use them.

Data type alchemy

After you determine the data type of something, you may decide that you don't like it and want to change it. Centuries ago, so-called *alchemists* devoted countless hours trying in vain to convert lead to gold. Of course, we now know this feat is impossible. Today the closest mankind has come to this goal is to convert personal income into tax dollars. Fortunately, because computers bear little resemblance to reality, you can convert between data types by using a few simple functions. Table 15-3 lists the VBA conversion

functions. Each accepts some kind of expression (text, number, or calculation) and tries to convert it to the data type specified in the table. If the
function can make sense of what you send it, everything works fine. If it
can't, VBA displays an error dialog box.

**Table 15-3   VBA Functions for Converting from One Data Type
to Another**

Function	Data Type It Converts To
CBool	Boolean
CByte	Byte
CCur	Currency
CDate	Date
CDbl	Double
CInt	Integer
CLng	Long
CSng	Single
CVar	Variant
CStr	String

So, you ask, when do you need to use these things? You need to use them
whenever you call a function that demands a certain data type but you don't
have any data of that type lying around. For example, suppose that you want
to find out how many characters are needed to print the number 100. If you
had this information as a string, you could simply call the VBA Len function,
but because all you have is a number, you can't. (Go ahead and run the
statement ?Len(100) from the Immediate window.) The answer is to convert
the number to a string first by using the CStr function. Try running this
statement from the Immediate window:

```
?Len(CStr(100))
```

VBA is much happier now because you explicitly converted the number 100
to the string 100 and VBA returns 3 as the result.

The following subroutine uses the CDate function to convert a string entered
by the user into a date/time value. It also uses several other functions that
we introduced in this chapter. Try running the procedure, DaysAlive, from
the Immediate window. Enter your birth date into the InputBox dialog box,
and the procedure will tell you how many days you've been alive.

```
Sub DaysAlive()
    Dim strBDay As String
    Dim datBDay As Date
    Dim lngDays As Long

    ' Ask the user for their birthdate
    strBDay = InputBox("When were you born:")

    ' Test to see if they entered something
    If strBDay <> "" Then

        ' Check to see if it is a date
        If IsDate(strBDay) Then

            ' Convert string to a date
            datBDay = CDate(strBDay)

            ' Compute the days alive
            lngDays = DateDiff("d", datBDay, Date)

            ' Tell the user the answer
            MsgBox "You've been alive for " & _
              lngDays & " days."
        End If
    End If
End Sub
```

Although this procedure may seem a bit complicated, it is only so because VBA is so particular about data types. When you write your own procedures, you need to be sensitive to data types as well.

Chapter 16
Creating User Forms

• •

In This Chapter

▶ Adding user forms to your projects

▶ Creating controls on your custom forms

▶ Writing code to make your forms work

• •

*E*very once in a while, when you are in an application, you need to pause and say, "Hey, user! I need some information in order to keep going!" Of course, *you* can't really say anything to the user; you need to make your program say it. One way to do so is to create custom dialog boxes — forms that spring to attention and make the user take notice. This chapter discusses the new, shared forms package that's part of Office 97, Microsoft Forms. Microsoft Forms replaces the individual dialog building tools of Word and Excel, and it's even used by PowerPoint. Access, of course, being ever the individualist, has its own forms and doesn't use Microsoft Forms.

To use Microsoft Forms effectively, you need to know three things:

1. How to design a form (called a User Form by the Office documentation).

2. How to display a form and find out whether the user clicked OK or Cancel.

3. How to set and retrieve information on and from the form.

This chapter provides details of all three pieces of the puzzle.

Getting Started with User Forms

In this chapter, we show you how to create and display a simple form that contains just a few controls. To start off, look at how you add a form to an existing project.

The example we use in this chapter is a small Word template for printing addresses. The template is designed to position the address on a page so that it fits nicely in a standard windowed envelope. When you create a new document by using the template, the template displays a form that enables you to enter name and address information. Just like a cooking show on television, we start with a *half-baked* version of the template that contains a place to put the address information but no form or VBA code. You get to add that yourself by following the steps in this chapter.

Before you can start, however, you need to copy the sample template file from the disk that came with this book to your hard drive. Furthermore, because the file is a template, you must copy the file to the Office 97 templates directory. Normally, all Office 97 templates are stored in the C:\Program Files\Microsoft Office\Templates directory. So, before you do anything else, copy the sample file for this chapter, called EnvPrt1.dot, to this directory.

If you installed Office 97 to a directory that differs from the default one, you'll need to figure out where to put the template file.

Adding a user form

Now that you've copied the sample template file to your hard drive (see "Getting Started with User Forms" if you haven't copied the file), you need to open the template in Word and display the Visual Basic Editor.

This chapter builds upon a single example to demonstrate the power of VBA user forms. Each series of steps is dependent upon the series that precedes it. Follow all the steps in this chapter to get a complete picture of user forms, and refer to the section "Getting Started with User Forms" for instructions on how to load and use the sample file for this chapter.

1. **Launch Microsoft Word.**

2. **Choose File⇨Open to open the unfinished version of the template.**

   Word displays the Open dialog box.

3. **Select Document Templates (*.dot) from the Files of Type drop-down list.**

4. **Locate the EnvPrt1.dot file in the templates directory and click OK.**

   Word opens the template file.

5. **Choose Tools⇨Macro⇨Visual Basic Editor (or press Alt+F11) to display the VBE.**

   The VBE appears in the foreground. The Projects window contains several projects, including one for EnvPrt1.dot.

VBA treats user forms like any other project component. You add new ones to a project using menu commands. To add a new user form to the sample project, follow these steps:

1. **In the Projects window, click on the sample project (it's the one labeled UserForms) to make sure that it is the active one.**

2. **Choose the Insert⇨UserForm command.**

   VBA inserts a new user form into the project. Now, your screen ought to look like the one shown in Figure 16-1.

If you look closely at Figure 16-1, you may notice a few things about the VBE that are different from other chapters you may have read so far. First of all, a big, gray blob is in the center of the screen. That, my friend, is a blank user form. Don't worry. You get a chance to put stuff on it soon enough.

The second thing that you may notice is the small window floating above the VBE's upper-left corner. As the window's title implies, this is your toolbox. You use it to select and create different types of controls (text boxes, labels, list boxes, and so on) on the user form.

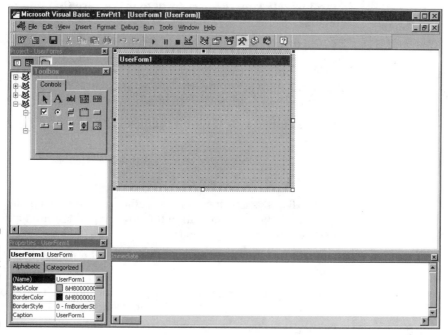

Figure 16-1:
This is what a fresh, new user form looks like.

Lastly, in the lower-left corner you see the VBE Properties window filled with lots of entries. If you've worked through some of the other examples in this book, you may have glanced at it. With code modules, however, it's not very interesting because it only contains a single entry. Because there are so many ways to describe user forms, though, it is sure to contain a great many items whenever you select a user form in the VBE.

Sizing the form

One of the first things that you probably want to do after you create a user form is to make sure that it's the right size. You can use two ways to do this. If your manual dexterity is accurate enough, you can drag the borders of the user form. Try it in the following steps.

This chapter builds upon a single example to demonstrate the power of VBA user forms. Each series of steps is dependent upon the series that precedes it. Follow all the steps in this chapter to get a complete picture of user forms, and refer to the section "Getting Started with User Forms" for instructions on how to load and use the sample file for this chapter.

1. **In the VBE, click on the user form to make sure that it is actually selected.**

   The VBE displays a shaded border around the form to show you that you've selected it. At each corner of the form and at the midpoint of each side, you see small squares. Three of the squares (those on the lower right side) are white, the others are black. You use the white squares to change the size of the form.

2. **Move the mouse over the white square in the lower-right corner of the form.**

   The mouse cursor changes to a diagonal line with arrows at each end.

3. **Click and hold the left mouse button.**

   The VBE displays another shaded rectangle along the inside border of the form. This is your indication that you've just initiated a resize operation.

4. **While still holding the mouse button, drag the mouse a small distance.**

   The inner shaded rectangle moves with your mouse. This shows you how large or small the form will become when you stop sizing it.

5. **Release the mouse button.**

   VBA resizes the form based on the last mouse position.

While this method of resizing a form works quite nicely for large changes, it can often be difficult to make minor changes by using the mouse. In these cases you may want to try the other method for resizing a form — by setting its Height and Width properties directly.

Our sample requires a form of a certain size. Follow these steps to set the size to exact amounts:

1. Select the Properties window in the VBE by clicking on its title bar.

2. Scroll down through the list of properties until you find the Height property.

3. Use the mouse to highlight the current property setting.

You see something like what's shown in Figure 16-2.

Figure 16-2:
You can change property values by highlighting them in the Properties window.

4. Type 160 as the new value and press Enter.

VBA changes the height of the form in the window automatically as soon as you press Enter.

5. Scroll through the list again until you find the Width property (it's near the end of the list).

6. Highlight the current property setting, type in 285 as the new value, and press Enter.

VBA changes the width of the form in the window.

All user form measurements (for both forms and controls) are expressed in pixels. Keep this in mind as you design forms. You don't want to create forms that are too big to display on computers running at 640 x 480 pixel resolution.

Setting form properties

After you have established the size of your form, you can change a few more of its properties that affect its appearance and how you use it in VBA code. First, use the Properties window to find the Name property. Here's a hint: It's actually listed as "(Name)" and appears at the top of the list. Change the name to "frmAddressInfo".

Next, find the Caption property in the Properties window. A form's caption is what shows up in the title bar. When you create a new user form, VBA assigns an arbitrary caption like UserForm1. To help your users understand what the form does, you need to change this caption to something more descriptive, such as Enter Address Information.

Adding Control to Forms

Congratulations! You've just created a new user form! Of course, it's not very functional right now. Your users would probably not find it amusing to be confronted by a completely blank dialog box. To remedy this situation you need to create some controls.

You create controls on user forms by drawing them with the mouse. You use the toolbox, mentioned earlier, to tell VBA what type of control you want to draw by clicking on a control's icon. Table 16-1 lists each type of control you can create by using the toolbox. You've probably used most of the controls in other applications, so we don't spend a lot of time explaining what the controls are. Instead, we focus on using them on your own forms and on programming them using VBA.

Practice makes perfect

If you've never used a drawing program or another form designer, it may take a while for you to become comfortable creating controls. The process can be described as art, as well as science. Like any art, the only way to become proficient is to practice. Try following the next series of steps to create a label and text box on the form.

This chapter builds upon a single example to demonstrate the power of VBA user forms. Each series of steps is dependent upon the series that precedes it. Follow all the steps in this chapter to get a complete picture of user forms, and refer to the section "Getting Started with User Forms" for instructions on how to load and use the sample file for this chapter.

Table 16-1   VBA Includes a Number of Controls in the Toolbox

Icon	Control	What You Use It For
	Selector	You use this tool to select controls already on the form, not to create new controls.
	Label	You use this tool to display labels for other controls and other types of static text.
	Text Box	You use this tool to provide a place for users to type information.
	Combo Box	This tool is kind of like a text box, because users can type in it, but it also includes a list that they can choose from.
	List Box	Hey, it's a list of items. What else can we say?
	Check Box	You use check boxes to represent yes/no options.
	Option Button	You normally use option buttons inside a frame control to give the user a fixed set of options to choose from.
	Toggle Button	Toggle buttons work like option buttons except that they are rectangular and look more like command buttons.
	Frame	You can use frames with option or toggle buttons to create a set of options. You can also use them to group related controls.
	Command Button	You use command buttons to represent actions that the user can take.
	Tab Strip	Tab strips look like the tops of file folders. You can use them like option or toggle buttons to give users a set of options to choose from.
	Multi Page	Sometimes called a tab control, multi-page controls combine a tab strip with an area where you can place other controls. Only one page of a multi-page control is visible at any given time.
	Scroll Bar	You use scroll bars to provide users with a fixed range of numerical values to choose from. Users can click and/or drag a scroll bar to change the value.
	Spin Button	Spin buttons are similar to scroll bars in that they represent a range of numbers. Clicking the buttons changes the value by a positive or negative increment.
	Image	You use image controls to hold pictures or other graphic elements to make your forms prettier.

1. **Click on the user form to select it.**

   You may notice that the toolbox is only visible when a form is active.

2. **Click on the Label control in the toolbox.**

3. **Move the mouse over the user form.**

   The mouse cursor changes to cross-hairs with a big letter *A* hanging off to one side.

4. **Click on one of the grid dots in the upper-left corner and drag the mouse until the bounding rectangle is about 2 dots high by 10 dots wide.**

   As you drag the mouse, VBA draws a rectangle on the form. This rectangle shows you how big the control will be when you stop dragging, as demonstrated in Figure 16-3.

Figure 16-3: Dragging the mouse shows you where the new control will go.

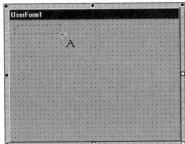

5. **Release the mouse button.**

   VBA creates a new label control with the same dimensions as the shaded rectangle. Figure 16-4 shows what the label looks like. Note that VBA assigns it a default caption of Label1.

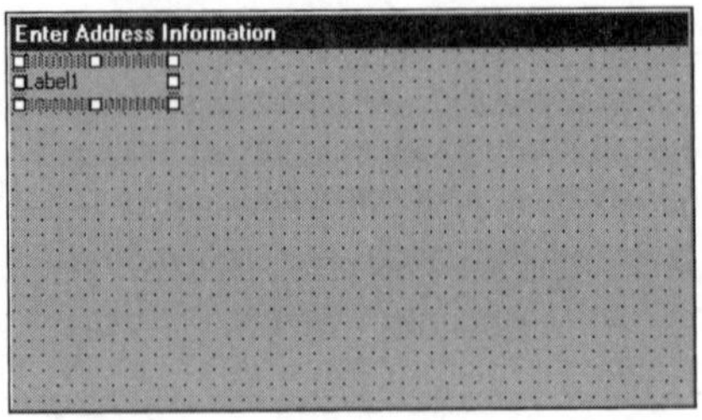

Figure 16-4: VBA creates the new control when you release the mouse button.

If you make a mistake, you can correct both the size and the position of the control. To do either one, you must first make sure that the control is selected. If it is selected, VBA draws a shaded border around the control and you see white boxes (called *sizing handles*) along the edges. If a control is not selected, click on that control with the left mouse button to select it.

This chapter builds upon a single example to demonstrate the power of VBA user forms. Each series of steps is dependent upon the series that precedes it. Follow all the steps in this chapter to get a complete picture of user forms, and refer to the section "Getting Started with User Forms" for instructions on how to load and use the sample file for this chapter.

To change a control's size, do the following:

1. **Make sure the control is selected.**

2. **Move the mouse over one of the white sizing handles.**

   The mouse cursor changes to display opposing arrowheads.

3. **Click the left mouse button and drag the mouse until the gray rectangle shows the desired size.**

   VBA draws the rectangle whenever you move or resize a control.

4. **Release the left mouse button to finish the operation.**

   VBA changes the control's size.

If you make a mistake, you can also undo it. Just choose the Edit⬄Undo command or press Ctrl+Z.

Moving a control is accomplished in a similar manner. Follow the next set of steps to see what we mean.

This chapter builds upon a single example to demonstrate the power of VBA user forms. Each series of steps is dependent upon the series that precede it. Follow all the steps in this chapter to get a complete picture of user forms, and refer to the section "Getting Started with User Forms" for instructions on how to load and use the sample file for this chapter.

1. **Make sure that the control is selected.**

2. **Move the mouse over the control's border *without* touching the white sizing handles.**

   The mouse cursor changes to a four-headed arrow. Figure 16-5 shows what this looks like.

3. **Click the left mouse button and drag the mouse until the gray rectangle shows the desired position.**

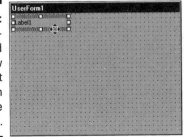

Figure 16-5:
A four-headed arrow means that you can move the control.

4. Release the left mouse button to finish the operation.

VBA moves the control.

Now that you're an expert on creating labels, try to create a text box. We don't give you step-by-step instructions, but the process is essentially the same as it is for labels. (Face it — if we provided step-by-step instructions for every control on the form, this chapter would be the only one in the book!) Look at Figure 16-6, and try to create a text box like the one shown.

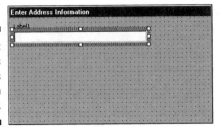

Figure 16-6:
Text boxes and labels go hand in hand.

Setting control properties

After you've drawn a few controls on a form, take the time to set some properties by using the VBE Properties window. Although you can set properties by using VBA code, it makes sense to use the Properties window to set those properties whose values won't change while your program runs.

Because VBA has different kinds of controls, the properties of each control vary. One property that all controls have in common, however, is the Name property. Each control needs to have a unique name because that's how VBA tells controls apart. When you first create a control VBA assigns it an arbitrary name like TextBox1. You may want to change this name to something more meaningful, especially if you're going to refer to the control in VBA code.

This chapter builds upon a single example to demonstrate the power of VBA user forms. Each series of steps is dependent upon the series that precedes it. Follow all the steps in this chapter to get a complete picture of user forms, and refer to the section "Getting Started with User Forms" for instructions on how to load and use the sample file for this chapter.

To change the name of a text box that you just created, do this:

1. **Make sure the text box is selected.**

2. **Select the Properties window by clicking on its title bar.**

3. **Scroll to the top of the list of properties until you see the (Name) entry.**

   VBA always places the Name property at the top of the list.

4. **Highlight the existing text (TextBox1) by using the mouse, type** txtName, **and press Enter.**

   VBA changes the name of the text box to txtName. We use this new name in our example code throughout this chapter to refer to the text box and the data that it contains.

Another common property that some controls share is the *Caption* property. Caption controls the text displayed in a label and on the title bar of a user form. If the dialog box that you can create in the preceding example is going to make sense to the end user, you need to change the label's caption. Follow the next series of steps to see what we mean.

This chapter builds upon a single example to demonstrate the power of VBA user forms. Each series of steps is dependent upon the series that precedes it. Follow all the steps in this chapter to get a complete picture of user forms, and refer to the section "Getting Started with User Forms" for instructions on how to load and use the sample file for this chapter.

1. **With the Properties window still selected, click on the drop-down list just below its title bar.**

   When the list opens you see one entry for each control on the form as well as one for the form itself.

2. **Select the entry for Label1.**

   Notice that VBA selects the label on the form. This is another way to select controls. Cool, isn't it?

3. **Scroll through the list of properties to find the Caption property.**

   The current value should read Label1.

4. **Highlight the current value, type** Name:, **and press Enter.**

   VBA immediately changes the caption of the label on the form.

As you can imagine, controls can have many different properties. We can't go over each and every one of them here. If we did, you'd need a wheelbarrow to carry this book! For most of the properties, you can deduce their purposes from their names. For others, just place the cursor in the property value cell in the Properties window and press F1. VBA opens the help file to show you a description of the property.

To round out the example, you must create a whole bunch more controls. Figure 16-7 shows what the finished form should look like. In addition to several more labels and text boxes the form features a combo box and two command buttons. To create these controls from scratch, draw and position them on the form, as shown in Figure 16-7. Set each control's Name and Caption properties to the values shown in Table 16-2. Table 16-2 also shows the values for some other properties that you need to change as well.

Figure 16-7:
The finished
form
controls a
lot more
controls.

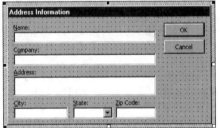

If you don't want to create all these controls from scratch, you can simply open the finished version of the template. It's called EnvPrt2.dot and is also located on the diskette that came with this book.

Making Forms Say "Hi, There!"

After you have a form built, you still need to show it to the user. When the form appears, the user can view the information, make changes, and then tell you that they're finished, by clicking the OK or Cancel button.

Show me the form

VBA user forms have a method called Show that opens the form and waits for the user to take action. You can try this out by running the following line of code from the Immediate window:

```
frmAddressInfo.Show
```

Table 16-2	Controls That Make Up the Sample Address Dialog Box		
Control	*Name*	*Caption*	*Other Properties*
Label	Label1	Name:	
Text Box	txtName		
Label	Label2	Company:	
Text Box	txtCompany		
Label	Label3	Address:	
Text Box	txtAddress		Height = 25.5, MultiLine = True
Label	Label4	City:	
Text Box	txtCity		
Label	Label5	State:	
Combo Box	cboState		
Label	Label6	Zip Code:	
Text Box	txtZipCode		MaxLength = 10
Command Button	cmdOK	OK	Default = True
Command Button	cmdCancel	Cancel	Cancel = True

VBA opens the form on top of the host application, in this case Microsoft Word. While the form is open, try to select the Word document by clicking it. Ha! Fooled you! You can't select the document. In fact, you can't do anything with Word as long as the form is open. That's because user forms always open modally. When a form is *modal*, you must close the form before you can interact with the host application.

Because you haven't added any code to the form's buttons yet, to close the form you must click the close button in the upper-right corner.

So, where do you put the code to open a form? You can put it anywhere you want. For this example, however, you want the code to run whenever a user creates a new document based on the template. Fortunately for you, Word makes this easy, and the next series of steps proves it.

This chapter builds upon a single example to demonstrate the power of VBA user forms. Each series of steps is dependent upon the series that precedes it. Follow all the steps in this chapter to get a complete picture of user forms, and refer to the section "Getting Started with User Forms" for instructions on how to load and use the sample file for this chapter.

1. **In the VBA Projects window, expand the sample project to view the Microsoft Word Objects folder.**

2. **Expand this folder to view the ThisDocument object.**

   ThisDocument is a special type of Word object that represents the document where the VBA code that you type lives.

3. **Select the ThisDocument object in the Properties window and press F7.**

   VBA displays the code window for the ThisDocument object.

4. **From the object list at the top of the code window, select the Document object.**

   VBA creates an empty procedure for the object's New event. This event is triggered when a user creates a new document based on the template and it's exactly where you want to put your code.

5. **In the body of the empty Document_New procedure, enter the following line of code:**

```
frmAddressInfo.Show
```

   The code window now looks like the one in Figure 16-8 (except for the comments, which we added).

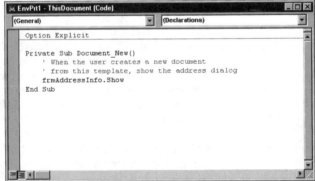

Figure 16-8:
Adding code to the New event runs it when a new document is created.

You can test this code out by creating a new document based on the template. First, however, you need to add some code to the form itself, which we discuss in the following sections.

Adding some intelligence

In the VBA world, you have two ways to deal with a modal user form. You can close it (as we mention in the preceding section) or you can hide it. You close a form by using the Unload procedure with the name of the form. For example, you use code like this to close the address form:

```
Unload frmAddressInfo
```

If you happen to run the code from the form itself you can use a shortcut. The keyword Me always refers to the form that contains the VBA code, so you can rewrite the above statement like this:

```
Unload Me
```

Hiding a form is a bit different. To hide a form, you call that form's Hide method, as in

```
frmAddressInfo.Hide
```

Again, you can use Me to refer to the form that contains the running VBA code, so the following statement is also valid:

```
Me.Hide
```

Now, why may you want to hide a form rather than close it? Well, if you close a form you can't tell what the user has entered! You can tell what a user has entered when you hide a form, however, because the form is still hanging around in memory; it's just invisible.

This chapter builds upon a single example to demonstrate the power of VBA user forms. Each series of steps is dependent upon the series that precedes it. Follow all the steps in this chapter to get a complete picture of user forms, and refer to the section "Getting Started with User Forms" for instructions on how to load and use the sample file for this chapter.

On the address form, you need to add code to the OK and Cancel buttons that hide and/or close the form. Follow these steps to add the code:

1. **Select the address form (frmAddressInfo) in the VBA Projects window and press F7.**

   VBA displays the code window for the form.

2. **From the Object list at the top of the code window, select the cmdCancel entry.**

VBA displays an empty procedure for the Cancel button's Click event. (The name of the Cancel button is cmdCancel, which is why you selected that from the list.)

3. Inside the body of the procedure, enter the following two lines of VBA code:

```
Unload Me
ActiveDocument.Close
```

This is the code that runs if the user presses the Cancel button. The code closes the form and then the active document (the new document created from the template).

4. From the Object list, select the cmdOK entry.

VBA displays an empty procedure for the OK button's Click event.

5. Inside the body of the procedure, enter the following line of VBA code:

```
Me.Hide
```

You want to add more code later, but for now this simply hides the form when the user presses the OK button. Your code window now looks like the one in Figure 16-9.

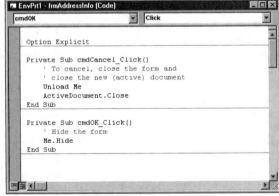

Figure 16-9: VBA runs this code when the buttons are clicked.

```
EnvPrt1 - frmAddressInfo (Code)
cmdOK                              Click

Option Explicit

Private Sub cmdCancel_Click()
    ' To cancel, close the form and
    ' close the new (active) document
    Unload Me
    ActiveDocument.Close
End Sub

Private Sub cmdOK_Click()
    ' Hide the form
    Me.Hide
End Sub
```

Reading and Writing Form Data

The last thing you need to do to complete this chapter's example is to add code that reads data from and writes data to the controls on the form. After you master this, you can use the data to perform a variety of tasks.

Initializing the controls

As it turns out, controls on user forms are just like any other object in VBA. They all have properties and methods that you can use to manipulate them. Most of the controls have some property (or properties) that you can use to set their values. In our address template example, we tell you to set the values of several controls when the form opens.

As the form opens, VBA triggers its Initialize event. This is your opportunity to take action (such as setting the values of a few controls) before the form opens and the user starts to interact with it. In this example, you need to add some values to the State combo box and set some default values for other controls.

This chapter builds upon a single example to demonstrate the power of VBA user forms. Each series of steps is dependent upon the series that precedes it. Follow all the steps in this chapter to get a complete picture of user forms, and refer to the section "Getting Started with User Forms" for instructions on how to load and use the sample file for this chapter.

To initialize the controls on the form as it opens, follow these steps:

1. **Make sure the code window for the address form is still showing.**

   If the code window is not showing, you can display it by following Step 1 from the example in the preceding section.

2. **From the Object list at the top of the code window, select the UserForm entry.**

   This is the entry for the form itself. VBA displays an empty procedure for the form's Click event. We don't care about this event, but you can leave the procedure in the code window.

3. **From the Procedure list at the top of the form, select the Initialize entry.**

   VBA creates another empty procedure, this time for the Initialize event. This empty procedure is where you can write code that runs when the form is first opened.

4. **Inside the body of the procedure, enter the following lines of VBA code:**

```
With cboState
    .AddItem "CA"
    .AddItem "DC"
    .AddItem "HI"
    .AddItem "NY"
```

(continued)

(continued)

```
        .AddItem "VA"
        .AddItem "WA"
End With
```

The With keyword is another neat VBA shortcut. It enables you to work with an object over and over again without having to type it each time. This code is calling the AddItem method of the State combo box. As you can probably guess, AddItem adds new entries to the list. (Note that you can add more states if you want. We just added a few for brevity's sake.)

5. **Now enter the following two lines of VBA code just below those that you just typed:**

```
txtCity.Text = "Richmond"
cboState.Text = "VA"
```

These statements set default values for the City and State controls by setting their Text properties. Your code window should now look like the one shown in Figure 16-10.

Figure 16-10: This code readies the form by populating the combo box and setting control values.

```
EnvPrt1 - frmAddressInfo (Code)                          _ □ ×
cmdOK                    ▼    Click                        ▼

Private Sub UserForm_Initialize()
    ' Load a few states into the combo box
    With cboState
        .AddItem "CA"
        .AddItem "DC"
        .AddItem "HI"
        .AddItem "NY"
        .AddItem "VA"
        .AddItem "WA"
    End With

    ' Set some default avlues
    txtCity.Text = "Richmond"
    cboState.Text = "VA"
End Sub
```

A quick test

At this point, you can test the form to see if the Initialization code is working properly. To test your code, however, you want to create a new document based on the template. To do this, do the following:

This chapter builds upon a single example to demonstrate the power of VBA user forms. Each series of steps is dependent upon the series that precedes it. Follow all the steps in this chapter to get a complete picture of user forms, and refer to the section "Getting Started with User Forms" for instructions on how to load and use the sample file for this chapter.

1. **Choose File⇨Save (or Press Ctrl+S) to save your changes to the template.**

2. **Switch back to Microsoft Word and choose File⇨New to open the New Document dialog box.**

   You see an icon in the list labeled EnvPrt1.dot. This is the template you are working on.

3. **Select the EnvPrt1.dot template and click the OK button.**

   At this point, Word creates a new document based on the template. If everything works properly, VBA opens the address form. Figure 16-11 shows what this looks like.

4. **Click the Cancel button.**

   Both the form and the document disappear. The section "Adding some intelligence," earlier in this chapter, shows the code that does this. (You could have also clicked the OK button, but you haven't added any interesting code to this button's Click event yet.)

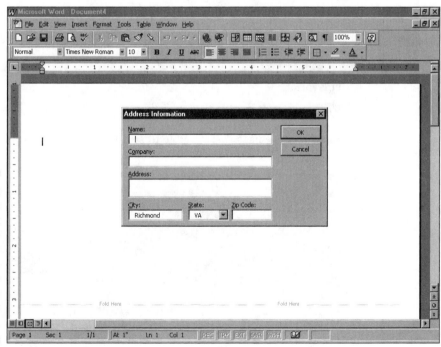

Figure 16-11:
The address form that you see when you create a new document from the template.

Reading data back

Time to add the cool code that actually turns this chapter's example into something useful. (The code in this section also demonstrates how to read the values from controls on the form.) When the user clicks the OK button, VBA takes the data on the form and stuffs it into the text box on the newly created Word document. Of course, this means that you have to add some more code to the OK button's Click event.

This chapter builds upon a single example to demonstrate the power of VBA user forms. Each series of steps is dependent upon the series that precedes it. Follow all the steps in this chapter to get a complete picture of user forms, and refer to the section "Getting Started with User Forms" for instructions on how to load and use the sample file for this chapter.

Follow these steps to add the proper code:

1. **Switch back to the VBA Editor and make sure that the form's code window is showing.**

2. **Scroll through the code window to find the cmdOK_Click procedure.**

   The procedure needs to contain one line of code, which you add in the example in the section "Adding some intelligence."

3. **Just above the existing line of code, enter the following variable declaration:**

```
Dim strText As String
```

   The procedure uses this variable to store the address information prior to plastering it on the document.

4. **Just below the existing code, enter the following:**

```
strText = txtName & vbCrLf
If Len(txtCompany) > 0 Then
    strText = strText & txtCompany & vbCrLf
End If
strText = strText & txtAddress & vbCrLf & _
  txtCity & ", " & cboState.Text & " " & _
  txtZipCode

ActiveDocument.Shapes("txtAddressBox"). _
  TextFrame.TextRange.Text = strText

Unload Me
```

Your code window now looks something like the one shown in Figure 16-12.

Figure 16-12:
This code is
the meat of
the template.

```
EnvPrt1 - frmAddressInfo (Code)
cmdOK                              Click

Private Sub cmdOK_Click()
    Dim strText As String

    ' Hide the form
    Me.Hide

    ' Build up the address information:
    ' First the name
    strText = txtName & vbCrLf
    ' Then the company if it's not blank
    If Len(txtCompany) > 0 Then
        strText = strText & txtCompany & vbCrLf
    End If
    ' Then the address, city, state, and zip code
    strText = strText & txtAddress & vbCrLf & _
        txtCity & ", " & cboState.Text & " " & _
        txtZipCode

    ' Put text in the text box on the document
    ' and format it if necessary
    ActiveDocument.Shapes("txtAddressBox"). _
        TextFrame.TextRange.Text = strText

    ' Unload the form
    Unload Me
End Sub
```

This code does three things. First, it builds up the address information one chunk at a time. You may notice that we refer to controls on the form (for example, strText = txtName & vbCrLf) but we don't include any properties. That's because all controls have a default property that returns or sets the value of the control. Saying txtName is really the same as saying txtName.Text. Default properties let you save a few keystrokes.

The next thing the code does is to stick the address information into the text box on the document. The line of code that begins with ActiveDocument is the one that does it.

Finally, the last line of code closes the form. (Remember it's still open, just hidden.) You always want to close a form whenever you're finished using it.

The Grand Finale

If you have followed all the examples in this chapter, you are now ready to test your Word template. To do so, make sure that you save the changes to the template and then close the file in Word. Next, create a new document based on the template in the example of the section "A quick test" earlier in this chapter. When the new document opens, Word displays the custom form. Enter some address information into the fields on the form, and click the OK button. If everything works as planned, Word takes that information and sticks it in a text box on the document. You see something like what's shown in Figure 16-13. Note that the border of the text box is invisible. We use it only to place the information precisely on the page.

Now that you've worked through a simple example, you have all the knowledge you need to create more complicated dialog boxes. The basics are the same. You add a user form to your project, draw some controls, and add some code. The rest is up to your imagination.

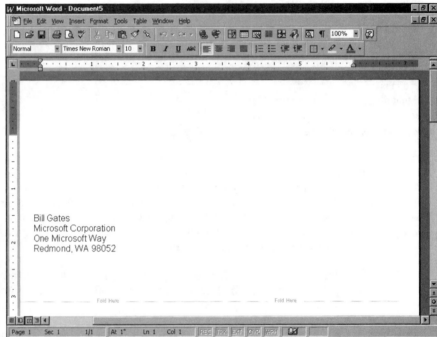

Figure 16-13:
The end result of running the code in the template.

Chapter 17

Planning for Trouble
and Knowing How to Handle It

. . . .

In This Chapter

▶ Avoiding trouble in the first place

▶ Exploring the debugging tools for VBA

▶ Using Breakpoints and Watches

▶ Stepping through your code to stomp out the bugs

▶ Facing differences with Access

▶ Trapping errors before they trap you

▶ Employing error handling in your code

. . . .

*R*arely in life do things go exactly as planned. The same holds true for
your applications. It's very difficult to know from the onset how all the
chips will fall once your end user gets a hold of your application. For that
very reason, you need to plan for the unexpected and take advantage of the
VBA error-handling capabilities. Of course, you won't find a substitute for
rolling out an application that has been thoroughly tested in the confines of
your office. After all, you want to be the one to find the application coding
boo-boos — don't leave that up to your customer.

This chapter starts off with a tour through the debugging tools that are at
your service and ends up with instructions on using error handling in your
applications.

Getting the Bugs Out

You can encounter three different types of errors in your Office 97 applications — syntax, run-time, and logic. You need to be ready to handle all three.
Syntax errors are the easy ones to handle. Your code won't compile if a
syntax error is detected. To weed these out along the way, compile your
code by choosing Compile Project⇨Debug.

Access enjoys a slightly different development environment than the rest of its Office siblings. When compiling code in Access, you have three different menu selections on the Debug menu to choose from: Compile Loaded Modules, Compile All Modules, and Compile And Save Modules. *Loaded modules* refer to the modules that are currently open in design mode.

The other two error types are not so easy to deal with. Run-time errors, as the name implies, don't rear their ugly heads until you are actually running your application, whereas logic errors are slightly more devious. Sometimes you may not even realize you have a logic error because, although an incorrect result is produced, you're not faced with a blatant error message as you are with syntax and run-time errors. By using the debugging tools, you can work to stomp out any run-time errors and test your code to rid it of any lurking logic errors.

Avoiding bugs

No magic formula exists to writing bug-free code, but here are a few helpful hints to keep in mind as you develop your applications.

- ✔ **Use Option Explicit:** Doing so requires you to declare variables before using them.

- ✔ **Use Auto List Members:** Why not let VBA help you select a valid property, method, event, or data type?

- ✔ **Use Auto Quick Info feature:** VBA prompts you with the correct syntax for a given function, walking you through argument by argument, as shown in Figure 17-1.

- ✔ **Declare with care:** Take a few extra moments to make sure that you declare variables as the proper data type and keep the scope as tight as possible. If only one procedure needs a certain variable, you have no reason for that variable to be global!

- ✔ **Reuse code that you know works:** If you've written similar code before that you know works, take advantage of it and drag it into your current work area.

- ✔ **Use Auto Syntax checking:** We realize that at times this feature can be annoying, but it helps nip syntax errors in the bud.

- ✔ **Test, test, and test some more:** Again, bugs that could have been caught with some simple test by the developer are inexcusable.

Figure 17-1:
Auto Quick
Info helps
you write
better code
the first
time
around.

Opening the debugging toolbox

Are you one of those people who writes perfect code that doesn't require any testing and never breaks? If you are, you are probably about one of the two people in the world. If you are with the majority, you need to test your code before moving it into production, and you may have the occasion to debug a particularly nasty mishap in your applications. Whether you use the debugging tools for testing or troubleshooting doesn't really matter — you just need to know this stuff!

Visual Basic Editor debugging tools

A number of debugging tools are available to you, such as the Immediate window, Breakpoints, Locals, and Watch windows, Step statements to walk through your code, and more! In this section, we point out what you have available and give you a little practice using these tools, too!

Immediate window

We can start off easy with something that is likely already familiar to you — the Immediate window. Throughout many of the chapters in this book, we utilize the Immediate window to run code snippets.

The Immediate window can also evaluate expressions, check variable values, set values, and receive messages from your code (by using the Debug.Print statement) while your code is executing. The Immediate window could have been called the CodeRunner, ValueChecker, ValueSetter, MessageGetter window, but that was too much to put in the title bar and would cause havoc with authors and trainers.

To see for yourself what the Immediate window can do, follow these steps:

1. **Open Word if it's not already running and open** C:\Dummies\Chapter 17\Debug.doc.

    Debug.doc can be installed from the disk that came with this book. This document contains some simple code that you can use to test out some of your new tools.

2. **Start the VBE by using the Alt+F11 shortcut keys.**

    The VBE is opened.

3. **Open the Immediate window if it's not visible by using the Ctrl+G shortcut keys.**

4. **Type** powersof2 **and press Enter.**

    The PowersOf2 subroutine runs and then returns a number of statements to the Immediate window, as shown in Figure 17-2.

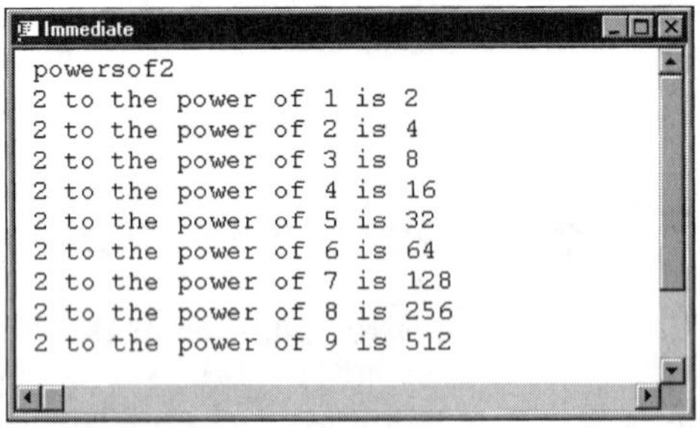

Figure 17-2:
Revisiting
your
friend the
Immediate
window.

```
Immediate
powersof2
2 to the power of 1 is 2
2 to the power of 2 is 4
2 to the power of 3 is 8
2 to the power of 4 is 16
2 to the power of 5 is 32
2 to the power of 6 is 64
2 to the power of 7 is 128
2 to the power of 8 is 256
2 to the power of 9 is 512
```

Breakpoints

Breakpoints are these neat little markers that stop your code dead in its tracks. More technically speaking, a breakpoint is a point in your code at which your function or subroutine pauses execution. Breakpoints are actually the backbone of your debugging efforts. You can think of breakpoints as the lock on the toolbox. Most of the tools are inaccessible if no breakpoints are around.

To set a breakpoint, you place your cursor on the line of code that you want to pause on and choose Debug⇨Toggle Breakpoint. As the command *toggle* implies, you can turn breakpoints on and off with this command. You can opt to have multiple breakpoints within your code as well. To clear all breakpoints in your code, choose Debug⇨Clear All Breakpoints.

Now that you know how to pause your code with a breakpoint, you can dive into the toolbox and check out what's happening in your code. While in break mode you can

- ✔ Use the Immediate window to reset variable values and check values
- ✔ Refer to the Locals window to see the value of all the variables currently in use (you can also make changes to the values)
- ✔ Refer to the Watches window to see the values of specific expressions or variables
- ✔ Use the Add Watch dialog box to set up additional expressions to watch
- ✔ Start single stepping through your code, line by line
- ✔ Set the next line of code to be executed

Using our simple code example in Debug.doc, you can practice setting a breakpoint.

1. **While still in the Visual Basic Editor for the Debug.doc project, locate the Modules folder in the Project window and open the folder.**

   See the section "Immediate window" earlier in this chapter for the steps that take you into the Debug.doc project.

2. **Open the Code module by double-clicking the Code module icon under the Modules folder.**

3. **Place your cursor on the Next statement and choose Debug⇨Toggle Breakpoint.**

   Doing so sets a breakpoint, as seen in Figure 17-3.

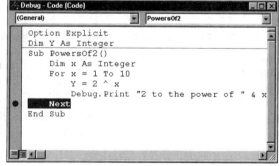

Figure 17-3:
Setting a
breakpoint
in your
code.

```
Debug - Code (Code)
(General)                    PowersOf2
    Option Explicit
    Dim Y As Integer
    Sub PowersOf2()
        Dim x As Integer
        For x = 1 To 10
            Y = 2 ^ x
            Debug.Print "2 to the power of " & x
        Next
    End Sub
```

Variable watch

The Locals and Watches windows provide a neat set of debugging tools for your VBA code. Rather than going back and forth to the Immediate window to check values, you can utilize the Locals and Watches windows to keep a finger on the pulse of the variables in your code procedures. The *Locals window,* when visible, automatically displays the values of all of the declared variables in the current procedure — at no extra charge to your application. You can watch the variables as they are being updated automatically each time you suspend code execution.

In order to take advantage of the Locals window, however, you must have your code in break mode and the window must be visible. If you run your code procedure and do not take any breaks, the variables have no value after the code has completed execution.

For purposes of testing your code, you can even change the value of a variable in the Locals window. To make a change to a value, simply select the existing value and enter a new value.

Take a look at the Locals window in action. Now that we have a breakpoint set in the PowerOf2 subroutine, we can open the Locals window to check the values of x and y when code execution is halted.

1. **Run the PowersOf2 subroutine again by using the Immediate window. (Hint: Type** powersof2 **and press Enter.)**

   This time you only see one statement sent to the Immediate window, because the subroutine has been paused on the Next statement.

2. **Open the Locals window by choosing <u>V</u>iew⇨Loca<u>l</u>s Window, as shown in Figure 17-4.**

   Because code has been halted on the first run through of the For..Next loop, the value of x is still 1, and y is currently 2 ($2^1=2$).

3. **Choose Run⇨Continue to continue execution of the PowersOf2 subroutine.**

4. **Refer back to the Locals window.**

   If the window is hidden, simply reselect <u>V</u>iew⇨Loca<u>l</u>s Window.

   At this point, you are in the second pass through of the For..Next loop, and the values of x and y have been updated accordingly.

The Locals window, as you can see in Figure 17-4, lists the local variables in use, their current values, and their data type. You can also use the Calls Stack button to open the Call Stack dialog box, which lists the procedures that have most recently been called in the current code. But what about

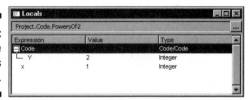

Figure 17-4:
Visiting the
Locals
window.

module level and global variables? Where are they represented? Good question, and you may have already noticed that the first variable in the list can be expanded. This variable displays all module level variables in the current module. The bad news, however, is that global variables are not accessible from the Locals window. You have to rely on checking that in the Immediate window or setting up a Watch variable.

Next on the docket is the Watches window. The Locals window just keeps tab on the values of the variables whereas the *Watches window* can keep an eye out for a particular variables value and take action! You decide which variables you want to keep a *watch* on. To do so, you can add a watch by choosing Debug⇨Add Watch.

By using our same subroutine, you can set a watch to halt execution when a certain condition is true.

1. **Choose Debug⇨Clear All Breakpoints to remove any breakpoints you have set.**

2. **Add a watch expression by choosing Debug⇨Add Watch.**

   The Add Watch dialog box opens.

3. **In the Expression box, type** x=5 **and set the watch type to break when the expression is true, as shown in Figure 17-5.**

   The Watch is created but is out of context before you run the procedure, as shown in Figure 17-6. This is normal operating procedure, so don't be alarmed!

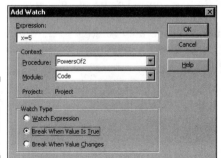

Figure 17-5:
Adding
a Watch
variable.

Figure 17-6: Your Watch variable has been created.

Figure 17-7: Your code is paused when the watch expression is true.

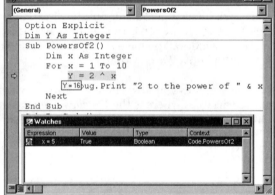

4. **Now, try running the PowersOf2 code either by using the Immediate window as shown in previous examples or by clicking the Run button while the subroutine is selected.**

   The code is halted when the value of the watch expression (x=5) is true, as seen in Figure 17-7.

Part of adding a watch is deciding what action to take when VBA sees the value you are looking for. You may decide to break the code, so you can check other application variables or make modifications to values.

The watch expression can be a variable, a property, a function call, or any other valid Basic expression. Similar to the Locals window, watch expressions are updated each time you enter break mode. You also need to include the context of the watch, which is essentially where you want to watch for the expression. The context includes the procedure name, module name, and VBA project.

Save yourself some typing. You can add watch variables easily by dragging a selected expression from a code window into the Watch window.

Don't overdo it. When setting up a watch expression, limit the guard duty to a specific procedure or module whenever possible. Selecting all procedures or all modules slows down your code execution, because the watch expression is evaluated after each statement is executed.

What you can do with a watch besides tell time? As mentioned earlier, you can determine how VBA responds to your watch expression. Here are your list of options:

- **Watch Expression:** Works like a Locals variable. The expression value is updated when you enter break mode.

- **Break When Value Is True:** Your code halts execution and enters break mode as soon as your watch expression becomes true.

- **Break When Value Changes:** Your code halts execution and enters break mode as soon as your choose expression value changes.

Don't want to be bothered with setting up watches ahead of time? You can use the *Quick Watch* to check the current value of a variable, property, or other expression on the fly, or rather at the last minute because you didn't have a watch already set up. To check a variable's value using quick watch, simply select the expression from either the code window or the Immediate window and then press Shift+F9 or choose Debug⇨Quick Watch.

VBA has another cool feature built-in called *Data Tips.* When your code is in break mode, you can hover your mouse over an expression or variable, and a data tip pops up with the current value. Take another look at Figure 17-7 and you'll see the data tip for the variable *Y*.

Do you know where your code has been?

The *Calls Stack* is your ticket to finding out what procedures have been called prior to a break in code execution. This feature can be useful when you have procedures calling multiple other procedures. In the case of an error, the call stack can help you trace back your steps and try to figure out where the error occurred. For example, in the code module in the sample Debug.DOC, you have a simple subroutine that runs your PowersOf2 subroutine. If you pause code execution while in the PowerOf2 subroutine and look at the call stack, you can see that RunCode called PowersOf2, as shown in Figure 17-8.

Ready, set, stop, continue

Breakpoints, in conjunction with the Step statements (which we are about to explore), are extremely useful for working out the kinks in your code. After you enter into break mode, you may need to terminate execution completely or continue running the code procedure. The *Continue* button and menu

Figure 17-8:
Trace your
procedure
calls with
the Call
Stack.

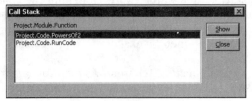

command (Run⇨Continue) restarts your code from the current point of execution until the procedure is either finished or another breakpoint is encountered.

Another important command is *Reset,* which resets all the variables used in the current code procedure. This command is useful for starting back at square one with your code procedure! To reset your code that is currently in break mode, choose Run⇨Reset.

Stepping through code

After you enter into break mode, you can work on debugging and/or testing your code by using the step statements. By stepping through your code, you can pinpoint what statement is causing your code to fail.

Generally, when debugging or testing your code, you want to single through your code for which VBA has the *Step Into* command. After you are in break mode, choose Debug⇨Step Into to execute the next line of code. You can continue single stepping throughout the rest of your code procedure if desired.

Save yourself some time by using the shortcut for single stepping — F8.

Sometimes you may call another procedure that you know already works without a problem. In walks the *Step Over* command that executes the called procedure as a unit and then leaves you waiting at the next statement in the current procedure. To Step Over a procedure, choose Debug⇨Step Over. If you accidentally single step into a called procedure, don't worry — VBA has another step command just for you.

The *Step Out* command executes the remaining code in the current called procedure. For example, if you are stepping through the following code where Foo1 calls Foo2, you can use Step Out to continue executing Foo2 and then pause upon re-entering Foo1.

```
Sub Foo1
    'Run some code here
    Foo2
    'Run some other things
End Sub

Sub Foo2
    'This is called from Foo1
    'Run some other code
End Sub
```

In addition to the stepping statements, some additional commands can affect where and how you continue running your code.

✔ **Run To Cursor:** While in break mode, you can place your cursor on a given line of code and command VBA to chase down your cursor with the Debug➪Run To Cursor command. Along the way, VBA runs all the code between the last run line of code and the line identified at the finish line. This feature enables you to avoid stepping through large loops and pick up single stepping later on in the procedure.

✔ **Set Next Statement:** By using the Set Next statement you can control where your code continues executing. This feature can be useful if you want to skip execution of some code statements.

✔ **Show Next Statement:** This feature simply identifies the next statement to be executed. If you have been looking around your code while in break mode, this command can be useful to return the cursor to the line that will execute next.

Access 97 debugging tools

For the most part, Access shares the same debugging tools as found in the VBE. The main difference is that the Locals, Watches, and Immediate windows are packaged up into one all-inclusive window called the Debug window, as seen in Figure 17-9.

Error Handling Unleashed

In this section we look at the basic constructs used in error handling and how to trap those little nasty problems when they occur. Think of error handling in code like wearing your seat belt in a car or a safety helmet while riding your mountain bike. You hope never to need these safety precautions, but they can save your life (and in the case of code, your reputation as a developer) in the case of a mishap.

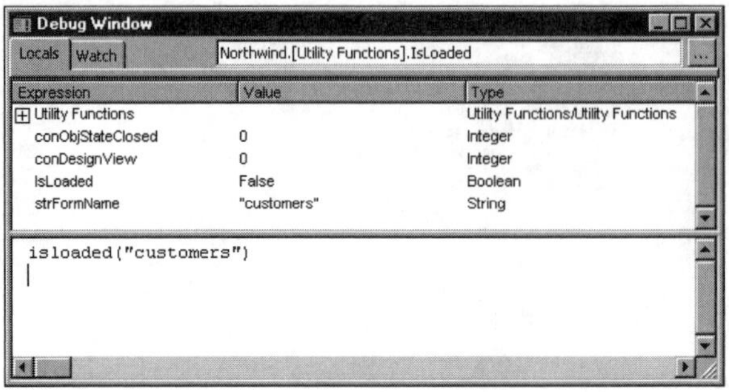

Figure 17-9:
The Access
all-inclusive
Debug
window.

To start with, consider this simple subroutine that carries out some calculations:

```
Sub CalcForMe(Y as Integer)
    Dim x as Integer
    X=10
    Debug.Print x/y
End Sub
```

Try running the CalcForMe code by following these steps:

1. **Open Word if it's not already running.**

2. **Start the VBE by using the Alt+F11 shortcut keys.**

   The VBE is opened.

3. **Create a new module by choosing Insert⇨Module.**

4. **Type** Sub CalcForMe (Y as Integer).

5. **Complete the subroutine by entering the remaining lines of code as shown:**

   ```
   Dim x as Integer
   X=10
   Debug.Print x/y
   ```

6. **Open the Immediate window if it's not already visible by choosing View⇨Immediate Window.**

   From the Immediate window, you can run the code with different values of *Y*.

7. **In the Immediate window, type in** CalcForMe(5) **and press Enter.**

   Doing so returns a result of 2. So everything seems to be working fine, right? If you said "yes," reserve judgment for a moment.

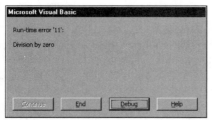

Figure 17-10:
An
unfriendly
run-time
error
message.

8. Try this step again by typing `CalcForMe(0)` **and press Enter.**

This time trouble arises and you are faced with a run-time error for attempting to divide by zero.

When you carry out the division of *x/y,* if *Y* is zero you receive a divide by zero error, as seen in Figure 17-10. VBA does alert you to the problem, but for an end user, this is an admittedly unfriendly, and maybe even scary, message. Not only that, but what is a user to do when faced with this dialog box — Debug? End? How on earth would your user know what to do from here?

As the developer, your job is to shield your end user from such messages. You can anticipate that this error may occur if y=0, and you can handle this problem in a number of ways. You can explicitly check the value of *Y* and exit the routine if Y=0. That will work for you and avoid the error message, but informing the user as to what's happening would be a nice touch. Consider this code as an alternative in which you check for the divide by zero error and provide a nicer message with the following code:

```
Sub CalcForMe(Y as Integer)
    On Error GoTo Err_CalcForMe
    Dim x as integer
    X=10
    Debug.Print x/y
    Exit Sub
Err_CalcForMe:
    If Err.Number = 11 Then
        Y = InputBox("Please enter a number other
    than zero", "Value of Y")
        Resume
    End If
End Sub
```

Yes, we just threw a bunch of new stuff at you. Now, we'll dissect some of these new items and talk about how to add error handling to your procedures.

On error do this

One of the basic error-handling statements is the On Error, which comes in three varieties for your coding pleasure:

- ✔ On Error GoTo *line label*
- ✔ On Error Resume Next
- ✔ On Error GoTo 0

In the previous code procedure, CalcForMe, we used the On Error GoTo *line label* to handle any possible errors. You may find the On Error GoTo *line label* quite odd — after all this is not a language that uses line numbers or labels. *Line labels* assist you in moving to a specific location within your code. For example, when a code procedure includes an On Error GoTo *line label* command and an error is encountered, code execution continues at the specified line label. Keep in mind, however, that the specified line must be in the same subroutine or function as the On Error statement.

Next on the line up is the On Error Resume Next, which we refer to as poor man's error handling. If you start off your procedure with an On Error Resume Next, you are telling your code that if a run-time error occurs, simply skip ahead to the next statement and ignore the error. This statement can certainly be useful at times, and it take a lot less effort than the full-blown error handling we are suggesting, but it's not 100 percent bulletproof. For example, consider this simple code snippet:

```
Sub KeepErrorsAway()
    On Error Resume Next
    'Code here
End Sub
```

If an error is encountered, the code continues to roll forward, but no corrective actions are taken and no notification of an error is given.

Finally, you have the On Error GoTo 0 statement, which actually turns off the error handling running in the current procedure. In general, this On Error variety is used by the developer while debugging code.

If you don't use an On Error statement, any run-time error that occurs is fatal. Your end user sees a not-so-friendly error message and the code stops executing.

If you opt for the On Error GoTo *line label* route, you need to know how to create one of these. Actually, doing so is quite straightforward. Simply type in the line label and end it with a colon, such as `MyLineLabel:`.

Resume code execution

Now that you know how to trap the error with the On Error statements, what happens next? You should be aware of different flavors of the Resume statement:

- ✔ Resume
- ✔ Resume Next
- ✔ Resume *line label*

The *Resume* statement restarts code execution on the line that encountered the error. Generally, you would use the Resume statement when you make provisions for fixing the error through code. You may even ask the user to make a correction, such as re-inputting a value and trying to re-execute the code. *Resume Next,* as we've already covered, continues code execution on the line following the error. The Resume Next command may stand by itself or be part of the On Error statement as we showed you earlier — On Error Resume Next. Finally, the *Resume line label* statement resumes code execution at the specified line label.

Elvis has left the building

What's wrong with the following code?

```
Sub NoProblemsHere()
    On Error GoTo Err_NoProblemsHere
    Msgbox " This code works just fine!"
Err_NoProblemsHere:
    Msgbox "Problem encountered with this code"
End Sub
```

We did a nice job including error handling, except for one large omission. Even if no errors are encountered, the second message box statement is still executed. You need to include an exit routine in your procedures with error handling. If you have no errors, then you don't want your error handing code to run, right? To exit your procedure, simply place an Exit Sub or Exit Function statement before the error-handling section. In the preceding example, you can fix this subroutine by including an Exit Sub command before the Err_NoProblemsHere line label.

Doing it up right with error handling

Now that we've introduced the components, take a look at the basic structure that your error-handing routine should resemble:

```
Sub HandleErrors()
    On Error GoTo Err_HandleErrors
    'Code here

    'If no error, be sure to exit before error handling
    Exit Sub

Err_HandleErrors:
    'Code to handle the error, notify user, etc.
    Resume Next
End Sub
```

To prevent error-handling code from running when no error has occurred, don't forget to place an Exit Sub or Exit Function directly before the error-handling code.

In the error-handling portion of your procedure, you may handle the error and resume execution at the same point, continue execution at the next line, or end the procedure altogether. Your actions are guided by the purpose of your code procedure.

Try out your new error-handling skills by wrapping the following subroutine with error handling:

```
Sub CanYouBreakMe()
    Dim BirthDay As Date, Y As Integer
    BirthDay = InputBox("Enter your b-day")
    Y = DateDiff("d", BirthDay, Date)
    MsgBox "You are " & Y & " days old"
End Sub
```

First of all, can you break this code? If you enter a string value into the input box you get a run-time error, which is something you want to avoid. To see what we mean, try the following:

1. Open Word if it's not already running.

2. Start the VBE by using the ALT+F11 shortcut keys.

The VBE is opened.

3. **Create a new module for your code by choosing Insert⇨Module.**

   (If you want, you can skip this step and add this subroutine to an existing module.)

4. **Type** `Sub CanYouBreakMe ().`

5. **Complete the subroutine by entering the remaining lines of code:**

```
Dim BirthDay As Date, Y As Integer
BirthDay = InputBox("Enter your b-day")
Y = DateDiff("d", BirthDay, Date)
MsgBox "You are " & Y & " days old"
```

   Now, the real work begins. You need to add error handling to this subroutine.

6. **Add the following line right after the** Sub CanYouBreakMe() **statement:**

```
On Error Goto Err_CanYouBreakMe
```

   If you're going to have the code go to a line label, you had better make sure that the line exists.

7. **Create the line label** `Err_CanYouBreakMe` **right before the End Sub statement.**

   If you don't remember how, type the following:

```
Err_CanYouBreakMe:
```

   Now, you need to handle the error.

8. **Type the following to trap for the case when the user enters a string value which causes a type mismatch error. (Hint: It's error number 13.)**

```
If Err.Number = 13 Then
    Msgbox "Please enter a valid date"
    Resume
Else
    Exit Sub
EndIf
```

   If the error is due to a type mismatch, you inform the user that they need to enter a valid date and then present the input box again. If the error is something else, you gracefully leave the function by using the Exit Sub.

9. **Add an** `Exit Sub` **command directly before the error handler takes over.**

   If the error never occurs, you want to leave the subroutine.

Your revised subroutine should look something like this:

```
Sub CanYouBreakMe()
    On Error Goto Err_CanYouBreakMe
    Dim BirthDay As Date, Y As Integer
    BirthDay = InputBox("Enter your b-day")
    Y = DateDiff("d", BirthDay, Date)
    MsgBox "You are " & Y & " days old"
    Exit Sub
Err_CanYouBreakMe:
    If Err.Number = 13 Then
        Msgbox "Please enter a valid date"
        Resume
    Else
        Exit Sub
    EndIf
End Sub
```

As the developer, you need information about an error when it occurs, such as its error number and description. When an error occurs in VBA, information about the particular error is stored in the Err object.

In the CanYouBreakMe subroutine, you specifically checked for the error number by using the number property of the Err object — Err.Number. Knowing the specific type of error can assist you in planning your next set of actions. Additionally, you can check the error description by using Err.Description.

The property values stored in the Err object only reflect the most recent error.

Part IV

Doing Cool Stuff with VBA and Office

The 5th Wave — By Rich Tennant

"THIS IS YOUR GROUPWARE?! THIS IS WHAT YOU'RE RUNNING?! WELL HECK — I THINK THIS COULD BE YOUR PROBLEM!"

In this part . . .

Ready for some fun? It's time to put the basics that appear in all the other parts to use in some real-world examples. We dive into Excel, Word, PowerPoint, and Access to discover neat developments — such as using VBA to make coffee or water the plants.

No, actually we stick to real deliverables — charting in Excel, augmenting mail merge in Word, presenting cool slide shows in PowerPoint, and automating report generation in Access.

Pull out your party shoes — it's time to rock 'n roll!

Chapter 18

Programming Excel Pivot Tables

● ●

In This Chapter

▶ Discovering the power of Excel pivot tables

▶ Finding out how pivot tables are put together

▶ Writing VBA code to create custom queries based on pivot tables

● ●

*W*hen it comes to creating applications using Microsoft Excel, it's hard to beat the power of an Excel pivot table. *Pivot tables* are first-class data analysis tools that let you slice, dice, mince, and chop large amounts of data into digestible bits of information. Unfortunately, not everyone is comfortable using pivot tables in their raw form. Therefore, in this chapter we show you how to write VBA code to control pivot tables, giving you the opportunity to attach any pretty user interface to them that you want.

The Nature of the Beast

Before you can start to program pivot tables, you need to understand them and how they are constructed. Pivot tables are extremely complex animals. In fact, VBA devotes no fewer than 10 object types comprising hundreds of properties and methods to represent pivot tables. (Chapter 4 has more information about object types in general.)

Why pivot?

Pivot tables take large amounts of raw data and perform numerous cross-tabulations of the data based on values in various fields. Figure 18-1 shows an example of a data table based in Microsoft Excel. The data table is part of the sample file for this chapter, Chap18.xls, which you can install from the disk that came with this book. We queried nearly all the tables in the Access Northwind Traders sample database to create the data in this sample file. The data in the sample file contain information on sales, along with the associated product category, customer country, employee, supplier, and order date.

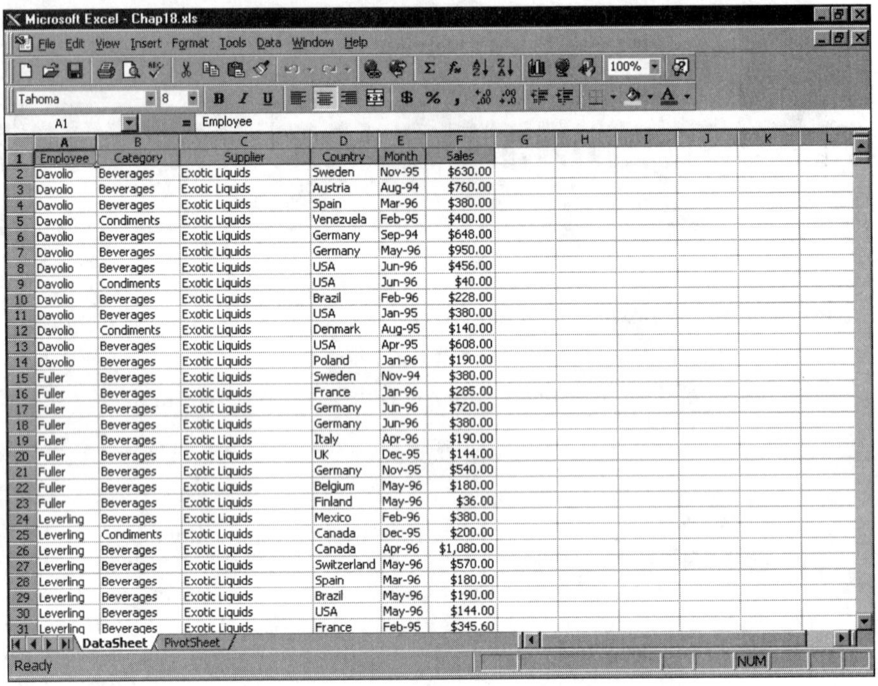

	Employee	Category	Supplier	Country	Month	Sales
2	Davolio	Beverages	Exotic Liquids	Sweden	Nov-95	$630.00
3	Davolio	Beverages	Exotic Liquids	Austria	Aug-94	$760.00
4	Davolio	Beverages	Exotic Liquids	Spain	Mar-96	$380.00
5	Davolio	Condiments	Exotic Liquids	Venezuela	Feb-95	$400.00
6	Davolio	Beverages	Exotic Liquids	Germany	Sep-94	$648.00
7	Davolio	Beverages	Exotic Liquids	Germany	May-96	$950.00
8	Davolio	Beverages	Exotic Liquids	USA	Jun-96	$456.00
9	Davolio	Condiments	Exotic Liquids	USA	Jun-96	$40.00
10	Davolio	Beverages	Exotic Liquids	Brazil	Feb-96	$228.00
11	Davolio	Beverages	Exotic Liquids	USA	Jan-95	$380.00
12	Davolio	Condiments	Exotic Liquids	Denmark	Aug-95	$140.00
13	Davolio	Beverages	Exotic Liquids	USA	Apr-95	$608.00
14	Davolio	Beverages	Exotic Liquids	Poland	Jan-96	$190.00
15	Fuller	Beverages	Exotic Liquids	Sweden	Nov-94	$380.00
16	Fuller	Beverages	Exotic Liquids	France	Jan-96	$285.00
17	Fuller	Beverages	Exotic Liquids	Germany	Jun-96	$720.00
18	Fuller	Beverages	Exotic Liquids	Germany	Jun-96	$380.00
19	Fuller	Beverages	Exotic Liquids	Italy	Apr-96	$190.00
20	Fuller	Beverages	Exotic Liquids	UK	Dec-95	$144.00
21	Fuller	Beverages	Exotic Liquids	Germany	Nov-95	$540.00
22	Fuller	Beverages	Exotic Liquids	Belgium	May-96	$180.00
23	Fuller	Beverages	Exotic Liquids	Finland	May-96	$36.00
24	Leverling	Beverages	Exotic Liquids	Mexico	Feb-96	$380.00
25	Leverling	Condiments	Exotic Liquids	Canada	Dec-95	$200.00
26	Leverling	Beverages	Exotic Liquids	Canada	Apr-96	$1,080.00
27	Leverling	Beverages	Exotic Liquids	Switzerland	May-96	$570.00
28	Leverling	Beverages	Exotic Liquids	Spain	Mar-96	$180.00
29	Leverling	Beverages	Exotic Liquids	Brazil	May-96	$190.00
30	Leverling	Beverages	Exotic Liquids	USA	May-96	$144.00
31	Leverling	Beverages	Exotic Liquids	France	Feb-95	$345.60

Figure 18-1: This raw data is used to create a pivot table.

Over 2,000 rows of data are in the table. Making sense of all the data on your own can be difficult, to say the least. For instance, what if you want to know how much seafood Nancy Davolio sold to French customers last January? If you take on this task by yourself, you need to search through all the rows and total up each data field that meets your specified criteria. Excel pivot tables, on the other hand, can do this for you in much less time than your own computations take.

Pivot table wizardry

Figure 18-2 shows an Excel pivot table (also included in Chap18.xls) based on the Northwind Traders data. This pivot table summarizes the information and displays it by employee and product category. We created this table by running the Excel Pivot Table Wizard. The wizard walks you through the creation of a pivot table by asking a few simple questions. Even we use the Pivot Table Wizard because it's so helpful.

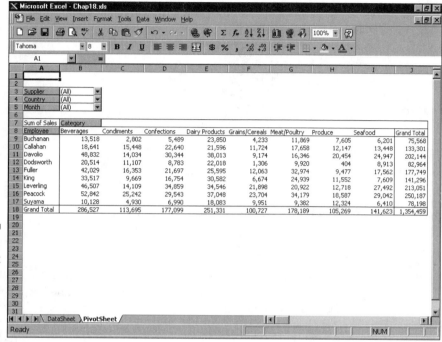

Supplier	(All)								
Country	(All)								
Month	(All)								
Sum of Sales	Category								
Employee	Beverages	Condiments	Confections	Dairy Products	Grains/Cereals	Meat/Poultry	Produce	Seafood	Grand Total
Buchanan	13,518	2,802	5,489	23,850	4,233	11,869	7,605	6,201	75,568
Callahan	18,641	15,448	22,640	21,596	11,724	17,658	12,147	13,448	133,301
Davolio	48,832	14,034	30,344	38,013	9,174	16,346	20,454	24,947	202,144
Dodsworth	20,514	11,107	8,783	22,018	1,306	9,920	404	8,913	82,964
Fuller	42,029	16,353	21,697	25,595	12,063	32,974	9,477	17,562	177,749
King	33,517	9,669	16,754	30,582	6,674	24,939	11,552	7,609	141,296
Leverling	46,507	14,109	34,859	34,546	21,898	20,922	12,718	27,492	213,051
Peacock	52,842	25,242	29,543	37,048	23,704	34,179	18,587	29,042	250,187
Suyama	10,128	4,930	6,990	18,083	9,951	9,382	12,324	6,410	78,198
Grand Total	286,527	113,695	177,099	251,331	100,727	178,189	105,269	141,623	1,354,459

Figure 18-2:
This pivot table makes data much more manageable.

If you've never used the Pivot Table Wizard before, you can follow the steps below to create a new pivot table based on the data in the sample file. If you're a pivot table master, on the other hand, you may want to skip this section of the book.

To create a pivot table, do the following:

1. Launch Microsoft Excel, and open the sample file for this chapter (Chap18.xls).

You see the worksheet that contains the pivot table as shown in Figure 18-2.

2. Click the DataSheet worksheet tab.

Excel displays the worksheet that contains the pivot table's raw data.

3. Click the right mouse button on the DataSheet worksheet tab.

Excel displays a shortcut menu.

4. Select the Move or Copy command.

Excel displays the Move or Copy dialog box, as shown in Figure 18-3.

Figure 18-3:
Create a
copy of the
data
worksheet
in a new
workbook
by using
this
dialog box.

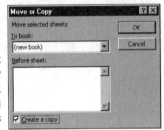

5. **From the To book drop-down list select (new book).**

6. **Click the Create a copy check box.**

7. **Click the OK button.**

   Excel creates a new workbook and copies the DataSheet worksheet to the new workbook. (This action may take some time because of the large amount of data.)

8. **Choose the Data⇔Pivot Table Report command.**

   Excel displays the Pivot Table Wizard screen, as shown in Figure 18-4. Note that you can base a pivot table on data in an Excel worksheet or an external database.

Figure 18-4:
The Pivot
Table
Wizard can
use Excel
data or an
external
database.

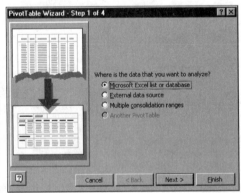

9. **Click the Next button.**

   Excel displays the second page of the wizard, which prompts you for the data range. The range $A$1:$F$2156 is already selected.

10. Click the Next button again.

Excel displays the third page of the wizard (see Figure 18-5). This page is where you drag fields from the database onto the pivot table diagram to define the original structure for the pivot table.

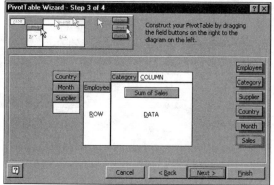

Figure 18-5:
Drag fields onto the diagram to create the pivot table.

11. Drag the fields from the right-hand side of the form to the pivot table diagram, as shown in Figure 18-5.

When you're done, you have the Employee field in the Row area, Category in the Column area, Sum of Sales in the Data area, and the remaining fields in the Page area in the diagram's upper-left corner. Note that Excel changed Sales to Sum of Sales. This is because Excel always needs to perform a calculation (such as sum or average) on the data in the pivot table.

12. Click the Finish button.

Excel adds a new worksheet to the workbook and creates the pivot table, as shown in Figure 18-6.

You can change the number format of the data in the pivot table to make it more pleasing to look at. Right-click anywhere in the data area and select Field from the shortcut menu. Click the Number button from the dialog box that appears and choose a number format (such as $#,##0).

Tables, fields, and items

When the time comes to write VBA code to control pivot tables, you need to know what the pieces are that make up a pivot table. Figure 18-7 shows another view of a finished pivot table; the pivot table shown in this figure is marked up to show you the parts that make up a pivot table.

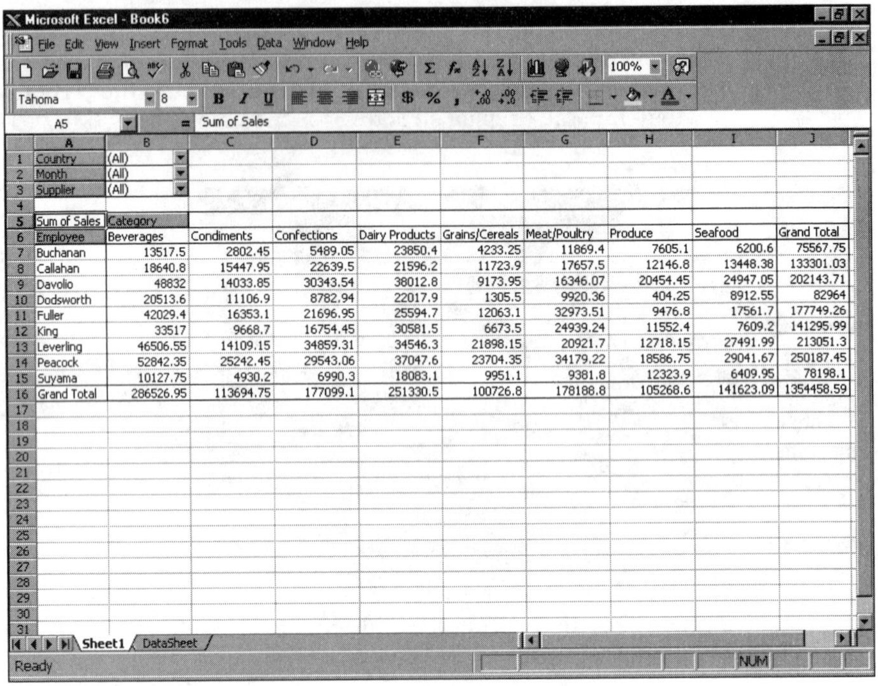

Sum of Sales	Category								
Employee	Beverages	Condiments	Confections	Dairy Products	Grains/Cereals	Meat/Poultry	Produce	Seafood	Grand Total
Buchanan	13517.5	2802.45	5489.05	23850.4	4233.25	11869.4	7605.1	6200.6	75567.75
Callahan	18640.8	15447.95	22639.5	21596.2	11723.9	17657.5	12146.8	13448.38	133301.03
Davolio	48832	14033.85	30343.54	38012.8	9173.95	16346.07	20454.45	24947.05	202143.71
Dodsworth	20513.6	11106.9	8782.94	22017.9	1305.5	9920.36	404.25	8912.55	82964
Fuller	42029.4	16353.1	21696.95	25594.7	12063.1	32973.51	9476.8	17561.7	177749.26
King	33517	9668.7	16754.45	30581.5	6673.5	24939.24	11552.4	7609.2	141295.99
Leverling	46506.55	14109.15	34859.31	34546.3	21898.15	20921.7	12718.15	27491.99	213051.3
Peacock	52842.35	25242.45	29543.06	37047.6	23704.35	34179.22	18586.75	29041.67	250187.45
Suyama	10127.75	4930.2	6990.3	18083.1	9951.1	9381.8	12323.9	6409.95	78198.1
Grand Total	286526.95	113694.75	177099.1	251330.5	100726.8	178188.8	105268.6	141623.09	1354458.59

Figure 18-6: This is the finished pivot table.

In general, each distinct field in the source database (whatever you based the pivot table on) is referred to as a *pivot field*. This pivot table is made up of six pivot fields: Category, Country, Employee, Month, Supplier, and Sales. The gray buttons on the pivot table represent every pivot field except the Sales field. In this example, the Sales field is known as the *data field* and is shown in the data area.

Excel also categorizes pivot fields according to their location on the pivot table. As you can see from the illustration, Category is a *column field,* Employee is a *row field,* and the rest (except for Sales, of course) are *page fields*. Each field, in turn, is made up of individual *pivot items* created by the distinct values in the database. The Employee pivot field, for example, has nine pivot items — one for each employee in the database.

Getting the answers that you want

Now, back to the problem of finding out how Ms. Davolio's sales were in January 1996 in France. After you build a pivot table, you can reorient it to see just the slice of data that you want. (You can find out about how to use the Pivot Table Wizard to build a pivot table in the section "Pivot table

Page fields

Column field

Pivot items

Pivot table

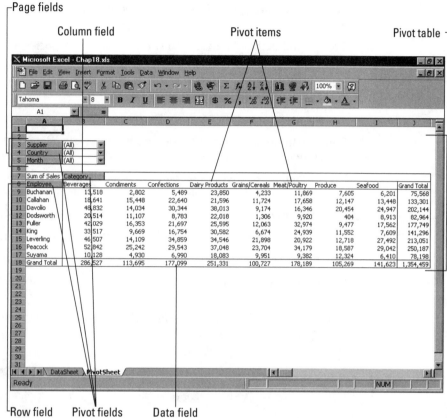

Figure 18-7:
This field
guide to
pivot tables
can help
you locate a
table's
parts.

Row field   Pivot fields   Data field

wizardry" in this chapter.) Because most people can only see in two dimensions at a time (3-D glasses for computer screens are hard to come by), other fields in the database are summarized as *pages*. Every pivot field except for those shown in the rows and columns is considered a page. You can limit the data that is shown in a page or you can view all the information.

To find out how Nancy's sales in France during January 1996 were, follow these steps:

1. **Click the Employee button and drag it over the page fields at the top of the worksheet.**

   As you drag the button over the page fields, Excel draws a horizontal gray bar underneath the mouse indicating the drop position.

2. **Release the mouse button while the Employee button is over the page fields.**

   Excel rebuilds the pivot table to show product categories for all employees, as shown in Figure 18-8.

3. **Click the Supplier page field button and drag it over the cell labeled Total in the first column of the pivot table.**

   As you drag the button, Excel draws a vertical gray bar.

4. **Release the mouse button while you have the Supplier button positioned over the Total cell.**

   Excel rebuilds the pivot table again, listing all the suppliers in the database in the leftmost column.

5. **Click the arrow button to the right of the Country page field.**

   Excel displays a list of all the distinct country values in the database.

6. **Select France from the list.**

   Excel updates the pivot table to show only those sales to customers in France.

7. **Click the arrow button to the right of the Employee page field and select Davolio from the list.**

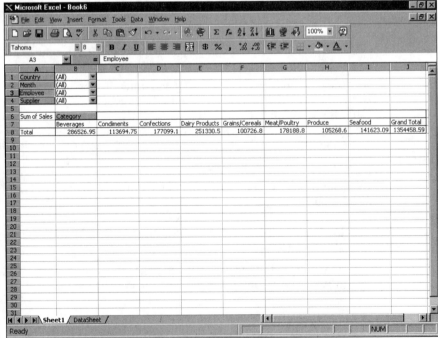

Figure 18-8: Changing the Employee field from a row field to a page field alters the structure of the pivot table.

8. Click the arrow button to the right of the Month page field and select Jan-96 from the Month list.

Excel updates the pivot table after each change. Now, the pivot table looks like the one in Figure 18-9. As you can see from the figure, Ms. Davolio had $1,875 in seafood sales to French customers in January 1996.

 If you want, you can see the sales totals for all employees in France during January 1996. You can have more than one row or column field. Just drag another page field onto the row or column labels to adjust the appearance of a pivot table.

Customizing Pivot Tables with VBA

The first section of this chapter, "The Nature of the Beast," explains elements like *page field* and *pivot item,* which is all very nice, but what do those things have to do with VBA? Well, you must understand terms like page field and pivot item if you're going to control pivot tables with VBA.

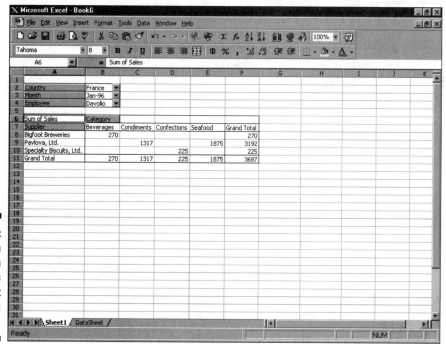

Figure 18-9: You can limit data in page fields to see just what you want.

The sample application that we chose for this chapter (Chap18.xls) is a simple user form that you can use to select the orientation for a pivot table. After you make your selections, the application copies the resulting data to a new worksheet. Why is this useful? Despite how easy it is to use pivot tables, some people become overwhelmed by them. Plus, it is easy to mess them up by, say, dragging a pivot field completely off the pivot table! Not everyone knows how to correct the damage after such an error is made. For this reason, you may want to provide your users with a simpler interface that has just a few options. Our application is a simpler user interface than that of a pivot table.

As shown in Figure 18-10, the form used by our application features combo boxes for each field in the pivot table. From these combo boxes, users can select which item(s) they want to view. They can also select all items in any given field to be displayed simultaneously. Two other combo boxes let users select how to orient the data. You write the VBA code to manipulate the pivot table behind the scenes in the section "Moving fields around" later in the chapter.

Figure 18-10:
This form
simplifies
users'
choices.

Filling the lists

To start off, you want to populate the controls on the form with pivot field names and pivot item values. You may think that this requires a lot of VBA code, but it doesn't. Thanks to the many different objects and collections that make up a pivot table, the task of adding names and values to the controls is actually rather easy.

First, you need to open the sample file for this chapter. We've already built the form for you. Phew! You just need to add the VBA code. Follow these steps:

1. **Open Chap18.xls if it isn't already open.**
2. **Press Alt+F11 to display the Visual Basic Editor (VBE).**

3. **In the Projects window, find the form frmPick.**

4. **Double-click the form's icon in the Projects window to display the form in design view.**

5. **Select the Country combo box and press F4 to open the Properties window.**

When you open the Properties window notice that the name of the combo box is *Country* — the same name as the pivot field. The same holds true for the other combo boxes (except for the two at the bottom of the form). You can see why we named the controls the same as the pivot fields in a moment.

Because the process that you use to load items into each list box is the same, you can create a generic subroutine to handle the task. Using the sample file Chap18.xls and building on the last series of steps, try this:

1. **Press F7 to open the form's code window.**

   Note that we've already written some of the code for you.

2. **Move the cursor to the end of the module and enter the following VBA code:**

```
Private Sub FillList(ctl As Control, _
  pvf As PivotField)

    Dim pvi As PivotItem

    With ctl
        .Clear
        .AddItem "(All)"
        For Each pvi In pvf.PivotItems
            .AddItem pvi.Value
        Next
        .ListIndex = 0
    End With
End Sub
```

The FillList procedure accepts a control (any one of the combo boxes) and a pivot field as parameters. After clearing any existing items from the list, the procedure adds an entry — "(All)" — which selects all the items in the pivot field. It then uses a For Each loop to loop through each pivot item in the specified pivot field, adding each item to the combo box's list. Finally, the procedure sets the combo box's ListIndex property to 0. This action selects the first item in the list, "(All)".

Now that you have a generic subroutine, you need to call it from somewhere. The obvious choice is the form's Initialize event, which is triggered when the form opens. Follow these steps to add the required code:

1. **Select UserForm from the object list at the top left of the code window.**

   VBA adds an empty procedure for the form's default event, Click.

2. **Select Initialize from the procedure list at the top right of the code window.**

   VBA adds an empty procedure for the form's Initialize event.

3. **Inside the body of the UserForm_Initialize procedure, add the following VBA code:**

```
Dim pvt As PivotTable
Dim pvf As PivotField

Set pvt = PivotSheet.PivotTables(1)
With pvt
    For Each pvf In .PivotFields
        With pvf
            If .Orientation <> xlDataField _
            And .Orientation <> xlHidden Then
                Call FillList(Controls(.Name), pvf)
                cboRows.AddItem .Name
                cboColumns.AddItem .Name
            End If
        End With
    Next

    cboRows.Text = .RowFields(1).Name
    cboColumns.Text = .ColumnFields(1).Name
End With
```

This bit of VBA code sets a reference to the pivot table living on the PivotSheet worksheet and then loops through each of its pivot fields by use of a For Each loop. Also, the code uses an If..Then statement to check the Orientation property of each field. For those of you who just scratched your heads and asked aloud "what did they just say?," we can provide a definition or two. The *Orientation property* dictates where on the pivot table the field appears, and the If..Then statement filters out the data field and all other hidden fields.

For the remaining fields, the UserForm__Initialize procedure calls the FillList procedure, which passes a control reference as well as a reference to the pivot field. Now, you can see why we named the controls in the way that we did. The piece of code, Controls(.Name), refers to the control on the form whose name is the same as the pivot field. Neat trick, huh?

In addition to listing each pivot item through the call to FillList, the procedure also adds the pivot field name to the cboRows and cboColumns combo boxes. These combo boxes let you specify how to orient the data.

Lastly, the procedure sets the text of the cboRows and cboColumns combo boxes to the names of the pivot table's RowField and ColumnField, respectively. As we mention in the section "Tables, fields, and items" in this chapter, a pivot table maintains collections for the fields in the rows and columns.

We can use a statement such as RowFields(1).Name because we only have one row field and one column field. If you have more than one field in either the rows or columns, you end up with more than one item in the RowFields and ColumnFields collections. In other words, the code in the last series of steps counts on the fact that only one row field exists. If more than one row field is being manipulated, you have to write more code.

We've provided a subroutine that opens the form. You can test the form by running the procedure, StartPivotTool, from the Immediate window. If you do, you should see all the combo boxes properly populated with values. Hopefully you're impressed with how little code it took to do that. The procedure got all the information it needed from the pivot table (and its fields and items).

Moving fields around

Time to add the code that reorients the pivot table to the sample file that we use throughout this chapter. This task, too, is quite easy. All you need to do is tell each field to which area you want it to go (row, column, or page). Follow the steps listed below to add the VBA code to change the pivot table's structure:

1. Select cmdOK from the object list at the top-left of the code window.

VBA adds an empty procedure for the OK button's default event, which is Click.

2. Inside the body of the procedure, add the following VBA code:

```
Dim pvt As PivotTable
Dim pvf As PivotField
Dim wks As Worksheet
Dim i As Integer
```

(continued)

(continued)

```
If cboRows.Text = cboColumns.Text Then
    MsgBox "You must choose different fields " & _
    "for rows and columns.", vbExclamation
    Exit Sub
End If

Set pvt = PivotSheet.PivotTables(1)
With pvt
    .ColumnFields(1).Orientation = xlPageField
    .RowFields(1).Orientation = xlPageField
    .PivotFields(cboColumns.Text).Orientation = _
    xlColumnField
    .PivotFields(cboRows.Text).Orientation = _
    xlRowField

    For Each pvf In .PivotFields
        With pvf
            If .Orientation = xlPageField Then
                .CurrentPage = Controls(.Name)
            End If
        End With
    Next
End With
Unload Me
```

Notice in the code that the procedure first checks to see if the fields chosen
for the row and column refer to the same pivot field. While it's perfectly
acceptable to do this (the result is a summary for a single field), it doesn't
make sense for our example. If the user chooses the same field, the procedure issues a warning and terminates.

Otherwise, the procedure sets a reference to the pivot table and then
changes the orientation of individual fields. It starts by changing the orientation of the existing row and column fields to page fields with the following
two lines:

```
.ColumnFields(1).Orientation = xlPageField
.RowFields(1).Orientation = xlPageField
```

At this point, every field is now a page field. The procedure then creates new
row and column fields based on the user's selections:

```
.PivotFields(cboColumns.Text).Orientation = _
xlColumnField
.PivotFields(cboRows.Text).Orientation = _
xlRowField
```

The procedure uses the field names stored in the cboRows and cboColumns combo boxes to refer to the desired pivot fields.

Finally, the procedure loops through the remaining page fields, setting the CurrentPage property of each. The *CurrentPage property* controls what value is selected in the page fields. Remember that, in this example, the FillList procedure is used to populate each combo box with field item values as well as an (All) entry.

Copying the results

The last thing the procedure must do is to copy the resulting data from the pivot table to a new worksheet. Because the structure of the data is constantly changing, you may think that this task is difficult. That's not true. Thanks to some handy properties of a pivot table it, too, is easy.

Figure 18-11 shows yet another view of a pivot table. This time we've highlighted several distinct Excel ranges that you can access through properties of a PivotTable object. These properties include ColumnRange, RowRange, DataBodyRange, DataLabelRange, PageRange, TableRange1, and TableRange2. Each of these properties returns an Excel Range object.

Because the result of these properties is a Range object, you can call any Range object property or method. To add the VBA code that copies data to a new worksheet, follow these steps:

1. **Place the cursor at the bottom of the cmdOK_Click procedure, just** *before* **the End With statement.**

2. **Enter the following VBA code:**

```
Set wks = ActiveWorkbook.Worksheets.Add
For Each pvf In .PageFields
    i = i + 1
    wks.Cells(i, 1) = pvf.Name
    wks.Cells(i, 2) = pvf.CurrentPage
Next

.TableRange1.Copy wks.Cells(i + 2, 1)
```

(continued)

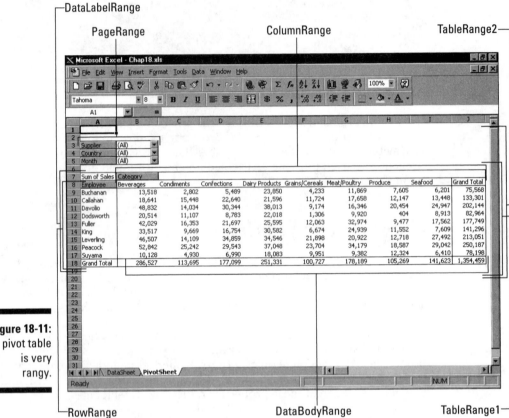

Figure 18-11:
A pivot table
is very
rangy.

(continued)

```
With wks.Cells(i + 2, 1).CurrentRegion
    If chkAutoFormat Then
        .AutoFormat xlRangeAutoFormatList2
    Else
        .EntireColumn.AutoFit
    End If
End With
```

The first block of VBA code adds a new worksheet to the active workbook, storing a reference to it in the wks variable. It then loops through each page field in the pivot table, printing the field's name and current page to the worksheet.

The next line of code references the pivot table's TableRange1 property, calling its Copy method. Keep in mind that TableRange1 returns a Range object. That's where the Copy method is defined. The Copy method accepts a destination range as a parameter, which the procedure sets to a cell on the newly created worksheet.

The last block of code calls a method of the destination cell's current region. The current region is the range of non-blank cells that surround the current cell. If the AutoFormat check box on the form is checked, the procedure calls the region's AutoFormat method, selecting the List2 format scheme. Otherwise, the procedure calls the AutoFit method of the region's EntireColumn property. This does not apply a format but at least displays all the data.

Give It a Try

If you have followed the examples throughout this chapter, you now have a working example. To test it out

1. **Switch to Excel and create a new workbook.**

2. **Choose Tools⇨Macro⇨Macros.**

   Excel opens the Macros dialog box.

3. **Select the StartPivotTool macro and click the Run button.**

   Excel displays the pivot field selection form.

4. **Select some entries from the combo boxes (it doesn't matter what you select).**

5. **Click the OK button.**

   Excel creates a new worksheet in the active workbook and copies the results of the pivot table to it. Figure 18-12 shows the results of a query similar to the one that we created earlier (in the section "Pivot table wizardry") with just the pivot table.

Pivot tables are very powerful tools but you need to invest some time finding out how to use them. For those users that only want a limited number of choices, you can create customized dialog boxes that give them access to only the information that they want.

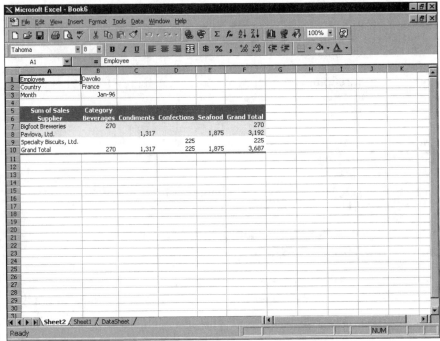

Figure 18-12:
The results
of a custom
pivot table
query.

Chapter 19

Charting Excel Data

• •

In This Chapter
▶ Finding out what makes a chart
▶ Creating charts easily by using VBA
▶ Changing chart options with VBA

• •

*A*h, where would Corporate America be without charts? These days, middle managers won't believe anything unless it's in a printed report and upper management won't believe anything unless you hand them a four-color, three-dimensional, bi-axial, doughnut chart with data labels. If you're developing applications in Excel, then sooner or later (probably sooner) you'll need to create a chart by using VBA. In this chapter, we explore the complex world of Excel charts and give you the lowdown on building ones that will impress even the pickiest CEO.

What's in a Chart, Anyway?

When it comes to complexity, Excel charts are at the top of the heap. Just about every little bit of data and every little option is represented by one or more objects that you can play with by using VBA. Figure 19-1 shows a sample Excel chart. Several of the chart's key components are recognizable as normal chart thingies, such as the x- and y-axes, data series, and legend. You may not have heard of other components before, such as walls and floor.

If you hold the mouse over any part of an Excel chart, Excel displays a tool tip window that tells you what the part is.

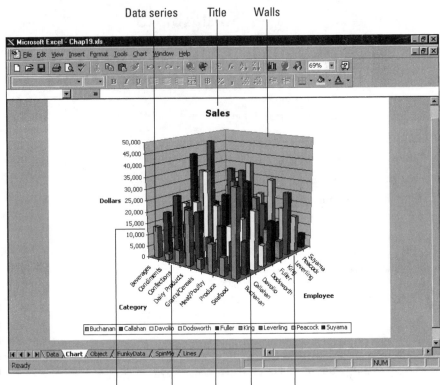

Figure 19-1:
Charts have
many parts.

Where Are the Charts?

Excel charts reside in two places in two different manners — as separate
sheets (tabs) in a workbook and as objects embedded on a worksheet. The
example shown in Figure 19-1 is a chart that occupies its own sheet. Figure
19-2 shows the same chart; however, this time the chart is embedded on a
worksheet.

You need to be aware of where a chart lives because Excel treats the two
charts differently when it comes to VBA. Depending on a chart's location,
Excel uses different code structures for charts. Charts that live on their own
sheet are known simply as Charts and are represented by a collection of the
Workbook object. Therefore you can write VBA code such as the following
line to find out how many chart sheets are in a workbook:

```
Debug.Print ActiveWorkbook.Charts.Count
```

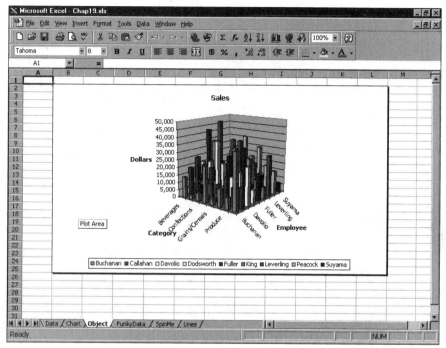

Embedded charts, on the other hand, are known to Excel as *ChartObjects* and are contained within a Worksheet object. The sample file for this chapter, C:\Dummies\Chap19.xls, contains an embedded chart on the Object worksheet (see Figure 19-2). As an example of using ChartObjects, you count the embedded charts on the worksheet using code like the following:

```
Debug.Print Sheets(3).ChartObjects.Count
```

The distinction between Charts and ChartObjects is important, because to change the characteristics of an actual chart you must use ChartObject. For instance, to remove the legend from a chart on its own sheet you can write code like the following line:

```
ActiveWorkbook.Charts(1).HasLegend = False
```

The following statement does *not* work, however, for an embedded chart:

```
Sheets(3).ChartObjects(1).HasLegend = False
```

If you try to run this code, VBA tells you that the object doesn't support the property. That's because a ChartObject is not a Chart. Fortunately, every ChartObject has a Chart property that refers to the actual Chart it contains. Therefore, this code works just fine:

```
Sheets(3).ChartObjects(1).Chart.HasLegend = False
```

So, you ask, why does Excel need a separate object? The answer is that a ChartObject has properties that apply to the frame in which the chart lives. For example, does the frame have a border? Is it shaded? Obviously, if a chart is all by itself on its own sheet, then it doesn't need these properties.

ChartWizard — One-Step Charts

In this chapter, we have to assume that you know how to create charts by using the standard Excel interface. We just don't have the time to explain how to do it. Instead, we're going to jump right into writing VBA code to create charts. With that in mind, you can find no simpler way to create a chart by using VBA than to use the ChartWizard method. *ChartWizard* is a method of a Chart and is the Excel VBA equivalent of a Cuisinart. It accepts a heap of parameters, including the source range for the chart's data, and creates a chart in a single line of code. Shazam!

Figure 19-3 shows the VBA Object Browser open to the ChartWizard method. Look at all those parameters (shown at the bottom of the Object Browser dialog box)! Table 19-1 summarizes each parameter, including the expected data type and what it's used for. Fortunately, most of the parameters for the ChartWizard method are optional.

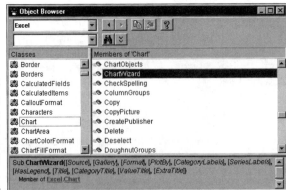

Figure 19-3: The ChartWizard has a whole gang of parameters.

Table 19-1	ChartWizard Parameters	
Parameter	*Data Type*	*Description*
Source	Range	Source data for the chart. Must include the heading rows and/or columns if applicable.
Gallery	Integer	Chart type. Must be one of the constants defined in the xlChartType class.
Format	Integer	A number from 1 to 10 representing the built-in auto format for each chart type.
PlotBy	Integer	How data is to be plotted. Must be xlRows or xlColumns.
CategoryLabels	Integer	Number of rows or columns containing category labels.
SeriesLabels	Integer	Number of rows or columns containing series labels.
HasLegend	Boolean	True to create a legend.
Title	String	The chart's title text.
CategoryTitle	String	The category axis label.
ValueTitle	String	The value axis label.
ExtraTitle	String	The series axis label for 3D charts, or the secondary axis label for 2D charts.

Excel usually picks reasonable default values if you decide not to specify some of the parameters.

To see how easy it is to create a chart by using the ChartWizard method, follow these steps:

1. **Launch Excel, open the sample file for this chapter (C:\Dummies\Chap19.xls), and make sure the Data sheet is selected.**

   Click the tab at the bottom of the workbook if the Data sheet isn't selected.

2. **Press Alt+F11 and then Ctrl+G.**

   Excel opens the Visual Basic Editor (VBE) and then VBA displays the Immediate window.

3. Execute the following line of code from the Immediate window:

```
ActiveWorkbook.Charts.Add
```

Excel creates a new chart on its own sheet in the workbook. You can switch back to Excel if you want to see the chart, although it's not very exciting because it has no data.

4. Execute the following line of code from the Immediate window (make sure to type it all on one line):

```
ActiveChart.ChartWizard
Worksheets("Data").Range("A6:I15"), xl3DLine, 3,
xlColumns, 1, 1, True, "Sales"
```

Excel creates a three-dimensional line chart from the data on the Data worksheet. Figure 19-4 shows what the chart looks like.

So what did that marvelous little line of code in Step 6 do? It told the chart where to get the data (from range A6:I15 on the Data worksheet), what type of chart to create (3-D line, format number 3), how to plot the data (in columns), how many rows and columns to use as labels (1 for both), to include a legend (the True constant), and what to use as the title (Sales). You can't get much more economy out of a line of code than that!

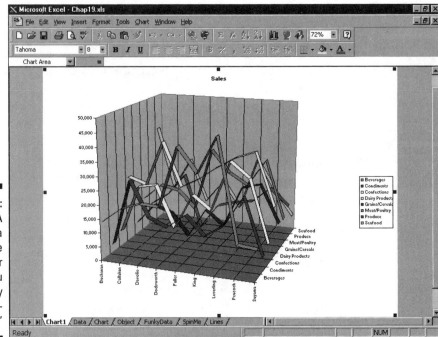

Figure 19-4:
VBA
creates a
3-D line
chart faster
than you
can say
"Chart-
Wizard."

A Few Cool Chart Tricks

Creating a chart by using the ChartWizard method seems easy, and it is, but sometimes things do get complicated. For instance, the data that we use in the example from the "ChartWizard — One-Step Charts" section of this chapter, is contained in one nice, contiguous block. What happens if the data that you want to chart is spread out all over the place? Take, for instance, the FunkyData worksheet (shown in Figure 19-5). The category and value information is scattered across the worksheet in many different cells. How can you create a chart from that?

Organizing a Union

If you ever find yourself staring at pieces of data strung out all over a worksheet, consider using the Excel Union method to gather them together. *Union* is like glue that you can use to bond discontinuous ranges into a single Range object. After you have the single Range object, you can send it to the ChartWizard method.

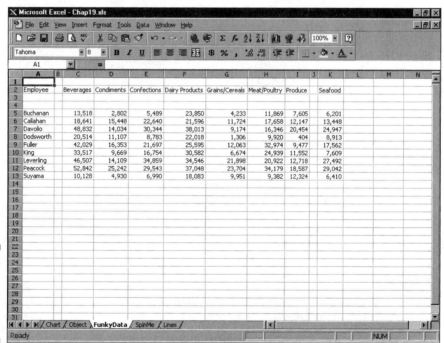

Figure 19-5: How can you create a chart from this mess?

To use Union to build an embedded chart from the data in the sample worksheet that we use throughout this chapter (Chap19.xls), do this:

1. **Press Alt+F11 to open or switch to the VBA editor, and then choose Insert⇨Module.**

   VBA adds a new module to the project.

2. **Type the following VBA code to create a new subroutine called CreateFunkyChart:**

```
Sub CreateFunkyChart()
    Dim chtNew As ChartObject
    Dim rngInput As Range

    With Worksheets("FunkyData")
        Set chtNew = _
        .ChartObjects.Add(100, 150, 300, 150)

        Set rngInput = Union( _
        .Range("A2"), _
        .Range("A5:A13"), _
        .Range("C2:I2"), _
        .Range("C5:I13"))

        chtNew.Chart.ChartWizard rngInput, _
            xlLine, 1, xlColumns, 1, 1
    End With
End Sub
```

This procedure begins by creating a new embedded chart on the worksheet. Remember the ChartObjects collection from the "Where Are the Charts?" section of this chapter? The procedure creates a new ChartObject by calling the Add method. Those numbers you see define the position and size (left, top, height, and width) of the new ChartObject. You express the values in points. (If you're not a typography buff, a *point* is $1/72$ of an inch.)

After charting the ChartObject, the procedure defines an Excel Range object by using the Union method. Union accepts up to 30 individual Range objects and glues them together. In this case, we use four objects that represent various pieces of data on the worksheet.

Finally, the procedure calls the ChartWizard method of the Chart contained in the ChartObject's Chart property. Are you sick of the word *Chart* yet?

Run the procedure from the VBA Immediate window by typing **CreateFunkyChart** and press Enter. Figure 19-6 shows what the finished product looks like. Note that the chart lives on the worksheet rather than on a sheet of its own.

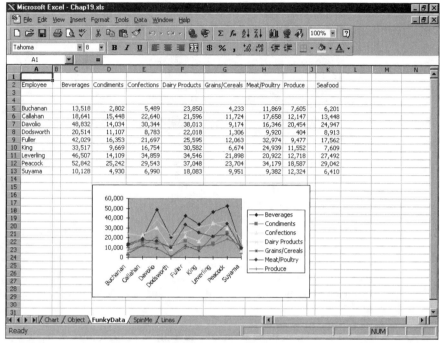

Figure 19-6:
The Union
method
helps you
create
order from
chaos.

Adding a new series

Every Chart object has a SeriesCollection property that returns a reference to a collection of the data series that comprises the chart. Like other collections, the SeriesCollection collection has Add and Remove methods so that you can create and delete individual data series. Creating a new series is much like creating the chart itself. You must organize the input data and tell Excel what to do with it.

To see how to add the seafood data from the FunkyData worksheet to the chart, continue using the sample file Chap19.xls and follow the steps listed below:

1. **Open the Visual Basic Editor by pressing Alt+F11 from Excel.**

2. **Select a blank line in the code module that you create in the example of the preceding section and type the following VBA code to create a new subroutine called AddSeries:**

```
Sub AddSeries()
    Dim cht As Chart
    Dim rngInput As Range
```

(continued)

(continued)

```
    With Worksheets("FunkyData")
        Set cht = .ChartObjects(1).Chart

        Set rngInput = Union( _
            .Range("K2"), _
            .Range("K5:K13"))

        cht.SeriesCollection.Add _
            rngInput, xlColumns, 1
    End With
End Sub
```

This procedure begins by setting a reference to the embedded chart. It then calls the Union method to create a single Range object from the header (cell K2) and the data range (K5:K13). Finally, the procedure calls the Add method of the chart's SeriesCollection collection, which passes the input range as well as values that indicate the data is column oriented and is the first row in the data series label.

Figure 19-7 shows the revised chart after the AddSeries procedure runs. Note the addition of the seafood series.

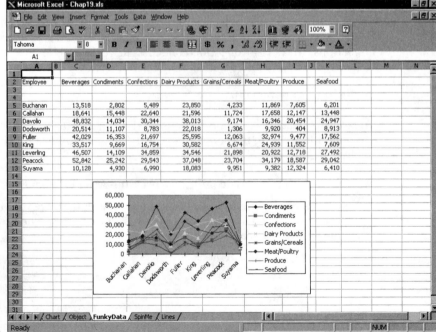

Figure 19-7: You can easily add a new series by using the Series Collection collection.

Properties for sale

You can change about a gazillion chart properties by using VBA. Everything
from chart titles to category labels to series colors and patterns to background bitmaps. In this section, we show you a few examples of how to
change properties with VBA. However, if you want the complete lowdown on
chart properties, you need to spend some time with your friend the Object
Browser. (See Chapter 5 for more details about the Object Browser.)

One set of eye-catching properties relates to three-dimensional charts. You
can write VBA code to alter the 3-D view by changing these properties. This
is something Microsoft demonstrates quite often. Here, we create a procedure called RotateActiveChart that progressively alters the rotation and
elevation of a three-dimensional chart. The code for the procedure is shown
below and is included in the sample file, Chap19.xls:

```
Sub RotateActiveChart()
    Dim intOld As Integer
    Dim i As Integer

    With ActiveChart
        intOld = .Rotation
        For i = 0 To 180 Step 5
            .Rotation = i
        Next
        .Rotation = intOld

        intOld = .Elevation
        For i = -90 To 90 Step 5
            .Elevation = i
        Next
        .Elevation = intOld
    End With
End Sub
```

As you can see, the procedure uses a For..Next loop to move through the
rotation values 0 through 180 and the elevation values –90 through 90 in
increments of 5. When you run this procedure, the effect is an animated
chart. We admit that the functionality this provides is a bit dubious, but
your boss is sure to be impressed.

To test this code, we created a simple 3-D surface chart on the SpinMe
worksheet. Before you run the procedure, make sure that you click on the
edge of the chart object once to select it. If you don't, ActiveChart can't
refer to anything and VBA complains. After you select the chart object, run
the RotateActiveChart from the Macros dialog box. Wheeee! Look at it go!

Point me at the data

After you create a chart, you can use its properties to examine the actual data that is being plotted. Each data series has a Values collection that contains one element for each value in the series. Series objects also have an XValues collection that contains one element for each label on the x-axis. Furthermore, each Series also has a Points collection that represents each point on the chart. Each Point object has properties that let you change things, such as the marker, color, or label text. By using all these properties together, you can do some really neat things.

To finish up this chapter, we show you an example of what can be done. (It's a lot of code, so we don't make you type it in yourself; just sit back and follow along as we explain how it works.) Figure 19-8 shows a line chart that plots sales information by category and salesperson. Although the number of points is relatively small, it's not readily apparent who sold the most product in each category. We think that labels need to be on the chart to point out this information. That's what the following procedure does:

```
Sub AddLabels()
    Dim serAny As Series
    Dim varMax As Variant
    Dim varValues As Variant
    Dim lngMax As Long
    Dim strLabel As String
    Dim i As Long

    ' Turn screen updates off
    Application.ScreenUpdating = False

    ' Loop through all the series
    For Each serAny In ActiveChart.SeriesCollection

        ' For each series...
        With serAny
            ' Turn off all data labels
            .HasDataLabels = False

            ' Find the maximum value
            varMax = 0
            For i = 1 To UBound(.Values)
                If .Values(i) > varMax Then
                    varMax = .Values(i)
                    lngMax = i
                End If
```

```
            Next

            ' Build the label text
            strLabel = .Name & vbLf & _
              Format(.Values(lngMax), "Currency") _
            & vbLf & "(" & .XValues(lngMax) & ")"

            ' Turn on the max point's label
            .Points(lngMax).HasDataLabel = True

            ' Put the text in the label
            With .Points(lngMax).DataLabel
                .Interior.ColorIndex = 2
                .Text = strLabel
            End With
        End With
    Next

    ' Turn screen updates back on
    Application.ScreenUpdating = True
End Sub
```

This procedure works by looping through each data series on the active
chart. For each one, it removes the data labels and then loops through all
the values in the series. By comparing each value against a variable, varMax,
the procedure eventually finds the maximum value in the series. After the
maximum value is found, the procedure stores the number of the data point
in another variable, lngMax.

After the procedure finds the maximum data point, it constructs the text for
a data label by using the name of the series (obtained from its Name property), the actual value (from the Values property), and the category label
(from the XValues property). The procedure turns on the data label for just
the maximum value point by using the following line of code:

```
.Points(lngMax).HasDataLabel = True
```

Then the procedure sets the text and interior color of the point's data label
and repeats the process for each data series in the chart. To see this procedure in action, follow these steps:

1. **Switch to Excel and click on the tab at the bottom of the workbook to
   select the Lines chart sheet.**

   Excel displays the Lines chart (refer to Figure 19-8).

2. **Choose Tools⇨Macro⇨Macros, select the AddLabels macro, and click
   the Run button.**

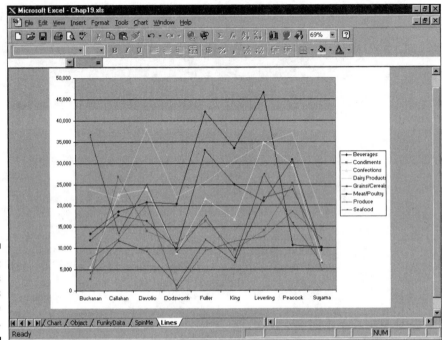

Figure 19-8:
What this
chart needs
is some
labels.

Excel runs the procedure and labels appear on the chart a moment later.
The chart now looks like the one shown in Figure 19-9. Now, you can see
exactly who sold the most in each category. As with just about everything in
Office 97, spending some time poking around in the Object Browser helps
you get the most out of a program's capabilities (in this case, Excel charts).

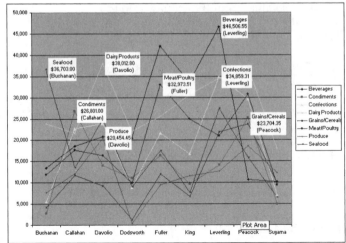

Figure 19-9:
The labels
make the
information
clearer.

Chapter 20

Hard-Core Find and Replace in Word

- -

In This Chapter

▶ Solving business problems with VBA

▶ Automating a search and replace operation

▶ Capitalizing on the DIR function

▶ Opening, closing, and saving documents programmatically

▶ Using With..End With and For Each..Next constructs

- -

*T*his chapter is the first in a series of two that dive into the depths of Word VBA for everyday useful purposes. Here, it is our hope that you have fun and apply the concepts that we discuss throughout the book. You may be familiar with the Find and Replace capabilities within Word, which are rather sophisticated. We plan to take Find and Replace a step further with VBA.

The Challenge

Here's the scenario for the chapter. Sit back as we describe the playground upon which you are about to unleash your VBA talents. You are a consultant for the Upper East Side Volleyball Club, which is undergoing a minor crisis and asks if you can help. They produce hundreds of documents per season: league schedules, tournament schedules, clinic sign-up forms, and member notifications. The problem is, with the recent change in management and the new club location (and name — the club is going to be called Old Dominion Volleyball Club), all of the documents that have been produced for the summer and fall seasons need to be updated, which means days and days of manual effort. Can you help out the volleyball club? But of course.

First of all, you need to gather all the new information from the club.
Table 20-1 shows what they need modified in all their existing documents:

Table 20-1	Changes Needed in All Documents	
Item	*Old Information*	*New Information*
Club Name	Upper East Side Volleyball Club	Old Dominion Volleyball Club
St. Address	1282 East Main Street	200 Dominion Hills Road
Zip Code	23222	23060
Phone	(804) 999-1100	(804) 4VB-CLUB
President Name	Sandy McBeach	Karen "Bumpset" Dig'emUp

Planning the Attack

Are you up to the challenge of helping your old clients, the Upper East Side
(Old Dominion) Volleyball Club? By using VBA within Word, you can assist
with their transition and make it as painless as possible. The club's new
president, Karen Dig'emUp, has provided you with a sampling of schedules
and documents. But before you begin to help them, a valuable exercise is to
think about how you can do this manually. No, you aren't going to do the
work manually, but just think about it.

You need to open each document, run the find and replace dialog box for
each piece of information that you need to change, and then save the
document. Although the Find and Replace dialog box is powerful and easy to
use, as shown in Figure 20-1, you have multiple pieces of information to
replace in hundreds of documents. If, for instance, you can run a find and
replace for one item in 30 seconds, and a document has five pieces of
information that need your attention, you can finish one document in 2.5
minutes. Now, consider doing this for 500 documents. We can do the math
for you — 2.5 minutes times 500 documents is approximately 21 hours!
Pretty soon, you're facing a serious time commitment. And what happens if
this tragedy happens again next year? You'd have to make the time invest-
ment all over again.

Next, take a quick look at one of the sample documents, as shown in Figure
20-2. This sample is one of hundreds of schedules that have already been
created for the Fall leagues and, as you can see, it is strewn with old information! We encourage you to look through some of the sample documents

Figure 20-1:
The
Find and
Replace
dialog box
found in
Word.

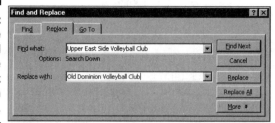

so that you can size up what you are dealing with. These sample documents from the volleyball club are included in the Clubdocs directory for Chapter 20. You may notice that in addition to main document text, information in the header and footer sections needs to be changed.

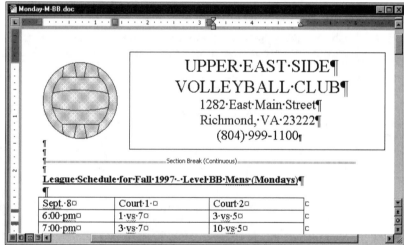

Figure 20-2:
Example of
a typical
document
that needs
modifications.

Okay, so how can you take advantage of VBA to automate this process? At a very basic level, you can automate the Find and Replace portion of the process. We take you through the steps that do this in the following section "Up, Up, and Away with VBA to Save the Day," but this still requires that you open each document.

Up, Up, and Away with VBA to Save the Day

Throughout the sections of this chapter, we walk you through the development of the code that can solve the volleyball club's problem. In this section, we want you to programmatically open each document, run the code to replace all the old information with the new information, and save the document. Sound like fun? Here you go. . . .

Creating somewhere to write our code

Before you can start to solve the volleyball club's dilemma, you need to create a new document and module to store your code.

1. Open Word, if it's not already open.

2. Choose File⇨New to create a new document, select Blank Document as the document type in the New dialog box, and click OK.

3. At this point, you may want to save your document with a user-friendly name, such as Dominion.doc.

4. Choose Tools⇨Macro⇨Visual Basic Editor to start up the Visual Basic Editor.

The Visual Basic Editor appears.

5. Choose Insert⇨Module to create a new module.

A new code window opens, which is called Module1 by default. Notice that an Option Explicit statement is already included. Remember that Option Explicit requires you to explicitly declare all variables before you use them within your code. This is a great safety net to set up in any code you ever write. Chapter 11 discusses the use of Option Explicit in greater detail if you would like more information.

6. Rename Module1 by changing the (Name) property in the Properties window to VBCode.

Notice that the title bar of your code window changes accordingly.

Setting up constants

From Table 20-1, you can see what information has changed for the purpose of this chapter's example, and you can create constants within your new module that reflect new and old information. Ideally, you want to declare these constants in the Declarations section of your new module (VBCode) so that they can be accessed from any procedure. If you continue through this chapter, you use these constants later on in the chapter, in the section "Search and replace."

In the Declarations section, type in the following constants:

```
Const OldClubName = "Upper East Side"
Const NewClubName = "Old Dominion"
Const OldAddress = "1282 East Main Street"
Const NewAddress = "200 Dominion Hills Road"
Const OldZipCode = "23222"
Const NewZipCode = "23062"
Const OldPhoneNum = "(804) 999-1100"
Const NewPhoneNum = "(804) 4VB-CLUB"
Const OldPresName = "Sandy McBeach"
Const NewPresName = "Karen ""Bumpset"" Dig'emUp"
```

When you search for the old values through VBA code, the values must be an exact match. Be sure that if a space is between an area code and a phone number in your documents, that you also include one when setting up your constants. Also, if the phone number appears with and without an area code, you need to set up an additional search constant here.

By using constants, rather than typing in your exact values in code procedures, you gain lots of flexibility as you continue programming. If values change down the road, you can come to this one location in the Declarations section to make changes to the old and new values and then rerun the code.

In addition to all the information constants, we have included two more: one to store the location of the existing documents that need to undergo modification and the other to store the location for saving the revised documents. For safety reasons, we recommend that you leave the existing documents intact and save the new, revised documents to a new location. That way, you can always revert back to the old documents in case of any unexpected trouble.

Add the following constants to the bottom of your constant listing in the Declarations section:

```
Const OldLocation = "c:\data\clubdocs\"
Const NewLocation = "c:\data\clubnewdocs\"
```

In order to test out your code, you need to copy the sample documents for the Volleyball Club from C:\Dummies\Chapter 21\ClubDocs installed from the disk and then move that folder to the directory C:\Data. You also need to create a directory to store the revised documents. In this chapter, we write the code assuming that you have placed your old documents in C:\Data\Clubdocs\ and have created a new directory C:\Data\Clubnewdocs\. If you have elected to go with a different directory structure, be sure that you modify the OldLocation and NewLocation constants accordingly.

Opening our documents

For purposes of this chapter, we are assuming that all of the volleyball club's documents reside in one directory. If not, we could adjust the programming logic to handle this as well, but with this assumption you can handle the single directory scenario.

We utilize the VBA Dir function to get a reference to our documents, one by one, from the specified directory. Before you rush into searching and replacing, get the basics of how to open documents from a directory down and then you can modify the code further.

Later in this section, you enter the following subroutine. For now, just take a quick look through it:

```
Sub OpenDocuments()
    'Set up variables for the document name and path
    Dim DocName As String
    Dim DocPath As String

    'Get the name of the first document in this directory
    DocName = Dir(OldLocation)

    'Loop through documents and modify them
    Do While DocName <> ""
        DocPath = OldLocation & DocName
        Documents.Open FileName:=DocPath

        'Search and replace code will enter in here

        ActiveDocument.Close
        'Get the name of the next document
        DocName = Dir()
    Loop

End Sub
```

1. **In the code window, type** Sub OpenDocuments() **and press Enter.**

   Notice that an End Sub statement is added for you automatically. Now, you are ready to start to write your code.

2. **Type the following statements in the code window:**

```
Dim DocName As String
Dim DocPath As String
```

   This action declares two string variables — one to store the name of the current document and one to store its full path.

   It is a good idea to document your code as you go. Although we aren't asking you to do it here in this step list, taking a few extra keystrokes to add comments can help you when you come back to your code in a few months or can help someone else if they need to understand what you've coded.

3. **Type the next line of code into the code window:**

```
DocName = Dir(OldLocation)
```

   In this line of code, you're using the Dir function to return the name of the first document in the directory specified by the constant OldDirectory (C:\Data\Clubdocs) and store it in the DocName variable.

   If you installed this chapter's sample files from the disk with this book and moved them to a directory other than C:\Data\Clubdocs, you need to change the path in the OldDirectory constant to the file path that you use.

4. **Next, set up a Do While loop by typing this line of code in the Code window:**

```
Do While DocName <> ""

Loop
```

   This loop continues looping through all the documents in the OldLocation until no more documents are left! In more technical terms, it continues to execute until the Dir function no longer returns a document name.

   Next, you can add code to be executed each time that you cycle through the loop.

5. **In the code window, type these statements right after the Do While statement:**

```
DocPath = OldLocation & DocName
Documents.Open FileName:=DocPath
```

By using the name of the document and the directory that stores the document, you set the DocPath variable to be the full path of the current document and then you use the Open method of the Documents collection to open it.

6. To finish out the subroutine, type in the following statements:

```
'Search and replace code will enter in here
ActiveDocument.Close
DocName = Dir()
```

Later in this chapter, in the section "Finishing touches," you add the search and replace code, but for now you can enter a comment to act as a place holder. After you have carried out all our modifications on the document, you close the document with the Close method of the ActiveDocument object.

Finally, you get the next document in the directory by using the Dir function again, but this time you do not pass in a directory name. This current directory is assumed and passes the name of the next document into the variable DocName. When the Loop statement is reached, the subroutine cycles through these steps again for as long as you have new documents in the directory.

Before you start on the search and replace code, a good idea is to verify that this code actually works. To test out your code, you should first verify that you have properly set the constant OldLocation to indicate the directory in which the volleyball club's documents are stored. After you do that, follow these steps:

1. Place your cursor on the line and press F9 to set a breakpoint on the ActiveDocument.Close statement.

Pressing F9 is a great shortcut for Debug⇨Toggle Breakpoint.

2. Press the Run button on the toolbar or choose Run⇨Run Sub/User Form to run the code.

The code pauses when it reaches breakpoint. If all goes well, you see one of the Volleyball club's documents open in Word. Toggle over to Word by using Alt+F11 to see if everything worked properly.

3. Return to your code and continue the execution of the code by pressing F5.

Your code pauses again when it reaches the breakpoint. When this happens, you need to verify that the next document opened properly.

4. Press Alt+F11 to toggle to Word.

You should find an open document different than the one that you encountered at the first pause in code execution.

If this code appears to be working correctly, continue on to the "Search and replace" section of this chapter.

Now is a good time to save your work if you haven't done so yet. Choose File➪Save in the VBE or click the Save button to do so.

Search and replace

Now that you can successfully open documents through code, you need to handle the searching and replacing of the old information. Because there are five items that you want to change, you can either write the search and replace code five times or pass in the values to search and replace as arguments. Certainly, we always strive for reusable components, so here you go:

1. **In your code window, type in the following to create another subroutine in your VBCode module:**

```
Sub SearchReplace(FindIn As Range, OldVal, NewVal)
```

The subroutine requires three arguments in order to run properly. These arguments include a document range (FindIn), the old text to find (OldVal), and the new text that is to replace the old text (NewVal).

2. **Type the following code into the new subroutine:**

```
With FindIn.Find
    .Text = OldVal
    .Replacement.Text = NewVal
    .Execute Replace:=wdReplaceAll
    .Forward = True
    .Wrap = wdFindContinue
End With
```

This code is a With..End With construct that searches within the range for the old value and replaces it with the new value.

By using the Find property of the Range object that is passed into the SearchReplace subroutine, you can set find and replace values. If you manually use the Find and Replace dialog box in Word, you have to enter what you want to find and what you want to replace it with, as well as your selections for some other assorted options. This is essentially what you do here, but you use code instead. The Text and Replacement.Text properties in the last code block are obviously setting Find and Replace options. However, the actual replacement occurs with the Execute Replace:=wdReplaceAll statement, which gives the command to run the replacement for all instances of the found text.

Yes, this search and replace is fantastic but it has limitations. It can't read minds — not yours, and certainly not your customer's. If the Volleyball club is not consistent in their spelling of the president's name or the layout of the phone number, your search and replace routine can not possibly change all instances of these pieces of information. Your code can only be as good as the data that you provide it. If, for example, the phone number appears with and without an area code, you need to include replacements for both cases.

Also, before you set up the values that you want to search for and replace, be certain that you want to change all instances of these values. If, for example, you had a document that states *"Formerly the Upper East Side Volleyball Club,"* your code is not smart enough to bypass this text when it does its search and replace. So what are we saying here? If you want to use this code to make modifications, consider using it to also add text to the documents, such as a reference to the old club's name. Just remember to add this text after you carry out your search and replace on the club's name.

Setting the range

Somehow we need to pass the SearchReplace subroutine a valid range. Actually, passing the valid range is the most difficult part of this code solution. You may think that a find and replace operation within code works in the same manner as the user interface feature. Sadly, this is not true (as we discovered while writing this book). Although you can easily search and replace text on the main document, to check headers and footers is slightly more complex, because a document can have different headers and footers for each section. By using the Section collection of a document, you can loop through each section and check the main text, the header, and the footer to ensure that you don't miss anything.

Are you unfamiliar with sections within a Word document? *Sections* are simply separate parts of a document that can have their own properties, such as margins, headers, and footers. Sections can be useful for document development when you need to have different headers and footers for different chapters, or when you want to have a section with two columns of text. For more information, see on-line help in Word.

1. **In your Code window, type in the following line of code to create another subroutine in your VBCode module:**

```
Sub FixDocuments(OldVal, NewVal)
```

This subroutine needs to receive the old and new values from the main driving subroutine — OpenDocuments.

2. **Next, you need to declare a variable with the following code so that you can store a section object:**

```
Dim DocSection As Section
```

3. **To complete the subroutine, type in the following code for the For Each..Next loop:**

```
For Each DocSection In ActiveDocument.Sections
    Call SearchReplace(DocSection.Range, OldVal, _
    NewVal)
    Call SearchReplace(DocSection.Headers.Item _
    (wdHeaderFooterPrimary).Range, OldVal, NewVal)
    Call SearchReplace(DocSection.Footers.Item _
    (wdHeaderFooterPrimary).Range, OldVal, NewVal)
Next
```

You use this For Each..Next loop to cycle through all the sections of the current document. Each section places a call to the SearchReplace subroutine along with its required arguments. As you can see, the SearchReplace subroutine is called three times — once for the main document, once for the header, and once for the footer.

That's a lot to digest, but all you are really doing is checking the header, footer, and main body text in each section of a document. The code looks scarier than it really is. Each call to SearchReplace feeds in the three required arguments. The OldVal and NewVal are easy to understand, but the first argument is slightly more complex. The first argument needs to be a range object. In the first call, you set the entire section as the range by using the DocSection.Range command. Then, in order to check the header, you use the Headers collections of the section to set the primary header as the current range, and then you do the same exact thing for the footer section.

Finishing touches

Now, if you have followed the steps throughout this chapter, you are ready to return to the OpenDocuments subroutine and actually tie in some search and replace code. You need to place a call to FixDocuments for each value that you want to search and replace and then finish up by saving the modified document to a new directory.

1. **Return to the OpenDocuments subroutine, either scroll to it in the Code window or select it from the procedure list box.**

2. **Move the cursor one line below the comment that you left as a placeholder for the search and replace code.**

Hint: The comment ('Search and replace code will enter in here) is located in the middle of the Do While loop.

3. In the Do While loop, type the following code:

```
Call FixDocuments(OldClubName, NewClubName)
Call FixDocuments(OldAddress, NewAddress)
Call FixDocuments(OldZipCode, NewZipCode)
Call FixDocuments(OldPhoneNum, NewPhoneNum)
Call FixDocuments(OldPresName, NewPresName)
```

This code calls FixDocuments five separate times, once for each piece of the information that needs to be changed.

FixDocuments requires two arguments, OldVal and New Value. In these Call statements, you pass in constant values that are set up in the Declarations section.

The keyword Call is not required, but including it can make your code easier to read.

4. Type the following code statement after the last Call statement:

```
ActiveDocument.SaveAs NewLocation & DocName
```

This code statement saves the modified document to the new directory you have set up. The statement uses the SaveAs method of the document object to save the active document in the new directory by its current name.

Your completed OpenDocuments subroutine now looks as ours does in Figure 20-3.

Figure 20-3:
The completed subroutine Open-Documents.

```
Dominion - VBCode (Code)
(General)                    OpenDocuments

Sub OpenDocuments()
Dim DocName As String
Dim DocPath As String

DocName = Dir(OldLocation)

Do While DocName <> ""
    DocPath = OldLocation & DocName
    Documents.Open FileName:=DocPath
    Call FixDocuments(OldClubName, NewClubName)
    Call FixDocuments(OldAddress, NewAddress)
    Call FixDocuments(OldZipCode, NewZipCode)
    Call FixDocuments(OldPhoneNum, NewPhoneNum)
    Call FixDocuments(OldPresName, NewPresName)
    ActiveDocument.SaveAs NewLocation & DocName
    ActiveDocument.Close
    DocName = Dir()
Loop
End Sub
```

Did You Forget Error Handling?

True, we did not include error handling in this chapter's code, and we probably deserve a slap on the hand. We chose not to include it so that you could concentrate on some of the code that may be rather new to you. Once you have verified that the code works, you should incorporate error handling into your code procedures to plan for the unexpected. What could go wrong, you ask? Lurking problems can include not finding any documents in the directory or running out of disk space on your hard drive.

Ready, Set, Go!

After all that hard work, it's definitely time for a rest. Why not kick your feet back and watch your VBA code modify all the Volleyball Club's documents? To do this, follow these steps:

1. **You can return to your document and choose Tool⇨Macro⇨Macros to open the Macros dialog box.**

   The Macros dialog box opens, as shown in Figure 20-4.

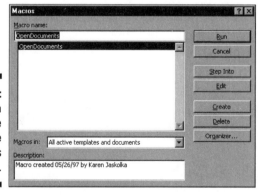

Figure 20-4: Running a subroutine from the Macros dialog box.

2. **Select OpenDocuments (it should be your only choice) and click Run.**

   Allow your code a few minutes to run. You can gauge your progress by watching Word's title bar. As each new document is opened, the title bar is updated.

Are you wondering why your other subroutines aren't appearing in the list? Actually, the Macros dialog box is rather smart. It only includes the subroutines that do not require any arguments.

3. **Open some documents in the C:\Data\Clubnewdocs directory to check out your handiwork, such as the modified document shown in Figure 20-5.**

Congratulations! If you have followed each section of this chapter, you made it through the chapter successfully. Now you can agree that you can do really cool stuff with VBA.

Figure 20-5:
Proof that
your code
works —
even in the
header
section!

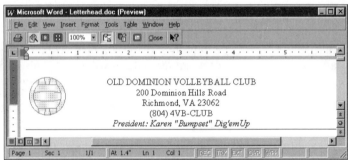

Chapter 21

Making Mail Merge Work for You

● ●

In This Chapter

▶ Taking something as basic as mail merge and augmenting it with VBA

▶ Creating a user form

▶ Populating a combo box

▶ Distributing your Word solutions

● ●

*M*icrosoft Word boasts some impressive mail-merge capabilities that are both flexible and easy to use. However, to merge data, an end user must go through a number of steps, an action which can get repetitive but is necessary. Here, using VBA, we streamline the process for your end user by providing a much simpler interface for mail merge.

As you may have guessed, considering Word's extensive object model, MailMerge is a property of a document. If you have merged data into a document, you can access the methods and properties of the MailMerge object, such as getting a listing of data fields available in the data source, and actually setting the data source via VBA. In the chapter, we run through a practical example of developing an add-in to Word that automates the mail-merge process for a specific database. We start by creating a simple user interface form that allows the end user to select the data source. Then, using the form selection, we add all the available merge fields to the current document.

Mapping Out Our Course

We begin this chapter by making a reference to the database that will supply a listing of possible data sources for our mail merge. To facilitate the selection of the data source, we also walk through the basics of creating a user form that drives the mail-merge process. After a data source is selected, our code will merge all data fields into the current document and show either data or the merge field codes. After we have completed these tasks, we take a moment to discuss how you can distribute such a solution to your end users.

Setting the Stage

Before we can run off building user forms and writing code, we need a storage receptacle for all our great work, as well as a database reference to serve as our source for table names. Follow the next series of steps to start that process.

The goal of this chapter is for you create a powerful Word mail-merge add-in. To that end, each series of steps in this chapter builds on the previous set of steps. Follow the steps in sequence to make the add-in work properly.

1. **Open Word, if it's not already open.**

2. **Create a new document template by choosing File⇨New.**

   Click the template option in the Create New option group, which is set to Blank document by default. Click OK.

3. **Save your template by choosing <u>F</u>ile⇨<u>S</u>ave and name the template something that you can remember, such as MailMerge.dot.**

4. **Start up the Visual Basic Editor (VBE) by choosing <u>T</u>ools⇨<u>M</u>acro⇨<u>V</u>isual Basic Editor.**

   The VBE appears.

5. **Create a new module by choosing <u>I</u>nsert⇨<u>M</u>odule.**

   A new code window opens, which is called Module1 by default.

   Notice that an Option Explicit statement is already included and you should not mess with it. Option Explicit is like a friend who provides a little tough love once in a while because it requires that you explicitly declare all variables before using them within your code.

6. **In the Declarations section of your Code module, set up the following global constant to store the name and path of the database file:**

```
Global Const DBpath = "C:\Program Files\
          Microsoft Office\Office\Samples\Northwind.mdb"
```

7. **Rename Module1 to Code by changing the (Name) property in the Properties window for Module 1.**

   Notice that the title bar of your code window changes accordingly.

If you accepted the default installation directory for Office, your sample Access database should be in the path identified in Step 6. If not, simply modify the constant to meet your needs.

Didn't install the sample applications when you installed Office 97? No problem. Simply set the DBpath constant to the name of any database on your hard drive. If your database gauge is on empty, you can use the Wine List.mdb in C:\Dummies\Chapter 3 installed from the disk.

Creating a User Form

Now we can create a simple user form that gives the end user a list of available data tables for a mail merge. If you need to brush up on the ins and outs of forms, please refer to Chapter 16, which is devoted entirely to forms development.

Getting out the Tinker Toys

The goal of this chapter is for you to create a powerful Word mail-merge add-in. To that end, each series of steps in this chapter builds on the previous set of steps. Follow the steps in sequence to make the add-in work properly.

1. To create a new form, choose Insert⇨UserForm.

A new form is inserted into your VBA project, as shown in Figure 21-1.

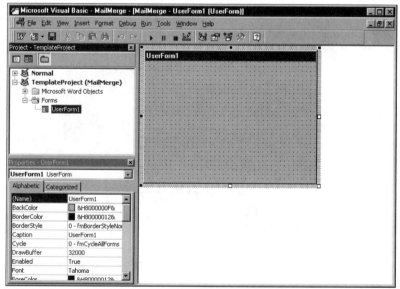

Figure 21-1:
Creating a new user form.

2. **Rename the form** frmMailMerge, **which is only slightly more exciting than** UserForm1, **by changing the (Name) property in the Properties window.**

3. **Also in the Properties window, change the form caption to Select Mail Merge Source.**

   Notice that, when your caption change is committed, the title bar of your form is updated accordingly, as shown in Figure 21-2.

   Now you are ready to add controls to this lovely new form, but first you better be sure you have your Toolbox handy.

4. **If your form toolbox is not handy, select the form and then choose** View➪Toolbox.

5. **Add a combo box control to frmMailMerge that will present a list of all the tables in our selected database.**

   For now, leave all the default settings; you return in a later step to write the code that populates the combo box.

   In this chapter, we assume that adding controls to a form does not present you with a challenge. If we are mistaken, Chapter 16 covers user forms development.

6. **Add a check box control under the combo box control, change the caption to** Show data in merge fields, **and rename the control to** chbxData.

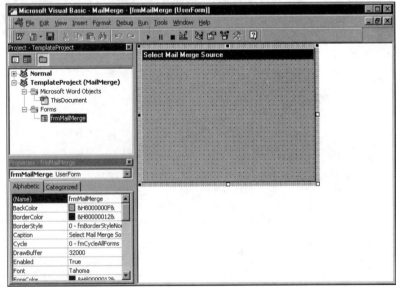

Figure 21-2: Making some minor form property modifications.

7. **Add two command buttons (cmdOK and cmdCancel), position them under the check box control, and change the caption property of these buttons to OK and Cancel.**

Doing so gives your form a more user-friendly appeal. Command Button1 and CommandButton2 usually don't excite your end users! The completed form is shown in Figure 21-3.

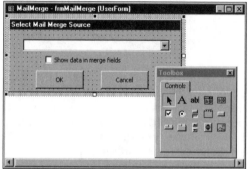

Figure 21-3:
Viewing our
completed
form in
design
mode.

Time to write the code to make your form go!

Okay, so we have this beautiful user form that does absolutely nothing at this point. The combo box list is empty, the OK and Cancel buttons don't work, and the check box couldn't care less whether it's checked or not. Never fear, VBA is here (and so are we — to give you a hand).

We can start with the easy hits. When the user presses the OK button, you want to call a mail-merge procedure that we have yet to write. Think about how you want the mail merge: you want to pass the name of the table that the user selects from the combo box, as well as the value of the check box that determines how the merge fields are displayed. Based on our data needs, the MergeIt procedure requires two arguments — the name of the table selected in the combo box and the value of the check box indicating whether data or merge fields are displayed in the final document.

The goal of this chapter is for you to create a powerful Word mail-merge add-in. To that end, each series of steps in this chapter builds on the previous set of steps. Follow the steps in sequence to make the add-in work properly.

1. **Select the OK button and choose View➪Code.**

A new subroutine, named Private Sub cmdOK_Click( ), is created. The code you place in this subroutine runs when the OK button is clicked. The VBE created a subroutine for the Click event instead of another event because Click is the default event.

If you want to write code for another event, you select the appropriate object and event from the object and procedure lists in the form's code window.

You can also right-click the button to expose the shortcut menu and select View Code to see the code for the Click event — default event.

2. **Complete the cmdOK_Click subroutine as shown here:**

```
Private Sub cmdOK_Click()
    Call MergeIt(Me.ComboBox1.Text, Me.chbxData)
    Unload Me
End Sub
```

As we have mentioned, MergeIt requires two arguments. You can see in our Call statement that we pass in the text value of the combo box control and the value of the check box. We use the keyword Me, which is how the form refers to itself. Me.Combobox1.Text is interpreted by VBA as "give me the text property of the combobox1 object on the current form." The second statement in the cmdOK_Click subroutine simply closes the form using the Unload command.

There is nothing wrong with putting in a placeholder to a procedure that doesn't yet exist because we don't intend to click the OK button until the code is written. And, if you try to run the code behind the OK button at this point, the code will fail.

3. **Select the Cancel button and choose View⇨Code.**

A new subroutine, named Private Sub cmdCancel_Click( ), is created.

4. **Complete the cmdCancel_Click subroutine as shown here:**

```
Private Sub cmdCancel_Click()
    Unload Me
End Sub
```

When the user presses the Cancel button, the form closes by using the Unload command.

Now, the real challenge is populating the combo box with the table names from the selected database set up as a global constant — DBpath. This code needs to run in the Initialize event of the user form. The Initialize event is triggered when the user form opens.

5. **While viewing the code window for the user form, select Initialize from the Procedure list box.**

As soon as you select this event name, a new subroutine is created, listed as Private Sub UserForm_Initialize( ) in the code window.

6. **Inside the new subroutine, set up the following variables:**

```
'Declare variables for Access db and TableDef
Dim db As Database
Dim td As TableDef
```

The *db* variable represents the database that is the source of the mail merge, and the *td* variable represents an Access table definition.

Next, you open the database using the OpenDatabase method of the default workspace in the Jet Database Engine. From Word, we can use Data Access Objects (DAO) to access our Access database of choice. No, we aren't really opening Access; we're taking a back door through the Jet Database Engine, which is really the brains behind Access anyway. DAO is the object model of Jet, and we can use its objects and methods just as we do in other Office applications. Remember, we set up DBpath as a global constant in our code module.

7. **Enter the following comment and code statement that sets the reference to the NorthWind database after the variable declaration statements:**

```
'Open the set database, as per DBpath in declarations
Set db = DBEngine.Workspaces(0).OpenDatabase(DBpath)
```

Now that you have a reference to the desired database, you can access its list of table definitions using the TableDefs collection.

Next, use the For Each..Next construct to loop through the TableDefs collection of the current database, and then add the name of each tabledef to the combo box list using the AddItem method of the combo box. (If only it were that easy.) You also need to filter out the system table, because its inclusion could confuse the user.

8. **Add the following looping construct to the UserForm_Initialize subroutine:**

```
'Loop through names of tables and add to combo box
For Each td In db.TableDefs
  'Skip the table if it's a system table (MSys...)
  If (td.Attributes And dbSystemObject) = 0 Then
    ComboBox1.AddItem td.Name
    End If
Next
```

9. **To finish off our subroutine, shut down the reference to the database using the Close method of the database object by adding the following lines of code:**

```
'House cleaning  -close the database
db.Close
```

We refer to this as good housekeeping. After you are finished with your toys (or objects), you need to put them away.

So far, so good

At this point, test your user form to ensure that the UserForm_Initialize subroutine properly constructs the combo list by following the next series of steps.

REMEMBER

The goal of this chapter is for you to create a powerful Word mail-merge add-in. To that end, each series of steps in this chapter builds on the previous set of steps. Follow the steps in sequence to make the add-in work properly.

1. **To test the form, ensure that it's the active object by selecting the form in the VBE.**
2. **Choose Run⇨Run Sub/UserForm or press F5.**

   Your user form opens in Word, awaiting your response, as shown in Figure 21-4. At this point, you cannot test the OK button because we haven't written the MergeIt code, but you can try out the combo box and the Cancel button.

Select Mail Merge Source
Show data in merge fields
OK
Cancel

Figure 21-4: Our homemade Select Mail Merge Source dialog box.

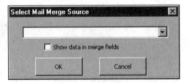

3. **Verify that the combo box contains a list of tables from the NorthWind database, as shown in Figure 21-5.**

Select Mail Merge Source
Categories
Customers
Employees
Order Details
Orders
Products
Shippers
Suppliers

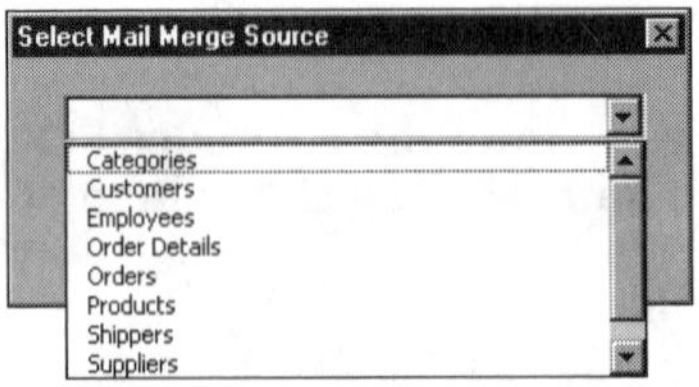

Figure 21-5: Verification that our form Initialize code is working!

If you have no tables in your combo box, check the Global Const DBpath to ensure that it points to a valid database and verify that tables actually exist in it.

Writing Some Module Code

At this point, your user form is ready to go and your VBA code actually populates a pick list of tables in the combo box to feed into the mail-merge routine. Be sure to pat yourself on the back before moving forward. You just put a virtual smiley face on your code! Now, you can write some more cool VBA code.

The goal of this chapter is for you to create a powerful Word mail-merge add-in. To that end, each series of steps in this chapter builds on the previous set of steps. Follow the steps in sequence to make the add-in work properly.

1. **Open your Code module by double-clicking on it.**

2. **Under your global constant declaration, type** `Sub RunMailMerge()` **and press Enter.**

   This creates a new subroutine that we will use to have the form open within Word.

3. **Add the following statement, which uses the Show method of the form object, to your new subroutine.**

   ```
   frmMailMerge.Show
   ```

   Later in this chapter, we call the RunMailMerge subroutine to start the mail-merge process.

4. **Now, create the MergeIt subroutine by typing** `Sub MergeIt(tbName As String, ShowMergeFields As Boolean)` **in the code window of your module and pressing Enter.**

   Remember, MergeIt needs two arguments — table name and check box value. The table name arrives as a string value, whereas the check box control on the form passes a Boolean value.

   To begin the subroutine, declare a variable to store a mail-merge data field.

5. **Insert the following statement to the top of the subroutine:**

   ```
   Dim Fld As MailMergeDataField
   ```

   Next, we can start working our mail-merge magic. You need to add code to select form letters as the document type and then set up the data source for the mail merge based on the table selected on the user form. The table name is passed into the MergeIt subroutine as an argument.

6. **Type the following statements as the next line of code in the subroutine:**

```
'Takes active document as merge document
ActiveDocument.MailMerge.MainDocumentType =
 wdFormLetters

'Opens data source based on form selection
ActiveDocument.MailMerge.OpenDataSource Name:= _
 DBpath, ConfirmConversions:=False, ReadOnly:=False, _
 LinkToSource:=True, AddToRecentFiles:=False, _
 PasswordDocument:="", PasswordTemplate:="", _
 WritePasswordDocument:="", _
 WritePasswordTemplate:="",_ Revert:=False, _
 Format:=wdOpenFormatAuto, _ Connection:="TABLE " & _
 tbName, SQLStatement:= _
 "SELECT * FROM [" & tbName & "]", SQLStatement1:=""
```

First, we selected the active document as the document to receive the gift of mail merge. For the purposes of this example, we are using form letters as the document type, but you could easily modify this, or add a programmatic selection box.

Next, we set the arguments of the OpenDatabase method of the MailMerge object for the current document. Notice that we use DBpath as the name of the database for the Name argument. Also, the argument tbName that is passed into MergeIt comes in handy for setting the Connection and SQLStatement arguments.

7. **Activate the main merge document with the EditMainDocument method and then proceed to add data fields to the document by typing the following code at the end of the subroutine:**

```
ActiveDocument.MailMerge.EditMainDocument

'Loops through all fields in data source and adds _
'as merge items
For Each Fld In _
 ActiveDocument.MailMerge.DataSource.DataFields
  Selection.Font.Bold = True
  Selection.TypeText Fld.Name & ":    "
  Selection.Font.Bold = False
  ActiveDocument.MailMerge.Fields.Add _
   Range:=Selection.Range, Name:= Fld.Name
  Selection.TypeText vbCrLf
Next
```

The For Each..Next loop cycles through all the fields in the DataFields collection of the DataSource object for the mail merge of the active document. Then, we turn on font bolding and add the name of the field to the document. Finally, we use the Add method of the Fields collection (which is the collection that represents all the merge fields on a document) to add each field as a merge field.

Hold on, we're almost finished with this. You haven't forgotten about the check box value that is still sitting around waiting to be used, have you?

To round out the subroutine, make sure that, if the Show data in merge fields check box is checked, the field codes toggle. The field codes are visible by default, so you need to hide the field codes and display the actual data from the data source.

8. Type the following code as the next statement in the subroutine:

```
'If user chose to see data, toggle field codes
If ShowMergeFields = True Then
    ActiveDocument.MailMerge.ViewMailMergeFieldCodes _
    = wdToggle
End If
```

Try It Out

Before we move on and package up this great code in an add-in and distribute it, we need to make sure that it works.

The goal of this chapter is for you to create a powerful Word mail-merge add-in. To that end, each series of steps in this chapter builds on the previous set of steps. Follow the steps in sequence to make the add-in work properly.

1. Switch to Word and then create a blank document by choosing File⇨New and clicking OK.

2. Choose Tools⇨Macro⇨Macros to open the Macros dialog box, and then select the subroutine RunMailMerge and click OK.

The Select Mail-Merge Source user form opens.

3. Select a table from the combo box and click OK.

Wait a few moments as Word gathers the data from your Access table and places the merge fields in your new document, as shown in Figure 21-6, which displays all the fields from the Customers table in the NorthWind sample database that comes with Access. Assuming that all goes well (and why shouldn't it?), you can proceed with the final steps.

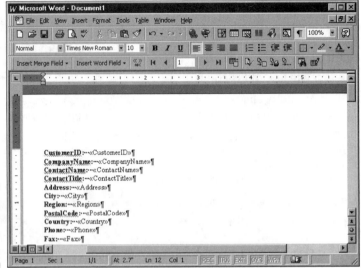

Figure 21-6:
Testing our
mail merge
code.

If you need to take a look at our code, open our version of MailMerge.dot in
C:\Dummies\Chapter 21 installed from the disk.

Finishing Touches

We aren't quite finished. When we tested the code it worked because we still
have our document template open. So how can we distribute this to end
users without their having to open MailMerge.dot?

We're glad you asked. Even though we could have placed this code in a
regular Word document, we chose to place it in a template. We did this for a
very good reason — you can load templates as global templates or add-ins.
You can slice this order one of two ways. You can opt to have users load
MailMerge.dot as an add-in on an as-needed basis, or you can place
MailMerge.dot in the Startup directory so that it loads automatically when
Word is launched.

To place MailMerge.dot in the Startup directory so that it loads automatically, you need to know where the Startup directory is. If you are uncertain,
check the path for Startup files on the File Locations tab of the Options
dialog box. To open the Options dialog box, choose Tools⇨Options. Then
copy MailMerge.dot into that directory using Explorer.

When you restart Word, you can open the Templates and Add-Ins dialog box
to verify that MailMerge.dot has been loaded. To open this dialog box,
choose Tools⇨Templates and Add-Ins.

Chapter 22

Making PowerPoint Presentations Come Alive

In This Chapter

▶ Creating a presentation from a text file

▶ Adding slide show effects by using VBA

▶ Building dynamic presentations that respond to your users' wishes

*I*t took a long time, but PowerPoint now has its own development environment — thanks, of course, to VBA. Because Office 97 is still so new, little real world evidence can explain what people are doing with PowerPoint and VBA. Overall, however, VBA is good for two things. First, you can use VBA to help you build your presentation. This means that you can write code to construct and edit slides as well as set slide show properties. Second, you can use VBA to create dynamic presentations. No longer are you limited to a strict linear path. You can use VBA to branch to different parts of a presentation. In this chapter, we explore several ways that you can use VBA to accomplish these goals.

Constructing Presentations by Using VBA

In Chapter 9, we explain the basics of the PowerPoint object model, including how to create slides one at a time by using VBA. If you want to add a slide to an existing presentation, we suggest that you take a detour and read Chapter 9. Another, more efficient way to create slides, especially if you have the information stored somewhere else (such as in a database or word processing document), is to import slides from a text file. The key is to format the text file to make it look like an outline. In this section, we show you how to take a text file and create a glitzy slide show using less than 30 lines of code.

Figure 22-1 shows a text file that we've provided on the sample diskette (it's called Widgets.txt). Tab characters at the beginning of a line create the indentations that you see in this figure. This is how you create an outline that PowerPoint can understand. Lines with no indentation are treated as titles while the others comprise the body of a slide.

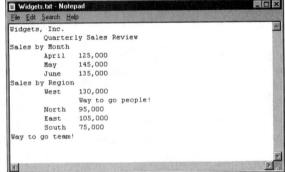

Figure 22-1:
You can quickly and easily create a presentation for this text file.

Importing text-file data

What we show you here is so easy that we have to create just a single subroutine and add VBA code as we go along. First, create a new procedure in a new presentation:

Each series of steps in the section "Constructing Presentations by Using VBA" builds on the results of the steps that precede it. To create the slide show from a text file, be sure to follow all the steps in this section.

1. **Launch Microsoft PowerPoint.**

   PowerPoint displays its opening dialog box, as shown in Figure 22-2.

2. **Select the Blank Presentation option and Click OK.**

   PowerPoint displays the New Slide dialog box.

3. **Select the blank slide option in the lower-right corner and click OK.**

   PowerPoint displays a new, blank slide.

4. **Press Alt+F11.**

   PowerPoint displays the VBA editor.

5. **Choose the Insert➪Module command.**

   VBA adds a new module to your project and displays its code window.

6. **Add the following procedure to the code window:**

```
Sub CreatePresentation()
    Dim strTextFile As String
    Dim objPres As Presentation
    Dim intLastSlide As Integer
    Dim strTemplate As String
    Dim objSlide As Slide

    strTextFile = "C:\DUMMIES\WIDGETS.TXT"

    Set objPres = Presentations.Add
    objPres.Slides.InsertFromFile strTextFile, 0
End Sub
```

7. **Edit the path in the strTextFile variable to reflect the path to the sample Widgets.txt file on your computer. (This step is necessary only if you used a path other than C:\Dummies when you loaded the sample files onto your computer.)**

Figure 22-2:
The
PowerPoint
opening
dialog box.

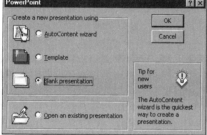

Don't worry about the extra variables in the procedure. You use them later on in the section titled "Setting slide show options." The last two lines of code in the procedure are the ones that do most of the work. The second-to-last line creates a new presentation by calling the Add method of the Presentations collection. The very last line inserts the contents of the file as an outline.

The zero at the end of the last line of code tells PowerPoint where to put the new slides. Because this is a new presentation, you have to specify zero because there are no existing slides. However, you can use the InsertFromFile method to insert slides at any point in an existing presentation.

To test the procedure as it stands, follow these steps:

1. **Switch back to PowerPoint.**

2. **Choose the Tools⇨Macro⇨Macros command.**

   PowerPoint displays the Macros dialog box. You see your new procedure, CreatePresentation in the list. If you don't, open the Macro in the
   drop-down list and select All open presentations.

3. **Select the CreatePresentation macro from the list and click the Run
   button.**

   PowerPoint runs the procedure. It creates a new presentation and
   inserts the data from the text file. Figure 22-3 shows the finished
   product. Granted, it's not very pretty yet. You do that in the section
   "Dressing it up" later in this chapter.

Go ahead and close the newly created presentation when you're done
looking at it.

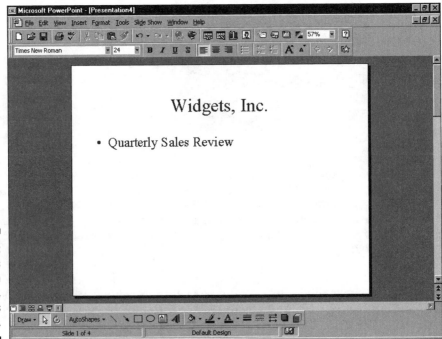

Figure 22-3:
This
presentation
isn't pretty,
but it's
a start.

Dressing it up

Each series of steps in the section "Constructing Presentations by Using VBA" builds on the results of the steps that precede it. To create the slide show from a text file, be sure to follow all the steps in this section.

After you create the slides, you can start to dress up your presentation. Apply a design template first:

1. **Switch to the VBA editor (or press Alt+F11).**

2. **Insert the following lines at the bottom of the CreatePresentation subroutine, just before the words** End Sub:

```
strTemplate = "C:\Program Files\Microsoft " & _
  "Office\Templates\Presentation Designs\" & _
  "Notebook.pot"
objPres.ApplyTemplate strTemplate
```

This code applies the Notebook presentation theme to the newly created presentation.

3. **Edit the path to Notebook.pot to reflect the file's location on your hard disk. (This step is necessary only if you changed the default path when you loaded Office 97 onto your computer.)**

You can also pick a different template if you don't like how Notebook.pot looks.

Of course, you can modify the properties of the presentation, one at a time, by using VBA code. But unless you're the type of person who likes to count the grains of sand at the beach, this is not the best approach. It's much better to use one of the design templates that ship with PowerPoint, because they were created by professional designers. You can even create your own!

Laying out your slides

When you import slides from a text file, PowerPoint — knowing no better — creates them using the Title and Text layout style. That is, PowerPoint treats lines with no indentation as the title of each slide and all other lines as the body of the slide. Chances are, however, that you want to specify different layouts for some slides in the presentation. In our example, we want to make the first slide the title slide for the presentation (the slide that tells people what the presentation is all about). We also want to remove the text from the last slide, leaving just the title. Fortunately, this is easy. You just set each slide's Layout property.

To add the code to do this, follow the next series of steps.

Each series of steps in the section "Constructing Presentations by Using VBA" builds on the results of the steps that precede it. To create the slide show from a text file, be sure to follow all the steps in this section.

1. **Move your cursor to the bottom of the CreatePresentation procedure if it's not already there.**

2. **Enter the following VBA code:**

```
objPres.Slides(1).Layout = ppLayoutTitle
intLastSlide = objPres.Slides.Count
objPres.Slides(intLastSlide).Layout = _
  ppLayoutTitleOnly
```

The first line in the code fragment looks fairly straightforward. It sets the Layout property of the first slide (slide 1) to the constant ppLayoutTitle. This coding creates a title slide.

To set the layout of the last slide, you can type an exact slide number, but what if the number of slides change? Our code handles this nicely. The second line of code, in the preceding fragment, computes the last slide's number by simply looking at the total number of slides (given by the Count property of the Slides collection). The procedure then uses this number to specify the last slide, setting its Layout property to ppLayoutTitleOnly.

PowerPoint defines constants for each distinct layout style. You can find a list of them in the Object Browser. Just find the entry for ppSlideLayout in the Classes list.

Setting slide show options

Now, you can have some fun with the presentation! Many people (read as *bosses*) are impressed when you add slick effects to your slide presentations. As you know, anything that you can do through the user interface, you can also do by using VBA. Follow the next set of steps to add some transition effects to the slides in your presentation:

Each series of steps in the section "Constructing Presentations by Using VBA" builds on the results of the steps that precede it. To create the slide show from a text file, be sure to follow all the steps in this section.

1. **Move your cursor to the bottom of the CreatePresentation procedure if it's not already there.**

2. **Enter the following VBA code:**

```
For Each objSlide In objPres.Slides
    With objSlide.SlideShowTransition
        .EntryEffect = ppEffectFade
        .AdvanceOnTime = True
        .AdvanceTime = 5
    End With
Next
```

This code sets up a For Each loop that loops through each slide in the newly created presentation. It then uses a With statement to set various properties of each slide's SlideShowTransition object.

For Each loops and the With statement are covered in Chapter 13.

EntryEffect defines the slide show effect used to introduce the slide. The procedure sets this to ppEffectFade, which produces a gradual fading in and out of each slide. (It's very soothing to watch!)

Like the layout options, PowerPoint defines constants for every slide transition. Look for the ppEntryEffect object in the Object Browser Classes list.

If you want the slide show to advance automatically, you must set two additional properties, AdvanceOnTime and AdvanceTime. Setting AdvanceOnTime to True tells PowerPoint, "Yes. Advance this slide automatically." You then set AdvanceTime to the number of seconds (five in this case) that you want each slide to be displayed.

Welcome to the Big Show

It's now time to fire off the slide show. To do that, you need to write just a little more VBA code. Follow this next set of steps to finish the procedure.

Each series of steps in the section "Constructing Presentations by Using VBA" builds on the results of the steps that precede it. To create the slide show from a text file, be sure to follow all the steps in this section.

1. **Move your cursor to the bottom of the CreatePresentation procedure if it's not already there.**

2. **Enter the following VBA code:**

```
With objPres.SlideShowSettings
    .AdvanceMode = ppSlideShowUseSlideTimings
    .LoopUntilStopped = True
    .Run
End With
```

The code in the preceding section, "Setting slide show options," modifies the slide show settings for each slide. Slide show settings that are for the presentation itself are stored in, appropriately, the SlideShowSettings object. This code fragment sets the AdvanceMode property to ppSlideShowUseSlide Timings, which tells PowerPoint to advance each slide by using the timing information that you set up. The procedure also sets the LoopUntilStopped property to True. As you can probably guess, this line tells PowerPoint to continue running your masterpiece until you yell "Uncle!" — er, that is, until you press Esc.

Finally, the procedure calls the Run method. This is what actually kicks off the slide show. You can test the complete procedure by following these steps:

1. **Press Ctrl+S and enter a file name to save the presentation that contains the VBA code you've been working in this section.**

2. **Switch to PowerPoint by pressing Alt+Tab.**

3. **Choose the Tools⇨Macro⇨Macros command.**

   PowerPoint displays the Macros dialog box. If you don't see the CreatePresentation procedure, open the Macro in drop-down list and select All open presentations.

4. **Select the CreatePresentation macro from the list and click the Run button.**

   PowerPoint runs the procedure. After a small delay, the finished slide show starts to run. Figure 22-4 shows the opening screen. Note how the layout is different from the slide in Figure 22-3. The appearance of the slide changes when you make it a title slide.

Building Dynamic Presentations

Not everyone can be a dynamic presenter, so maybe dynamic presentations are the next best thing. By *dynamic* we mean a presentation that can take different paths, depending on the interests of the person presenting or viewing it. Prior to Office 97, creating dynamic presentations was difficult if not impossible. Now, as you can see in this section, it's easy.

Our sample presentation

To demonstrate the possibilities of dynamic presentations, we've created a very simple presentation and included it on the sample diskette. The filename is Widgets.ppt and the sample contains information on a fictitious company. Figure 22-5 shows the first slide of the presentation in slide show view. The viewer can take three different paths: Clicking on the text near the bottom of the slide takes the viewer to further information on either the company itself, its products, or its contact information.

Although we've taken the time to create the presentation, you need to add the VBA code that is necessary to make the presentation dynamic.

Setting up hyperlink jumps

The first task you need to perform to make the presentation dynamic is to establish the jumps to other slides in the presentation. These jumps let the viewer go directly to the information he or she wants to see. Normally, we have you open the code window and start to type but, believe it or not, you don't need any code to make this jumping process work!

Every object you place on a slide can have a custom action associated with it. Specifically, whenever you move the mouse over an object or you click an object, you can tell PowerPoint to do something. If you want, you can tell PowerPoint to run some VBA code. In fact, we show you how to do this in the section "Responding to mouse movement" in this chapter. But you can also jump to another slide by using a new feature of PowerPoint 97, hyperlinks.

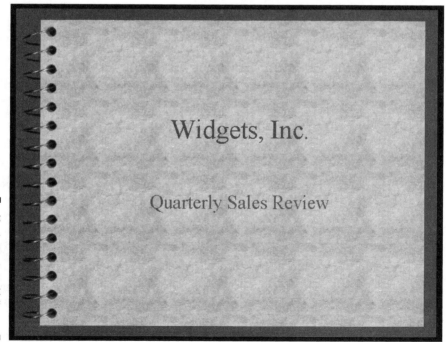

Figure 22-4:
A complete, running slide show, with effects, at the touch of a button!

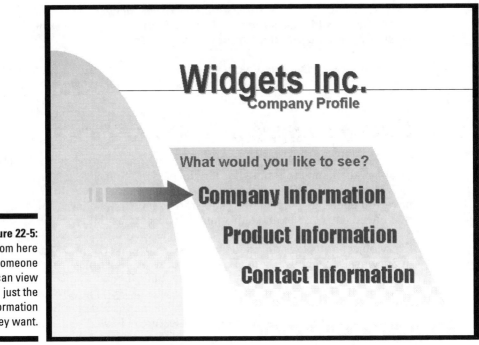

Figure 22-5:
From here
someone
can view
just the
information
they want.

If you've ever surfed the Web you may be familiar with the concept of hyperlinks. *Hyperlinks* are simply destinations that are associated with an object (like a picture) or some text on a Web page. The same concept applies to PowerPoint 97. You can associate a destination with each object on a slide, that destination being another slide in the same presentation! Of course, you can also set up hyperlinks to your favorite Internet site as well.

Each series of steps in the section "Building Dynamic Presentations" is founded on the results of the steps that precede it. To create a dynamic, interactive presentation by using VBA, be sure to follow all the steps in this section.

To set up links from the first slide to other slides in the presentation, follow these steps:

1. **Open the sample presentation for this section, Widgets.ppt.**

   PowerPoint displays the first slide in the presentation. If for some reason you don't see the first slide, press the Home key.

2. **Select the text box that contains the words Company Information.**

   PowerPoint draws a gray border around the text, as shown in Figure 22-6. It's important that the text box, and not the text inside it, is selected. If you see a blinking cursor, then you've selected the text. Click once on the gray border to select the text box.

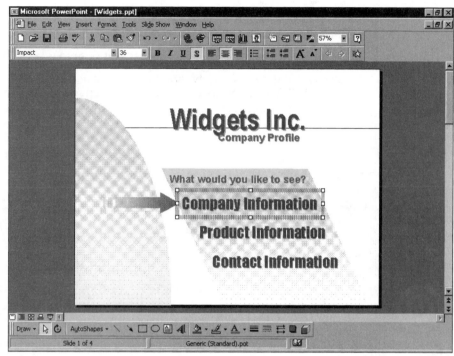

Figure 22-6:
The gray
border tells
you that
you've
selected
the text box.

3. Choose Slide Show⇨Action Settings.

PowerPoint displays the Action Settings dialog box for the text box, as
shown in Figure 22-7. Using this dialog box, you can dictate what
happens when a user clicks an object with the mouse.

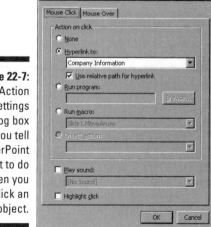

Figure 22-7:
The Action
Settings
dialog box
lets you tell
PowerPoint
what to do
when you
click an
object.

4. Select the Hyperlink to option button.

PowerPoint enables the drop-down list next to the option button.

5. Open the Hyperlink to drop-down list and select Slide.

PowerPoint displays the Hyperlink to Slide dialog box, as shown in Figure 22-8. This box lists each slide in the active presentation and shows a thumbnail version of the selected slide.

Figure 22-8:
You create a hyperlink to another slide when you select the slide from this dialog box.

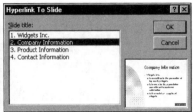

6. Select the Company Information slide from the list and click OK.

PowerPoint closes the Hyperlink to Slide dialog box and returns you to the Action Settings dialog box. Company Information now shows in the drop-down list.

7. Click OK to close the Action Settings dialog box.

8. Repeat Steps 2 through 7 for the two other text boxes, Product Information and Contact Information, to create hyperlinks to the Product Information and Contact Information slides, respectively.

Assuming that you got all the hyperlinks set up properly, you can now jump to any slide in the presentation directly from the front page. To test this, follow these steps:

1. Choose View⇨Slide Show to open the presentation in a slide show window.

PowerPoint opens the presentation in a full screen slide show.

2. Click the text Contact Information with the mouse.

PowerPoint displays the Contact Information slide, which is actually the fourth slide in the presentation.

3. Press the Home key to return to the first slide.

4. Click the text Product Information with the mouse.

PowerPoint displays the Product Information slide.

5. Press the Esc key to end the slide show.

If PowerPoint doesn't jump to the right slide or nothing happens at all when you click the mouse on the hyperlinks, reopen the Action Settings dialog box for the misbehaving text box and make sure that the settings are correct.

Adding navigation buttons

Jumping to a particular slide is nice, but what if you want to get back to the first screen or just browse through each screen? If you need this type of functionality you can augment the hyperlinks that you create with a set of navigation buttons on each slide. The advantage to having buttons on each slide is that the person viewing the presentation always has a consistent set of controls at their fingertips.

In this section, we show you how to add buttons to go to the next slide, the previous slide, and back to the first slide. Just follow the next set of steps.

Each series of steps in the section "Building Dynamic Presentations" is founded on the results of the steps that precede it. To create a dynamic, interactive presentation by using VBA, be sure to follow all the steps in this section.

1. Make sure that the presentation sample is open in PowerPoint.

2. Choose View⇨Master⇨Slide Master.

PowerPoint displays the slide master screen, as shown in Figure 22-9. Any objects that you place on the slide master are visible on every slide in the presentation.

3. If the Drawing toolbar is not already visible, choose the View⇨Toolbars⇨Drawing command to display it.

Refer to Figure 22-9 to see the Drawing toolbar along the bottom of the screen.

4. Click the AutoShapes button on the Drawing toolbar.

PowerPoint displays a list of AutoShape categories.

5. Click the Action Buttons command.

PowerPoint displays the Action Buttons tool palette, as shown in Figure 22-10. All of the controls on this palette are designed to respond in one way or another to mouse clicks.

6. Click the Home action button.

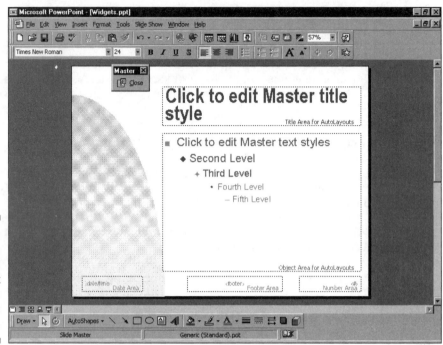

Figure 22-9:
Put stuff on
the slide
master that
you want to
appear on
every slide.

Figure 22-10:
The Action
Buttons tool
palette.

It's the one that looks like a little house with a chimney. Your mouse
cursor changes to crosshairs which indicates that you can now draw
the object on the slide.

**7. Click and drag the mouse onto the surface of the slide master to draw
a small back button.**

Figure 22-11 shows what you want the button to look like. Make it large
enough to be clicked easily but small enough so that it's not obtrusive.
As soon as you draw the button, PowerPoint opens the Action Settings
dialog box. PowerPoint has already selected a Hyperlink to the first
slide in the presentation.

8. Click the OK button to close the Action Settings dialog box.

Figure 22-11:
The Home
action
button
hyperlinks
to the
first slide in
one step.

9. **Repeat Steps 4 through 8 to create Next and Previous action buttons next to the Home button.**

10. **Choose View⇨Slide to close the slide master when you're done.**

As you can see from the example, the built-in action buttons can save you time if you want to hyperlink to other slides in the presentation. They don't give you the design flexibility of other objects, however.

If you click and drag on the dark line at the top of the palette, you can *tear off* Office 97 tool palettes. When you tear off a palette, it stays displayed on the screen instead of disappearing. This makes it easy to select multiple tools from the same palette because you don't have to constantly reopen the Auto Shapes list.

Now that you've created the buttons, choose the View⇨Slide Show command and run the slide show to test the buttons. Notice that the buttons don't appear on the first slide. That's because PowerPoint maintains a separate master for the title slide. Move to one of the other pages, however, and you see the buttons. Click them to move through the presentation.

Responding to mouse movement

We mention that you can also run code instead of using simple hyperlinks, and we know that you've been champing at the bit to write some. In this section, we show you how to call a simple procedure when you move the mouse over a slide's text boxes.

Each series of steps in the section "Building Dynamic Presentations" is founded on the results of the steps that precede it. To create a dynamic, interactive presentation by using VBA, be sure to follow all the steps in this section.

To begin, write the procedures that you want to call. Follow the steps listed below to create some VBA procedures inside the slide presentation:

1. **With the presentation still open, press Alt+F11 to open the VBA editor.**

2. **From the Projects window, under the Widgets.ppt project, select Slide1.**

   VBA highlights Slide1, the VBA component that corresponds to the presentation.

3. **Press F7.**

   VBA opens the code window for the presentation.

4. **Create a new procedure in the code window by typing the following VBA code:**

```
Sub MoveArrow(intShapeNumber As Integer)
    Dim shpShape As Shape

    Set shpShape = ActivePresentation.Slides(1). _
      Shapes(intShapeNumber)

    With SlideShowWindows(1).View.Slide. _
      Shapes("AutoShape 13")
        .Top = shpShape.Top
        .Left = shpShape.Left - .Width
    End With
End Sub
```

   This creates a procedure that accepts the number of a shape on the title slide as an argument. It then positions the arrow shape just to the left of it.

5. **Now create three new subroutines by typing the following VBA code after the End Sub line of the procedure that you just created:**

```
Sub MoveArrowCompany()
    Call MoveArrow(6)
End Sub

Sub MoveArrowContact()
    Call MoveArrow(8)
End Sub

Sub MoveArrowProduct()
    Call MoveArrow(7)
End Sub
```

These procedures call the first procedure, passing the shape number of one of the three text boxes. You must create these procedures because you can't call procedures that accept arguments from a PowerPoint shape. The code window now looks like the one shown in Figure 22-12.

Figure 22-12:
This tiny bit
of VBA
code
causes the
arrow on
the title
slide to
jump
around.

```
Widgets.ppt - Slide1 [Code]
(General)                          MoveArrow
Option Explicit

Sub MoveArrow(intShapeNumber As Integer)
    Dim shpShape As Shape

    Set shpShape = ActivePresentation.Slides(1). _
    Shapes(intShapeNumber)

    With SlideShowWindows(1).View.Slide. _
    Shapes("AutoShape 13")
        .Top = shpShape.Top
        .Left = shpShape.Left - .Width
    End With
End Sub

Sub MoveArrowCompany()
    Call MoveArrow(6)
End Sub

Sub MoveArrowContact()
    Call MoveArrow(8)
End Sub

Sub MoveArrowProduct()
    Call MoveArrow(7)
End Sub
```

Now that the code is written all you need to do is hook it up to the text boxes on the slide. To do this, you use the Action Settings dialog box, just as you do for hyperlinks:

1. **Switch back to PowerPoint from the VBA editor.**

2. **Select the Company Information text box on the title slide.**

   PowerPoint draws a gray rectangle around the text box to show you that the text box is selected.

3. **From the Slide Show menu, select the Action Settings command.**

   PowerPoint displays the Action Settings dialog box for the text box.

4. **Click the Mouse Over tab on the Action Settings dialog box.**

   PowerPoint shows you an identical dialog box, except that the action you define here takes place when you move the mouse over the object.

5. **Click the Run macro option button.**

   PowerPoint enables the macro list just below the option button.

6. **Open the drop-down list and select Slide1.MoveArrowCompany from the list.**

7. **Click OK to close the Action Settings dialog box.**

8. **Repeat Steps 2 through 7 for the two other text boxes, Product Information and Contact Information, selecting the Slide1.MoveArrowProduct and Slide1.MoveArrowContact procedures, respectively.**

Start the slide show and move the mouse over the text boxes to test the procedures. Of course, the procedures are fairly trivial, but you can use the same technique to run sophisticated procedures, as well.

Chapter 23

Automating Access Reports

● ●

In This Chapter

▶ Creating a form for selecting multiple reports

▶ Printing multiple reports at the same time

▶ Making Access forms look and act professionally

● ●

*T*o date, Access has been by far the most popular of the Office applications with which to create applications. Unlike its siblings, whose development capabilities evolved from simple macro languages, Access was designed from the beginning to let people create custom applications. As such, it offers rich development capabilities. In short, you can do lots of stuff with Access! In this chapter, we show you how to create a simple application that demonstrates how to use Access forms and reports together with VBA.

What's the Point?

The sample application that we've chosen for this chapter uses a sample database that includes a number of simple reports. The application is a form that lets you choose one or more reports from a list and then preview or print them all in one step. Why would you want to do this? Chances are good that you're going to have lots of reports as part of your application, many of which you print on a regular basis (daily, weekly, monthly, and so on). Rather than print reports one at a time while hunched over your computer, wouldn't it be nicer if you could simply select the ones you want to print and then go play golf? That's what our little sample application lets you do.

Figure 23-1 shows the main screen for the application that you create, which is made up of a single Access form, a list box, some option buttons, and a few command buttons. Using this form, you'll be able to select one or more reports, decide whether to preview or print them, and even cancel the process, if you want.

Figure 23-1:
Using this
form you
can print or
preview one
or more
reports.

Rather than spend a lot of time in this chapter telling you how to create the form, we've included the form (*sans* VBA code) in the sample database, Chap23.mdb, on the disk that came with this book (in the \Chapter 23 folder). We've also included the finished form in the same database, à la Julia Child's magic oven, in case you want to see what it does without having to add all the code yourself. So why not get started?

Don't Write Code; Use a Table!

The first item of business is to fill the list box with the names of reports. You could write VBA code to perform this task, but there's a better way — use a table. You can use tables to supply the rows to a list or combo box. The advantage of using a table is that adding or removing items from the list is easier. You simply add or delete items from the table. If you were to use VBA, you'd have to edit your code each time you wanted to make a change.

We created a table in the sample database that consists of a single field. Into this table, we put one row for each report in the database. Figure 23-2 shows the table in datasheet view. Note that the rows in the table must match the names of reports exactly; otherwise, VBA becomes very cranky when we try to run one of the reports.

Figure 23-2:
This table
contains a
list of all the
reports
in the
database.

The only thing you need to do with the rows is to get them to show up in the list box on the form. Follow the steps listed below to make that happen:

1. **Open the sample database, Chap23.mdb, in Access.**

   This sample database is in the C:\Dummies\Chapter 23 folder.

2. **Click the Forms tab.**

   You should see a list of all the forms in the database, including the one for this example, PrintReports.

3. **Select the PrintReports form in the database window and click the Design button.**

   Access opens the form in design view.

4. **Select the list box by clicking it with the mouse.**

   The Properties window now shows the properties for the list box, like the one shown in Figure 23-3. If you don't see the Properties window, choose View⇨Properties to display it.

5. **Click the All tab of the Properties window to display all the properties for the list box.**

6. **Find the Row Source property in the list and select the blank space next to it by clicking in the region.**

   As soon as you click in the blank region next to the property name, Access displays two buttons. The first button contains a down arrow and the second contains an ellipsis.

7. **Click the down arrow button.**

   Access displays a list of all the tables in the database.

8. **Select the Reports table from the list.**

   The Properties window should now look like the one in Figure 23-4. You don't need to change any of the other settings just yet.

9. **Click the Save button on the toolbar or press Ctrl+S to save the form.**

In the last set of steps, you told Access to display all the rows from the Reports table in the list box. To test this, close the form and reopen it in form view by clicking the Open button on the database toolbar. You should see the form (refer to Figure 23-1) with three rows in the list box. If you don't, open the form in design view and verify that the Row Source property value is correct.

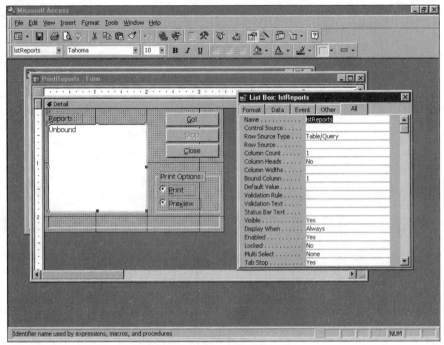

Figure 23-3:
Selecting
the list box
in design
view
shows its
properties.

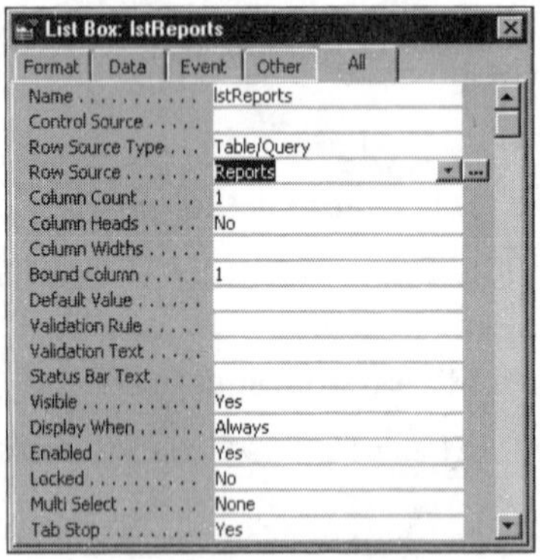

Figure 23-4:
Change the
Row Source
property to
show rows
from the
Reports
table.

Choose All You Want

But wait — you're not finished with the list box yet. You see, you want the
user to be able to select multiple items from the list for printing. Right now,
you can select only one item at a time. To see what we mean, open the form
and try to select more than one report from the list. You can't. Each time
you select another item, the first item becomes deselected.

Of course, you can give your users the ability to select multiple items in many ways.The easiest way by far is to convert the list box from one that allows only single selections into one that allows multiple selections. After you convert the list box to allow multiple selections, you can write VBA code to tell which rows in the list are selected and which aren't. Just follow the next set of steps.

You must follow the steps in this chapter in sequence to create the application that enables the user to preview or print one or more selected reports from a single dialog box.

1. **Open the form in design view again.**

2. **Select the list box by clicking it with the mouse.**

   Access updates the Properties window to display the list box's properties.

3. **Scroll through the list of properties until you find one called Multi Select and select it.**

   The current setting should be None. This means that you can select only one item from the list at a time.

4. **Open the drop-down list of property values by clicking the down-arrow button.**

   Access displays the three possible values for the Multi Select property: None, Simple, and Extended.

5. **Select** Simple **from the list of property values.**

   The Properties window should now look like the one in Figure 23-5.

6. **Click the Save button on the Toolbar or press Ctrl+S to save the form.**

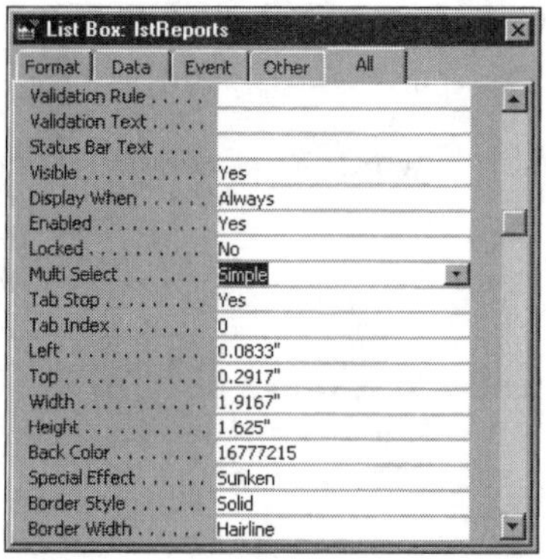

Figure 23-5:
Change the
Multi Select
property to
Simple to
select
multiple
items.

List Box: lstReports	
Format	Data	Event	Other	All
Validation Rule	
Validation Text	
Status Bar Text	
Visible	Yes
Display When	Always
Enabled	Yes
Locked	No
Multi Select	Simple
Tab Stop	Yes
Tab Index	0
Left	0.0833"
Top	0.2917"
Width	1.9167"
Height	1.625"
Back Color	16777215
Special Effect	Sunken
Border Style	Solid
Border Width	Hairline

By following these steps, you just created what's known as a *simple multi-select list box*. It's called simple because it's simple to select more than one item from the list. You select items by clicking them with the mouse. The items stay selected until you click them again. To test your new multi-select list box, follow these steps:

1. **Close the form.**

2. **Open the form in form view by clicking the Open button on the database window.**

   Again, you should see the form as we originally presented it in Figure 23-1.

3. **Click the first item in the list.**

   Access highlights the item.

4. **Click the second item in the list.**

   Access highlights this item as well. Your form should now look like the one shown in Figure 23-6 with the first two items selected.

Figure 23-6:
A multi-select list box lets you pick more than one item at once.

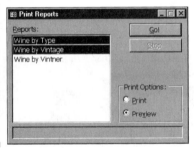

5. **Now click the first item in the list again with the mouse.**

   Access removes the highlighting.

That's how a simple multi-select list box works — click once to select, click again to deselect.

An extended multi-select list box (the other option of a Multi-Select property) enables you to select multiple items, but you must hold down a key when you select each one. The extended box works just like Windows Explorer in which you highlight a range of items by holding down the Shift key as you click the mouse. In the case of Explorer, you highlight individual items by holding down the Ctrl key and clicking.

Who Selected What?

The next step in building the report selection form is to add some VBA code that can tell which reports, if any, the user has selected. This function is a bit tricky because more than one item may be selected. Single-select list boxes (those with a Multi-Select property of None) can't have more than one item selected. You can always tell which item is selected, therefore, by inspecting the list box's Value property. Trying to use the Value property with a multi-select list box, on the other hand, is only asking for trouble.

For multi-select list boxes, you need to use another property called *Selected*. Selected is kind of unique in that, unlike most properties, it requires an argument. You feed the Selected property a row number and it tells you whether that row is selected by returning either True or False.

The Selected property makes determining which items are selected relatively easy. You simply loop through all the items in the list, asking the Selected property whether the item is highlighted in each loop iteration. Follow the next set of steps to add to this chapter's example the VBA code that does this.

You must follow the steps in this chapter in sequence to create the application that enables the user to preview or print one or more selected reports from a single dialog box.

1. **Close the form if it's already open and re-open it in design view by clicking the Design button on the database window.**

2. **Click the Code button on the Toolbar or choose <u>V</u>iew⇨<u>C</u>ode.**

   Access opens the form's code window. The window should be empty except for the words *Option Compare Database* and *Option Explicit* at the top of the page.

3. **Open the Object drop-down list at the top-left of the code window and select the cmdGo entry from the list.**

   VBA creates an empty procedure for the Go buttons click event called cmdGo_Click. Your code window should look like the one in Figure 23-7.

Figure 23-7:
Start with the empty event procedure for the Go button's click event.

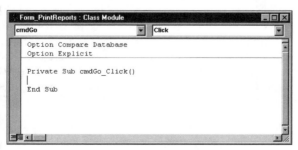

4. Type the following code into the body of the procedure:

```
Dim intCount As Integer
Dim strReport As String

For intCount = 0 To lstReports.ListCount - 1
  If lstReports.Selected(intCount) Then

    strReport = lstReports.ItemData(intCount)

    MsgBox strReport

  End If
Next
```

Your code window should look like the one shown in Figure 23-8.

5. Click the Save button on the toolbar or press Ctrl+S to save the form.

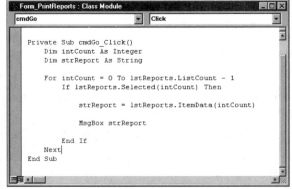

Figure 23-8:
This code finds all the selected reports in the list.

So what have you just done? To find out, examine the VBA code. First, you declared two variables — an Integer (intCount) and a String (strReport). The procedure uses intCount to loop through all the rows in the list box. It uses strReport, on the other hand, to store the name of a selected report, after it determines which ones are selected.

After declaring the variables, the procedure enters a For..Next loop, moving through the values 0 through lstReports.Count – 1. What exactly is lstReports.Count – 1? LstReports is the list box containing the reports and its Count property tells you how many items are in the list. The reason you need to start at 0 and subtract 1 from the total count is that rows in Access list and combo boxes are numbered starting at 0, not 1 — strange but true.

Once inside the loop, the procedure uses the Selected property we just mentioned. It passes the row number stored in intCount and uses the return value in an If..Then statement. If the Selected property returns True because a particular row is selected, the If condition succeeds and the rest of the code runs.

Right now, the rest of the code is just two lines, but you add more in following sections of this chapter. For now, those two lines of code grab the name of the selected report and display it in a message box. To get the name of the report, the procedure uses another neat little property of list boxes — the ItemData property. Like Selected, ItemData asks for a row number and returns the actual value in that row. Using ItemData you can find out the value of any row in the list, whether or not the row is selected!

You can use the ItemData property with single-select list boxes and combo boxes too! You aren't limited to multi-select list boxes.

To test your code, follow the steps listed in the preceding section to select one or more items from the list. After you select some items, click the Go button. Access should display the name of each selected report in a message box. In the next section, "Cranking Out Reports," we replace the call to MsgBox with code to print or preview the reports.

Cranking Out Reports

You're halfway home now. Finding out what reports are selected is the hardest part of this chapter's exercise. The rest is pretty straightforward VBA code and a little window dressing.

You must follow the steps in this chapter in sequence to create the application that enables the user to preview or print one or more selected reports from a single dialog box.

The next thing to add to the form is the code that actually prints the reports. You may already know that you can use the OpenReport method of the DoCmd object of Access to print reports. You use that, along with the option group on the form, to give the user the option to print or preview the report. Follow these steps:

1. **Open the form's code window by first opening the form in design view and then chooseing View⇨Code.**

   You should see the code in the cmdGo_Click procedure that you created in the preceding section, "Who Selected What?"

2. Remove the line of code containing the MsgBox statement.

You no longer need this because you verified in the section "Who Selected What?" that the For..Next loop works as it should.

3. Type the following VBA code in place of the MsgBox statement:

```
If grpPrintOptions.Value = 1 Then
   DoCmd.OpenReport strReport, acNormal
Else
   DoCmd.OpenReport strReport, acPreview
End If
```

Your code window should now look like the one in Figure 23-9.

4. Click the Save button on the toolbar or press Ctrl+S to save the form.

```
Form_PrintReports : Class Module

cmdGo                              Click

Private Sub cmdGo_Click()
    Dim intCount As Integer
    Dim strReport As String

    For intCount = 0 To lstReports.ListCount - 1
        If lstReports.Selected(intCount) Then

            strReport = lstReports.ItemData(intCount)

            If grpPrintOptions.Value = 1 Then
                DoCmd.OpenReport strReport, acNormal
            Else
                DoCmd.OpenReport strReport, acPreview
            End If
        End If
    Next
End Sub
```

The rather simple bit of code you just added checks the Value property of the form's option group. An Access option group takes on the value of the option button that's currently selected. Inspect the option buttons in design view; note that the button labeled Print has the value 1 and the other, labeled Preview, has the value 2. The If..Then statement in the sample code, therefore, determines whether the user wants to print or preview the reports.

The code goes on to execute the OpenReport method of the DoCmd object, passing the name of the report as the first argument. Depending on which option button the user selected, the procedure passes either acNormal or acPreview as the second argument to OpenReport. These are constants that tell DoCmd to print or preview the report, respectively.

If you're unfamiliar with the wacky DoCmd object in Access, check out Chapter 10.

You can test the code by opening the form in form view and selecting one or more reports from the list. Unless you have excess paper lying around, make sure the Preview option button is selected instead of the Print button. Click the Go button to run the reports. Access should open each one in print preview mode. Figure 23-10 shows what this looks like. You can see the two selected reports trying in vain to hide behind the selection form.

Adding Error Handling

One more bit of business needs to be addressed — handling errors in the procedure. Good programmers (of which you are undoubtedly one) put error handling in every procedure they write. Error handling is particularly important in this procedure. Why? If a user decides to send a report directly to the printer, and then clicks the Cancel button on the Printing dialog box, Access generates an error. Unless you add code to cope with this error, the procedure blows up in your user's face. Not only is this messy, but your user won't like it very much when it happens.

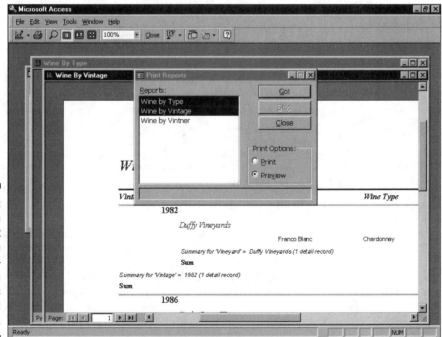

Figure 23-10:
You can see that the code works — there are two reports open behind the form.

We discuss coping with errors in Chapter 17. If you're unfamiliar with the general principles, visit that chapter.

To keep this error from appearing and bothering your user, you need to trap any error and see if it is the specific error caused when a user cancels the printing of a report. Every error that can occur in an Access application has a unique number. The error associated with canceling a report is 2501. Follow the next set of steps to add an error handler that filters this out and prevents the user from seeing the error message.

You must follow the steps in this chapter in sequence to create the application that enables the user to preview or print one or more selected reports from a single dialog box.

1. **Reopen the code window for the form.**

2. **Near the top of the cmdGo_Click procedure, right after the variable declarations, type the following line of code:**

```
On Error Goto HandleError
```

This establishes the error handler. If an error occurs while the procedure is running, VBA will jump to the label HandleError within the procedure.

3. **At the bottom of the procedure, after the Next statement, add this code:**

```
AllDone:
   Exit Sub
HandleError:
   Select Case Err.Number
     Case 2501
     Case Else
        MsgBox Err.Description, vbExclamation
   End Select
   Resume AllDone
```

This code defines both the exit point for the procedure and the error handler itself.

Now, if an error occurs, VBA will execute the Select Case statement inside the error handler. You can see from the code that the Select Case statement looks specifically for error 2501 by checking the Number property of the VBA Err object. If error 2501 occurs, VBA does nothing except resume execution at the AllDone label, effectively ending the procedure. For all other errors, the procedure displays a message box containing the error message (which you get from the Err object's Description property).

Letting the User Cancel

If you've followed along with this chapter's example so far, you should now have a fully functional addition to any application. The form that you create prints or previews reports and correctly handles errors that may occur while doing so. If you have an existing application, you can easily import the form (along with the Reports table) into your application's MDB file and use it there.

One nice feature to have is the option for users to cancel the printing process right from the report selection form. In case you were wondering, that's what the Stop button is for on the form. Adding this functionality is really quite easy, requiring only a few lines of code. To add it to your copy of the form, follow the next set of steps.

1. **Open the report selection form's code window.**

2. **At the top of the module, just *above* the declaration for the cmdGo_Click procedure, add the following module-level variable declaration:**

```
Dim Cancelled As Boolean
```

The cmdGo_Click procedure will use this variable to tell whether the Stop button has been clicked.

3. **Within the body of the cmdGo_Click procedure, add the following line of code just *before* the For statement:**

```
Cancelled = False
```

This resets the variable to False before starting the loop, so that, if the user cancels printing and then starts it again, the procedure doesn't quit prematurely.

4. **Next, find the If..Then statement that contains a reference to the DoCmd object.**

5. **Put the cursor just *after* the End If statement, click once with the mouse, and add the following VBA code:**

```
DoEvents
If Cancelled Then
   Goto AllDone
End If
```

This If..Then statement checks the value of the Cancelled variable and jumps to the AllDone label if it is True. The DoEvents statement makes sure the user has time to click the Stop button while the procedure is running.

6. Open the Object list at the top-left of the code window and select the cmdStop entry.

VBA creates an empty procedure called cmdStop_Click for the Stop button's Click event.

7. Inside the body of the cmdStop_Click procedure, type the following line of code:

```
Cancelled = True
```

You probably guessed that's what you needed to do, didn't you? This sets the value of the Cancelled variable to True when the user clicks the Stop button. When VBA processes the For..Next loop, the If..Then statement that you just added causes VBA to jump out of the loop, ending the procedure.

This technique can be useful whenever you have a long running process. The most important thing to include is the DoEvents statement. This gives your user a chance to click the button while the procedure is running. Normally, VBA takes over and doesn't relinquish control to the user until the running procedure is finished. DoEvents is a way of telling VBA, "Hey, give somebody else a turn, will ya?"

Juggling the Buttons

The piece of functionality you just added to your form is nice, but it does give rise to another problem. Now that your users can click the Stop button while the procedure is running, what happens if they click the Go button instead? You know what happens — the printing process starts again!

The simplest way to handle this problem is to disable the Go button before starting the printing process so that the user can't click it again. Then you can enable the button so that, when the procedure finishes printing, your user can print some more reports. You've probably worked with other applications that do something similar. To add this to the sample form, follow the next set of steps.

You must follow the steps in this chapter in sequence to create the application that enables the user to preview or print one or more selected reports from a single dialog box.

1. Open the form's code window.

2. **Near the top of the cmdGo_Click procedure, just *after* the On Error statement, add this VBA code:**

```
cmdStop.Enabled = True
cmdStop.SetFocus
cmdGo.Enabled = False
```

This code disables the Go button. Before doing so, however, it enables the Stop button and makes it the active control by calling its SetFocus method. You have to add this code because Access won't let you disable the control that has the focus, and the Go button *will* have the focus because the user just clicked it!

3. **Near the bottom of the procedure, just *after* the AllDone label, add this code:**

```
cmdGo.Enabled = True
cmdGo.SetFocus
cmdStop.Enabled = False
```

These statements reverse the process. They enable the Go button, make it the active control, and then disable the Stop button.

Not too painful a process, huh? You now have a form that responds intelligently to what's going on inside its VBA code.

You can use this technique in other applications. Disabling controls while you're running code helps keep users from getting into trouble.

Dressing Up the User Interface

The remainder of this chapter is devoted to adding a few features that dress up the way the form's user interface looks and works. Specifically, you're going to add a status bar that tells the user what report is currently being printed. You're also going to create code that deselects each report in the list as the report is printed.

You must follow the steps in this chapter in sequence to create the application that enables the user to preview or print one or more selected reports from a single dialog box.

Many applications have some type of status indicator that tells the user what a control does or what action is currently happening. Providing good feedback is an important aspect of any application. We provided a label on the report selection form to act as a status bar. All you need to do is add the code to put text in it:

1. **Open the form's code window.**

2. **In the cmdGo_Click procedure, find the line of code that reads, strReport = lstReports.ItemData(intCount).**

3. **Just after this statement, add the following two lines of VBA code:**

```
lblStatus.Caption = "Now printing " & strReport
DoEvents
```

The name of the label is lblStatus. The first statement sets its Caption property to some static text plus the name of the currently printing report. The DoEvents statement gives Access time to refresh the form before starting to print the report.

4. **Further down in the procedure, just after the AllDone label, add this line of code:**

```
lblStatus.Caption = ""
```

This statement is important because it clears any text from the label control. If you don't include this line of code, the name of the last report printed becomes stuck in the label even after it finishes printing.

The only thing left to do is to add one more line of code to deselect the report from the list as the report is printed. The reason for doing this is twofold. First, it gives the user additional feedback. The user sees each report removed from the list as it's printed, assuring him that the process is moving ahead. Second, if the user decides to cancel the printing process halfway through, he or she doesn't need to manually deselect the reports that have already been printed.

So, to finish the report selection form, follow these steps.

1. **Open the form's code window.**

2. **Locate the second DoEvents statement in the cmdGo_Click procedure.**

    You can find it just before the line of code that reads If Cancelled Then.

3. **Just *before* the DoEvents statement, add this line of code:**

```
lstReports.Selected(intCount) = False
```

The Selected property is introduced at the beginning of this chapter. This statement simply sets the Selected property to False for the current row. When you set it to False, Access deselects the current item.

The Whole Deal

Well, that's it! If you have followed the steps throughout this chapter, you just created a useful form that you can add to any Access application to help automate the reporting process. Though this is a simple example, it demonstrates several techniques that you can use with Access forms and reports.

Here's what the finished code module looks like:

```
Dim Cancelled As Boolean

Private Sub cmdGo_Click()
  Dim intCount As Integer
  Dim strReport As String

  On Error GoTo HandleError

  cmdStop.Enabled = True
  cmdStop.SetFocus
  cmdGo.Enabled = False

  Cancelled = False

  For intCount = 0 To lstReports.ListCount - 1
    If lstReports.Selected(intCount) Then

      strReport = lstReports.ItemData(intCount)

      lblStatus.Caption = "Now printing " & _
        strReport
      DoEvents

      If grpPrintOptions.Value = 1 Then
        DoCmd.OpenReport strReport, acNormal
      Else
        DoCmd.OpenReport strReport, acPreview
      End If

      lstReports.Selected(intCount) = False

      DoEvents
```

(continued)

(continued)

```
If Cancelled Then
        Exit For
      End If
    End If
  Next

AllDone:

  lblStatus.Caption = ""

  cmdGo.Enabled = True
  cmdGo.SetFocus
  cmdStop.Enabled = False

  Exit Sub
HandleError:
  Select Case Err.Number
    Case 2501
    Case Else
      MsgBox Err.Description, vbExclamation
  End Select
  Resume AllDone
End Sub

Private Sub cmdStop_Click()
  Cancelled = True
End Sub
```

As we mentioned at the beginning of the chapter, you can also find this by looking at the finished version of the form, called `PrintReports (done)`, in the Chap23.MDB database that's on the disk. And we've even included comments!

Part V
The Part of Tens

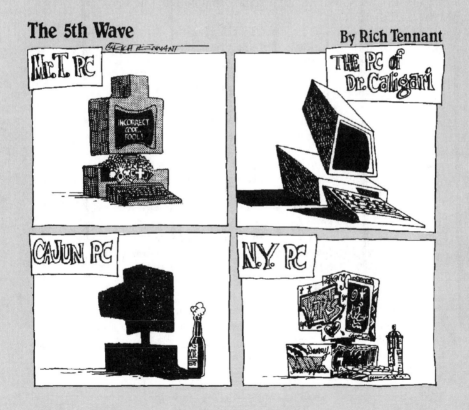

In this part . . .

Welcome to the signature Part of Tens — a section that no *...For Dummies* book would ever dream of sitting on the shelf without. Can you guess what's in this part? Please select from the following:

(a) Tons of useful information that couldn't fit anywhere else

(b) Stuff that means more as you make your way through the rest of the book

(c) Cool stuff that deserved its own special little place

If you answered a, b, and c, you are correct — it's a little bit of each. Your gold star's in the mail!

Venture through each chapter and prepare to be surprised by all the great tidbits you can pick up. First, we alert you to migration opportunities — that's the corporate lingo for some stuff you need to deal with that may not be fun. Then we draw a roadmap of places you can go and things you can see on your quest for more knowledge and experience with Visual Basic for Applications in Office 97. We leave you with an appendix that uncovers the awesomeness of the Office Developer Edition.

This part contains lots of twists and turns, from migration to more Web-based resources, so have a safe trip and always wear a seatbelt!

Chapter 24

Ten Tips for Migrating Your Applications to Office 97

- -

In This Chapter

▶ Your old macro code — where is it?

▶ Property values get picky about types (strong-typing)

▶ Reminders about 16-bit components that need replacements

▶ API calls living in a 32-bit world

▶ WordBasic is dead, and other gotchas

▶ PowerPoint changes, and the possible pain

▶ Excel reference changes with automation code

▶ Access conversion tips

▶ References that can really help

- -

As with any change, a little bit of pain or cleanup is bound to occur. The move to Office 97 is no exception. End users instantly have access to lots of great new functionality and you, the developer, inherit lots of new and cool development tools. The downside, if you can forgive us for stating the obvious, is you have the chore of testing your custom application in Office 97.

Where did my code go?

If you plan to convert any of your documents and workbooks or presentations from previous versions of Office, it may appear that your code or module sheets are missing. Don't despair. Your macro code is accessible via the Visual Basic Editor.

To view your code,

1. Select <u>M</u>acro from the <u>T</u>ools menu and then choose <u>V</u>isual Basic Editor.

2. Locate the Modules in the Project Explorer window.

3. Double-click the Modules folder to view its contents.

4. Locate the code that you are interested in.

When your old Word templates are opened by Word 97, each WordBasic procedure is converted into its own module. If your Word template had 100 procedures, you now have 100 modules, each containing exactly one procedure. Sounds a bit unwieldy. You may want to consider reorganizing your procedures into only a few modules. Now, what about that closet of yours?

Strong typing (You mean I have to hit the keys harder?)

The biggest across-the-board change with the introduction of VBA is that Office 97 type libraries now use *strong-typing* for property values. What does this mean? The VBA code of your older applications may not compile if you have used inappropriate data types in statements that reference properties. As an example, consider the ControlSource property of a control in Access. In previous versions of Access, you could set this property equal to a null value, as seen in the following code snippet:

```
Controlname.ControlSource = Null
```

In Office 97, the ControlSource property value requires a string value. If you need to set the ControlSource property to Null, the proper way to do it now is to set it equal to the Empty String, as seen here:

```
Controlname.ControlSource = ""
```

This change is a very devious one in Office 97. If you are wondering why this change is such a big deal, you probably are under the impression that problems such as this are caught by the code compiler. Unfortunately, you won't know you have a problem until you run the application that failed to use strong-typing. If your old code from previous versions of Office is not working, verify that all your variables match the property data types.

16-bit stuff no longer works!

If your move to Office 97 is accompanied by a move to a 32-bit operating system, you may have 16-bit issues to deal with, in addition to general Office 97 changes. The following 16-bit components need to be addressed:

✔ Any function calls to 16-bit DLLs need to be converted to 32-bit DLLs. DLLs are dynamic link libraries. If you aren't familiar with them, it's unlikely that you have anything to worry about here.

✔ 16-bit ActiveX Controls (previously know as OLE Custom Controls), such as a Calendar Control, need to be replaced with 32-bit equivalents.

✔ ODBC drivers for non-Microsoft databases need updated 32-bit drivers. (Office 97 includes the family ODBC drivers for Win32, such as SQL Server.)

Although this all sounds depressing, you really don't need to do much to fix the problem. If 32-bit counterparts are available for your 16-bit DLLs, Active X Controls, and ODBC drivers, you can switch to them. Availability will guide you.

API unpleasantness

Take a look at the item that is likely to present you with the greatest challenges — handling your API calls.

API is an acronym for *Applications Programing Interface*. Simply put, an API is composed of the functions that make Windows applications go. If you are unfamiliar with what an API call is all about, it's unlikely that you have to deal with this, unless you've inherited someone else's code. If you're forced to deal with someone's code, where do you want us to send the bamboo shoots?

What happens to all those great 16-bit API calls you have capitalized on in your 16-bit applications when you port them to 32-bit applications? All of your 16-bit API calls need to be examined and changed to 32-bit API calls. Sounds straightforward so far, but keep reading.

The good news is that some of the 32-bit API calls have additional functionality that you can capitalize on and some API calls have more robust replacements that you can migrate to when you are ready. The bad news is that some API calls are no longer supported in Win32. In any event, you have no escape from visiting each and every 16-bit API call declaration to prepare it for Win32. Plainly speaking, 16-bit applications need to call 16-bit APIs and 32-bit applications need to call 32-bit APIs, so this task is not optional.

You need to go through a number of steps to ensure that your applications continue to work as intended in the new 32-bit arena:

1. **Locate all your API declarations in your application and any applicable add-in libraries.**

   (API functions are declared in the Declarations section of modules, so be sure that you check these thoroughly.)

2. Reference Win32 API documentation to see what your next steps are.

Does the API call still exist? Has its functionality changed at all? Are there new arguments to worry about?

If your API call is still valid in Win32, continue with the next few steps. If not, you need to remove the API declaration and subsequent usage in your application. This means going through your code and finding every instance of the API call. If you fail to remove any remnants, your code won't run.

3. Check your function name for case sensitivity.

This alteration is a very sneaky change that you must learn to live with in a 32-bit world. API function names in Win 32 are now case sensitive.

If you are one of those people that likes to keep CAPS LOCK on, this is one more reason to turn it off!

4. Check for integer arguments.

The 32-bit API calls use long integers for arguments and return values, not short integers as were used in 16-bit API calls. You need to make the necessary changes to the API declaration statement (in your Declarations section of your application module) and then check each usage of the function to be sure that the arguments that are passed to the API call are long integers as well.

5. Check for string arguments.

The 32-bit API now has two versions of every API call — ANSI and Unicode.

If you are dying to know why some API calls have two versions, here's your answer. ANSI functions can only handle languages with 255 characters or less. Languages such as Japanese are left essentially without an API call. If you are using the Japanese version of Microsoft Access, for example, you want to utilize the Unicode version of your API calls.

You need to alias your API function with the proper new function name, which is likely to be the ANSI version. By providing an alias, which is the real name of the API call, you avoid changing all references to it throughout your code. If you do not alias the function, you get an error message that lets you know that the specified function can't be found.

Take the Win16 GetWindowText API call as an example, which returns a window caption. The 16-bit call GetWindowText is now represented by GetWindowTextA (ANSI) and GetWindowTextW (Unicode) in the Win32 API.

The following statement is an example of the Win 16 API declaration for the GetWindowText function:

```
Declare Function GetWindowText Lib "User" (ByVal hWnd As
        Integer, ByVal lpString As String, ByVal aint As
        Integer) As Integer
```

To use the same API call in the 32-bit world, you need to make a number of modifications to the function declaration, as shown in bold text in the following statement:

```
Declare Function GetWindowText Lib "User32" Alias
        "GetWindowTextA" (ByVal hwnd As Long, ByVal
        lpString As String, ByVal cch As Long) As Long
```

The changes that were made have been bolded in the Win32 API declaration and are listed here:

1. Verified that the API call is still valid in the 32-bit API.

2. Changed the library reference to the 32-bit library "User32".

3. Changed the short integer (Integer) argument types to long integers (Long).

4. Added an alias ("GetWindowTextA") so the function can run properly, because GetWindowText no longer exists under its old name.

For more information, reference "Porting Your 16-Bit Microsoft Office-Based Solutions to 32-Bit Microsoft Office" at www.microsoft.com/OfficeDev/TechInfo/porting.htm and download a Win32 API reference from www.microsoft.com/officedev/techinfo/win32api.exe

WordBasic is dead, and other gotchas

Now that Word enjoys VBA along with its other siblings in the Office suite, what happens to all that great WordBasic code that you slaved over? When your templates (which contain the code) are opened in Word 97, your WordBasic code is converted to VBA, as shown in Figure 24-1. However, if VBA is not familiar with some of the WordBasic commands, such as StartOfDocument and EditCopy, these commands are represented as methods of the WordBasic object.

The short story is that your applications built in Word can continue to function once converted to Word 97. So, perhaps our subtitle indicating that WordBasic is dead is a bit misleading. It is, however, strongly recommended that you rewrite your applications to capitalize on the power of VBA. You may wonder why you even need to bother to change your code to VBA if it still works. We can give you a few reasons: performance, efficiency, and future maintenance.

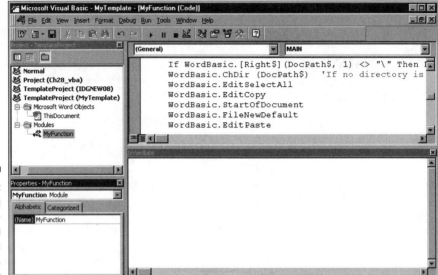

Figure 24-1:
Witnessing
a conver-
sion from
WordBasic
to VBA.

A few words of caution:

- **One-way conversion:** This WordBasic to VBA conversion process can't be undone by saving the file back as Word 6.0 or 95 format. If you resave your template as Word 6.0/95, all the VBA is *removed* and you are left with neither VBA nor your original Word Basic.

- **Old syntax errors bite now:** If you have any WordBasic syntax errors that you never caught, VBA finds them. In fact, VBA refuses to compile your code properly until you find syntax errors and fix them!

- **Code in Normal.dot is a no-no:** Developers ought to refrain from using the Normal template as a code repository, because all code stored in Normal must be public.

If you have been blissfully putting WordBasic code into your Normal template, we are here to inform you that the honeymoon is over. You want to move any code out of the Normal template or save your Normal.dot file under a different name before attempting a conversion to Word 97. In Word 97, the Normal template must be public and therefore cannot be protected from tampering.

Please reference "WordBasic Migration to Visual Basic" at www.microsoft.com/WordDev/TechInfo/wbmgrat.htm for more information.

PowerPoint changes for your own good, even though they ouch!

If you haven't done any development in PowerPoint prior to picking up this book, then you are unlikely to experience any migration-related pain. All your presentations probably will convert without a hitch. But what about those custom applications? In Chapter 9 we introduce new and improved object model of PowerPoint, which has been modified to be more consistent with its Office peers. The object model still contains top level objects, such as Application, Presentation, and Slide, but you find that some of the sub-objects have either been renamed, removed, or replaced.

Although the newly expanded object model provides you with lots of new capabilities, there is an unpleasant side effect of these object model changes. If you have any solutions that use the object model for PowerPoint 95, they need to be revised for PowerPoint 97. To determine if your applications are affected, review your usage of objects and refer to the new object model.

For more specific conversion information, you may want to read "Migrating Solutions to PowerPoint 97" at www.microsoft.com/PowerPointDev/TechInfo/ppt97mig.htm

I asked for a worksheet, not a workbook

Some of your older Automation code that used Excel as an Automation server may not work if you used the CreateObject, GetObject, or CreateLink functions. For example, in previous versions of Excel, the following code statement would return a pointer to the first worksheet in the workbook.

```
Set xlObj=GetObject("filename.xls")
```

However, the same code in Excel 97 returns a pointer to the entire workbook. Any applications using these functions need to be revised accordingly or you may experience some unanticipated behaviors.

For more information see "Migrating Solutions to Microsoft Excel 97" at www.microsoft.com/ExcelDev/TechInfo/xl97mig.htm

You can't go back, and other access tips

Planning a conversion to Access 97? If you're a seasoned Access developer, then you are all too familiar with the fact that conversion is a one-way street. After you convert a database to Microsoft Access 97, you can't open that database in earlier versions of Microsoft Access, nor can you save it back as an older version. Ouch! Always be safe and make a copy of your database before running it through a conversion of any sort.

The following are a number of conversion issues for Access 97 that we want to point out to you:

✔ New reserved words to watch out for.

✔ Old syntax continues to work, but it's time to change it! In the next version of Access you may not be so lucky as to have the old Access 1.1 code constructs still working for you. (The time has come to trade in your db.OpenSnapshot commands for the proper replacement — db.OpenRecordSet.)

✔ You need to convert more than MDB files. Don't forget that your Add-Ins and Libraries need to move to Access 97, as well.

✔ Take advantage of the Access capability to convert your macro-generated menus to command bars. Your old menus continue to work, but you need to plan on using CommandBars.

Before attempting a conversion, we highly recommend reading "Microsoft Access 97 Conversion Issues" at www.microsoft.com/AccessDev/AccWhite/acc97cnv.htm

Check out the Microsoft Web site

Throughout this chapter, we provide a number of Web addresses found at www.microsoft.com where you can go and find additional information. Microsoft wants you to move to Office 97, and in our opinion has done an excellent job in providing pertinent conversion information. We strongly encourage you to surf around and take advantage of this information that Microsoft has compiled for you.

Chapter 25

Ten Sources of Cool and/or Free Stuff for Office 97 and VBA

• •

In This Chapter

▶ Getting some new Office Assistants

▶ Finding free software for Office 97 and VBA

▶ Locating useful information on the Web

• •

*A*s much as we'd like to, we can't give you every bit of information you need about Office 97 development and VBA in such a short book. So to finish off this text, we decided to clue you in on where you can go to get more information and even some free stuff! Everything we mention in this chapter is available through the Internet, and most of it comes from Microsoft. So fire up your Web browser and take a peek at what we found.

As with everything on the Internet, we can't guarantee that the Web sites listed here will still be around when you read this book. Nor can we assure you of the content quality that you find on these Web sites. This chapter does not constitute a guarantee or endorsement of any kind, so use what you find at your own risk.

New Assistants

As if enough disk space weren't already consumed by Office Assistants, you can get more assistants for free from Microsoft. Point your Web browser at `http://www.microsoft.com/officefreestuff/office/assistants.htm` and you'll get a list of Assistants available for download. Among the characters you find there is our all-time favorite, Earl the cat (see Figure 25-1).

Earl has a very enviable outlook on life (he is a cat, after all) and will keep you in stitches with his goofy antics. Of course, more reserved Assistants are available, too, such as the Genius, Hoverbot, and Earl's distant cat cousin, Scribble; but what's the sense of wasting megabytes of disk space if you can't have fun?

Figure 25-1:
Earl the cat has the right attitude for Office development.

Go Beyond Help at Microsoft

Looking for more detailed information than on-line help provides? Check out the Microsoft Beyond Help Web site. Beyond Help is brought to you by some of the top product experts at Microsoft and offers numerous tips and tidbits to help make working with Office easier and more fun. You can see from Figure 25-2 that their emphasis is on getting things done fast and with flair.

You can find Beyond Help at `http://www.microsoft.com/officefreestuff/officehelpextras`.

VBA Companion free evaluation

VBA Companion, from APEX Software, is a reference tool that shows information on components like Microsoft Office and ActiveX controls. Like the VBA Object Browser on steroids, the Companion gives detailed reports on

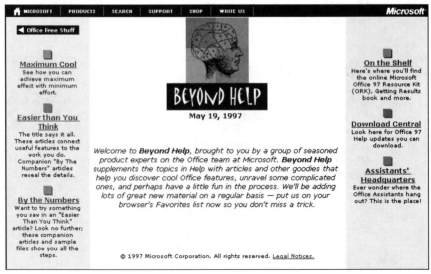

Figure 25-2:
Beyond Help is a watering hole for your knowledge thirst.

object, properties, and methods. Figure 25-3 shows the main window. One nice thing about VBA Companion is that, unlike Object Browser, you can use it without running one of the Office products. You can download an evaluation version that works with ActiveX controls from the APEX Web site at `http://www.apexsc.com/ocxedition.html`.

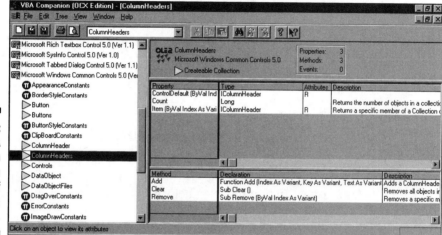

Figure 25-3: VBA Companion gives you loads of information on objects.

Word 97 sample code

If Word is your primary development tool and you're new to Word 97, you can get a whole pile of sample code from Microsoft. Microsoft has made available samples from the Word Development Kit that show the difference between the old WordBasic (boo! hiss!) and VBA (hooray!). All in all, you can examine more than 70 different procedures. You can find the examples in WRDKEX97.EXE at `http://www.microsoft.com/officedev/freestuff`.

ODE AutoDemo

Also on the Office Developer's Web site at `http://www.microsoft.com/officedev/freestuff` is a self-running demo of Office 97 Developer Edition (ODE). We cover the ODE in detail in the Appendix to this book. You can see what Microsoft has to say about the ODE by downloading the demo file.

Free issue of Access/Office/VBA Advisor

Access/Office/VBA Advisor magazine, from Advisor Publications, is a monthly journal covering all aspects of Office development. It features monthly columns on programming issues as well as feature articles on various Office products. You can request a free issue of the magazine by visiting the Advisor Web site at `http://www.advisor.com`.

Free issue of Microsoft Office Developer's Journal

The Cobb Group, a publisher of many software-related journals, is offering a free issue of its *Microsoft Office Developer's Journal*. This monthly periodical focuses on Office programming and design issues. You can sign up for a free issue at `http://www.cobb.com/adj/free1001.htm`.

Get informed with Informant

A new player in the Office development magazine game is Informant Communications Group. The group offers yet another source of information for those seeking Office application help in the form of *Microsoft Office & Visual Basic for Applications Developer* magazine. Like *Access/Office/VBA Advisor* and *Microsoft Office Developer's Journal*, *Microsoft Office & Visual Basic for Applications Developer* features articles for people who develop applications with Microsoft Office 97 and VBA. You can get the nitty-gritty details from Informant's Web site at `http://www.informant.com`.

Start your day right

Begin each new day with a tidbit of information for getting the most out of Microsoft Office. Check out the Office Tip of the Day at `http://www.tipworld.com/office.html`.

And much, much more . . .

We could go on and on, but we don't really know what kind of help or tool you're after. Your best bet is to try one of the Web search engines to locate more information on Microsoft Office and VBA. Our favorite search engine is Digital's Alta Vista (`http://www.altavista.digital.com`) but others are available, such as Yahoo!, Lycos, Magellan, Infoseek, and Excite. If you don't have a preference, check out the Microsoft search page (see Figure 25-4) at `http://www.microsoft.com/search/default.asp`. The page enables you to search all of the Microsoft Web site or use one of the other popular search engines from one convenient page.

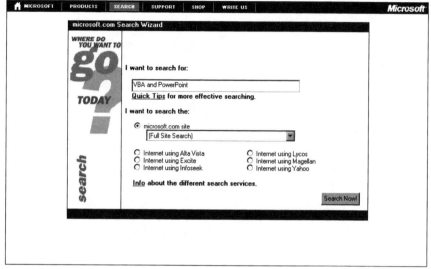

Figure 25-4:
The
Microsoft
search
page can
help you
find the
information
you need.

Appendix

About the Office 97 Developer Edition

• •

*U*nless you've been living under a rock lately, you've no doubt heard the buzz about the Office 97 Developer Edition (known among the *in* crowd as the ODE). After all, this is a book on Office 97 development, you're an Office 97 developer, and the ODE is for people like you. So what is this thing anyway? We explore that very issue in this chapter where we explain the top things that you need to know about the ODE. Although we can't cover every single aspect of the ODE in detail, we do give you enough information to sound intelligent when you talk about it to your boss. Besides, that's what it's all about anyway, right?

Now that we've said that, we think that, after you read this appendix, you'll definitely want to get a copy of the ODE if you haven't already. The ODE is filled with all kinds of useful information as well as programs that you can use to make the development of Office applications easier.

What is the ODE?

We start off with the most basic question of all — what is the ODE? You have Microsoft Office 97. Do you need something else in order to develop applications? Actually, no, you don't. Of course, that depends on your definition of *need*. You see, the ODE is really a set of tools, utilities, and documentation that you can use *with* Office 97, not something that you absolutely need to have.

If you want to get more information about the ODE before you plunk down the bucks for it, check out the Office Developer Web site at http:// www.microsoft. com/officedev

What you get with the ODE

Of course, before you plunk down your hard-earned cash for another piece of software, it makes sense to know what's in the one that you think you want to buy. In this section, we give you an overview of the ODE contents.

Access runtime license

One big reason to buy the ODE is that it provides you with the ability to distribute your Access applications to people who don't own a copy of Access. Not only does the ODE give you some tools that make it easy to do this, ODE includes a piece of paper from Microsoft that says you can do this without paying Microsoft any more money.

Access Setup Wizard

Setting up an Access application can be complex. Lots of files need to be installed, icons need to be created, and so on. The Access Setup Wizard helps walk you through the process, step by step. The end result is a customized setup program that your users can run to install your application. What could be easier? We cover the setup wizard in the section "Using the Setup Wizard" in this chapter.

Access replication tools

Access 97 includes an advanced feature called *replication*. In a nutshell, replication gives you the ability to make special copies of an Access database (called *replicas*) and pass them out to different people in your organization. These people can then do whatever they want to the data (add new records, change records, and delete records). You can then ask for the replicas back and synchronize them with one another. The end result is that all of the copies end up with the same data once again.

Although you don't need the ODE to create and synchronize replicas, it does come with some tools that may make managing replication easier. The Replication Manager application comes only with the ODE and lets you see graphically who has your replicas and which ones need to be synchronized. By using other tools in the ODE, you can also set up synchronization schedules, processing replicas automatically with no intervention on your part.

We decided not to cover replication in this book because it's an advanced feature of one product in the Office 97 suite. Besides, if you understand what replication is, it's easy to make it work with Access. Consider using the tools in the ODE, however, if you have lots of replicas spread out all over the place or you need to schedule automatic, unattended synchronization.

Access source code control integration

If you work with other developers on a project, you know that sometimes it's hard to manage everyone's efforts. You need to make sure that each person has the parts of the application that they need to do their job. You also have to make sure that one developer doesn't inadvertently overwrite another developer's changes. To make this easier for Access developers, the ODE ships with an Access add-in that links Access to a source code control program.

If you've never worked with source code control before, you can think of the source code control program as a librarian, whose job it is to maintain the source files that make up an application. Anyone can go to the library to browse the information there, but only one person can check out a specific copy of a book at any given time. Source code control works much the same way. A central database or source code is maintained, and developers can use this to create versions of the application for testing. If a developer needs to make a change to a source file, he or she must *check it out* from the database. After making changes, the developer then checks the file back in. This approach prevents developers from stomping all over each other's changes.

The ODE comes with an add-in that links Access to a source code control program so that multiple developers can work on the same database project at the same time. To use this, however, you need to have a source code control program such as the Microsoft Visual SourceSafe. If you don't have such a program, the add-in can't do you any good.

Access and VBA manuals

If you find yourself yearning for the good old days of printed manuals, the ODE has two of them for you. You get both *Building Applications with Microsoft Access 97* and the *Microsoft Office/Visual Basic Programmer's Guide* when you purchase the ODE. The former details how you can create applications by using Microsoft Access. Because the *Building Applications* book only covers Access, it can go into a lot more detail than we do in this book. The latter text shows you how to utilize VBA in all of the Office products.

ActiveX controls

If you're looking for a way to spruce up your user interfaces, you may consider using some of the ActiveX controls that come with the ODE. These controls are like the controls that you find in Access or Microsoft Forms but are much more complex, providing additional functionality that you can't find in normal controls. Later in this chapter, in the section "Creating great user interfaces with ActiveX controls" we show you how to use two of these controls with a VBA user form.

Windows 95 Help Workshop

For the real professional or adventurous developer, the ODE includes the Help Workshop for Windows 95. This tool helps you manage and create Windows 95 help files that you can distribute with your application. As help file builders go, the Help Workshop is pretty lightweight. You still need an editor to create the help topics, but the Help Workshop can help you tie them all together in a help file.

Windows API text file and viewer

As powerful as VBA is, it can't do everything. For example, suppose that you want to find out how much free disk space you have. VBA does not have a built-in function that can tell you this information — but the *Windows Application Programming Interface* (API) does have one. The Windows API is a huge set of functions that people who build Windows applications (such as Word or Excel) use. These functions are part of Windows, so they're always available. But how do you call them from VBA?

The answer is a strange construct called a Declare statement. Declare statements tell VBA where to find functions that aren't part of VBA itself. And such statements can be tricky to construct. For example, take a look at the Declare statement for the function that retrieves free disk space:

```
Declare Function GetDiskFreeSpace Lib "kernel32" _
  Alias "GetDiskFreeSpaceA" (ByVal lpRootPathName _
  As String, lpSectorsPerCluster As Long, _
  lpBytesPerSector As Long, lpNumberOfFreeClusters As _
  Long, lpTtoalNumberOfClusters As Long) As Long
```

Do you want to code that from scratch? Of course you don't. That's what the Windows API text file and viewer is for. The viewer lets you look up all the functions in the Windows API and then copy them to your VBA program. Figure A-1 shows the viewer's main screen. You can see the list of functions as well as the Declare statement for the GetDiskSpaceFree function.

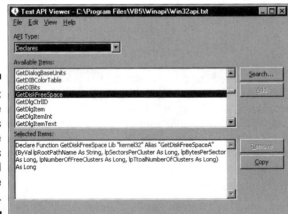

Figure A-1: The Windows API text file view helps you find Declare statements.

MSDN Library Sampler

It seems that every month, more and more information is made electronically with CD-ROMs being the media of choice for large volumes of data. Microsoft took advantage of the space left over on the ODE CD-ROM by filling it with a special edition of the Microsoft Developer Network (MSDN) Library. This on-line resource contains thousands of pages of documentation to help you develop, deploy, and support Office applications. We show you how to use this valuable resource in the section "Getting answers with MSDN Sampler" in this chapter.

Access developers really like the ODE

One of the first things you may notice about the ODE is that it favors Access developers over other Office 97 programmers. It has more tools and features that are designed to work with Access than the other applications in the Office suite. The primary reason for this is that the ODE replaced a product called the Access Developer's Toolkit (*ADT*). The ADT, as the name implies, was designed exclusively for Access developers. As Microsoft beefed up the rest of the Office family with cool developer functionality, however, it no longer made sense to offer something that was strictly for Access developers. If you don't spend most of your time writing Access applications, however, don't despair. All Office programmers can still use lots of things in the ODE.

Setting up the ODE tools

Installing the ODE Tools is relatively easy. You just put the ODE CD-ROM into your computer (preferably in the CD-ROM drive) and the welcome program launches automatically.

If the welcome screen does not appear automatically, you may have the Windows *AutoPlay* feature turned off. To open the welcome screen manually, run the Autorun.exe program in the root directory of the CD-ROM.

Click the button at the top of the welcome screen to start the ODE Tools setup program. You are prompted to supply an install directory (which defaults to a subdirectory of your main Office 97) as well as what type of install to perform (Typical, Custom, or Minimal) by clicking on the appropriate button. Choosing the Custom installation is a pretty good idea; the section "What you get with the ODE" in this chapter discusses what the ODE components do. Pick only those components that you intend to use.

When you're done choosing the components to install, click the OK button to finish the installation. The setup program copies the required files and creates a program group labeled Microsoft ODE Tools.

Distributing Access applications royalty-free

If you happen to be an Access developer, you can take advantage of an ODE feature that used to be in the old ADT, a royalty-free runtime license for your Access applications. What does this mean? Normally your users must have a copy of Access installed on their computers before they can use your application. Although this does give them the power to use Access to create their own applications, it can become costly — especially in companies with lots of computers.

With the runtime license you can distribute fully functional versions of your applications to users that don't have a copy of Access. And the best part is that you don't have to give Microsoft any more of your money! Runtime applications are the ideal solution for large organizations and for developers who want to sell commercial programs to the public.

Using the Setup Wizard

To make it simple to distribute your applications, Microsoft ships a utility called the Access Setup Wizard. The wizard itself is actually an Access application that leads you, the developer, through a series of steps where you tell it what files you want to distribute, along with various program options. The wizard them gathers up all the required files, copies them to a location on your hard disk where you can find them easily, and creates a setup program for your users to install your application.

You launch the wizard from the Microsoft ODE Tools program group on the Start menu. When you do this, Access opens and the setup wizard database loads. You are then left staring at the introduction screen. This is the starting point for new applications and the screen includes some descriptive information that concerns what the wizard does. To create a setup program for your Access database, follow these steps:

1. **Click the Next button.**

   The next screen that appears, shown in Figure A-2, is where you tell the setup wizard what files to include as part of your application. You must supply at least one file, usually your application's main Access database.

2. **Click the Add button to add a new file to the list.**

   When you click the Add button you are presented with a dialog box that lets you select which file to add.

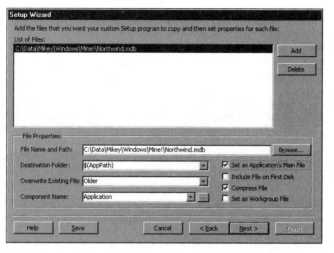

Figure A-2:
You tell the
wizard what
files to
install by
using this
screen.

3. Choose an Access database from the list of files and click OK. (It doesn't really matter which database you choose for this example.)

You are returned to the first screen and the wizard fills in information about the file on the form, including the file's path and eventual destination. For the destination, you can hard-code the name of a folder or you can choose from a list of locations that are determined when the user runs the setup program.

4. Mark the check box labeled Set as Application's Main File.

This tells the setup wizard that the database you just added is the one that needs to be opened when the user runs your program.

5. Click the Next button.

In the next screen, you define the shortcuts that the setup program can create. You need to define at least one shortcut for you application's main database file. After all, how else can your users run your program?

6. Click the Add button.

This adds a new entry to the list of shortcuts.

7. In the Description field on the form, enter a description of the shortcut, such as My Cool Application.

This description is then used as the label for the shortcut when it is created.

8. Click the Next button.

The screen you now see is used to define special Registry settings for your application. Unless you really know a lot about the Windows Registry, just skip this screen.

9. **Click the Next button again.**

This next screen presents you with a list of optional components that you can install along with your application. The one at the top of the list is Microsoft Access Run-Time Version. If you don't intend to require your users to own a copy of Access in order to run your application, you need to select this option.

10. **Click the runtime option to select it.**

11. **Click the Next button one more time.**

The setup wizard now informs you that it must include a workgroup file with your application.

12. **Click OK to close the dialog box.**

The setup wizard returns you to the main form.

13. **Click the Next button again to skip the component selection screen.**

You use one of the final screens in the wizard to define program options, such as the name, version number, and default installation directories.

14. **Fill in the information on the screen (use your imagination) and click the Next button twice.**

You now see the screen shown in Figure A-3. This is where you tell the setup wizard what type of installation program to create and where to store the files. As you can see, you have the option of dividing the files so that they fit on 1.44MB diskettes, putting them on a CD-ROM, or placing them all in a network directory for easy setup over a LAN.

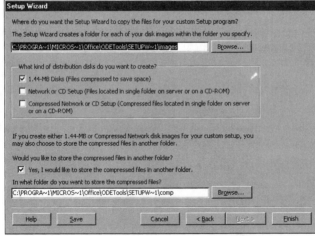

Figure A-3:
Your use this screen to tell the wizard what type of setup program to create.

15. Click the Finish button.

The setup wizard asks you if you want to save your selections in a template file. *Template files* store all your options so you can run the setup wizard another time.

16. Click Cancel to close the dialog box, and go get a cup of coffee.

At this point the wizard collects all the files it needs to create your diskette images, compresses them to make them smaller, and copies them to another location on your hard disk. This can take a very long time. When the wizard is done, however, you're ready to copy the files to floppy disks and give them to your users.

Running the Setup program

After the setup wizard finishes its job, running the resulting setup program is simple. Just find the directory where the wizard created the disk images (it's usually a subdirectory underneath the ODE tools directory) and run the Setup.exe program.

Figure A-4 shows what the main screen looks like. Does it look familiar? It should. The setup wizard uses the same technology that Office itself does. You can see from the figure that your selections for application name have been included on the dialog box.

Follow the instructions on the dialog boxes to select an installation directory and setup options. The dialog boxes are identical to those used by the Office 97 setup program so they may be very familiar to you.

Figure A-4:
Your custom setup program looks just like one from Microsoft.

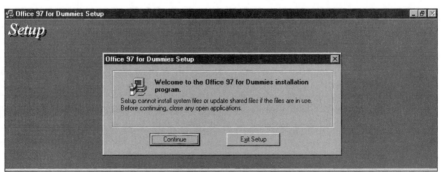

Advanced options

While we just don't have time to cover them here, a number of advanced options are available through the setup wizard. For example, you can define different setup profiles, such as Typical, Custom, and Minimal, just like Office 97 does. As you add files to your setup program by using the wizard, you can tell the wizard which profile they are to be installed with.

Spend some time looking through the setup wizard for more examples and ideas. The wizard comes with a help file, too. Don't forget to use it to find out more about what the setup wizard can do.

Creating great user interfaces with ActiveX controls

One very cool feature of the ODE is a set of ActiveX controls. (The *X* is silent, by the way.) ActiveX controls are like the other controls in Access and Microsoft Forms except that they aren't part of the application but are, instead, separate software components. If you're not familiar with Microsoft Forms, you may want to check out Chapter 16.

Because ActiveX controls are separate components, you can add them to your application one by one as you need them. This process is like ordering *a la carte* at a restaurant. Table A-1 lists the different controls that come with the ODE and what each is used for.

Table A-1	ActiveX Controls that Ship with the ODE
Control	*Purpose*
Common Dialog Control	Displays common windows dialog boxes, such as File Open, File Save, and Print
Image List Control	Acts as a little warehouse for images that you can use with other ActiveX controls, such as the Toolbar and Tree View controls
Internet Transfer Control	Lets you connect to other computers by using two different Internet protocols, HTTP and FTP
List View Control	Creates a list of items that you can display along with icons (This is the control used by Windows Explorer to list files.)
Progress Bar Control	Shows progress of a task as a bar that increments from 0 to 100 percent
Rich Text Box Control	Lets you enter text *and* formatting onto a form
Slider Control	Like the volume meter on a stereo, this control lets you select from a range of distinct values
Status Bar Control	Creates status bars on forms with areas for printing text and other information
Tab Strip Control	Creates the tabs on a tabbed dialog box
Toolbar Control	Displays a custom toolbar with buttons that you can create, manipulate, and program

Control	Purpose
Tree View Control	Displays a hierarchical view of information (this is the same control used by Windows Explorer to display directories)
UpDown Control	Sometimes called a spinner, this control lets you click arrow buttons to change a value
Winsock Control	Gives you access to networking information and control

Adding controls to your project

To demonstrate the power of ActiveX controls, you can create a simple example by using Microsoft Forms in either Word, PowerPoint, or Excel. Follow these steps:

1. **Launch Word, PowerPoint, or Excel (it doesn't matter which).**

2. **Press Alt+F11 to open the VBE.**

3. **Select the UserForm command from the Insert menu.**

   This command adds a new, blank user form to your project.

4. **Select the Additional Controls command from the Tools menu.**

   VBA opens a dialog box that lists all the ActiveX controls available on your system. You may be surprised at how many are available.

5. **Scroll through the list of controls until you find one labeled Microsoft ProgressBar Control, version 5.0.**

6. **Mark the check box next to the control's description.**

7. **Scroll through the list some more until you find one labeled Microsoft Slider Control, version 5.0.**

8. **Mark the check box next to this control's description and click OK.**

   You may notice that your toolbox has changed to include two new icons. These are the ActiveX controls that you just added to your project.

Using controls on a form

After you've added the controls to your project, you can use them just like any other control. You draw them on the form, set their properties, and respond to their events in the same manner. To demonstrate this by using the Progress Bar and Slider controls, follow these steps:

1. Use the mouse to draw a text box, a slider, and a progress bar on the blank user form.

(If you've never created controls before, you may want to turn to Chapter 16.) Your form ought to look like the one shown in Figure A-5.

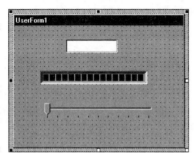

Figure A-5:
Create this
simple form
to test
some
ActiveX
controls.

2. Choose View➪Code to open the form's code window.

3. Type the following VBA code into the code window:

```
Private Sub Slider1_Scroll()
    TextBox1.Text = Slider1.Value
    ProgressBar1.Value = Slider1.Value * 10
End Sub
```

This code runs whenever you drag the button on the slider control. It sets the value of both the text box and the progress bar based on the new value of the slider control.

4. Open the Immediate window (press Ctrl+G) and run the following line of code:

```
UserForm1.Show
```

VBA opens the form on top of your application.

5. Click the slider's button with the mouse and drag it from left to right.

As you drag, the Scroll event fires, running the code that you typed into the code window. The code reads the value from the slider control and writes it to the text box. It also sets the value for the progress bar control to 10 times the value of the slider control.

This works because the slider control is used to select from a finite range of values. The default range is 0 through 10. You can change this in form design view by using the Properties window.

This is just a simple example that uses very simple controls. Some controls, such as the Tree View control, are extremely complex. After you become familiar with using controls, however, you ought to find working with ActiveX controls quite easy. They are, after all, just controls with properties, methods, and events.

Getting answers with MSDN Sampler

Every developer needs information, and to satisfy this need the ODE comes with a special edition of the Microsoft Development Network (*MSDN*) Library. The MSDN Library is a CD-ROM based reference tool that lets you browse and search through literally tens of thousands of pages of information.

You can sign up for a subscription to the full version of the MSDN Library, which comes on two compact discs and contains information for all types of programmers, including those who program with strange languages like C++. A subscription entitles you to quarterly updates with new information added each time.

The edition of the MSDN Library that ships with the ODE is an abridged version, containing only information relevant to Office developers. You can use it to look up answers to migration, development, and troubleshooting questions.

You install the Sampler right from the ODE opening screen. Click the middle button to launch the MSDN setup program. You are prompted for an install directory and given the choice of two installation options. One of the options copies the indexes used by the Library's browser (think of them as the card catalog) to your hard disk, the other option doesn't. The first option takes up more space but gives you quicker searches.

Navigating the InfoViewer window

When you install the Library Sampler you find a new icon in your ODE Tools group called Microsoft ODE Tools Sampler. The icon launches Microsoft InfoViewer, the program that reads information from the CD-ROM. Figure A-6 shows the InfoViewer screen. The main points of interest are the Contents pane, on the left, and the Topic pane, on the right.

You must insert the ODE CD-ROM into your CD-ROM drive before launching the program. If you don't, InfoViewer complains that it can't find the CD and asks you where it is.

If you know what you're after, you can use the Contents pane to find the right document. You expand the outline just like you do in Windows Explorer. Each of the books represents a main topic category and the individual pages are separate articles that you can read.

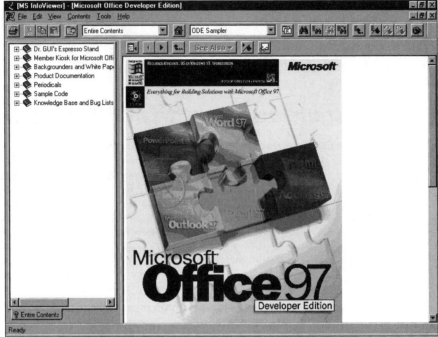

Figure A-6:
The
InfoViewer
main screen
showing the
MSDN
Library
Sampler.

For instance, suppose that you want to take a look at the object model for Microsoft PowerPoint. You can start at the top-level categories and drill down until you find the topic you are after. To try it out, follow these steps:

1. **Insert the ODE Tools CD-ROM and launch the MSDN Library Sampler.**

   If you've already used the Sampler, InfoViewer displays the topic you last looked at.

2. **In the Contents pane, click the plus sign (+) next to Product Documentation to expand the list of products for which documentation is included.**

3. **Click on the plus sign next to Microsoft PowerPoint to expand the list again, this time revealing the documentation for PowerPoint.**

   Beneath Microsoft PowerPoint are two more icons that look like books: Microsoft PowerPoint Objects and Microsoft PowerPoint Object Model Chart.

4. **Click on the plus sign next to Microsoft PowerPoint Object Model Chart to expand the list again.**

   This time you see a document titled, "PowerPoint Object Model Chart."

5. Double-click the document.

After a short delay while the CD-ROM drive finds the right piece of information, InfoViewer displays the document in the Topic pane. You can scroll around the pane by using the scroll bars to see it all.

Searching for topics

Of course, if you don't know where to find the right document, the Contents pane is not of much use. This situation is where the value of the MSDN Library Sampler comes in, though. You see, it has a very powerful search engine that lets you find information in any of the Library's documents quickly and easily.

As an example, suppose that you want to find out how to perform linear regression analysis by using Microsoft Excel. If you enjoy inflicting pain on yourself, you can browse through each Excel-related document using the Contents pane. A better (and practically painless) way is to use the built-in query tool. To do so

1. Select the Tools⇨Query command or press Ctrl+Q to open the Query dialog box.

In the Query dialog box, a space is provided for you to enter your query, as well as options for controlling the scope of the search.

2. Type excel linear regression **into the first field on the dialog box (where it says "Type the word(s) you want to find:").**

Note that the search engine is case insensitive, meaning that it matches *Excel* even though you type *excel*.

3. Click the Query button.

After your CD-ROM drive whirs for a bit, InfoViewer opens the Query Results window. This window shows all the documents in the Library that contain the words you search for — in this case, *excel, linear,* and *regression.* It even ranks them based on the number of times the words appear.

4. Double-click the first one in the list.

InfoView displays the documentation for the Excel LINEST worksheet function. This function is used to perform linear regression anaylsis.

When you open a document window the Query Results window disappears. To make it come back, press Ctrl+R.

Press Ctrl+S to synchronize the Contents pane with the Topic pane. This shows you where the current document is in the overall contents.

You can choose from many different ways to perform queries so that you find exactly the information that you're looking for. You can even define subsets of topics to search in rather than searching the entire CD-ROM. Consult on-line help of the MSDN Library Sampler for more information.

Index

IDG Books Worldwide, Inc., End-User License Agreement

READ THIS. You should carefully read these terms and conditions before opening the software packet(s) included with this book ("Book"). This is a license agreement ("Agreement") between you and IDG Books Worldwide, Inc. ("IDGB"). By opening the accompanying software packet(s), you acknowledge that you have read and accept the following terms and conditions. If you do not agree and do not want to be bound by such terms and conditions, promptly return the Book and the unopened software packet(s) to the place you obtained them for a full refund.

1. **License Grant.** IDGB grants to you (either an individual or entity) a nonexclusive license to use one copy of the enclosed software program(s) (collectively, the "Software") solely for your own personal or business purposes on a single computer (whether a standard computer or a workstation component of a multiuser network). The Software is in use on a computer when it is loaded into temporary memory (RAM) or installed into permanent memory (hard disk, CD-ROM, or other storage device). IDGB reserves all rights not expressly granted herein.

2. **Ownership.** IDGB is the owner of all right, title, and interest, including copyright, in and to the compilation of the Software recorded on the disk(s) or CD-ROM ("Software Media"). Copyright to the individual programs recorded on the Software Media is owned by the author or other authorized copyright owner of each program. Ownership of the Software and all proprietary rights relating thereto remain with IDGB and its licensers.

3. **Restrictions on Use and Transfer.**

    (a) You may only (i) make one copy of the Software for backup or archival purposes, or (ii) transfer the Software to a single hard disk, provided that you keep the original for backup or archival purposes. You may not (i) rent or lease the Software, (ii) copy or reproduce the Software through a LAN or other network system or through any computer subscriber system or bulletin-board system, or (iii) modify, adapt, or create derivative works based on the Software.

    (b) You may not reverse engineer, decompile, or disassemble the Software. You may transfer the Software and user documentation on a permanent basis, provided that the transferee agrees to accept the terms and conditions of this Agreement and you retain no copies. If the Software is an update or has been updated, any transfer must include the most recent update and all prior versions.

4. **Restrictions on Use of Individual Programs.** You must follow the individual requirements and restrictions detailed for each individual program. These limitations are also contained in the individual license agreements recorded on the Software Media. These limitations may include a requirement that after using the program for a specified period of time, the user must pay a registration fee or discontinue use. By opening the Software packet(s), you will be agreeing to abide by the licenses and restrictions for these individual programs that are detailed on the Software Media. None of the material on this Software Media or listed in this Book may ever be redistributed, in original or modified form, for commercial purposes.

5. **Limited Warranty.**

   (a) IDGB warrants that the Software and Software Media are free from defects in materials and workmanship under normal use for a period of sixty (60) days from the date of purchase of this Book. If IDGB receives notification within the warranty period of defects in materials or workmanship, IDGB will replace the defective Software Media.

   (b) **IDGB AND THE AUTHORS OF THE BOOK DISCLAIM ALL OTHER WARRANTIES, EXPRESS OR IMPLIED, INCLUDING WITHOUT LIMITATION IMPLIED WARRANTIES OF MERCHANTABILITY AND FITNESS FOR A PARTICULAR PURPOSE, WITH RESPECT TO THE SOFTWARE, THE PROGRAMS, THE SOURCE CODE CONTAINED THEREIN, AND/OR THE TECHNIQUES DESCRIBED IN THIS BOOK. IDGB DOES NOT WARRANT THAT THE FUNCTIONS CONTAINED IN THE SOFTWARE WILL MEET YOUR REQUIREMENTS OR THAT THE OPERATION OF THE SOFTWARE WILL BE ERROR FREE.**

   (c) This limited warranty gives you specific legal rights, and you may have other rights that vary from jurisdiction to jurisdiction.

6. **Remedies.**

   (a) IDGB's entire liability and your exclusive remedy for defects in materials and workmanship shall be limited to replacement of the Software Media, which may be returned to IDGB with a copy of your receipt at the following address: Software Media Fulfillment Department, Attn.: *Microsoft Office 97 Programming with VBA For Dummies*, IDG Books Worldwide, Inc., 7260 Shadeland Station, Ste. 100, Indianapolis, IN 46256, or call 800-762-2974. Please allow three to four weeks for delivery. This Limited Warranty is void if failure of the Software Media has resulted from accident, abuse, or misapplication. Any replacement Software Media will be warranted for the remainder of the original warranty period or thirty (30) days, whichever is longer.

   (b) In no event shall IDGB or the authors be liable for any damages whatsoever (including without limitation damages for loss of business profits, business interruption, loss of business information, or any other pecuniary loss) arising from the use of or inability to use the Book or the Software, even if IDGB has been advised of the possibility of such damages.

   (c) Because some jurisdictions do not allow the exclusion or limitation of liability for consequential or incidental damages, the above limitation or exclusion may not apply to you.

7. **U.S. Government Restricted Rights.** Use, duplication, or disclosure of the Software by the U.S. Government is subject to restrictions stated in paragraph (c)(1)(ii) of the Rights in Technical Data and Computer Software clause of DFARS 252.227-7013, and in subparagraphs (a) through (d) of the Commercial Computer–Restricted Rights clause at FAR 52.227-19, and in similar clauses in the NASA FAR supplement, when applicable.

8. **General.** This Agreement constitutes the entire understanding of the parties and revokes and supersedes all prior agreements, oral or written, between them and may not be modified or amended except in a writing signed by both parties hereto that specifically refers to this Agreement. This Agreement shall take precedence over any other documents that may be in conflict herewith. If any one or more provisions contained in this Agreement are held by any court or tribunal to be invalid, illegal, or otherwise unenforceable, each and every other provision shall remain in full force and effect.

Installation Instructions
for the Disk

● ●

*T*he disk stuck to the back of this book contains the sample files that you need for the steps in certain chapters. All the files and directories on the disk are compressed into a self-extracting file for your convenience.

These instructions assume that your computer meets the minimum system requirements for Office 97 — Windows 95 or NT on a computer with at least 16MB of RAM. Of course, your computer also needs to have a 3^1/$_2$-inch disk drive. Also, please read the "IDG Books Worldwide, Inc. End-User License Agreement" that precedes this page before you decide to use the disk.

You access those eminently useful sample files on the disk by following these steps:

1. **Insert the disk into your disk drive.**

2. **Choose Start➪Run.**

   The Run dialog box appears.

3. **Type** A:\97vba.EXE **in the Open text field and click OK.**

   You see a dialog box for the extraction utility. The box wants to know which directory that you want the sample files to go in. We suggest that you choose the default directory C:\Dummies because that's the structure that we refer to in the chapters. If you choose another directory or disk drive, be aware that some of the code we create in this book refers to this default directory structure. Just replace our drive or directory references with yours, as appropriate.

4. **Click the Unzip button.**

   The self-extracting file creates all the chapter subdirectories (such as \Chapter 20) and puts the appropriate sample files in each subdirectory.

5. **Click OK when prompted that your files have been unzipped successfully.**

6. **Close the extraction utility by clicking the close button.**

That's all you have to do!

If, after following these instructions, you still have problems installing the sample files from the disk attached to this book, please call the IDG Books Worldwide Customer Service phone number: 800-762-2974 (outside the U.S.: 317-596-5261).

IDG BOOKS WORLDWIDE REGISTRATION CARD

Visit our Web site at http://www.idgbooks.com

ISBN Number: __0-7645-0182-8__

Title of this book: __Microsoft Office 97 Programming With VBA For Dummies__

My overall rating of this book: ❑ Very good [1] ❑ Good [2] ❑ Satisfactory [3] ❑ Fair [4] ❑ Poor [5]

How I first heard about this book:

❑ Found in bookstore; name: [6] _____ | ❑ Book review: [7]
❑ Advertisement: [8] _____ | ❑ Catalog: [9]
❑ Word of mouth; heard about book from friend, co-worker, etc.: [10] | ❑ Other: [11]

What I liked most about this book:

_____

_____

What I would change, add, delete, etc., in future editions of this book:

_____

_____

Other comments:

_____

Number of computer books I purchase in a year: ❑ 1 [12] ❑ 2-5 [13] ❑ 6-10 [14] ❑ More than 10 [15]

I would characterize my computer skills as: ❑ Beginner [16] ❑ Intermediate [17] ❑ Advanced [18] ❑ Professional [19]

I use ❑ DOS [20] ❑ Windows [21] ❑ OS/2 [22] ❑ Unix [23] ❑ Macintosh [24] ❑ Other: [25]_____

(please specify)

I would be interested in new books on the following subjects:

(please check all that apply, and use the spaces provided to identify specific software)

❑ Word processing: [26] _____ | ❑ Spreadsheets: [27] _____
❑ Data bases: [28] _____ | ❑ Desktop publishing: [29] _____
❑ File Utilities: [30] _____ | ❑ Money management: [31] _____
❑ Networking: [32] _____ | ❑ Programming languages: [33] _____
❑ Other: [34]

I use a PC at (please check all that apply): ❑ home [35] ❑ work [36] ❑ school [37] ❑ other: [38] _____

The disks I prefer to use are ❑ 5.25 [39] ❑ 3.5 [40] ❑ other: [41]_____

I have a CD ROM: ❑ yes [42] ❑ no [43]

I plan to buy or upgrade computer hardware this year: ❑ yes [44] ❑ no [45]

I plan to buy or upgrade computer software this year: ❑ yes [46] ❑ no [47]

Name: _____ Business title: [48] _____ Type of Business: [49] _____

Address (❑ home [50] ❑ work [51]/Company name: _____)

Street/Suite# _____

City [52]/State [53]/Zip code [54]: _____ Country [55] _____

❑ **I liked this book!** You may quote me by name in future IDG Books Worldwide promotional materials.

My daytime phone number is _____

IDG BOOKS WORLDWIDE

THE WORLD OF COMPUTER KNOWLEDGE®